FUNDAMENTALS OF DECISION MAKING
AND PRIORITY THEORY

WITH
THE ANALYTIC HIERARCHY PROCESS

VOL. VI OF THE AHP SERIES

THOMAS L. SAATY

Library of Congress Cataloging-in-Publication Data
Saaty, Thomas L.

Fundamentals of Decision Making and Priority Theory
with the Analytic Hierarchy Process

CIP 93-86891
ISBN 0-9620317-6-3

1. Priorities   2. Decision Making
3. Analytic Hierarchy Process (AHP)

Thomas L. Saaty
University of Pittsburgh
322 Mervis Hall
Pittsburgh, PA 15260
Phone: 412-648-1539
Email: saaty@katz.pitt.edu

Printed and Bound in the United States of America

Published by:
RWS Publications   Phone: 412-414-5984
4922 Ellsworth Avenue   Fax: 412-681-4510
Pittsburgh, PA 15213   www.rwspublications.com

THOMAS L. SAATY

University of Pittsburgh
322 MERVIS HALL
PITTSBURGH, PA 15260
WORK: (412) 648-1539 HOME: (412) 621-6546

Fundamentals of Decision Making and Priority Theory
with the Analytic Hierarchy Process
Vol. VI of the AHP Series

CONTENTS

PREFACE

This work is the outcome of many years research into a very practical, yet simple way to facilitate group decision making. This method allows participants to build their own assumptions and to avoid technical thinking which they would be unable to understand or do on their own.

From 1963 to 1969, this author worked at the Arms Control and Disarmament Agency (ACDA) in the Department of State in Washington. Significant resources were spent to engage some of the world's leading thinkers in mathematical economics, utility theory, game theory, and conflict resolution over a period of several years to study the problem of arms negotiation carried out with the Soviet Union in Geneva to reduce the very large accumulation of nuclear weapons. A major problem in using that kind of thinking and research was that negotiators and other nontechnical people neither could learn nor apply the findings of these scholars. There was a two culture chasm in thought and language that could not be bridged. Why is communication on such an important matter between the scientist and the user so difficult? Is it a problem of understanding the issues, or is it lack of communication with simpler tools intrinsic to both ways of thinking? How do we use such tools in group decision making and what if there are groups that are in conflict --- can we assist them by negotiating the issues?

This book is about making decisions the natural way which we call the Analytic Hierarchy Process (AHP). It involves assumptions about what people are observed to do with their biological equipment. They should not need to steep themselves for long in technical training to organize their thinking and discover what judgments they hold. They should be able to approach a decision problem by posing and answering the right kind of questions.

There are two kinds of decisions: intuitive and analytical. Intuitive decisions are not supported by data and documentation and may appear arbitrary. A surprising amount of corporate decision making is of the intuitive type. The person charged with making the decision accumulates a lot of information, probably biased by his own values, goes in a room and comes out with a decision. This model is a poor basis from which to operate a large corporation. Such a decision is weak on several grounds. It is difficult to get it accepted by others particularly because the decision maker is unable to justify it with persuasive logic. In addition, the judgments may not be rooted in anything explicit, the other participants cannot identify a place to add their knowledge, or the decision maker himself may have difficulty in synthesizing his own and his subordinates' expertise. Such a decision would be hard to review in the future for learning purposes. Besides being weak decisions, no one around the manager can learn what went into the decision and what was good or bad about it. There is no learning or creation of a process through group participation.

Analytical decision making, when used collectively in a corporation, leads to shared values. Decisions that are required by corporations metamorphose from individual to strategic to portfolio decisions. Usually the criteria that matter in all these differing levels of decision making are common and show up again and again. For example, customer satisfaction, technological advancement, and profit show up at all levels. An overall corporate perspective can be developed by simply observing the recurrent themes.

People must constantly make decisions in order to survive. We believe that they can make better decisions if they practiced decision making as a science. But there are those who believe that mathematics has nothing to do with decision making. They are probably unaware of the jumps they make in their thinking due to internal preferences. If the decision were to be laid out in full in the form of a hierarchy, one can easily see the need for numbers to distinguish among the different intensities of preference that give rise to the intuitive jumps. Our contention is that one cannot avoid the need for numbers to make tradeoffs. In fact most people are not versed in the use of numbers as required in decision methods.

The question then is: what do people do naturally that we can abstract, organize and improve upon, thus gradually making it into a

science of decision making?   Complex decision making needs
organized thinking to structure a problem. This structure can be
provided by a hierarchy or a network. It also needs numbers and a
modicum of mathematics to formalize judgments and make tradeoffs.
    The structure we adopt to represent the factors affecting a
decision constantly changes with the knowledge we have.   The
soundness of the decisions we make is relative to that knowledge.
    The following letter, written by Benjamin Franklin to Joseph
Priestly in 1722, is taken from: "Letter to Joseph Priestly", Benjamin
Franklin Sampler, 1956. It shows that he was aware of the need to do
something quantitative about decision making.

Dear Sir: In the affair of so much importance to you, wherein you ask
my advice, I cannot, for want of sufficient premises, advise you what
to determine, but if you please I will tell you how.   When those
difficult cases occur, they are difficult, chiefly because while we have
them under consideration, all the reasons pro and con are not present
to the mind at the same time; but sometimes one set present
themselves, and at other times another, the first being out of sight.
Hence the various purposes or information that alternatively prevail,
and the uncertainty that perplexes us. To get over this, my way is to
divide a sheet of paper by a line into two columns; writing over the one
Pro, and over the other Con.   Then, during three or four days of
consideration, I put down under the different heads short hints of the
different motives, that at different times occur to me, for or against the
measure.   When I have thus got them all together in one view, I
endeavor to estimate their respective weights; and when I find two, one
on each side, that seem equal, I strike them both out. If I find a reason
pro equal to some two reasons con, I strike out the three. If I judge
some two reasons con, equal to three reasons pro, I strike out the five;
and thus proceeding I find at length where the balance lies; and if, after
a day to two of further consideration, nothing new that is of importance
occurs on either side, I come to a determination accordingly.   And,
though the weight of the reasons cannot be taken with the precision of
algebraic quantities, yet when each is thus considered, separately and

comparatively, and the whole lies before me, I think I can judge better, and am less liable to make a rash step, and in fact I have found great advantage from this kind of equation, and what might be called moral or prudential algebra. Wishing sincerely that you may determine for the best, I am ever, my dear friend, yours most affectionately, B. Franklin.

Old Ben was on the right track and the subject of this book provides the algebraic precision he was lacking. How we measure and assign numbers to judgments and how we combine our measurements to make the right choices is critical in decision making.

Logic and feelings, emotions, intuition and experience are all part of our make up. Our approach to making decisions needs to consider intensities of judgment whatever the origin of that judgment. It is from an arithmetic of intensities that the AHP derives its priority scales and combines them into a single scale of overall priorities.

Peter Drucker writes in the Wall Street Journal on Tuesday, April 13, 1993: "We Need to Measure, Not Count." He goes on to say that

"Quantification has been the rage in business and economics these past 50 years. Accountants have proliferated as fast as lawyers. Yet we do not have the measurements we need.

Neither our concepts nor our tools are adequate for the control of operations, or for managerial control. And, so far, there are neither the concepts nor the tools for business control - i.e., for economic decision making. In the past few years, however, we have become increasingly aware of the need for such measurements.

It may take many years, decades perhaps, until we have the measurements we need in all these areas. But at least we know now that we need new measurements and what they have to be. Slowly, and still groping, we are moving from counting to measuring."

No philosopher has been more intensely concerned with questions of value than Nietzsche was. His early works dealt mainly with such questions. His masterpiece, *Thus Spoke Zarathustra*, revolves around evaluation concerns, as do most of his later works. He says, "All the scientists have to from now on prepare the way for the future task of philosophers. This task is the solution of the problem of value, the determination of the order of rank among values." (From "The Giants of Philosophy", Knowledge Products, Nashville, TN.)

The very definition of "true" knowledge reposes in the final analysis upon an ethical [value-laden] postulate. Values and knowledge are inevitably linked in and through actions... All action signifies an ethic, serves or disserves certain values. (From "Chance and Necessity", by Nobel Prize winner Jacques Monod)

These are the issues that concern us in this book. The first chapter gives a general introduction to hierarchies and priorities in decision making. Chapters 2 and 3 discuss judgments, paired comparisons and their numerical representation, consistency, and how to derive priority scale from these judgments. Chapter 4 is less technical than the previous two chapters, and gives a general understanding of a hierarchies and how to use them in decision making. Chapter 5 is concerned with the much-discussed rank preservation and reversal when new alternatives are added or old ones are deleted. Chapter 6 deals with a variety of applications of mostly hierarchies and of a holarchy in problems of benefits and costs, of risk, and of forecasting turnaround of the economy. and 9 provide the basic theory of measurement and ratio scales in hierarchic structures that require independence within levels and downward from level to level. Chapter 7 deals with small and large scale group decision making. Chapter 8 deals with dependence within and between levels of a hierarchy or the components of a system, and provides interesting examples of dependence in business problems. More significantly, this chapter shows that the well-known Bayes Theorem giving rise to posterior prediction in probability theory follows from the supermatrix approach developed in that chapter, and goes beyond that theorem by illustrating an application of dependencies in medical diagnosis. Chapter 9 summarizes some highlights of the AHP, with a discussion of difference scales and how to convert from relative to absolute measurement and conversely. Chapter 10 is a formalization of the theory in terms of axioms and theorems. Chapter 11 deals with advanced topics and some recent developments in the subject. Chapter 12 illustrates two examples of time-dependent judgments without much theoretical framework. The final chapter, Chapter 13, contains a generalization of the AHP to the continuous case of deriving ratio scales in the context of neural firing and provides illustrations of how visual images are formed.

In this second edition we corrected some errata and have added a small and useful appendix at the end. I am grateful to the many colleagues and friends who assisted me in writing this book.

Thomas L. Saaty, Pittsburgh, 2000

IMPORTANT NEW DEVELOPMENTS

This book has thoughts and ideas not found in other books on the subject of decision making so that we felt it was important to keep the book in print. However, extensions of the theory of relative measurement to larger and more complex systems have continued to grow. Since the publication of the first edition of this book about the fundamentals of hierarchic decision making, some significant developments have taken place. They are advances in the theory of network decisions with dependence and feedback between and among all the elements involved in a decision. That theory is called the Analytic Network Process (ANP). The ANP has been applied to a variety of complex decisions with benefits, opportunities, costs and risks and in particular how to synthesize the four outcomes developed under each of these into a single overall outcome by using the concepts of strategic criteria and negative priorities. Two books were published in 2005 on this subject. They are "Theory and Applications of the Analytic Network Process: Decision Making with Benefits, Opportunities, Costs and Risks" and "The Encylicon: a Dictionary of Decisions with Dependence and Feedback based on the Analytic Network Process" both also published by RWS Publications.

Thomas L. Saaty, Pittsburgh, 2007

CHAPTER ONE

HOW TO USE THE ANALYTIC HIERARCHY PROCESS

1. Introduction - The Need For a Multivalued Logic

Our world today consists of a set of complex interrelated problems which feed into one another. The world economy, for instance, depends on energy and other resources. The availability of energy depends on geography and politics. Politics depends on military strength. Military strength depends on technology. Technology depends on ideas and resources. Ideas depend on politics, resources depend on the economy. And the circle goes round and round. To the best of our understanding it is a system, that is, a network of interacting factors whose causes and effects cannot be easily differentiated. When we approach this system with our traditional reductionist logic, we tend to break it down into simple chains of reasoning in search of explanations. Then we piece these together without any prior logical rules to govern our attempts to obtain integrated, rational results.

Nearly all of us, in one way or another, have been brought up to believe that clear-headed logical thinking is our only reliable way to identify and solve problems. We are told that our feelings and our judgments must be subjected to the acid test of deductive thinking. But experience suggests that deductive thinking is not natural. Indeed, we have to be trained, and for a long time at that, before we can do it well. But deductive thinking concerning complex problems with many related factors often leads to sequences of ideas which are so tangled that their interconnections are not readily discerned.

At the same time we elect leaders in government and industry who make silent decisions. They often do not care or are unable to understand the problems they face. We assume that they have learned through experience. We want to believe that they have the talent to take in a wide diversity of information, put it together in some mysterious seat of the pants way, and come up with the "right answers". They seem to know intuitively, and we want to have faith that in some hidden way they have logically arrived at the "truth".

We have a lurking suspicion that the universe contains a primal, non-rational force that can be grasped only by the intuitive power of an imaginative genius. These charismatic leaders, like the Knights of the Roundtable, would then guide the brotherhood to the holy grail. But what takes place in the mind of this genius to grasp the essence of the forces operating to empower him to face complexity with serenity and assurance? Hugh Sidey writes in Time magazine (p.29 Aug. 17, 1981), "History shows that the Churchills, the Roosevelts, the Hitlers and the Stalins made almost as many mistakes as correct decisions in their designs, both good and evil. The call to action swept their people along. The polls showed grave doubts among the American people about where Ronald Reagan was taking us...but there is an irresistible appeal to fall in behind a man when he promises adventure even when one may not agree with him. Tennyson said it well: 'I myself must mix action, lest I wither by despair'."

Analytic decision making is a sought after science because in today's world we have complex decisions that affect many people who in turn can affect the next decision we make. To operate successfully, industry and government must organize their policies on the basis of both short and long term thinking. They must integrate and synthesize a diversity of data and information. They need to deal with intangibles side by side with tangibles that have different scales. How should these diverse scales be interpreted for decision making? Is it meaningful to mix dollars, tons, yards and hours directly? If not, to what scale are they converted and how are they combined? Conflicts and conflict resolution, from the family to the international arena, are legitimate concerns to promote peaceful coexistence and successful relationships. Good decision making should also address creative approaches to resolving differences.

This lack of integrative measurements and procedures to derive them is especially troublesome when we have to determine which of several options is the most desirable, or the least objectionable, as the case may be. Therefore, we need a new process by which to determine which objective outweighs another, at least in the near term. Since we are concerned with real-life problems we must recognize the necessity for trade-offs to best serve the common interest. Therefore, this new process should also allow for consensus building and compromise.

Individual knowledge and experience are inadequate when making decisions concerning the welfare and quality of life for a group. Participation and debate are needed both among individuals and between the groups affected. Here several aspects of group decision making have to be considered. The first is the need for discussion and exchange within the group to reach some kind of consensus on the given problem. The second is more significant. The holistic nature of the given problem necessitates that it be divided into smaller subject matter areas within which different groups of experts determine how each area affects the total problem. If this process is successful, one can then reconstruct the initial question and review the proposed solutions. A last and often crucial disadvantage of many traditional decision making methods is that they require specialized expertise to design the appropriate structure and then to embed the decision making process in it.

Thus we require that the new method should be

- simple in construct,
- adaptable to both groups and individuals,
- natural to our intuition and general thinking,
- encourage compromise and consensus building, and
- not require inordinate specialization to master.

At the core of the problems which our method addresses is the assessment of the benefits, the costs and the risks of the proposed solutions. We must answer questions such as the following: Which consequences weigh more heavily than others? Which aims are more important than others? What is likely to take place? What should we plan for and how do we bring it about? These and other questions demand a multicriteria logic. It has been demonstrated again and again, by practitioners who used the theory discussed in this book, that multicriteria logic gives different and often better answers to these questions than ordinary logic.

To make a decision one needs various kinds of knowledge, information and technical data. These concern

- details about the problem to be decided,
- the people or actors involved,
- their objectives and policies,
- the influences affecting the outcomes, and
- the time horizons, scenarios and constraints.

The set of potential outcomes or alternatives from which to choose is central in decision making. In laying out the framework for making a decision one needs to sort the elements in groupings or clusters that have similar influences or effects. One must also arrange them in some rational order to trace the outcome of these influences. Briefly, we see decision making as a process that involves the following steps:

(1)   Structure a problem as a hierarchy or as a system with dependence loops.

(2)   Elicit judgments that reflect ideas, feelings or emotions.

(3)   Represent those judgments with meaningful numbers.

(4)   Use these numbers to calculate the priorities of the elements of the hierarchy.

(5)   Synthesize these results to determine an overall outcome.

(6)   Analyze the sensitivity to changes in judgment.

These criteria are met by the decision making process covered in this book. We call it the *Analytic Hierarchy Process (AHP)*. It is a framework of logic and problem-solving that spans the spectrum from instant awareness to fully integrated consciousness by organizing perceptions, feelings, judgments and memories into a hierarchy of forces that influence decision results. The AHP is based on the innate human ability to use information and experience to estimate relative magnitudes through paired comparisons. These comparisons are used to construct ratio scales on a variety of dimensions both tangible and intangible. Arranging these dimensions in a hierarchic or network structure allows a systematic procedure to organize our basic reasoning and intuition by breaking down a problem into its smaller constituent parts. The AHP thus leads from simple pairwise comparison judgments to the priorities in the hierarchy.

In the simple and most common case the forces are arranged from the more general and less controllable to the more specific and controllable. Starting from time horizons and scenarios of the original problem we progress to the actors, then to their objectives and policies. Further development of the hierarchy moves to those affected by a decision and their objectives and policies. Finally the structure generates the alternative outcomes of a prediction or the available choices in a priority decision. Simple scenarios may have less elaborate structures. In principle, however, any decision problem can be represented by multiple structures, depending upon the nature of the decision, the importance of the outcome and the expertise of the decision makers.

Using the AHP, we have predicted, with consistent success, the outcome of U.S. presidential elections, the results of sports contests and the winners of chess matches. Another recent example is the use of the AHP to predict the value of the dollar versus the yen, done in 1986. Not long before then, the dollar was worth 240 yen. We forecast, with the participation of knowledgeable colleagues, that it would hover around 139 yen over the following several months. It did, and it stayed near that level for many years. The process has proved to be a powerful tool for prediction. Failure can occur when the forecasting effort does not allow for the full range of possibilities, or assumes that certain outcomes will happen because of limited awareness or prior assumptions of the forecaster. Forecasting must be laterally broad to allow for all sorts of forces that can shape the future. Too often, when a difficult decision is to be made, we hesitate as passive observers. The AHP allows us to become committed participants, who fully understand, appreciate, and weigh the influences of the forces that control the outcome.

We need to make a few final observations to further clarify the role of the AHP in deriving measurement. There is a dichotomy between what is commonly known as hard data and soft data in relating the mind to the mind and nature to the mind.

One of the greatest values of hard measurement with a scale and a unit is to make a correspondence between the dimensions of a natural setting such as the width of a river and the dimensions of materials needed to correspond to that setting such as the length of a bridge and the steel to go into it to span the river. Hard measurement is needed for implementation.

One of the greatest values of soft measurement with a relative scale is to order elements in a set according to priority in order to make a decision, design a plan, allocate one or several resources in proportion to priorities or to resolve a conflict among the elements.

It would seem that the difference between hard and soft measurement is similar to the difference between tactical and strategic thinking. The first applies directly to manipulate the real or physical world and the second applies to manipulate thought to adjust it to what is possible in the real world. Hard measurement must be consistent with what is known in nature, whereas soft measurement must be consistent with what is known in the mind.

Hard data about the world must be transformed to a kind of data that can be integrated with other qualitative information needed to think through a plan consistently. Hard data cannot be used for this purpose in the raw form it is obtained from natural measurement. It must take the same form as the rest of our soft data to allow us to combine and manipulate it to make it serve our goals and values. These goals and values themselves must be understood with the same kind of soft data. That is how the world is assimilated by the mind with satisfaction.

Note that both hard data and soft data relate to our understanding of how to deal with the world to satisfy our needs. They say nothing about the real "truth" of the world itself but only with our interpretation of it to conform with our own standards and values. Science and engineering are thought to use only hard data. But that is short of the real truth. The outcome of their measurements must always be interpreted by some intelligent mind and aligned with the goals and understanding of that mind.

In sum, it appears that the purpose of counting and measurement is to create correspondence concerning magnitudes. But abstractly there are two types of magnitudes. Those arising from the standards we establish on concrete objects through perception to which we apply hard measurement and those arising from standards we set on ideas deriving from perception and from thought to which we apply so-called soft measurement. We distinguish between soft and hard because our ideas are flexible and adaptable and hence accept changing data in contrast to nature which is less flexible. Because we have imagination it is easier to alter our thinking than it is to alter nature, even though we can sometimes alter nature with great effort. In the end it is soft data that determines the significance of hard data to our value system. The Analytic Hierarchy Process is our tool for generating the soft data needed for that purpose.

2. About Paired Comparison

In dealing with the objects and phenomena of the physical world, the physical sciences usually employ ratio scales to establish relations between them, by using the ratio of their measurements to compare them. Very few properties are measured on other than ratio scales. An example is temperature which is usually measured on an interval scale, meaning, that the difference in measurements is used for the comparison. However, the Kelvin scale is a ratio scale.

The AHP derives ratio scales of relative magnitudes of a set of elements by making paired comparisons. It proceeds from judgments on comparisons with respect to dominance, which is the generic term for expressing importance, preference or likelihood, of a property which they have in common, to their numerical representation according to the strength of that dominance and then derives a ratio scale. Thus decision making with the AHP is based on ranking activities in terms of relative ratio scales.

One needs eyes and sometimes hands to estimate how many times one object is larger than another. But when we deal with intangibles, which we do all the time, we must use our feelings instead of our senses to make such a comparison. Feelings do not distinguish very sharply between discrete entities. A person with a million dollars is a millionaire. To our perception so is one with only $990,000 because the ratio of their respective riches is nearly one.

The facility to make comparisons based on feelings and

interpreted by experience appears to be an intrinsic ability of consciousness. If we can operationalize this facility mathematically, we can also operationalize dealing with sense perception.

With intangibles, these comparison ratios evoke semantic expressions of relative magnitude used to represent feelings. These feelings express how much more an attribute is possessed by one element than by another taken as the unit. We shall show that paired comparisons of tangibles or intangibles can be used to create a ratio scale of absolute numbers which represent their "strength".

We note that there is a limit to the number of comparisons we can make and to the relative magnitude of these comparisons. If there are too many items to be compared or if the comparisons result in widely different numbers one resorts to clustering which will be discussed later.

3. Relative Measurement, An Example

Our first example demonstrates the ability of the AHP to quantify essentially emotional factors in a decision making problem. The methodology is also explained in detail in prior publication the first of which was T. Saaty, "The Analytic Hierarchy Process", first published by McGraw Hill Book Company 1980 and republished by RWS Publication, Pittsburgh, 1990.

Our example deals with a modern moral dilemma which society faces all too often. In a large city a heart has become available for transplant and three people have the necessary blood and tissue match. All are urgent cases with a prognosis of having only a few days or weeks to live without receiving a transplant. One is a 15 year old girl from a wealthy family, easily capable of affording the entire expense. The second is a poor 30 year old mother of three young children, with no insurance. The third is a married 35 year old scientist with no children, doing research on

AIDS with a possible breakthrough, whose insurance covers 50% of the cost. Who should get the heart, remembering that a heart transplant may or may not succeed, and even if it does, the patient may or may not survive for very long? The committee making the decision consists of a social worker, a doctor, a hospital administrator, and a lawyer.

The various elements of this decision problem are organized into a hierarchy of four levels shown in Figure 1-1. Each level has multiple nodes with respect to which the alternatives on the next level are compared. This figure is a realistic simplification of a larger hierarchy developed with the organ transplant staff at Pittsburgh's Presbyterian Hospital, a prominent transplant center. The *goal* on the first level is to select the "best" recipient for the heart. The second level of the hierarchy includes the *criteria* affecting the decision: Family, Medical History, Social Factors, and Funding. Family has to do with relatives of the patient and how deprived they would be by the patient's death. Medical History has to do with objective biological and hereditary facts favoring success of the transplant. Social Factors have to do with a patient's potential contributions to society. The third level includes subfactors or *subcriteria* which contribute to the complete assessment of each criterion. The subfactor Social Behavior, for instance, takes into account such things as criminal record (which in this case none of the candidates has and therefore all get the full value of the subcriterion). Funding has no subcriteria and connects directly to the fourth level, since funding can be summed up in one comparative step. The fourth, and final, level contains the *alternatives* which are to be prioritized. In this case they are the potential recipients of the heart.

The first step is to compare the elements in each level in pairs. In emotional cases such as this, much thought has to be given to the question whose job is it to decide what the factors of social worth are and how much credit the individuals should get. If no individual feels comfortable about making such decisions, one should form groups to think about them, and even to vote on them. It is important to spell out the decision making process in advance. We will revisit this issue in a later chapter.

The comparisons are made using judgments based on knowledge and experience to interpret data according to their contribution to the parent node in the level immediately above. Once all the pairwise comparisons in a group are completed a scale of relative priorities is derived from them. This process is repeated for all groups on all levels. The final step is a weighting process that uses these priorities synthesize the overall importance of the criteria, subcriteria and alternatives, and the highest ranking alternative is chosen.

The advantage of this approach is twofold. First, the structure of the problem represented in the hierarchy can be as elaborate as necessary to handle the complexity of the decision. Its design helps the decision makers to visualize the problem and its controlling factors. Second, the judgment process is so simple that they are in command of the problem as they see it.

The entire process of comparisons is predicated on the use of a unit (of measurement) assigned to the goal. The question asked in making a comparison between a pair of elements has two parts: Dominance: Which of the two elements has the property or meets the criterion more? Intensity: How much more? Dominance stands for importance established through experience, preference perceived in the present, or likelihood projected in the future. When making a comparison one chooses the smaller or lesser one of the pair as the unit and estimates the larger one as a multiple of that unit, based on the perceived intensity factor. As we shall see presently each criterion (subcriterion, alternative) is assigned a weight relative to a node in the next higher level. Since each of these nodes carries only its priority of the unit goal, the derived scale is suitably transformed through multiplication by the weights of the criteria so that each alternative receives its portion of the unit goal.

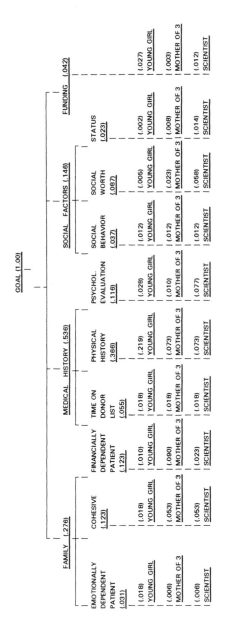

Figure 1-1 *Organ Transplant Hierarchy*

Let us now turn to how the judgments are recorded and the priorities derived from them.   We begin with the judgments for comparing the criteria of the second level with respect to the goal. They can be represented by the matrix below.   It is a square matrix with as many rows (and columns) as there are criteria connected to the goal.   The numbers in this matrix express the intensity of dominance of the criterion in the column heading over the criterion in the row heading.   Inasmuch as we are using the ratio scale, the matrix is reciprocal which means that the numbers, which are symmetric with respect to the diagonal, are inverses of one another, $a_{ij} = 1/a_{ji}$.   If one criterion is deemed to be five times more important than another, then the other is 1/5 as important when compared with the first.   The numbers in the Priorities column are the components of the eigenvector of the matrix, the inconsistency is a number closely related to the principal eigenvalue of the matrix.   These numbers are the result of simple computations which will be explained in detail in Chapter 3.

Goal	Family	Medical History	Social Factors	Funding	Priorities
Family	1	1/2	2	7	.276
Medical History	2	1	5	9	.536
Social Factors	1/2	1/5	1	5	.146
Funding	1/7	1/9	1/5	1	.042

Inconsistency = .034

Of the sixteen entries, four are ones, representing the four self comparisons on the diagonal.   Half of the remainder are reciprocals by virtue of the inverted comparison.   Thus all we need are six independent comparisons.   In general, $n(n - 1)/2$ comparisons are needed if n is the number of elements being compared in the triangle above the diagonal of ones.

The judgments are entered in the matrix in response to the question: How much more important is one criterion on the left side of the matrix, when compared with another at the top of the matrix, to justify a fair or rational heart transplant decision? When a criterion is compared with itself it is of equal importance and is assigned the value 1. The numbers 3, 5, 7, 9 correspond to the verbal judgments "moderately more", "strongly more", "very strongly more", and "extremely more", respectively. The numbers 2, 4, 6, 8 are used when a compromise is in order. This scale from 1 to 9 has proved to be the most appropriate. We shall discuss its choice in more detail in Chapter 3.   In our example, the value 2 representing "equal to moderate" is assigned to Medical History over Family, and its reciprocal value appears in the first row, second column position. "Equal to moderate" is also assigned to Family over Social Factors.   "Very strongly" is selected in favor of Family over Funding.   "Strongly" more important is assigned to Medical History over Social Factors. "Extremely" more important is selected for Medical History over Funding. Finally, "strongly" more important is assigned to Social Factors over Funding.

When the number of elements to be compared is reasonably small, between seven and nine, the priorities derived from the comparisons are very stable when small changes, one or two units in either direction, are made. A measure of the coherence of the judgments is the Inconsistency factor displayed at the bottom of the matrix.   It offers a clue whether to improve the judgments, by allowing the individual or the group to modify some of their estimates. There is a ceiling above which this factor indicates that the decision is not sound.   The judgments in our matrix are slightly inconsistent (0.034). The calculation of the Inconsistency factor will be presented in Chapter 3.

Now we turn our attention to the Priorities column. Its entries are the components of the eigenvector of the matrix. The computation of this vector is outlined in Chapter 3.   The significance of these numbers is that they represent the conversion of the pairwise comparisons of the criteria into a ratio scale. Thus, for instance, Medical History is nearly twice as important as Family which, in turn, is nearly twice as important as Social Factors. The eigenvector consolidates the sixteen relative intensity ratios of the matrix into four measures of intensity. This new scale is called the *derived* scale. It is an important property of this scale that the sum of the numbers is always 1.

The importance of this scale becomes apparent if we use the derived scale to form the matrix of the judgment ratios. For instance, instead of giving Social Factors over Family the intensity 2 we use the values in the derived scale to form 0.276/0.146. If we do this for all entries we obtain the matrix

Goal	Family	Medical History	Social Factors	Funding	Priorities
Family	1	.276/.536	.276/.146	.276/.042	.276
Medical History	.536/.276	1	.536/.146	.536/.042	.536
Social Factors	.146/.276	.146/.536	1	.146/.042	.146
Funding	.042/.271	.042/.536	.042/.146	1	.042

Inconsistency = .000

Observe that the Inconsistency is now 0. We shall later prove that when the judgments are consistent they coincide with their ratios from the derived scale.

Inconsistency is a natural human trait to allow for changing our minds when new facts come to light. For example a person may prefer an apple to an orange, an orange to a banana and still prefer a banana to an apple. This case is an example of the preferences being *intransitive*. Intransitivity is a strong indication of inconsistency. But preferences do not have to be intransitive to be inconsistent. For example one may prefer an apple twice as much as an orange and an orange three times as much as a banana but only prefer the apple five times as much as a banana. This would be inconsistent though an apple is still preferred to a banana. Despite the desirability of consistency, it cannot be forced on people and thereby invalidate their changing feelings.

If a comparison matrix is perfectly consistent, the priorities of the elements can be obtained by adding the numbers in each row and dividing each sum by the total sum of the rows, a process called normalization.

The next step in this example of the AHP is to repeat the procedure above for every criterion. The subcriteria under each criterion are compared as to their importance with respect to that criterion to derive their *local* priorities. To obtain the importance of each subcriterion relative to the overall goal, the local priorities are weighted (multiplied) by the priority of the parent criterion to obtain their *global* priorities with respect to the goal as shown in Figure 1-1. Finally the three alternatives, the candidates in this case, are compared with respect to each subcriterion, or criterion as in the case of Funding which has no subcriteria, and weighted by the overall priority of the subcriteria. The sum of these products taken for each alternative is the overall priority of that alternative.

In all, this abbreviated illustration would require $6 + 3 \times 3 + 3 \times 10 = 45$ judgments, agreed upon through a few hours of discussion. One should then perform a sensitivity analysis to determine how much effect a change in judgments would have on the final decision.

We continue our hypothetical case with the comparison matrix for the criterion Funding. The three pairwise comparisons answer the question: Which candidate can best fund the transplant and how much better when compared with another candidate?

The comparisons are

Funding .042	Young Girl(YG)	Mother of 3 (M)	Scientist (S)	Priorities	
				Local	Global
YG	1	7	3	.649	.027
M	1/7	1	1/5	.072	.003
S	1/3	5	1	.279	.012

Inconsistency .062

Observe that the global priorities are the product of the local priorities and the priority of the Funding criterion which we determined in the previous step.

The other matrices of judgment are given by:

Family .276	Emotionally Dependent Patient(EDP)	Cohesive (C)	Financially Dependent Patient(FDP)	Priorities	
				Local	Global
EDP	1	1/4	1/4	.111	.031
C	4	1	1	.444	.123
FDP	4	1	1	.444	.123

Inconsistency .000

Medical History .576	Time on Donor List (ToDL)	Physical History (PH)	Psychological Evaluation (PE)	Priorities	
				Local	Global
ToDL	1	1/7	1/2	.103	.055
PH	7	1	3	.682	.366
PE	2	1/3	1	.216	.116

Inconsistency .051

Social Factors .146	Social Behavior (SB)	Social Worth (SW)	Status (S)	Priorities	
				Local	Global
SB	1	1/3	2	.249	.037
SW	3	1	3	.594	.087
S	1/2	1/3	1	.157	.023

Inconsistency .051

Finally,

Emotionally Dependent Patient .031	Young Girl (YG)	Mother of 3 (M)	Scientist (S)	Priorities Local	Priorities Global
YG	1	3	3	.6	.018
M	1/3	1	1	.2	.006
S	1/3	1	1	.2	.006

Inconsistency   .000

Cohesive .123	Young Girl (YG)	Mother of 3 (M)	Scientist (S)	Priorities Local	Priorities Global
YG	1	1/3	1/3	.143	.018
M	3	1	1	.429	.053
S	3	1	1	.429	.053

Inconsistency   .000

Financially Dependent Patient .123	Young Girl (YG)	Mother of 3 (M)	Scientist (S)	Priorities Local	Priorities Global
YG	1	1/7	1/3	.081	.010
M	7	1	5	.731	.090
S	3	1/5	1	.188	.023

Inconsistency   .062

Time on Donor List .055	Young Girl (YG)	Mother of 3 (M)	Scientist (S)	Priorities Local	Priorities Global
YG	1	1	1	.333	.018
M	1	1	1	.333	.018
S	1	1	1	.333	.018

Inconsistency   .000

Physical History .366	Young Girl (YG)	Mother of 3 (M)	Scientist (S)	Priorities Local	Priorities Global
YG	1	3	3	.6	.219
M	1/3	1	1	.2	.073
S	1/3	1	1	.2	.073

Inconsistency   .000

Psycholog. Evaluation .116	Young Girl (YG)	Mother of 3 (M)	Scientist (S)	Priorities	
				Local	Global
YG	1	3	1/3	.243	.028
M	1/3	1	1/7	.088	.010
S	3	7	1	.669	.077

Inconsistency .007

Social Behavior .037	Young Girl (YG)	Mother of 3 (M)	Scientist (S)	Priorities	
				Local	Global
YG	1	1/7	1/3	.333	.012
M	7	1	5	.333	.012
S	3	1/5	1	.333	.012

Inconsistency .000

Social Worth .087	Young Girl (YG)	Mother of 3 (M)	Scientist (S)	Priorities	
				Local	Global
YG	1	1/5	1/9	.063	.005
M	5	1	1/3	.265	.023
S	9	3	1	.672	.058

Inconsistency .028

Status .023	Young Girl (YG)	Mother of 3 (M)	Scientist (S)	Priorities	
				Local	Global
YG	1	1/5	1/7	.075	.002
M	5	1	1/2	.333	.008
S	7	2	1	.592	.014

Inconsistency .014

Funding .042	Young Girl (YG)	Mother of 3 (M)	Scientist (S)	Priorities	
				Local	Global
YG	1	7	3	.649	.027
M	1/7	1	1/5	.072	.003
S	1/3	5	1	.279	.012

Inconsistency .062

It is instructive to study these matrices in some detail because they demonstrate how this process tempers potentially emotional decisions. For instance, the Scientist scores high in the Psychological Evaluation, in Status and as to Social Worth. But since these criteria have relatively low priorities he may not receive the highest overall priority. On the other hand, the Young Girl's high rating in Physical History may be of consequence because this criterion has a high overall priority.

In Table 1.1 we give the local priority of the three candidates for each of the corresponding criteria or subcriteria as applicable. We then weight each row by the priority of the criteria above it and sum to obtain the overall priorities on the right. In this case the young girl would be selected.

Table 1.1 Distributive mode synthesis of priorities

	EDP .031	C .123	FDP .123	ToDL .055	PH .366	PE .116	SB .037	SW .087	S .023	F .042	Overall Rank
YG	.6	.143	.081	.333	.6	.243	.333	.063	.075	.649	.358
M	.2	.429	.731	.333	.2	.088	.333	.265	.333	.072	.296
S	.2	.429	.188	.333	.2	.669	.333	.672	.592	.279	.346

Structural and Functional Dependence.

In relative measurement elements are compared with each other to derive values for them that are meaningful on a ratio scale. The approach itself makes these elements dependent on each other in measurement. We call this kind of dependence *structural dependence*. Another kind of dependence is *functional* dependence, where the elements depend on each other according to their functions or properties. This second type of dependence will be discussed later in the book. However, structural dependence highlights the presence of a criterion which is not usually considered important in measurement on scales with a unit. That criterion is the number of alternatives. It is of concern, for instance, in problems involving the allocation of limited resources. The more alternatives there are, the less of the resource each receives. Even though the elements are functionally independent, each depends on how many others there are, but not on any single one of them. In the heart transplant problem above we may think that the problem as stated here is solved as above. However, if there were additionally several candidates exactly like the young girl, should the non-uniqueness of the girl water down her priority and give the heart to the next runnerup? The answer is no, and in that situation the number of alternatives should not affect the choice. On the other hand, if the choice were to be made between two hats, a hat preferred on style to another may not be chosen if there were other copies of it depriving it of uniqueness. In this case the number of alternatives affects the decision. If it is desired to make a choice independent of the number of alternatives, instead of normalization (dividing by the sum) as in the distributive mode, one divides the local priorities of the candidates by the priority of the top ranking "ideal" candidate and then weights the results. This produces the following Table 1.2. For this example the ranks (but not the values) are as before.

Table 1.2 Ideal mode synthesis of priorities

	EDP .031	C .123	FDP .123	ToDL .055	PH .366	PE .116	SB .037	SW .087	S .023	F .042	Overall Rank
YG	1	.333	.111	1	1	.363	1	.094	.127	1	.639
M	.333	1	1	1	.333	.132	1	.394	.563	.111	.537
S	.333	1	.257	1	.333	1	1	1	1	.430	.623

Each new alternative is now pairwise compared with the ideal one and assigned its proportionate rank in the set. A well qualified new applicant may become the most preferred. No unpreferred one on all the criteria can affect the other's ranks (see Chapter 5).

Remark: In radar and sonar waveform propagation, information is preserved in phase which is unaffected by normalization of magnitude (as in the distributive mode.) In signal processing, to make noise effect more distinguishable on each trace, one divides all signal values by a constant, the largest value (as in the Ideal Mode). If the signals begin with the same amount of noise, the largest one will have the smallest noise.

4. Absolute Measurement, An Example [4]

Cognitive psychologists have recognized for some time that there are two kinds of comparisons that people are able to make - absolute and relative. In absolute comparisons alternatives are compared with a standard in one's memory that has been developed through experience. In relative comparisons alternatives are compared in pairs according to a common attribute, as we did throughout the heart transplant decision.

Absolute measurement (sometimes also called rating) is applied to rank independent alternatives from which the choice is made in terms of rating intensities for each of the criteria. For example, if ranking students is the objective and one of the criteria on which they are to be ranked is performance in mathematics, the mathematics ratings might be: excellent, good, average, below average, poor; or, using the usual school terminology, A, B, C, D and F. Relative comparisons are first used to set priorities on the ratings themselves. If desired a continuous curve may be fitted through the derived intensities. This concept may go against our socialization. However, it is perfectly reasonable to ask how much is an A preferred to a B or to a C. The judgment of how much an A is preferred to a B might be different under different criteria. Perhaps for mathematics an A is VERY STRONGLY preferred to a B, while for physical education an A is only MODERATELY preferred to a B. So the end result might be that the ratings are scaled differently. For example one could have the following scale values for the ratings:

	MATH	PHYSICAL EDUCATION
A	0.50	0.30
B	0.30	0.30
C	0.15	0.20
D	0.04	0.10
E	0.01	0.10

For many decisions it may be desirable to divide the ratings by the highest value. An alternative that is best for every criterion becomes the ideal with an overall rating of one. Thus the above example becomes:

	MATH	PHYSICAL EDUCATION
A	1.00	1.00
B	0.60	1.00
C	0.30	0.67
D	0.08	0.33
E	0.01	0.33

Finally, once the priorities (or scale values) for the ratings are established through relative measurement under each criterion, each student is scored by clicking off the appropriate rating under each criterion then weighting it by the importance of the criterion also obtained through comparisons and adding them up. Every individual gets a total overall score. The scores thus obtained may then be normalized by dividing by their sum so they can be compared on a percentage basis.

Absolute measurement requires intimate prior knowledge to make it possible to compare the ratings. One cannot whimsically assign judgments and hope for a meaningful outcome. In most decisions we have no such experience and prior knowledge and must apply relative comparisons to the alternatives themselves, as in the heart transplant example. Under absolute measurement, no matter how many new alternatives are introduced, or old ones deleted, the old ranks are unaffected by what new alternatives we look at. Absolute measurement is particularly useful in large scale and ongoing societal activities such as the school admission process. Most schools have long established criteria for admission that are quite independent of the current crop of students seeking admission. A student must meet the minimal standards to be admitted. In any situation where standards are well established and must be observed, absolute measurement should be used in preference to relative measurement.

In absolute measurement a hierarchy is developed in the usual way down to the level of criteria or subcriteria. The criteria or subcriteria are further divided into a level of intensities. Each criterion has intensity ratings listed under it. An example would be to take a criterion of performance and list under it the intensities excellent, very good, good, average, below average, poor and very poor. These are ratings that are then prioritized to determine their relative importance. The type and number of ratings for each criterion may be different. The alternatives are rated on the intensities. At times it may be desired to interpolate the value of an alternative according to an appropriately chosen curve for the intensities through them or according to subintensities. It is important to note that if we do not divide the intensities by the weight of the largest one, the priority of each criterion itself must be multiplied by the relative number of ratings under it to the total number of ratings under all the criteria. The same is true if different criteria have a different number of ratings. Otherwise an important criterion may become diluted merely because it has too many ratings under it. The computer program, Expert Choice, used in conjunction with the AHP does this automatically for the user.

The following example is concerned with choosing a site to locate the superconducting supercollider (SSC), a multi-billion dollar facility to carry out physics experiments. Here is a brief account of the study.

In January of 1987, the U.S. government administration proposed the construction of a superconducting supercollider. Thirty-five sites were initially proposed and it was the job of the Department of Energy with assistance from the National Academies of Sciences and Engineering to select the best site. A report was later issued which described how the committee doing the ranking chose the best site from among the eight finalists selected. Later, the author worked with Nicholas Rudenko and Christopher P. Sparta to apply the absolute mode of the Analytic Hierarchy Process and the "Expert Choice" software package. Information obtained directly from the "GAO Report to Congressional Requesters" was used to validate the ranking of the site finalists. Some of the information had to be summarized or interpreted because it was not given in explicit form, perhaps to preserve confidentiality. The criteria were:

A. GEOLOGY AND TUNNELING: (1) suitability of the topography, geology and associated geohydrology for efficient and timely construction of the proposed SSC underground structures; (2) stability of the proposed geology against settlement and seismicity and other features that could adversely affect SSC operations; (3) installation and operational efficiency resulting from minimal depths for the accelerator complex and experimental halls; and (4) risk of encountering major problems during construction.

B. REGIONAL RESOURCES: (1) proximity of communities within commuting distance of the proposed SSC facilities capable of supporting the SSC staff, their families, and visitors. Adequacy of community resources - e.g., housing, medical services, community services, educational and research activities, employment opportunities for family members, recreation, and cultural resources, all available on a nondiscriminatory basis; (2) accessibility to the site, e.g., major airport(s), railroad(s), and highway system(s) serving the vicinity and site; (3) availability of a regional industrial base and skilled labor pool to support construction and operation of the facility; (4) extent and type of state, regional and local administrative and institutional support that will be provided, e.g., assistance in obtaining permits and unifying codes and standards.

C. ENVIRONMENT: (1) significance of environmental impacts, constructing, operating, and decommissioning the SSC; (2) projected ability to comply with all applicable, relevant, and appropriate federal, state and local environmental/ safety requirements within reasonable bounds of time, cost, and litigation risk; (3) ability of the proposer, DOE, or both to reasonably mitigate adverse environmental impacts to minimal levels.

Note: the above subcriteria were developed from the

following 15 environmental factors: (1) Earth resources; (2) Water resources; (3) Air resources; (4) Noise/ vibration matters; (5) Ecological resources; (6) Health and safety matters; (7) Land use; (8) Socioeconomics; (9) Scenic/visual resources; (10) Cultural (historical, archaeological, and paleontological) resources; (11) Compliance with federal laws and regulations; (12) Compliance with state laws and regulations; (13) Compliance with local laws and regulations; (14) Alternative mitigative measures available; and (15) Cost effectiveness of mitigative measures.

D. SETTING: (1) ability of the proposed to deliver defendable title, in accordance with the schedule for land estates in land that will adequately protect the government's interest and the integrity of the SSC during construction and operation; (2) flexibility to adjust the position of the SSC in the nearby vicinity of the proposed location; and (3) presence of natural and man-made features of the region that could adversely affect the siting, construction and operations of the SSC.

E. REGIONAL CONDITIONS: (1) presence of man-made disturbances, such as vibration and noise, that could adversely affect the operation of the SSC; and (2) presence of climatic conditions that could adversely affect the construction and operation of the SSC.

F. UTILITIES: (1) reliability and stability of the electric-power-generating and transmission grid system. Flexibility for future expansion; and (2) reliability, quality, and quantity of water to meet the needs of the facility.

Paired comparisons and ratings were inferred from the condensed information available in the GAO report. To simulate the committee's thought processes and utilize the information provided in the report, the criteria listed in the report were condensed as follows:

Geology and Tunneling, Setting, and Regional Conditions - are given without subcriteria.

Regional resources - treated in the model in the detailed way described above.

Environmental - the three subcriteria were aggregated into one main criterion. 15 environmental factors were used to develop the ratings for this main criterion. The available information was used to indicate the number of factors that were rated Good and the number that were rated Satisfactory. If the site had 12 or more factors which were rated Good, we gave it a "Good" rating. If the site had less than 12 factors rated Good, we gave it a "Good/Satisfactory" rating.

Utilities - were not included in the final group of criteria because there was little discrimination among the sites as far as utilities were concerned.

Here everything proceeds with paired comparisons. The intensities are prioritized by comparing them in pairs as to their relative preference. The intensities of a criterion are each divided by the highest intensity among them so that the one with the largest value (the ideal) has a priority of one. This is done for each criterion. The resulting intensities are then weighted by the overall importance of their parent criterion. For each criterion or subcriterion immediately above the level of alternatives, each alternative is assigned the intensity that best describes it with respect to that criterion. The priorities of the intensities are then added for the alternative to give it an overall weight. How good absolute measurement is depends on the quality of the expert knowledge available to compare the intensities.

The hierarchy for the SSC problem is shown in Figure 1-2 followed by the ranking of alternatives according to the absolute mode of measurement. An alternative that is best on all criteria receives the value 1. All others receive a proportionate value. The outcome shown in Table 1.3 coincided with the committee ranking of the eight sites except that sites 4 and 6 are interchanged. What is important is that the best site, Texas, is the same. That is where the SSC will be located.

This example can also be done by paired comparisons, by adding alternatives one at a time. The ratio comparisons of a new alternative with any of the existing ones is supplied by the ratings of the two alternatives being compared with respect to a criterion. The priorities of the two alternatives are given by any of the two column vectors (See Chapter 5 on rank preservation and reversal.)

The final weights and ranking of alternatives depends on what criteria there are and on the weights of these criteria. If all the alternatives are not present at once but new ones arrive or old ones are deleted, new criteria may be introduced or the weights of the old criteria changed. As a result, the ranks of all the alternatives could now change. But there are other types of information that can also affect the ranks of alternatives. For example, the number of alternatives itself can affect their importance. Too much gold affects the value placed on gold. Also, what sort of alternatives there are in a collection can affect what value we attach to other alternatives. In other words, in many decision problems the assessment of the quality of an alternative depends on what other alternatives are considered. Absolute measurement rates alternatives one at a time and can only deal with independence, relative measurement can better deal with dependence. When it is desired to maintain the rank order of alternatives by introducing them one at a time, relative measurement is also the better alternative. We have already indicated that absolute measurement requires previous knowledge and experience to establish weights for the intensities. Relative measurement can be used for both preserving rank or allowing it to change. For most decision problems that have no precedent, relative measurement is the only meaningful approach.

In addition to dividing by the largest intensity for each criterion in absolute measurement, other variants of absolute measurement are:

1) Rating the alternatives using the intensities and then multiplying by the weight of that criterion and adding over the criteria.

2) Rating the alternatives using the intensities of a criterion, normalizing the weights of all the alternatives for each criterion, multiplying by the weight of that criterion and adding over the criteria.

3) Taking the logarithm of the intensity assigned to each alternative, multiplying it by the weight of the criterion and then adding. The result is the logarithm of the product of the intensities, each raised to the power of its criterion.

KEY TO FIGURE 1-2

GOAL	---	Determine the best site for DOE's supercollider
ACCESS	---	Accessibility to the site, e.g. major airports, railroads
ADEQUATE	---	Adequacy of community resources
ADMINIS.	---	Extent of state, regional and local administrative and institutional support
ENVIRON.	---	Environment
G/S	---	Good/Satisfactory
GEOLOGY	---	Geology and Tunneling
GOOD	---	Good
LABOR	---	Availability of regional industrial base and skilled labor pool
QUESTION	---	Questionable
REG COND.	---	Regional conditions
RESOURCE	---	Regional resources
S/Q	---	Satisfactory/Questionable
SATISFA.	---	Satisfactory
SETTING	---	Setting
L	---	Local Priority : Priority relative to parent node
I	---	Ideal priority

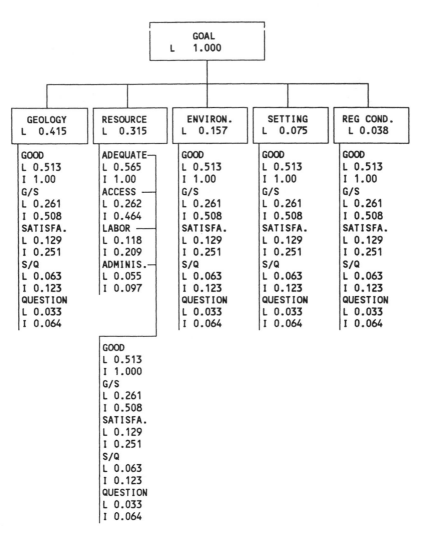

Note that only Resources had subcriteria and then intensities of subcriteria.
All others are criteria directly linked to intensities.

Figure 1-2 *Criteria and intensities for rating the eight sites*

Table 1.3 Rating of Sites on the Intensities

ALTERNATIVES	RESOURCE GEOLOGY .4153	RESOURCE ADEQUATE .1778	RESOURCE ACCESS .0825	RESOURCE LABOR .0370	ADMINIS. .0174	ENVIRON. .1570	SETTING .0747	REG COND. .0383	TOTAL
1 ONE	GOOD	GOOD	GOOD	GOOD	GOOD	GOOD	GOOD	G/S	.981
2 TWO	GOOD	GOOD	GOOD	GOOD	GOOD	G/S	G/S	SATISFA.	.857
3 THREE	GOOD	GOOD	SATISFA.	GOOD	GOOD	G/S	G/S	GOOD	.824
4 FOUR	GOOD	S/Q	GOOD	SATISFA.	GOOD	GOOD	GOOD	G/S	.798
5 FIVE	GOOD	SATISFA.	SATISFA.	GOOD	SATISFA.	GOOD	SATISFA.	SATISFA.	.708
6 SIX	GOOD	SATISFA.	GOOD	SATISFA.	SATISFA.	G/S	SATISFA.	G/S	.674
7 SEVEN	SATISFA.	SATISFA.	GOOD	GOOD	SATISFA.	G/S	GOOD	SATISFA.	.438
8 EIGHT	SATISFA.	SATISFA.	SATISFA.	GOOD	GOOD	GOOD	G/S	SATISF.	.429

Remark: In both relative and absolute measurement one can assign a zero directly to an alternative or to an intensity used to rate an alternative without involving that alternative or that intensity in a paired comparison process.

5. Why is AHP Easy to Use?

Despite the rigorous mathematical foundations of the AHP, it still meets the criteria of simplicity to use by both practitioners and academics steeped in their specialization without complete prior knowledge of the development of the theory. Here are some reasons people have given why the AHP is easy to use that has caused its widespread in both academia (with more than 50 Ph.D.'s awarded in it so far) and in top level decision making in corporations and governments (see bibliography at end of book).

- People find it natural and are usually attracted rather than alienated by it.

- It does not need advanced technical knowledge and nearly everyone can use it. It takes me about an hour to introduce it to my students with Expert Choice and they go on to do substantial examples.

- It takes into consideration judgments based on people's feelings and emotions as well as their thoughts.

- It deals with intangibles side by side with tangibles. What we perceive with the senses is dealt with by the mind in a similar way to what we feel.

- It derives scales through reciprocal comparison rather than by assigning numbers pulled from the mind directly.

- It does not take for granted the measurements on scales, but asks that scale values be interpreted according to the objectives of the problem.

- It relies on simple to elaborate hierarchic structures to represent decision problems. With such appropriate representation, it is able to handle problems of risk, conflict, and prediction.

- It can be used to make direct resource allocation, benefit/cost analysis, resolve conflicts, design and optimize systems.

- It is an approach that describes how good decisions are made rather than prescribes how they should be made. No one living at a certain time knows what is good for people for all time.

- It provides a simple and effective procedure to arrive at an answer, even in group decision making where diverse expertise and preferences must be considered.

- It can be applied in negotiating conflicts by focusing on relations between relative benefits to costs for each of the parties.

6. Beyond AHP

In this age we have begun to question the absolute objectivity of science. The very demand for objectivity itself and its method of application is a value system. Knowledge and value are inseparable. Their vital connection is through action. We need to experience the process of knowledge generation in terms of what goal motivates their pursuit. Why we want this kind of knowledge and not that; who chooses to pursue that political path in defending a scientific theory; why this way of thinking is preferred by us to that way; how should we use the knowledge we have. The answers to these questions are not neutral. They are value laden. We cannot escape the fact that it is the species homo sapiens that is interested in this or that knowledge.

The goal of multicriteria decisions is to assist people to expand and relate knowledge to value and establish priorities for actions taken in light of that knowledge. But values and choices change and we must be careful not to fix the importance of value permanently. Tomorrow's criteria for what is best will not be those of today, nor the methods we use to attain value will always be considered the best.

Abstractly, multicriteria decision making involves the decomposition of a decision problem into a hierarchy of aggregates, sub aggregates, and still more specific sub sub aggregates, down to a level of alternatives to choose from. The object is to rank them. People make assumptions on how to do this ranking and the differences in methods is what kind of assumptions they make and what they assume that people can and cannot do in the form of judgments. There are several ways for multicriteria decisions represented in this audience. In terms of scales there are ordinal multicriteria thinkers, there are interval and utility thinkers, there are Pareto optimality thinkers and there are even nihilists who think that it is precisely because value is relative that we should not try to ask what is best. The Analytic Hierarchy Process elicits judgments in the form of paired comparisons which I believe is closer to how the mind functions and how our senses interpret sense data and even on a lower level how our biology works to derive information from multiple sources. I find it difficult to believe that there are built-in scales for each attribute that are used to measure every stimulus we encounter. I am an eclectic who believes that all our rationality must be used to further our well being. Let me tell you why I felt a strong need for my kind of approach to decision making. It must be done with simplicity because all people are decision makers and they cannot go to a school for many years to learn about it. It must be rigorous to the most profound mind yet simple and easy to follow. In saying this I should note that it has not been easy to spread this new scientific paradigm to practitioners of traditional approaches. I attribute this mostly to the natural human tendency to resist change because it creates the risk to obsolete the more traditional approaches to which people have committed their efforts and talents. History is replete with examples where revolutionary changes were induced by mounting problems that could not be solved without adapting the new approach. Our way to interpret the world must have both mathematical (quantitative) rigor - free of paradoxes and contradictions to be sure that our thinking is not getting in its own way - and also be easy to communicate and follow by the lay person. Yes, the lay person without too much dogmatizing by the experts and preferably independently of their assistance.

It was once thought that the human race could understand and control without definition of value. There are many today who think that our very survival depends on invoking values that serve us well. But we must agree on the values. We need to learn to resolve conflicts.

Our present day values come from the past. But we need others that come from a simulated future into which we are marching even now. We need ways to forecast that future to improve our actions today compatible with whatever values we have.

The emergence of different biological forms to perform survival tasks in nature is a slow and extremely varied process ranging from the minutest virus or plant to the complex human. It is endowed with organic means of locomotion, ingestion, reaction and so on. The response of life forms is varied and by no means always ideal. The behavioral direction of forms is not yet well defined. It is amorphous and depends on the variety of conditioning so that the chemistry of a form which it learns to generate in reaction to a problem depends on what it has learned to do in the past.

Hierarchic structures are ways to increase the variety and efficiency of behavioral performance of people in different situations. It need not always provide a simple ideal answer. An answer depends on the prior learning of people to examine a situation from many facets.

The behavioral component in a similar way to the physical component which defines hyperbolic geometry through inversion, it too defines a hyperbolic behaviometry by inversion from individual behavior to universal behavior. The points at infinity are mapped to the origin. Principles which one takes for granted for people (along lines of the parallel postulate) can be varied in the general behavioral scheme.

With the physical goes the goal of health and long life and full dimensional enjoyment of living. With behavior goes happiness and satisfaction, with a spiritual life goes security and courage, perseverance, empathy and love.

Although by no means exhaustive, these are the kinds of ultimate human goals that define the future of the human race. Decision making is an activity that enhances these goals.

Every optimization problem is relative to the factors chosen. It is always possible to include more factors so that the previous solution is no longer optimum. Therefore optimization is an attempt to obtain an answer whose impact is psychological. Most physical optima are themselves approximations to outcomes with constraints derived from our senses responding to stimuli. The perspective of a hierarchy is broader than that of an optimization problem. A best choice from a hierarchy is also an optimum. In turn it is relative. It has the advantage over a formal optimum in that it is derived with respect to a very broad perspective. By combining the two approaches, formal optimization would come closer to satisfying our idea of an absolute optimum. Take for example the classical problem of the brachistochrone. It assures a perfectly smooth trajectory seldom found in nature. How do we optimize if we include all sorts of contortions in the trajectory, along with friction, wind and gravity?

There are a number of areas that need further investigation and others in which ground needs to be broken. The reader is referred to the AHP literature for applications and theoretical developments in most of these areas:

(1) Generalization of the hierarchy and systems networks to manifolds.
(2) Deeper and more extensive research on continuous judgments.
(3) Test different group decision-making approaches on the same problem and search for common elements. Develop A, B, C guidelines for group participation in decision making.
(4) Investigate the relationship of the principal eigenvector to the Weber-Fechner power law.
(5) Develop applications of the AHP in game theory, particularly with respect to negotiation.

(6) Investigate the relationship of the AHP and optimization. Can the general optimization problem be solved using the AHP?
(7) Implement psychological studies to show how people's strength of feeling can be adequately represented by numerical scales.
(8) Study the sensitivity of priorities to the number of criteria and, more generally, to the size of the hierarchy.
(9) Sample opinions on how satisfied clients are with AHP outcomes.
(10) Formulate more cases using the AHP in resource allocation, planning, cost-benefit analysis and conflict resolution.
(11) Is there power in hierarchic formulation and judgments to make better predictions? How can it be tested?
(12) The AHP and risk analysis: put forth a definitive theory about the use of scenarios in risk analysis.
(13) Investigate the relationship between the AHP and artificial intelligence.
(14) Develop communication and causal languages using the AHP.

(15) How the AHP theory applies to the development of underlying constructs associated with the senses as hyperbolic geometry relates to vision through inversion.

7. Feedback Systems - A Generalization of Hierarchies

A hierarchy is a special case of a network system with feedback. Hierarchies use goals and criteria to capture influence and distribute it down to the alternatives. In a system one simply has priorities of interaction on various attributes. We will show in Chapter 8 that it is only when a system is evaluated by a control hierarchy that one can obtain from it multicriteria and goal directed priorities.

Most decision problems are analyzed by assigning weights to criteria based on some higher objectives. The alternatives are then rated with respect to these criteria and their priorities weighted and summed, as for example one does by using the composition principle (weighting the elements of a level by the priorities of their parent criteria and adding to obtain an overall priority for each element) of the Analytic Hierarchy Process. There are many decision problems in which the only way to establish weights for the criteria is to consider the alternatives themselves as the attributes in terms of which the criteria must be judged. This is a case of dependence of criteria on alternatives. Whenever a new alternative is added, the weights of the criteria are changed and as a result the weights and ranks of the original alternatives are changed. In the hierarchic approach the criteria weights are initially determined independently of the alternatives.

We now give a simple example of feedback that is concerned with the management of a water reservoir. Here we are faced with the decision to choose one of the possibilities of maintaining the water level in a dam. Levels can be Low (L), Medium (M) or High (H) depending on the relative importance of Flood Control (F), Recreation (R) and the generation of Hydroelectric Power (E), respectively, for the three levels. As in the car selection example, the first set of three matrices gives the prioritization of the alternatives with respect to the criteria and the second set, those of the criteria in terms of the alternatives. As is usual in this book, the eigenvector is the priority vector. Its derivation is discussed later in this book.

Which level is best for flood control?

Flood Control	Low	Med	Hi	Eigen-vector
Low	1	5	7	.722
Medium	1/5	1	4	.205
High	1/7	1/4	1	.073

Consistency Ratio .107

Which level is best for recreation?

Recreation	Low	Med	Hi	Eigen-vector
Low	1	1/7	1/5	.072
Medium	7	1	3	.649
High	5	1/3	1	.279

Consistency Ratio .056

Which level is best for power generation?

Hydro-electric Power	Low	Med	Hi	Eigen-vector
Low	1	1/5	1/9	.058
Medium	5	1	1/5	.207
High	9	5	1	.735

Consistency Ratio .101

At Low Level which attribute is satisfied best?

Low Level Dam	F	R	E	Eigen-vector
Flood control	1	3	5	.637
Recreation	1/3	1	3	.258
Hydro-electric power	1/5	1/3	1	.105

Consistency Ratio .033

At Intermediate Level which attribute is satisfied best?

Intermediate Dam	F	R	E	Eigen-vector
F	1	1/3	1	.200
R	3	1	3	.600
E	1	1/3	1	.200

Consistency Ratio .000

At High Level which attribute
is satisfied best?

High Level Dam	F	E	R	Eigen-vector
Flood control	1	1/5	1/9	.060
Recreation	5	1	1/4	.231
Hydroelectric power	9	4	1/6	.709

Consistency Ratio   .061

The six eigenvectors were then introduced as columns of the following supermatrix which represents the impact of the elements on the left on those on top.

	F	R	E	L	M	H
F	0	0	0	.637	.200	.060
R	0	0	0	.258	.600	.231
E	0	0	0	.105	.200	.709
L	.722	.072	.058	0	0	0
M	.205	.649	.207	0	0	0
H	.073	.279	.735	0	0	0

Here one must ensure that all columns sum to unity exactly. The final priorities for both, the level of the dam and for the criteria were obtained by multiplying this matrix by itself several times until the columns stabilize and become identical in each block.

Stabilization is obtained after a few multiplications. We have

	F	R	E	L	M	H
F	0	0	0	.241	.241	.241
R	0	0	0	.374	.374	.374
E	0	0	0	.385	.385	.385
L	.223	.223	.223	0	0	0
M	.372	.372	.372	0	0	0
H	.405	.405	.405	0	0	0

In the top right block we can read off the overall priority of each of the three criteria from any column, and read off the overall priorities of the three alternatives from any column of the bottom left block. It is clear from this analysis that for the kind of judgments provided, there is preference for a high dam with priority .405 and for hydroelectric power generation with priority .385.

References and Book Bibliography

1. Dyer, R.F. and E.H. Forman, 1991, "An Analytic Approach to Marketing Decisions", Prentice Hall, Englewood Cliffs, NJ.

2. Dyer, R.F. E.A. Forman, E.H. Forman, G. Jouflas, 1988, "Marketing Decisions Using Expert Choice", Expert Choice, Inc., Pittsburgh, PA.

3. Golden, B.L., E.A. Wasil, P.T. Harker (eds.), 1989, "The Analytic Hierarchy Process - Applications and Studies", Springer-Verlag, NY.

4.   Saaty, T.L., "Absolute and Relative Measurement With the AHP. The Most Livable Cities in the United States", Socio-Econ.Plann. Sci. 20/6, pp. 327-331, 1986.

5.   --------------, 1992, "Multicriteria Decision Making - The Analytic Hierarchy Process", RWS Publications, 4922 Ellsworth Ave., Pittsburgh, PA 15213.

6.   --------------, 1992, "Decision Making for Leaders", RWS Publications, 4922 Ellsworth Ave., Pittsburgh, PA 15213.

7.   --------------, 1991, "Analytical Planning", RWS Publications, 4922 Ellsworth Ave., Pittsburgh, PA 15213.

8.   ------------- and L.G. Vargas, 1991, "The Logic of Priorities", RWS Publications, 4922 Ellsworth Ave., Pittsburgh, PA 15213.

9.   ------------- and L. G. Vargas, 1991, "Prediction, Projection and Forecasting", Kluwer Academic Publishers, Boston, Mass.

10. ------------- and J.M. Alexander, 1989, "Conflict Resolution - The Analytic Hierarchy Process", Praeger, NY.

11. ------------- and E. Forman, 1993, "The Hierarchon", RWS Publications, 4922 Ellworth Ave., Pittsburgh, PA, 15213.

Books on the Analytic Hierarchy Process in other languages:

Chinese:
     Saaty, T.L., 1989, Analytic Hierarchy Process - Applications to Resource Allocation, Management and Conflict Resolution, Thomas L. Saaty, translated by Shubo Xu, Press of Coal Industry, China.

Xu, Shubo, 1988, "Applied Decision Making Methods - Analytic Hierarchy Process", Press of Tianjin University, Tianjin, China.

French:
Merunka, D., 1987, "La prise de decision en management", Vuibert Gestion, 63 Bd. St. Germain, Paris.
Saaty, T.L., 1984, "Decider Face a la complexite", Enterprise moderne d'edition, 17 Rue Viete, 75017 Paris.

German:
Richter, K. and G. Reinhardt, 1990, "Haben Sie heute richtig ent-scheiden?", Verlag Die Wirtschaft Berlin.
Weber, K., 1993, "Mehrkriterielle Entscheidungen", R. Oldenbourg Verlag GmbH, Munchen.

Indonesian:
Saaty, T.L., 1991, "Pengambilan Keputusan Bagi-Para Pemimpin, PT Pustaka Binaman Pressindo, Jakarta, Indonesia.

Japanese:
Tone, K., 1986, "The Analytic Hierarchy Process - Decision Making", Japanese Scientific and Technical Press, Tokyo.
Tone, K. and R. Manabe, 1990, "AHP Applications", Japanese Science and Technology Press, Tokyo.
Kinoshita, E., 1991, "Like or Dislike Mathematics: Decision Making with Mathematics", Denkishoin, Tokyo.
Kinoshita, E., 1993, "AHP Method and Applications", Sumisho Publishing Co., Tokyo.

Portuguese:
Saaty, T.L., 1991, "Metodo de Analise Hierarquica", translated by Wainer Da Silveira E. Silva, Ph.D., McGraw-Hill, Ltda. e Makron Books, Brasil.

Russian:

Kearns, K. and T.L. Saaty, 1991, "Analytical Planning: The Organization of Systems, translated by Revaz Vachnadze, Radio Moscow, Moscow.

CHAPTER TWO

BASIC THEORY OF THE ANALYTIC HIERARCHY PROCESS

1. Introduction

When one speaks of relative measurement, those of us trained in the physical sciences and in mathematics are likely to think of measuring things. For example, on a scale such as the yard or the meter, each with its units, we divide the corresponding lengths to get the relative lengths. But that is not what I mean by relative measurement. First, I ask what would I do if I did not have a scale to measure length to define the relative length of two objects? Henri Lebesgue [11] wrote:

> "It would seem that the principle of economy would always require that we evaluate ratios directly and not as ratios of measurements. However, in practice, all lengths are measured in meters, all angles in degrees, etc.; that is we employ auxiliary units and, as it seems, with only the disadvantage of having two measurements to make instead of one. Sometimes, this is because of experimental difficulties or impossibilities that prevent the direct comparison of lengths or angles. But there is also another reason.
> In geometrical problems, one needs to compare two lengths, for example, and only those two. It is quite different in practice when one encounters a hundred lengths and may expect to have to compare these lengths two at a time in all possible manners. Thus it is desirable and economical procedure to measure each new length. One single measurement for each length, made as precisely as possible, gives the ratio of the length in question to each other length. This explains the fact that in practice comparisons are never,

or almost never, made directly but through comparisons with
a standard scale."

But when we have no standard scales to measure things absolutely,
we must make comparisons and derive relative measurements from
them. The question is how, and what have we learned in this
process?

We should note that we are not talking about a proposed
theory that we can accept or reject. Comparisons leading to
relative measurement is a talent of our brains. It has been
neglected in science because we have not learned to formalize it in
harmony with the usual way of creating standard scales and
comparing or measuring things on them one at a time.

The cognitive psychologist Blumenthal [4] writes:

"Absolute judgment is the identification of the magnitude of
some simple stimulus, ..., whereas comparative judgment is
the identification of some relation between two stimuli both
present to the observer. Absolute judgment involves the
relation between a single stimulus and some information held
in short-term memory — information about some former
comparison stimuli or about some previously experienced
measurement scale... To make the judgment, a person must
compare an immediate impression with memory impression of
similar stimuli...."

Thus relative measurement through comparative judgment
is intrinsic to our thinking and should not be carried by us as an
appendage whose real function is not understood well or at all and
should be kept outside. It is not difficult to see that relative
measurement predates and is necessary for creating and
understanding absolute measurement. Some of the work reported
on here is now well known. But we need it for the subsequent
discussion that lays the foundation for relative measurement.

2. The Paradigm Case; Consistency

We will first show that when the judgments use measurements from a scale to form the ratios, the resulting matrix is consistent and deriving the scale is an elementary but fundamental operation. Later we generalize to the inconsistent case where the numerical values of the judgments are not taken from precise measurements but are ratios estimated according to knowledge and perception.

Let us assume that n activities are being considered by a group of interested people and that their tasks are

a. to provide judgments on the relative importance of these activities, and

b. to ensure that the judgments are quantified to an extent that permits a quantitative interpretation of the judgments among all activities.

Our goal is to describe a method for deriving, from these quantified judgments (i.e., from the relative values associated with pairs of activities), a set of weights to be associated with individual activities in order to put the information resulting from a and b into usable form.

Let A_1, A_2, ..., A_n be the activities. The quantified judgments on pairs of activities (A_i, A_j) are represented by an n-by-n matrix

$$A = (a_{ij}), \ (i,j = 1, 2, ..., n).$$

The problem is to assign to the n activities A_1, A_2, ..., A_n a set of numerical weights w_1, w_2, ..., w_n that reflect the recorded quantified judgments.

First we get a simple question out of the way. The matrix A may have several, or only few, non-zero entries a_{ij}. Zeros are used when the judgment is unavailable. The question arises: how many entries are necessary to ensure the existence of a set of weights that is meaningful in the context of the problem? The answer is: it is sufficient that there be a set of entries that interconnects all activities in the sense that for every two indices, i, j, there should be some *chain* of (positive) entries connecting i with j:

$$a_{ii_1}, a_{i_1 i_2}, a_{i_2 i_3}, \ldots, a_{i_s j},$$

Note that a_{ij} itself is such a chain of length 1. (Such a matrix A $= (a_{ij})$ corresponds to a strongly connected graph.) This gives precise meaning to the formulation of task b.

One of the most important aspects of the AHP is that it allows us to measure the overall consistency of the judgments a_{ij}. An extreme example of inconsistent judgments is if we judge one activity to be more important than another and the second more important than the first, $a_{ij} > 1$ and $a_{ji} > 1$. More subtle is the case when the judgments of three alternatives are not "transitive." We might judge one stone two times as heavy as the first, a third stone twice as heavy as the second, but the first and last to be of equal weight. In that case $a_{ij} \neq a_{ik} a_{kj}$. This example leads us to the

Definition - A $= (a_{ij})$ is *consistent* if:

$$a_{ij} a_{jk} = a_{ik}, \qquad i,j,k = 1,\ldots,n \qquad (1)$$

We see that such a matrix can be constructed from a set of n elements which form a chain (or more generally, a spanning tree, a connected graph without cycles that includes all n elements for its vertices) across the rows and columns.

To interpret our first theorem let us consider the following case. An adult and a child are compared according to their height. If the adult is estimated to be two and a half times taller, that may be demonstrated by marking off several heights of the child end to end. However, if we have an absolute scale of measurement with the child measuring w_1 units and the adult w_2 units, then the comparison would assign the adult the relative value w_2/w_1 and the child w_1/w_2, the reciprocal value. These ratios also give us the paired comparison values $(w_1/w_2)/1$ and $1/(w_2/w_1)$, respectively, in which the height of the child serves as the unit of comparison. Such a representation is valid only if w_1 and w_2 belong to a ratio scale so that the ratio w_1/w_2 is independent of the unit used, be it in inches or in centimeters, for example.   In this way, we can interpret all ratios as absolute numbers or dominance units.

Let us now form the matrix W whose rows consist of the ratios of the measurements w_i of each of n items with respect to all others.

$$W = \begin{bmatrix} w_1/w_1 & w_1/w_2 & \cdots & w_1/w_n \\ w_2/w_1 & w_2/w_2 & \cdots & w_2/w_n \\ \vdots & \vdots & & \vdots \\ w_n/w_1 & w_n/w_2 & \cdots & w_n/w_n \end{bmatrix}$$

It is easy to prove:

Theorem 2.1 *A positive n by n matrix has the ratio form* $A = (w_i/w_j)$, *i,j = 1,...,n, if, and only if, it is consistent.*

Corollary If (1) is true then A is reciprocal.

We observe that if W is the matrix above and w is the vector $w = (w_1, \ldots w_n)^T$ then $Ww = nw$. This suggests

Theorem 2.2 *The matrix of ratios* $A = (w_i/w_j)$ *is consistent if and only if n is its principal eigenvalue and* $Aw = nw$. *Further,* $w > 0$ *is unique to within a multiplicative constant.*

Proof The "if" part of the proof is clear. Now for the other half. If A is consistent then n and w are one of its eigenvalues and its corresponding eigenvector, respectively.   Now A has rank one because every row is a constant multiple of the first row. Thus all its eigenvalues except one are equal to zero. The sum of the eigenvalues of a matrix is equal to its trace, the sum of the diagonal elements, and in this case, the trace of A is equal to n. Therefore, n is a simple eigenvalue of A. It is also the largest, or principal, eigenvalue of A. Alternatively, $A = Dee^TD^{-1}$ where D is a diagonal matrix with $d_{ii} = w_i$, and $e = (1,...,1)^T$. Therefore, A and ee^T are similar and have the same eigenvalues [16]. The characteristic equation of ee^T is obviously $\lambda^n - n\lambda^{n-1} = 0$, and the result follows.

The solution w of $Aw = nw$, the principal right eigenvector of A, consists of positive entries and is obviously unique to within a positive multiplicative constant (a similarity transformation) thus defining a ratio scale. To ensure uniqueness, we normalize w by dividing by the sum of its entries.

Given the comparison matrix A, we can directly recover w as the normalized version of any column of A; $A = wv$, $v = (1/w_1,...,1/w_n)$. It is interesting to note that for $A = (w_i/w_j)$, all the conclusions of the well-known theorem of Perron are valid without recourse to that theorem. Perron's theorem says that a matrix of positive entries has a simple positive real eigenvalue which dominates all other eigenvalues in modulus and a corresponding eigenvector whose entries are positive that is unique to within multiplication by a constant.

Here, we concern ourselves only with right eigenvectors because of the nature of dominance. In paired comparisons, the smaller element of a pair serves as the unit of comparison. There is no way of starting with the larger of a pair and decomposing it to determine what fraction of it the smaller is without first using the smaller one as a standard for the decomposition.

If A is consistent, then a_{ij} may be represented as a ratio from an existing ratio scale, such as the kilogram scale for weight. It may also be represented by using a judgment estimate as to how many times more the dominant member of the pair has a property for which no scale exists, such as smell or customer satisfaction. Of course, if the measurements from an actual scale are used in the pairwise comparisons, the derived scale of relative magnitudes is not a new scale — it is the same one used to do the measuring. We note that any finite set of n readings $w_1, \ldots, w_n$ from a ratio scale defines the principal eigenvector of a consistent n by n matrix $W = (w_i/w_j)$.

With regard to the order induced in w by W, in general, we would expect for an arbitrary positive matrix $A = (a_{ij})$, that if for some i and j, $a_{ik} \geq a_{jk}$ for all k, then $w_i \geq w_j$ should hold. But when A is inconsistent, i.e., it does not satisfy (1), what is an appropriate order condition to be satisfied by the a_{ij}, and how general can such a condition be? We now develop conditions for order preservation that are essentially observations on the behavior of a consistent matrix later generalized to the inconsistent case. The ratio $(w_i/w_j)/1$ may be interpreted as assigning the ith activity the unit value of a scale and the jth activity the absolute value w_j/w_i. In the consistent case, order relations on w_i, $i = 1, \ldots, n$, can be inferred from the a_{ij} as follows: we factor out w_1 from the first row, w_2 from the second and so on, leaving us with a matrix of identical rows and $w_i \geq w_j$ is both necessary and sufficient for $A \leftrightarrow w$.

C. Berge [1] reports on a proposal by T. H. Wei [17] on the measurement of dominance or power of a player in a tournament through a pairwise comparison matrix $B = (b_{ij})$. Each row of B defines the standing of one player relative to the other players in the tournament. We have:

$$b_{ij} = \begin{cases} 0 \text{ if i loses to j} \\ 1 \text{ if i ties j (in particular } b_{ii} = 1) \\ 2 \text{ if i wins over j} \end{cases}$$

and thus $b_{ij} + b_{ji} = 2$. The overall power of each player i is <u>defined</u> as the ith component of $\lim_{k \to \infty} B^k e/e^T B^k e$, where B^k is the kth power of B. It coincides with a constant multiple of the ith component of the solution of $Bw = \lambda_{max} w$ where λ_{max} is the principal eigenvalue of the matrix B. From a set of arbitrary nonnegative numbers one obtains a ratio scale w. But under what conditions is the solution relevant to the b_{ij}?

There is a canon about order relations in A and correspondingly in w when A is consistent that we need to observe when A is inconsistent. We begin with a consistent matrix A. By successive application of the consistency condition (1) to each factor on the left of the condition itself, we obtain:

$$A = (1/n) A^2 = \ldots = (1/n)^{k-1} A^k = \ldots$$

and in normalized form

$$\frac{A}{e^T A e} = \frac{A^2}{e^T A^2 e} = \ldots = \frac{A^k}{e^T A^k e} = \ldots \tag{2}$$

which shows that every power of A must be considered in the preservation of consistency. When A is consistent, the consistency condition (1) can be stated in equivalent terms for an arbitrary power of A. This is a useful observation for developing an order condition to be satisfied when A is inconsistent. Here the power of A gives different measurements of dominance due to intransitivity; The normalized sum of the rows of A give dominance in paths of length one; those of A^2 in paths of length two and so on. If we define a sequence of successive series of these vectors, then its limit is the principal right eigenvector.

Five Conditions on A For Preserving Order

A weaker condition for order preservation than

(i) $(A)_i \geq (A)_j$ implies $w_i \geq w_j$

is,

(ii) $(Ae)_i \geq (Ae)_j$ implies $w_i \geq w_j$

where $(A)_i$ and $(Ae)_i$ denote the ith row and ith row sum of A, and its generalization to powers of A given in the normalized form:

(iii) $$\frac{(A^m e)_i}{e^T A^m e} \geq \frac{(A^m e)_j}{e^T A^m e} \qquad \text{implies } w_i \geq w_j$$

The condition for order preservation must include all powers of A, and is given here in terms of their sum. For sufficiently large integer $N > 0$, and for $p \geq N$,

(iv) $$\sum_{m=1}^{p} \frac{(A^m e)_i}{e^T A^m e} \geq \sum_{m=1}^{p} \frac{(A^m e)_j}{e^T A^m e} \qquad \text{implies } w_i \geq w_j$$

and by (2):

(v) $$\lim_{p \to \infty} \frac{1}{p} \sum_{m=1}^{p} \frac{(A^m e)_i}{e^T A^m e} \geq \lim_{p \to \infty} \frac{1}{p} \sum_{m=1}^{p} \frac{(A^m e)_j}{e^T A^m e} \qquad \text{implies } w_i \geq w_j$$

Theorem 2.3 *If A is consistent, then*

$$\lim_{p \to \infty} \frac{1}{p} \sum_{m=1}^{p} \frac{(A^m e)_i}{e^T A^m e} \to c w_i > 0$$

and (i) - (v) are true.

Proof Follows from $A^m = n^{m-1} A$ where n is the principal eigenvalue of A, and $A = (w_i/w_j)$.

It appears that the problem of constructing ratio scales from a_{ij} has a natural principal eigenvalue structure. Our task is to extend this formulation to the case where A is no longer consistent.

3. Small Perturbations and Ratio Scale Approximation

Because we are interested in the construction of an appropriate matrix W of ratios that serves as a "good" approximation to a given reciprocal matrix A, we begin by assuming that A itself is a perturbation of W. We need the following kind of background information.

For an unrepeated eigenvalue of a positive matrix A it is known [10,15,18] that a small perturbation $A(\epsilon)$ of A gives rise to a perturbation $\lambda(\epsilon)$ that is analytic in the neighborhood of $\epsilon = 0$ and small because $A(\epsilon)$ is reciprocal. The following known theorems give us a part of what we need.

Theorem 2.4 *(Existence): If λ is a simple eigenvalue of A, then for small $\epsilon > 0$, there is an eigenvalue $\lambda(\epsilon)$ of $A(\epsilon)$ with power series expansion in ϵ:*

$$\lambda(\epsilon) = \lambda + \epsilon\lambda^{(1)} + \epsilon^2\lambda^{(2)} + \ldots$$

and corresponding right and left eigenvectors $w(\epsilon)$ and $v(\epsilon)$ such that

$$w(\epsilon) = w + \epsilon w^{(1)} + \epsilon^2 w^{(2)} + \ldots$$
$$v(\epsilon) = v + \epsilon v^{(1)} + \epsilon^2 v^{(2)} + \ldots$$

Let Θ_{ij} be a perturbation of a reciprocal matrix A such that $B = (a_{ij} + \Theta_{ij})$ is also positive [6].

Theorem 2.5 *If a positive reciprocal matrix A has the eigenvalues $\lambda_1, \lambda_2,\ldots, \lambda_n$ where the multiplicity of λ_j is m_j with $\sum_{j=1}^{n} m_j = n$, then given $\epsilon > 0$ there is a $\delta(\epsilon) > 0$ such that if $|a_{ij} + \Theta_{ij} - a_{ij}| \le \delta$ for all i and j the matrix B has exactly m_j eigenvalues in the circle $|\mu_j - \lambda_j| < \epsilon$ for each $j = 1,\ldots,s$ where $\mu_1,\ldots,\mu_s$ are the eigenvalues of B.*

If A is a consistent matrix, then it has one positive eigenvalue $\lambda_1 = n$ and all other eigenvalues are zero. For a suitable $\epsilon > 0$ there is a $\delta(\epsilon) > 0$ such that for $|\Theta_{ij}| < \epsilon$ the perturbed matrix B has one eigenvalue in the circle $|\mu_1 - n| < \epsilon$ and the remaining eigenvalues fall in a circle $|\mu_j - 0| < \epsilon$, $j = 2,\ldots,n$.

Theorem 2.6 *If n is a simple eigenvalue of A which dominates the remaining eigenvalues in modulus, for sufficiently small ϵ, $n(\epsilon) \equiv \lambda_{max}$ dominates the remaining eigenvalues of $A(\epsilon)$ in modulus.*

When A is inconsistent, several conditions on a_{ij} and on w_i, along with uniqueness, must be met to enable us to approximate A by ratios. Our conditions are divided into two categories. One category deals with the order induced by a_{ij} as absolute numbers $(w_i/w_j)/1$ or $1/(w_j/w_i)$ from a standard scale, on the components of the scale w. The other category deals with the equality or near equality of the a_{ij} to the ratios w_i/w_j formed from the derived scale w.

When A is inconsistent, how do we construct W so that the order preservation condition (v) still holds? Later we address the other question; what conditions must A satisfy to ensure that w_i/w_j is a "good" approximation to a_{ij}?

Let us consider estimates of ratios given by an expert who may make small perturbations ϵ_{ij} in $W = (w_i/w_j)$. Comparisons by ratios allow us to write $a_{ij} = (w_i/w_j) \epsilon_{ij}$, $\epsilon_{ij} > 0$, i, j = 1,...,n. In that case, A takes the form $A = W \text{ o } E = DED^{-1}$ where $W = (w_i/w_j)$, $E = (\epsilon_{ij})$, D a diagonal matrix with w as diagonal vector, and o refers to the Hadamard or elementwise product of the two matrices. The principal eigenvalue of A coincides with that of E. The principal eigenvector of A is the elementwise product of the principal eigenvectors $w = (w_1,...,w_n)^T$, and $e = (1,...,1)^T$ of W and of E respectively [16].

The distinction we make between an arbitrary positive matrix and a reciprocal matrix is that we can control a step by step modification of a reciprocal matrix so that in the representation $A = W \text{ o } E = DED^{-1}$, the ϵ_{ij}, i, j = 1,...,n are small. The purpose is to ensure that perturbing the principal eigenvalue and eigenvector of W yields the principal eigenvalue and eigenvector of A.

Why do we need such a perturbation? Because we assume that there is an underlying ratio scale that we attempt to approximate. By improving the consistency of the matrix, we obtain an approximation of the underlying scale by the principal eigenvector of the resulting matrix.

Theorem 2.7 *w is the principal eigenvector of a positive matrix A if, and only if, $Ee = \lambda_{max}e$.*

Note that e is the principal eigenvector of E and E is a perturbation of the matrix e^Te. When $Ee \neq \lambda_{max}e$ the principal eigenvector of A is another vector $w' \neq w$ and $A = W'oE'$ where $E'e = \lambda_{max}e$.

Corollary w is the principal eigenvector of a positive reciprocal matrix $A = WoE$, if and only if, $Ee = \lambda_{max}e$ and $\epsilon_{ji} = (\epsilon_{ij})^{-1}$

Assume that A is an arbitrary positive matrix that is a small perturbation E of $W = (w_i/w_j)$. Then we have

Theorem 2.8 *(order preservation): A positive matrix A satisfies condition (v), if and only if, the derived scale w is the principal eigenvector of A, i.e., $Aw = \lambda_{max}w$.*

Proof We give two proofs of this theorem, the first is based on Perron's theorem and the second, which is more appropriate for our purpose is based on perturbation.

Let

$$s_k = \frac{A^ke}{e^TA^ke} \tag{3}$$

and

$$t_m = \frac{1}{m}\sum_{k=1}^{m} s_k \tag{4}$$

The convergence of the components of t_m to the same limit as the components of s_m is the standard Cesaro summability. Since,

$$s_k = \frac{A^ke}{e^TA^ke} \rightarrow w \text{ as } k \rightarrow \infty \tag{5}$$

where w is the normalized principal right eigenvector of A, we have

$$t_m = \frac{1}{m} \sum_{k=1}^{m} \frac{A^k e}{e^T A^k e} \rightarrow w \ as \ m \rightarrow \infty \tag{6}$$

For the second proof, first assume that A has only simple eigenvalues. Using Sylvester's formula:

$$f(A) = \sum_{i=1}^{n} f(\lambda_i) \frac{\pi_{j \neq i} (A - \lambda_i I)}{\pi_{j \neq i} (\lambda_j - \lambda_i)}, \quad \lambda_{max} = \lambda_1$$

we have on writing f(A) = A^k, dividing through by λ^k_{max}, multiplying on the left by (A - $\lambda_{max}I$) to obtain the characteristic polynomial of A then multiplying on the right by e we obtain:

$$\lim_{k \rightarrow \infty} \frac{A^k e}{\lambda^k_{max}} = cw, \ for \ some \ constant \ c > 0$$

Sylvester's formula for multiple eigenvalues of multiplicity m_i shows that one must consider derivatives of $f(\lambda)$ of order no more than m_i. However, it is easy to verify by interchanging derivative and limit, that when each term is divided by λ^k_{max} its value tends to zero as $k \rightarrow \infty$, and the result again follows.

Therefore, it is necessary to obtain the principal eigenvector w to capture order properties from A, but not sufficient to ensure that W = (w_i/w_j) is a good approximation to A. The method we use to derive the scale w from a positive inconsistent matrix must also satisfy the following conditions on what constitutes a good numerical approximation to the a_{ij} by ratios. The first two are local conditions on each a_{ij}, the second two are global conditions on all a_{ij} through the principal eigenvalue and eigenvector as functions of the a_{ij}.

Four Conditions for Good Approximations

1). Reciprocity

The reciprocal condition is a local relation between pairs of elements: $a_{ji} = 1/a_{ij}$, needed to ensure that, as perturbations of ratios, a_{ij} and a_{ji} can be approximated by ratios from a ratio scale that are themselves reciprocal. It is a necessary condition for consistency.

2). Homogeneity - Uniformly Bounded Above and Below

Homogeneity is also a local condition on each a_{ij}. To ensure consistency in the paired comparisons, the elements must be of the same order of magnitude which means that our perceptions in comparing them, should be of nearly the same order of magnitude. Thus we require that the a_{ij} be uniformly bounded above by a positive constant K and, because of the reciprocal condition, they are automatically uniformly bounded below away from zero:

$$1/K \leq a_{ij} \leq K, \quad K > 0, i, j = 1,\ldots,n$$

It is a fact that people are unable to directly compare widely disparate objects such as an apple and a watermelon according to weight. If they are not comparable, it should be possible to aggregate them in such homogeneous clusters to make the comparisons. For example, we put the apple with a grapefruit and a cantaloupe in one cluster, then the cantaloupe again, a honeydew melon and varying sizes of watermelons in another cluster. The relative measurements in the clusters can be combined because we included the largest element (the cantaloupe) in the small cluster as the smallest element of the adjacent larger cluster. Then the relative weights of the elements in the second cluster are all divided by the relative weight of the common element and multiplied by its relative weight in the smaller cluster. In this manner, relative measurement of the elements in the two clusters can be related and the two clusters combined after obtaining relative measurement by paired comparisons in each cluster. The process is continued from cluster to adjacent cluster.

3). Near Consistency

The near consistency condition which is global, is formed in terms of the (structural parameters) λ_{max} and n of A and W. It is a less familiar and more intricate condition that we need to discuss at some length. The requirement that comparisons be carried out on homogeneous elements ensures that the coefficients in the comparison matrix are not too large and generally of the same order of magnitude, i.e., from 1 to 9. Knowing this constrains the size of the perturbations ϵ_{ij}, whose sum as we shall see below, is measured in terms of the near consistency condition λ_{max}-n.

The object then is to apply this condition to develop algorithms to explore changing the judgments and their approximation by successively decreasing the inconsistency of the judgments and then approximating them with ratios from the derived scale. The simplest such algorithm is one which identifies that a_{ij} for which $a_{ij} w_j/w_i$ is maximum and indicates decreasing it in the direction of w_i/w_j. Another algorithm due to Harker [8] utilizes the gradient of the a_{ij}. In the end, we obtain either a consistent matrix or a closer approximation to a consistent one depending on whether the information available allows for making the proposed revisions in a_{ij}.

Because consistency is necessary and sufficient for A to have the form $A = (w_i/w_j)$, we use w to explore possible changes in a_{ij} to modify A "closer" to that form. We form a consistent matrix $W' = (w'_i/w'_j)$, whose elements are approximations to the corresponding elements of A. We have $a_{ij} = (w'_i/w'_j) \epsilon_{ij}, \epsilon_{ij} > 0$. We have the converse of: given a problem, find a good approximation to its solution; given a problem with its exact solution, use the properties of this solution to revise the problem, i.e. the judgments which give rise to a_{ij}. Repeat the process to a level of admissible consistency. (see below)

4). Uniform Continuity

Uniform continuity implies that w_i, $i = 1,\ldots,n$ as a function of a_{ij} should be relatively insensitive to small changes in the a_{ij} in order that the ratios w_i/w_j remain good approximations to the a_{ij}. For example, it holds in w_i as the ith component of the principal eigenvector because it is an algebraic function of λ_{max} (whose value is shown to lie near n because of 3), and of the a_{ij} and $1/a_{ij}$, which are bounded.

Let us now turn to more elaboration of the near consistency condition in 3). We first show the interesting result, that inconsistency or violation of (1) by various a_{ij} can be captured by a single number λ_{max}-n, which measures the deviation of all a_{ij} from w_i/w_j.

Assume that the reciprocal condition $a_{ji} = 1/a_{ij}$ and boundedness $1/K \le a_{ji} \le K$, where $K > 0$ is a constant, hold. Let $a_{ij} = (1 + \delta_{ij}) w_i/w_j$, $\delta_{ij} > -1$, be a perturbation of $W = (w_i/w_j)$, where w is the principal eigenvector of A.

Theorem 2.9 $\lambda_{max} \ge n$

Proof Using $a_{ji} = 1/a_{ij}$, and $Aw = \lambda_{max}w$, we have

$$\lambda_{max} - n = \frac{1}{n} \sum_{1 \le i \le j \le n} \frac{\delta_{ij}^2}{1 + \delta_{ij}} \ge 0 \qquad (7)$$

Theorem 2.10 *A is consistent, if and only if, $\lambda_{max} = n$.*

Proof If A is consistent, then because of (1), each row of A is a constant multiple of a given row. This implies that the rank of A is one, and all but one of its eigenvalues λ_i, $i = 1,\ldots,n$, are zero. However, it follows from our earlier argument that,

$$\sum_{i=1}^{n} \lambda_i = Trace(A) = n.$$ Therefore $\lambda_{max} = n.$ Conversely, $\lambda_{max} = n$, implies $\epsilon_{ij} = 0$, and $a_{ij} = w_i/w_j$.

From (2) we can determine the magnitude of the "greatest" perturbation by setting one of the terms equal to λ_{max}-n and solving for δ_{ij} in the resulting quadratic. An average perturbation value is obtained by replacing λ_{max}-n in the previous result by $(\lambda_{max}$-n$)/(n - 1)$.

A measure of inconsistency is obtained by taking the ratio of λ_{max}-n to its average value over a large number of reciprocal matrices of the same order n, whose entries are randomly chosen in the interval [1/K, K]. If this ratio is small (e.g., 10% or less - for example 5% for 3 by 3 matrices) [7], we accept the estimate of w. Otherwise, we attempt to improve consistency and derive a new w. After each iteration, we assume that the new matrix is a perturbation of W and its eigenvalue and eigenvector are perturbations of n and w, respectively.

In his experimental work in the 1950's, the psychologist George Miller [12], found that in general, people (such as chess experts looking ahead a few moves to decide on a good next move) could deal with information involving simultaneously only a few facts: seven plus or minus two. With more, they become confused and cannot handle the information. Since the individual needs to maintain consistency in his decision matrix, he cannot consider more than a few options at a time. This is in harmony with the established fact that for a reciprocal matrix (though not in general) the principal eigenvalue is stable for small perturbations when n is small.

We have seen that only order preserving derived scales w are of interest. There are many ways to obtain w from A. Most of them are error minimizing procedures such as the method of least squares:

$$\sum_{i,j=1}^{n} (a_{ij} - \frac{w_i}{w_j})^2 \qquad (8)$$

which also produces nonunique answers. Only the principal eigenvector satisfies order preserving requirements when there is inconsistency. We summarize with:

Theorem 2.11 *If a positive n by n matrix A is: reciprocal, homogeneous, and near consistent, then the scale w derived from $Aw = \lambda_{max}w$ is order preserving, unique to within a similarity transformation and uniformly continuous in the a_{ij}, i, j, = 1,...,n.*

Similar results can be obtained when A is nonnegative. Also we have extended this discrete approximation of A by W to the continuous case of A reciprocal kernel and its eigenfunction [14].

4. Structural properties of Positive Reciprocal Matrices

We make the following observations on the structure of reciprocal matrices. The elementwise product of two n by n reciprocal matrices is a reciprocal matrix. It follows that the set of reciprocal matrices is closed under the operation Hadamard product. The matrix e^Te is the identity: $e^Te = e^Teoe^Te = ee^T$ and A^T is the inverse of A, $AoA^T = A^ToA = e^Te$. Thus the set G of n by n reciprocal matrices is an abelian group. Because every subgroup of an abelian group is normal, in particular, the set of n by n consistent matrices is a normal subgroup ($EoWoE^T = W$) of the group of positive reciprocal matrices.

Two matrices A and B are *R-equivalent* (A R B) if, and only if, there are a vector w and positive constants a and b such that $(1/a) Aw = (1/b) Bw$. The set of all consistent matrices can be partitioned into disjoint equivalence classes. Given a consistent matrix W and a perturbation matrix E such that

Ee = ae, a > 0 a constant, we use the Hadamard product to define A′ = WoE such that $(1/a)$ A′w = $(1/n)$ Ww. A′ and W are R-equivalent. There is a 1-1 correspondence between the set of all consistent matrices and the set of all matrices A′ defined by such Hadamard products. An R-equivalence class Q(W) is the set of all A′ such that A′R W. The set of equivalence classes Q(W) forms a partition of the set of reciprocal matrices. It is known that all the elements in Q(W) are connected by perturbations E, E′, E″,..., corresponding to a fixed value of a > 0 such that (EoE′oE″..)e = ae. Thus given an arbitrary reciprocal matrix A, there exists an equivalence class to which A belongs.

DeTurck [5] has proved that: The structure group G of the set of positive reciprocal n x n matrices has 2n! connected components. It consists of nonnegative matrices which have exactly one nonzero entry in each row and column. These matrices can be written as D·S, where D is a diagonal matrix with positive diagonal entries and S is a permutation matrix, and the negatives of such matrices. The connected component G_0 of the identity consists of diagonal matrices with positive entries on the diagonal. If A is a positive reciprocal matrix with principal right eigenvector w = $(w_1, w_2,...,w_n)^T$ and DεG$_0$ is a diagonal matrix with positive diagonal entries $d_1, d_2,...d_n$ then $I_D(A) = DAD^{-1}$ is a positive reciprocal matrix with principal eigenvector w′ = $(d_1w_1,...,d_nw_n)^T$. The principal eigenvalue is the same for both matrices. If v = $(v_1,...,v_n)^T$ and w = $(w_1,...,w_n)^T$ are two positive column vectors, then conjugation by the diagonal matrix D_{vw} with entries $v_1/w_1,...,v_n/w_n$ on the diagonal maps A_w onto A_v. The corresponding diagonal matrix D_{wv} provides the inverse map. Moreover, D_{wv} maps the consistent matrix of A_w to the consistent matrix of A_v.

5. The AHP Metric

It is desirable to have a way to judge when two ratio scales are close. Let W = (w_i/w_j) be the matrix of ratios of the principal right eigenvector w = $(w_1,...,w_n)$ of the positive reciprocal matrix A and λ_{max}

be the corresponding principal eigenvalue and let $\sum\limits_{i=1}^{n} w_i = 1$. We define the Compatibility Index (S.I.) of a matrix of judgments and the matrix of derived eigenvector ratios as S.I. $= \dfrac{1}{n^2} e^T A \circ W^T e.$

Theorem 2.12: $\dfrac{1}{n^2} e^T A \circ W^T e = \dfrac{\lambda_{max}}{n}$

Proof: From $Aw = \lambda_{max} w$ we have

$$\sum_{j=1}^{n} a_{ij} w_j = \lambda_{max} w_i$$

and $\dfrac{1}{n^2} e^T A \circ W^T e = \dfrac{1}{n^2} \sum\limits_{i=1}^{n} \sum\limits_{j=1}^{n} a_{ij} \dfrac{w_j}{w_i} = \dfrac{\lambda_{max}}{n}$

Table 2-1 gives information on compatibility and consistency for different size judgment matrices. When we have two ratio scales, we can check their compatibility by forming the Hadamard product of the matrices of their ratios, with the transpose of the second matrix used.

Table 2-1 Relationship Between Consistency and Compatibility for a Different Number of Elements

Number of Elements (n)	Compatibility Index (S.I.)	λ_{max}	$C.I. = \dfrac{\lambda_{max} - n}{n-1}$	R.I.	C.R.= C.I./R.I.
3	1.017	3.052	0.026	0.52	0.05
4	1.053	4.214	0.071	0.89	0.08
5	1.089	5.444	0.111	1.11	0.10
6	1.104	6.625	0.125	1.25	0.10
7	1.116	7.810	0.135	1.35	0.10
8	1.123	8.980	0.140	1.40	0.10
9	1.129	10.160	0.145	1.45	0.10
10	1.134	11.341	0.149	1.49	0.10
11	1.137	12.510	0.151	1.51	0.10
12	1.141	13.694	0.154	1.54	0.10
13	1.144	14.872	0.156	1.56	0.10
14	1.146	16.041	0.157	1.57	0.10
15	1.147	17.212	0.158	1.58	0.10

EXAMPLES

Consider the Hadamard product:

$$\begin{pmatrix} 1 & 2 & 4 \\ 1/2 & 1 & 2 \\ 1/4 & 1/2 & 1 \end{pmatrix} \circ \begin{pmatrix} 1 & 1/3 & 1/5 \\ 3 & 1 & 3/5 \\ 5 & 5/3 & 1 \end{pmatrix} = \begin{pmatrix} 1 & 2/3 & 4/5 \\ 3/2 & 1 & 6/5 \\ 5/4 & 5/6 & 1 \end{pmatrix}$$

We have
$$\frac{1}{n^2} e^T A \circ B^T e = \frac{9\frac{1}{4}}{9} = 1.028$$

The ratio scale vectors corresponding to the two matrices are $\left[\dfrac{4}{7}, \dfrac{2}{7}, \dfrac{1}{7}\right]^T$ and $\left[\dfrac{3}{4.6}, \dfrac{1}{4.6}, \dfrac{.6}{6.6}\right]^T$ which by this measure are considered close. For further detail and examples, see my book: *The Analytic Network Process*.

6. Concluding Remarks

Measurement is quantitative information useful for discriminating among magnitudes and among orders of magnitudes. Numerical discrimination is different from cognitive discrimination. Creativity and understanding are linked to our cognitive ability and not to our ability to make precise measurements. It is rare that extreme precision is needed for any sort of understanding and discrimination. Even in science measurement and precision are subject to interpretation. It is the goals we pursue that need to be served and we are in control of the importance and meaningfulness of these goals as they serve our well being and survival. Precision in the preparation of drugs is necessary, but there is such flexibility that the same size pill is prescribed for all adults regardless of the size of their bodies. Precision in designing the gears of a clock is mandatory, but precision in time is one and only one aspect of experience that may have to be traded off with other factors. In fact, time is subjective and what is considered good in punctuality by some may be regarded as some kind of militancy by others. Strict punctuality is a human normative invention not respected in the biology of cells and in birth and death. The question is whether we can access the world directly and satisfactorily with the very judgments we use to evaluate measurement.

One way to generate measurement on different orders of magnitude is to use the senses to make distinctions and to extend their use to lower and higher magnitudes through instruments like the microscope and the telescope. The size of objects is simply one of a very large number of attributes known to the mind. Not all magnitudes have the capability to be infinite as in size and weight, length and time. Most properties such as the ability to love and the ability to excel do not belong to the senses but directly to the mind. The mind will usually bracket their extension in one or in a few orders of magnitudes. Things of the mind must often be defined in objects. Their extension may be theoretically assumed because it cannot be seen with the eyes, felt with the hands or experienced with the body. In principle if there were no people, there may not exist such properties. In fact these attributes could determined why we assign significance to properties in the real world.

References

1.   Berge, C., 1962, *Theory of Graphs and Its Applications*, Wiley, New York.

2.   Birkhoff, G., 1957, "Extensions of Jentzsch's Theorem", *Trans. Amer. Math. Soc.* 85, p. 219-227.

3.   Blocksma, M., 1989, *Reading the Numbers*, Penguin Group, Viking-Penguin Inc., New York.

4.   Blumenthal, A.L., 1977, *The Process of Cognition*, Prentice Hall.

5.   DeTurck, D.M., 1987, "The Approach to Consistency in The Analytic Hierarchy Process," *Mathematical Modeling* 9/3-5, pp. 345-352.

6.   Franklin, J.N., 1968, *Matrix Theory*, Prentice-Hall, Englewood Cliffs, NJ.

7.   Golden, B.L. and Q. Wang, 1989, "An Alternate Measure of Consistency", in *The Analytic Hierarchy Process - Applications and Studies*, eds, Golden, Wasil and Harker, Springer-Verlag, New York.

8.   Harker, P.T., 1987, "Alternative modes of questioning in the analytic hierarchy process", *Mathematical Modeling* 9, pp. 353-360.

9.   Kohlberg, E., and John W. Pratt, 1982, "The Contraction Mapping Approach to the Perron-Frobenius Theory: Why Hilbert's Metric?," *Mathematics of Operations Research* 7/2.

10.   Lancaster, P., and Miron Tismenetsky, 1985, "Linear Transformations and Matrices," *The Theory of Matrices, 2nd Ed. With Applications*, Academic Press, Inc., Orlando.

11.   Lebesgue, H., 1928, *Leçons sur l'integration, 2nd ed.*, Gauthier-Villars, Paris.

12.   Miller, G.A., 1956, "The Magical Number Seven Plus or Minus Two: Some Limits on our Capacity for Processing Information," *Psychological Review* 63, pp. 81-97.

13.   Saaty, T.L., 1996, *Multicriteria Decision Making: The Analytic Hierarchy Process*, 2nd ed. 2nd printing, RWS Publications, 4922 Ellsworth Ave, Pittsburgh, PA. Original version published by McGraw-Hill 1980.

14.   ------------ and L.G. Vargas, 1993, "A Model of Neural Impulse Firing and Synthesis", *Journal of Mathematical Psychology* 37, 200-219.

15.   Stewart, G.W., 1973, "Eigenvalues and Eigenvectors," *Intro. to Matrix Computations*, Academic Press, Inc., Orlando.

16.   Vargas, L.G., 1983, "Analysis of Sensitivity of Reciprocal Matrices," *Applied Mathematics and Computation* 12, pp. 301-320, Elsevier Science Publishing Co., Inc., New York.

17.   Wei, T. H., 1952, "The Algebraic Foundations of Ranking Theory," Thesis, Cambridge, MA.

18.   Wilkinson, J.H., 1965, *The Algebraic Eigenvalue Problem*, Clarendon Press, Oxford.

CHAPTER THREE

THE SCALE, CONSISTENCY, AND THE EIGENVECTOR

1. Introduction

In chapters 1 and 2 we introduced some basic concepts of the AHP, including the comparison matrix and the principal eigenvector, which contains the derived scale. Here we will justify our choice of the scale when there are obviously many alternatives. We will also examine inconsistency and give a table of inconsistency measures for random judgments. There is an overall measure of inconsistency in hierarchies and another in networks. We then illustrate the impact of changes in judgment on inconsistency. We use the notion of consistency to show why people cannot deal with a large number of alternatives simultaneously, an observation already known to psychologists on empirical grounds. In case of incomplete judgments, we describe a method due to Harker for completing some or all of them. Finally, we give two methods to determine the most inconsistent judgments and how to improve them if one should desire to do so.

2. The Scale

In the paired comparison approach of the AHP one estimates ratios by using a fundamental scale of absolute numbers. In comparing two alternatives with respect to an attribute, one uses the smaller or lesser one as the unit for that attribute. To estimate the larger one as a multiple of that unit, assign to it an absolute number from the fundamental scale. This process is done for every pair. Thus, instead of assigning two numbers w_i and w_j and forming the ratio w_i/w_j we assign a single number drawn from the fundamental 1-9 scale to represent the ratio $(w_i/w_j)/1$. The absolute number from the scale is an approximation to the ratio w_i/w_j. The derived scale tells us what the w_i and w_j are. This is a central observation about the relative measurement approach of the AHP and the need for a fundamental scale.

The names of Ernest Heinrich Weber (1795-1878) and Gustav Theodor Fechner (1801-87) stand out as one considers the subject of stimulus, response, and ratio scales. In 1846 Weber formulated his law regarding a stimulus of measurable magnitudes. He found, for example, that people while holding in their hand different weights, could distinguish between a weight of 20 g and a weight of 21 g, but not if the second weight is only 20.5 g. On the other hand, while they could not distinguish between 40 g and 41 g, they could between the former weight and 42 g, and so on at higher levels. We need to increase a stimulus s by a minimum amount Δs to reach a point where our senses can first discriminate between s and $s + \Delta s$. Δs is called the just noticeable difference (jnd). The ratio $r = \Delta s/s$ does not depend on s. Weber's law states that change in sensation is noticed when the stimulus is increased by a constant percentage of the stimulus itself. This law holds in ranges where Δs is small when compared with s, and hence in practice it fails to hold when s is either too small or too large. Aggregating or decomposing stimuli as needed into clusters or hierarchy levels is an effective way for extending the uses of this law.

In 1860 Fechner considered a sequence of just noticeable increasing stimuli. He denotes the first one by s_0. The next just noticeable stimulus [1] is given by

$$s_1 = s_0 + \Delta s_0 = s_0 + \frac{\Delta s_0}{s_0}s_0 = s_0(1+r)$$

having used Weber's law.

Similarly

$$s_2 = s_1 + \Delta s_1 = s_1(1+r) = s_0(1+r)^2 \equiv s_0 \alpha^2$$

In general

$$s_n = s_{n-1}\alpha = s_0\alpha^n \qquad (n = 0,1,2,\ldots)$$

Thus stimuli of noticeable differences follow sequentially in a geometric progression. Fechner noted that the corresponding sensations should follow each other in an arithmetic sequence at the discrete points at which just noticeable differences occur. But the latter are obtained when we solve for n. We have

$$n = \frac{(\log s_n - \log s_0)}{\log \alpha}$$

and sensation is a linear function of the logarithm of the stimulus. Thus if M denotes the sensation and s the stimulus, the psychophysical law of Weber-Fechner is given by

$$M = a \log s + b, \qquad a \neq 0$$

We assume that the stimuli arise in making pairwise comparisons of relatively comparable activities. We are interested in responses whose numerical values are in the form of ratios. Thus $b = 0$, from which we must have $\log s_0 = 0$ or $s_0 = 1$, which is possible by calibrating a unit stimulus. This is done by comparing one activity with itself. The next noticeable response is due to the stimulus

$$s_1 = s_0\alpha = \alpha$$

This yields a response $\log \alpha / \log \alpha = 1$. The next stimulus is

$$s_2 = s_0\alpha^2$$

which yields a response of 2. In this manner we obtain the sequence 1, 2, 3,... .

Our ability to make qualitative distinctions is well represented by five intensities: equal, moderate, strong, very strong, and extreme. We can make compromises between adjacent intensities when greater precision is needed. Thus we require nine values which, according to the previous discussion, should be consecutive. The following refinement of the above is also possible: equal, tad, weak, moderate, moderate plus, strong, strong plus, very strong, very very strong, and extreme. The resulting scale would then be validated in practice.

We use the scale of absolute values shown in Table 3.1 to make the comparisons. We deal with widely varying measurements of alternatives by grouping those of similar magnitude in clusters and then uniformizing the measurement with a pivotal alternative that appears in two adjacent clusters. We do this because in using judgments, people are usually unable to accurately compare the very small with the very large. But they can make the transition gradually from clusters of smaller elements to clusters of larger ones. This approach is the valid way to extend the 1-9 scale as far out as one wants. In any case one does not need to go too far out on the scale to set priorities against one's personal goals. Thus the problem is to find the right numbers to represent comparisons of objects that are close on some property. The 1-9 scale is a simple scale that serves well.

If the need arises for a judgment larger than 9, the larger element could be placed in another homogeneous set of comparisons and the 1-9 scale is also applied to that set.

Table 3.1 The Fundamental Scale

Intensity of Importance	Definition	Explanation
1	Equal Importance	Two activities contribute equally to the objective
2	Weak	
3	Moderate importance	Experience and judgment slightly favor one activity over another
4	Moderate plus	
5	Strong importance	Experience and judgment strongly favor one activity over another
6	Strong plus	
7	Very strong or demonstrated importance	An activity is favored very strongly over another; its dominance demonstrated in practice
8	Very, very strong	
9	Extreme importance	The evidence favoring one activity over another is of the highest possible order of affirmation
Reciprocals of above	If activity i has one of the above nonzero numbers assigned to it when compared with activity j, then j has the reciprocal value when compared with i	A reasonable assumption
Rationals	Ratios arising from the scale	If consistency were to be forced by obtaining n numerical values to span the matrix

Clustering is used to combine different homogeneous groups. When we have a situation like a_i preferred to a_j by 3 and a_j preferred to a_k by 5, implying that a_i is preferred to a_k by 15, we need not conclude that there is a need for a wider scale but that there is inconsistency in the judgments already given, because we know from the homogeneity requirement that there is no need for a number outside the scale.   No matter what finite scale one chooses to represent the outer limit of perception, 1 to 9 or 1 to α^n, inconsistency might seemingly require an even larger number. Instead of extending the scale one should look for better understanding of the inconsistency of judgments.

There are many situations where elements are close or tied in measurement and the comparison must be made not to determine how many times one is larger than the other, but what fraction it is larger than the other.   In other words there are comparisons to be made between 1 and 2, and what we want is to estimate verbally the values such as 1.1, 1.2, ..., 1.9.   There is no problem in making the comparisons by directly estimating the numbers.   Our proposal is to continue the verbal scale to make these distinctions so that 1.1 is a "tad", 1.3 indicates moderately more, 1.5 strongly more, 1.7 very strongly more and 1.9 extremely more.   This type of refinement can be used in any of the intervals from 1 to 9 and for further refinements if one needs them, for example, between 1.1 and 1.2 and so on.

Let us note that we are unable to distinguish between object sizes as they become very small or very large.   Sometimes we can with the aid of an instrument like the microscope or the telescope which bring things to our range of abilities, but we must then relate the new magnitudes to those we know best in our daily experience.   The idea of a logarithmic scale arises from saturation of the ability to make distinctions which happens at both ends of the scale.   What we have done with the 1-9 scale, which we are compelled to use, as we can use no other scale with clear understanding of magnitudes, is to piecewise linearize the logarithmic idea in a limited operational range of magnitudes.

Naturally if one uses actual measurements to form the ratios, one gets them back by solving for the derived scale because in the consistent case one gets back exactly what one puts in.   In fact Expert Choice, the implementation software package of AHP,

uses fractional values.   They allow one to put very close
approximations to whatever number one may think of between 1
and 9. But what arbitrary values would one assign to feelings. It
is better to have a well tested protocol to go from comparisons to
words to numbers validated to work in known situations, than to
guess at widely disparate numbers assigned to firm judgments
associated with perception.

There are undoubtedly a few situations with known scales
whose numbers can be used by an experienced person to form
ratios and one need not use the scale 1-9. But AHP was developed
to set priorities involving subjective understanding on all sorts of
alternatives and even on ranges of measurements of alternatives.
In that case the decision maker must exercise care in assessing
distinctions in his judgments and feelings and must put them in
smaller homogeneous ranges for which he is well equipped to
make unambiguous distinctions.

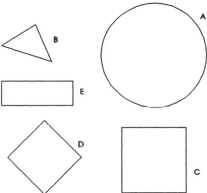

Figure 3-1 *Five areas to compare*

Figure 3-1 gives five areas to which the paired comparison
process and the scale can be tested.   One may approximate the
outcome by adding the rows of the matrix and dividing by the
total.   Compare the answer with A = .471, B = .050, C = .234,
D = .149, E = .096.

We have considered the use of all kinds of scales other than the 1-9 scale. One particular instance is the power scale, α^0, α^1, ..., α^n. There are several problems in using such a scale. Clearly one can choose the numbers 1, 2, 2^2, 2^3, or 1, 3, 3^2, or similar subsets that are already in the 1-9 scale. A rule is needed to identify the value of α, the base in the geometric scale, to be associated with a verbal expression. Note that if we find one counterexample that produces a poor result with such a scale, for whatever α one may choose, then we would no longer be tempted to try a power scale. It is difficult to see how a power scale would be as natural a representation of the semantic scale when comparing homogeneous alternatives.

If we extend the 1-9 scale in an extreme case to 100, the scale 1, α, ... , α^n with n = 100 can give astronomically large values even for small values of α near one. We not only have difficulty estimating such values, but lower down on the scale we could have a problem distinguishing between some of the small values.

Consider

$$n \; = \; 1 \quad 2 \quad 3 \quad 4 \quad 5 \quad 6 \quad 7 \quad 8 \quad 9 \quad 10 \quad \ldots \; 100$$

then

$$2^{n/2} \; = \; 2^{1/2} \quad 2^{1} \; 2^{3/2}\,2^{4/2}\,2^{5/2}\,2^{6/2}\,2^{7/2}\,2^{8/2}\,2^{9/2}\,2^{10/2}\ldots\,2^{100/2}$$

or

$$2^{(n-1)/2}= \; 1 \quad 2^{1/2} \quad 2^{1} \quad 2^{3/2} \quad 2^{4/2} \quad 2^{5/2} \quad 2^{6/2} \quad 2^{7/2} \quad 2^{8/2} \quad 2^{9/2} \quad \ldots \; 2^{99/2}$$

The last value is beyond our ability to compare it semantically, say with $2^{10/2}$. If instead of $\alpha = 2$ we use $\alpha = 1.009$ for example, it is difficult to distinguish between the scale values for very small n.

When the use of one of the two scales gives rise to a consistent matrix, the use of the other would make it inconsistent. There are situations where both matrices are inconsistent and there is reversal in the ranks of the first and second alternatives as represented by the two eigenvectors as in the following example

Scale	Matrix				Eigenvector
1-9	$\begin{bmatrix} 1 & 2 & 3 & 1 \\ 1/2 & 1 & 6 & 1 \\ 1/3 & 1/6 & 1 & 1/3 \\ 1 & 1 & 3 & 1 \end{bmatrix}$				$\begin{bmatrix} .3477 \\ .2939 \\ .0808 \\ .2775 \end{bmatrix}$
	C.R.		=		.062

Scale	Matrix				Eigenvector
$2^{(n-1)/2}$	$\begin{bmatrix} 1 & 2^{1/2} & 2^1 & 1 \\ .707 & 1 & 2^{2.5} & 1 \\ 1/2 & .176 & 1 & 1/2 \\ 1 & 1 & 2 & 1 \end{bmatrix}$				$\begin{bmatrix} .2966 \\ .3334 \\ .1064 \\ .2775 \end{bmatrix}$
	C.R.		=		.065

3. The Eigenvector

From linear algebra we know that for a given matrix A and a given vector b, the equation $Ax = b$ has a solution if the inverse A^{-1} exists which is the case if and only if $|A| \neq 0$. The fact that a homogeneous system of linear equations, $Ax = 0$, has a nonzero solution if $|A| = 0$ plays an important role in the judgment matrix of the AHP.

The matrix of paired comparisons in the AHP leads to the condition $Aw = \lambda_{max}w$ or $(A - \lambda_{max}I)w = 0$, a homogeneous system in the matrix $A - \lambda_{max}I$. A nonzero solution implies that the determinant $|A - \lambda_{max}I|$ is equal to zero. But this determinant is an nth degree polynomial in λ_{max}, where n is the order of A. This polynomial is equal to zero when λ_{max} is a root of the equation obtained by setting the determinant equal to zero and known as the characteristic equation of A. Such a root is known as a characteristic root or eigenvalue of the matrix A. Thus when λ_{max}

is an eigenvalue of A, the solution vector w is not identically equal to zero. Consider the homogeneous system $Aw = \lambda w$. The characteristic polynomial of an n by n matrix A has n zeros, λ_1, λ_2, ..., λ_n.

In the following we use the vector $e = (1, 1, ..., 1)^T$. All other vectors are column vectors.

Theorem 3.1   *If $A > 0$, w_1 is its principal eigenvector corresponding to the maximum eigenvalue λ_1, $\lambda_i \neq \lambda_j$ for all i and j, and w_i is the right eigenvector corresponding to λ_i then*

$$\lim_{k \to \infty} \frac{A^k e}{e^T A^k e} = c w_1$$

where c is some constant.

Proof   Because w_1, ..., w_n are linearly independent, we have: $e = a_1 w_1 + ... + a_n w_n$ where a_i, $i = 1,...,n$ are constants. On multiplying both sides on the left by A^k we have:

$$A^k e = a_1 \lambda_1^k w_1 + \cdots + a_n \lambda_n^k w_n = \lambda_1^k \left[a_1 w_1 + a_2 \left(\frac{\lambda_2}{\lambda_1} \right)^k w_2 + \cdots + a_n \left(\frac{\lambda_n}{\lambda_1} \right)^k w_n \right]$$ and again

multiplying on the left by e_k^T we have:

$$e^T A^k e = \lambda_1^k \left[b_1 + b_2 \left[\frac{\lambda_2}{\lambda_1} \right]^k + \cdots + b_n \left[\frac{\lambda_n}{\lambda_1} \right]^k \right]; \quad b_i = a_i e^T w_i$$

Since $w_1 > 0$, $b_1 \neq 0$, the theorem follows on putting $c = 1/e^T \cdot w_1$.

The proof of this theorem can be generalized to a nonnegative matrix, some power of which is positive. Because of its central relevance we need the following:

Definition - A matrix is irreducible if it cannot be decomposed in the form $\begin{bmatrix} A & 0 \\ B & C \end{bmatrix}$ where A and C are square matrices and 0 is the zero matrix.

Definition - A nonnegative, irreducible matrix A is *primitive* if and only if there is an integer $m \geq 1$ such that $A^m > 0$. Otherwise it is called *imprimitive*.

The graph of a primitive matrix has a path of length $\geq m$ between any two vertices.

From the work of Frobenius (1912), Perron (1907), and Wielandt (1950), we know that a nonnegative, irreducible matrix A is primitive, if and only if, A has a unique characteristic root of maximum modulus, and this root has multiplicity 1.

Theorem 3.2 *For a primitive matrix A*

$$\lim_{k \to \infty} \frac{A^k e}{\|A^k\|} = cw, \qquad \|A^k\| \equiv e^T A e$$

where c is a constant and w is the eigenvector corresponding to $\lambda_{max} \equiv \lambda_1$.

The actual computation of the principal eigenvector in Expert Choice is based on Theorem 3.1. It says that the normalized row sums of the limiting power of a primitive matrix (and hence also of a positive matrix) gives the desired eigenvector. Thus a short computational way to obtain this vector is to raise the matrix to powers. Fast convergence is obtained by successively squaring the matrix. The row sums are calculated and normalized. The computation is stopped when the difference between these sums in two consecutive calculations of the power is smaller than a prescribed value.

There is literally an infinite number of ways to estimate the ratio w_i/w_j from the matrix (a_{ij}). But we have already shown that our formulation with particular emphasis on consistency leads to an eigenvalue problem.

What is an easy way to get a good approximation to the priorities? Multiply the elements in each row together and take the nth root where n is the number of elements. Then normalize the column of numbers thus obtained by dividing each entry by the sum of all entries. Alternatively normalize the elements in each column of the judgment matrix and then average over each row.

We would like to caution the reader that for real applications one should only use the eigenvector derivation procedure because it can be shown that the approximations described above can lead to rank reversal in spite of its closeness to the eigenvector.

4. Consistency

Classically transitivity in ordered sets means that $i \geq j$, $j \geq k$ implies $i \geq k$ ($>$ preferred). Because we require that $a_{ij} \geq 1$ for $j \geq i$, consistency implies transitivity for $i \geq j => a_{ij} \geq 1$, $j \geq k => a_{jk} \geq 1$ and because of consistency we have $a_{ij}a_{jk} = a_{ik} \geq 1$ and hence $i \geq k$. Thus transitivity is a necessary condition for consistency. It is obviously not sufficient as, for example, when $a_{ij} = 2$, $a_{jk} = 3$, and $a_{ik} = 4$ shows. The AHP does not require that judgments be consistent or even transitive.

When A is consistent the entire set of entries can be constructed from a set of n judgments that form a chain across the rows and columns. Such a chain of interconnecting entries is given by: $a_{ii_1}, a_{i_1i_2}, a_{i_2i_3}, ..., a_{i_{n-1}j}.$

One might ask, if the judgments are totally random in nature, what kind of consistency would the AHP interpret them to have? The consistency of a matrix of such random judgments should be much worse than the consistency of a matrix of informed judgments. The measure can be used to compare and evaluate the goodness of the consistency of informed judgments.

The user of the AHP can often be perfectly consistent if he/she wishes to preserve the relation $a_{ij}a_{jk} = a_{ik}$ by using redundant judgments, from relations between previously given judgments. This method is something we do not necessarily recommend. Second, in theory, by deriving the scale of relative measurement from the fundamental scale through the principal eigenvector, one is able to capture second, third and higher order effects whose entries contain magnitudes for relations between the alternatives that can differ considerably from the entries of the original matrix.

Reciprocal, nonnegative matrices may have complex eigenvalues, but their sum is a real number. We note that since the maximum eigenvalue lies between the largest and the smallest row sums, a matrix whose columns are identical has an eigenvalue which is equal to the sum of any of its columns. A small perturbation of a consistent matrix leaves its maximum eigenvalue λ_{max} close to its value n. The remaining eigenvalues are perturbed closely to their zero values. The choice of perturbation most appropriate to describe the effect of inconsistency on the eigenvector depends on what is thought to be the psychological process involved in pairwise comparisons of a set of data. We assume that all perturbations of interest can be reduced to the general form $a_{ij} = (w_i/w_j)\epsilon_{ij}$. For example:

$$\frac{w_i}{w_j} + \alpha_{ij} = \frac{w_i}{w_j}\left[1 + \frac{w_j}{w_i}\alpha_{ij}\right] \equiv \left[\frac{w_i}{w_j}\right]\epsilon_{ij}$$

Consistency occurs when $\epsilon_{ij} = 1$.

Let us now develop a few elementary but essential results about consistent matrices. Writing out the system $Aw = \lambda_{max}w$ in detail, we have for the ith equation:

$$\lambda_{max} = \sum_{j=1}^{n} a_{ij}\frac{w_j}{w_i}$$

We define:

$$\mu = -\frac{1}{n-1}\sum_{i=2}^{n}\lambda_i$$

and note that $\sum_{i=1}^{n}\lambda_i = n$ because n is the sum of the diagonal elements known as the trace of A. This fact follows by expanding $|\lambda I - A| = (\lambda-\lambda_1)...(\lambda-\lambda_n)$ and equating coefficients. Now $\sum_{i=1}^{n}\lambda_i = n$ implies that $\mu = \frac{\lambda_{max}-n}{n-1}$; $\lambda_{max} \equiv \lambda_1$

and since

$$\lambda_{max}-1 = \sum_{j\neq i}a_{ij}\frac{w_j}{w_i}$$

we have

$$n\lambda_{max}-n = \sum_{1\leq i<j\leq n}\left[a_{ij}\frac{w_j}{w_i}+a_{ji}\frac{w_i}{w_j}\right]$$

and therefore

$$\mu=\frac{\lambda_{max}-n}{n-1}=\frac{1}{n-1}-\frac{n}{n-1}+\frac{1}{n(n-1)}\sum_{1\leq i<j\leq n}\left[a_{ij}\frac{w_j}{w_i}+a_{ji}\frac{w_i}{w_j}\right]$$

Substituting, $a_{ij} = (w_i/w_j)\epsilon_{ij}, \epsilon_{ij} > 0$ we arrive at the equation

$$\mu = -1+\frac{1}{n(n-1)}\sum_{1\leq i<j\leq n}\left[\epsilon_{ij}+\frac{1}{\epsilon_{ij}}\right]$$

We observe that as $\epsilon_{ij} \rightarrow 1$, i.e., as consistency is approached, $\mu\rightarrow 0$. Also, μ is convex in the ϵ_{ij}. This follows from the observation that $\epsilon_{ij} + 1/\epsilon_{ij}$ is convex (and has its minimum at $\epsilon_{ij} = 1$), and from the fact that the sum of convex functions is convex. Thus, μ is small or large depending on ϵ_{ij} being near to or far from unity, respectively (i.e., near to or far from consistency). Finally, if we write $\epsilon_{ij} = 1 + \delta_{ij}$, with $\delta_{ij} > -1$ we have

$$\mu = \frac{1}{n(n-1)} \sum_{1 \le i < j \le n} \left[\delta_{ij}^2 - \frac{\delta_{ij}^3}{1 + \delta_{ij}} \right]$$

We want μ to be near zero, or λ_{max} to be near to its lower bound n, and thus to approach consistency. It is interesting to note that $(\lambda_{max} - n)/(n - 1)$ is related to the statistical root mean square error. Indeed, let us assume that $|\delta_{ij}| < 1$ (and hence that $\delta_{ij}^3/(1 + \delta_{ij})$ is small compared with δ_{ij}^2). This is a reasonable assumption for an unbiased judge, who is limited by the "natural" greatest lower bound -1 on δ_{ij} (since a_{ij} must be greater than zero), and who would tend to estimate symmetrically about zero in the interval $(-1,1)$. Now, $\mu \to 0$ as $\delta_{ij} \to 0$. Multiplication by 2 gives the variance of the δ_{ij}. Thus, 2μ is this variance.

How to Estimate λ_{max}

There is a simple way to obtain the exact value (or estimate) of λ_{max} when the exact value (or estimate) of w is available in normalized form. Add the columns of A and take the scalar product of the resulting vector with the vector w. Thus from:

$$\sum_{j=1}^{n} a_{ij} w_j = \lambda_{max} w_i$$

we obtain

$$\sum_{i=1}^{n} \sum_{j=1}^{n} a_{ij} w_j = \sum_{j=1}^{n} \left[\sum_{i=1}^{n} a_{ij} \right] w_j = \sum_{i=1}^{n} \lambda_{max} w_i = \lambda_{max}$$

A Measure of Random Inconsistency

The *consistency index* of a matrix of comparisons is given by C.I. $=(\lambda_{max}-n)/(n-1)$. The *consistency ratio* (C.R.) is obtained by forming the ratio of C.I. and the appropriate one of the following set of numbers, each of which is an average random consistency index computed by E. Forman [2] for n $\leq$ 7 for very large samples (and by a number of other people for n > 7 for smaller samples). They create randomly generated reciprocal matrices using the scale 1/9, 1/8, ..., 1, ...8, 9 and calculate the average of their eigenvalues. This average is used to form the Random Consistency Index $\equiv$ R.I.

n	1	2	3	4	5	6	7	8	9	10
R.I.	0	0	.52	.89	1.11	1.25	1.35	1.40	1.45	1.49

n	11	12	13	14	15
R.I.	1.51	1.54	1.56	1.57	1.58

DeSchutter's Conjecture

John DeSchutter has conjectured the following relationship between the index R.I. and n, the size of the matrix:

$$R.I. = 1.98\frac{n-2}{n} = 1.98\left[1-\frac{n-1}{n(n-1)/2}\right]$$

where 1.98 is the average value of the ratio of each value computed so far from n = 3 to n = 15 divided by (n-2)/n for the corresponding value of n. Here (n-1) is the minimum number of judgments needed to measure consistency and n(n-1)/2 is the number elicited for redundancy. Alternatively, a plot of values of R.I. against n shows that the resulting curve approaches 1.98 as an asymptote, i.e., $\lim_{n\to\infty} R.I. = 1.98$. One may suspect that this value is actually equal to 2.

Why Tolerate 10% Inconsistency

Inconsistency may be thought of as an adjustment needed to improve the consistency of the comparisons. But the adjustment should not be as large as the judgment itself, nor so small that using it is of no consequence. Thus inconsistency should be just one order of magnitude smaller. On a scale from zero to one, the overall inconsistency should be around 10%. The requirement of 10% cannot be made smaller such as 1% or .1% without trivializing the impact of inconsistency. But inconsistency itself is important because without it, new knowledge that changes preference cannot be admitted. Assuming that all knowledge should be consistent contradicts experience which requires continued adjustment in understanding. Thus the object of developing a wide ranging consistent framework depends on admitting some inconsistency. By noting the Random Inconsistency Indices for different values of n, we distribute 10% proportionally by multiplying it by each of the R.I. values. These percentages are suggested by the R.I. values above. In other words, if the R.I. is equal to 1 for all n, we would allow 10% in all cases. However, for n = 3 and 4, the values are 0.52 and 0.89 and for n ≥ 5 it is greater than one. By convention we require the consistency ratio to be 5% and 8% for n = 3 and 4 respectively and 10% for all values of n ≥ 5. A plausible approach to the measurement of inconsistency has also been given by Golden and Wang [3].

5. Why Compare About Seven Elements

There are two explanations which one can give to justify the use of not many more than seven elements in a comparison scheme.

Consistency Explanation

In making pairwise comparisons, errors arising out of inconsistency in judgments affect the final answer. We distribute inconsistency proportionately among the alternatives because in computing the eigenvector, transitivities of all order are considered and the average is taken over all these transitivities. If the number of elements is small their relative priorities would be large. These priorities would be less affected by inconsistency adjustment. Thus for example if there are 10 homogeneous elements, each would have a relative priority of .10 and is unaffected by a 1% inconsistency distributed among the 10 so that its value would now be .10 ± .01. If the number of elements is large, the relative priority of each would be small and would be more affected by inconsistency. Still the number should be large enough to enable one to make redundant judgments to improve the validity of the outcome. For this reason seven elements is found to be a reasonable choice for high average priority and high validity.

Neural Explanation

This explanation has to do with the brain limit on the identification of simultaneous events. The perception or simultaneity span is the ratio of the buffer-delay time to the attentional integration time. Some psychologists have found that the more intense the stimulus the greater the perception or simultaneity span. The reason is that with increased intensity the time of rapid integration is reduced. The most common duration time estimate for the short term memory (buffer-delay) is 750 milliseconds and that for item-integration time is 100 milliseconds. Their ratio is about seven.

Illustrative Matrices

Here are examples of inconsistent matrices with their inconsistency indices:

1) $a_{12} = 2$, $a_{13} = 9$, a_{23} should be 9/2 but is 9 (twice what it should be)

$$\begin{bmatrix} 1 & 2 & 9 \\ .5 & 1 & 9 \\ 1/9 & 1/9 & 1 \end{bmatrix} \quad \begin{bmatrix} .582 \\ .367 \\ .051 \end{bmatrix}$$

$\lambda_{max} = 3.054$, C.I. = .027, C.R. = .046 (acceptable).

2) If we change just a_{12} from 2 to 3, we have $\lambda_{max} = 3.136$, C.I. $= .068$, C.R. $= 0.117$.

3) Interchange an element (a_{12}) with its reciprocal in

$$\begin{pmatrix} 1 & 2 & 4 & 8 \\ .5 & 1 & 2 & 4 \\ .25 & .5 & 1 & 2 \\ .125 & .25 & .5 & 1 \end{pmatrix} \quad get \quad \begin{pmatrix} 1 & .5 & 4 & 8 \\ 2 & 1 & 2 & 4 \\ .25 & .5 & 1 & 2 \\ .125 & .25 & .5 & 1 \end{pmatrix}$$

$\lambda_{max} = 4$ C.R. $= 0$ $\lambda_{max} = 4.250$ C.R. $= .092$

6. A Method for Incomplete Comparisons

When not all judgments are available, either because of the limitation or because the judge is unwilling or unsure to make a comparisons of two elements, Harker [4] provides the following suggestions:

- Have the decision maker provide judgments, such that at least one judgment is answered in each column, yields a matrix with some unknown ratio elements.

- Enter zero for any missing judgment in that matrix, and add the number of missing judgments in each row to the diagonal element in the row, producing a new matrix A.

- Calculate the weight w:

$$\lim_{k \to \infty} \frac{A^k e}{e^T A^k e} = cw$$

- Use the resulting w_i/w_j as a suggested value for the missing judgments to make it consistent with the judgments already provided.

- If needed, the decision maker can be guided to make additional judgments, that have the greatest impact on the weight w. One computes the larger absolute value of the gradient of w with respect to the (i,j) calculated using the following formula:

  x: right principal eigenvector = w, in AHP notation $Ax = \lambda_{max}x$

  y: left principal eigenvector $y^tA = \lambda_{max}y$

$$D^A_{\lambda_{max}} = \left[\frac{\partial \lambda_{max}}{\partial_{ij}} | i,j \right],$$

$$= \left[(y_i x_j) - (y_j x_i)/a_{ij}^2 \quad i>j \right]$$

where y is normalized so that $y'x = 1$.

Then $D^A_x = \left[\dfrac{\partial x}{\partial_{ij}} | i>j \right]$ is the matrix of gradients for the weights x and is given by:

$$\left[\begin{bmatrix} \tilde{A} - \lambda_{max}\tilde{I} \\ e \end{bmatrix}^{-1} \begin{bmatrix} \tilde{D}^A_{\lambda_{max}} x - \tilde{z} \\ 0 \end{bmatrix} \right]$$

where   I = n x n identity matrix

e = n dimensional row vector of ones

z = (z_k) = n dimensional column vector defined by:

$$z_k = \begin{cases} x_j & \text{if } k = i \\ -x_i/a_{ij}^2 & \text{if } k = j \\ 0 & \text{otherwise} \end{cases}$$

~ denotes the matrix or vector with its last row deleted.

The choice of the next (i,j) value is made according to:

$$(i,j) = \underset{(k,l) \, \epsilon \, Q}{arg \; max} \; (\| \; \partial x(A)/\partial_{ij} \; \|_\infty)$$

where Q is the set of unanswered comparisons and $\| \cdot \|_\infty$ denotes L_∞ or the Chebyshev norm.

Harker's Example

If:
$$A = \begin{bmatrix} 1 & 2 & 3 \\ & 1 & 2 \\ & & 1 \end{bmatrix}$$

then

λ_{max} = 3.0092027
x = (0.5396145, 0.2969613, 0.1634241)
y = (0.1634241, 0.2969613, 0.5396145)

After normalizing y so that $y^T x = 1$, we have:

y = (0.6177249, 101224806, 2.0396826)

The derivatives of the principal eigenvector are:

$$D_{\lambda_{max}}^A = \begin{bmatrix} 0 & 0.0320137 & -0.0213425 \\ 0 & 0 & 0.0320137 \\ 0 & 0 & 0 \end{bmatrix}$$

$$\begin{bmatrix} \tilde{A} - \lambda_{max}\tilde{I} \\ e \end{bmatrix} = \begin{bmatrix} -2.0092027 & 2 & 3 \\ 1/2 & -2.0092027 & 2 \\ 1 & 1 & 1 \end{bmatrix}^{-1}$$

$$= \begin{bmatrix} -0.2157468 & 0.0538129 & 0.5396146 \\ 0.0807193 & -0.2695597 & 0.2969613 \\ 0.1350274 & 0.2157468 & 0.1634241 \end{bmatrix}$$

and

$$\begin{bmatrix} \tilde{D}^A_{\lambda_{max}} x \\ \\ 0 \end{bmatrix} = \begin{bmatrix} 0.0060190 \\ 0.0052318 \\ 0 \end{bmatrix}$$

For each question, z and $\partial x / \partial_{ij}$ are:

(1,2) $z = \begin{bmatrix} 0.2969613 \\ -0.1349036 \\ 0 \end{bmatrix}$ $\dfrac{\partial x}{\partial_{12}} = \begin{bmatrix} 0.0703116 \\ -0.0612519 \\ -0.0090518 \end{bmatrix}$

(1,3) $z = \begin{bmatrix} 0.1634241 \\ 0 \\ -0.0599572 \end{bmatrix}$ $\dfrac{\partial x}{\partial_{13}} = \begin{bmatrix} 0.0342412 \\ -0.0141159 \\ -0.020125 \end{bmatrix}$

(2,3) $z = \begin{bmatrix} 0 \\ 0.1634241 \\ -0.0742403 \end{bmatrix}$ $\dfrac{\partial x}{\partial_{23}} = \begin{bmatrix} -0.0098114 \\ 0.0431281 \\ -0.0333168 \end{bmatrix}$

Therefore, (1,2) should be asked next.

The decision maker may decide to stop the questioning, or continue according to:

a.)   If the maximum absolute difference in the attribute weights from one question to the next (w^k and w^{k+1})

is less than or equal to a given constant $\alpha\%$ and $\ell = \frac{arg\ max}{1 \leq i \leq n} \quad |w_i^{k+1} - w_i^k|$ then the procedure would stop at the $(k+1)$ comparison if

$$\frac{|w_\ell^{k+1} - w_\ell^k|}{w_\ell^k} \leq \alpha$$

b.)   The next question derived from the gradient procedure would only be asked if it appears that the ordinal ranking could be reversed.

Due to the computational complexity of this task, a simplification can be made by using a sample of random spanning trees to calculate: a_{ij} = the current value of the $(i,j)^{th}$ question which has just been chosen.

a_{ij} = the largest path intensity in the set of all elementary paths   connecting i and j

$\underline{a}_{ij}$ = the smallest path intensity

Let u_{ij} = max $[1, a_{ij} - \underline{a}_{ij}]$
        L_{ij} = min $[1, a_{ij} - \underline{a}_{ij}]$

and define $P(w)$ to be a function which returns the ordinal ranking inherent in the cardinal ranking w; that is P: $R^n \rightarrow Z^n$ where Z^n is the n dimensional space of natural numbers. For example, if w = $(.15, .3, .2, .35)^T$ then $P(w) = (4, 2, 3, 1)^T$. Three rankings can be defined with this function:

$P_1 = P(w)$
$P_2 = P(w + \partial w/\partial_{ij} (a_{ij} + u_{ij}))$
$P_3 = P(w + \partial w/\partial_{ij} (a_{ij} - L_{ij}))$

P_1 =   current ordinal ranking
P_2, P_3 =   approximation to the ordinal ranking
if the $(i,j)^{th}$ comparison achieved its
max and min deviation, respectively.

If $P_1 = P_2 = P_3$, the next comparison is unlikely to alter the ordinal ranking.

Nonlinear responses

In the standard theory it is assumed that a_{ij} is an approximation to the ratio w_i/w_j. However, one could have situations in which a_{ij} is an approximation to some function of this ratio $f(w_i/w_j)^\alpha$ with $\alpha > 0$. The eigenvector problem can be written as $Aw^\alpha = \lambda_{max}w^\alpha$ where $w^\alpha = (w_1^\alpha, w_2^\alpha, ..., w_n^\alpha)$. Defining v to be equal to w^α leads to $Av = \lambda_{max}v$, a standard eigenvalue problem in the AHP.

7. Improving the Consistency of Judgments

There are two ways to identify the most inconsistent judgment and improve its value. One is to compare each a_{ij} with the corresponding ratio w_i/w_j from the eigenvector. That a_{ij} for which $a_{ij}w_j/w_i$ is largest (smallest) is the most inconsistent. The proposal is to change that a_{ij} to w_i/w_j. This adjustment would improve the overall consistency. In fact any change in a_{ij} in the direction of w_i/w_j improves inconsistency.

A second method that uses the gradient is due to Harker [5]. Although using the gradient is a more sophisticated way of computing inconsistency, it is less efficient because generally the judgment matrices are of small order. As in the previous section, it involves computing the matrix $D_{\lambda_{max}}^A$. The most inconsistent judgment has the largest absolute value and is the one to improve by changing it in a direction closer to the ratio of the corresponding components of the eigenvector.

References

1. Batschelet, E., 1973, "Mathematical Recreations and Essays", MacMillan, New York.

2. Forman, E.H., 1990, "Random Indices For Incomplete Pairwise Comparison Matrices", European Journal of Operational Research 48, 153-155.

3. Golden, B.L., E.A. Wasil, and P.T. Harker, editors, The Analytic Hierarchy Process, Springer-Verlag, New York, 1989.

4. Harker, P.T., 1987, "Incomplete Pairwise Comparisons in the Analytic Hierarchy Process," Mathematical Modelling 9/11, 837-848.

5. Harker, P.T., 1987, "Alternatives Models of Questioning in the Analytic Hierarchy Process", Mathematical Modelling 9, 353-360.

6. Saaty, Thomas L., The Analytic Hierarchy Process, McGraw Hill, 1980. Reprinted by the author, 1988 at Pittsburgh.

CHAPTER FOUR

HIERARCHIES AND HIERARCHIC SYNTHESIS

1. Introduction

A hierarchy is a representation of a complex problem in a multilevel structure whose first level is the goal followed successively by levels of factors, criteria, subcriteria, and so on down to a bottom level of alternatives. A hierarchy is also a convenient way to decompose a complex problem in search of cause-effect explanations in steps which form a linear chain. A simple illustration of a three level hierarchy is shown in Figure 4-1. The object of a hierarchy is to assess the impact of the elements of a higher level on those of a lower level or alternatively the contribution of elements in the lower level to the importance or fulfillment of the elements in the level above. This type of assessment is usually made by paired comparisons responding to an appropriately posed question eliciting the judgment. The mathematical definition of a hierarchy is given in Chapter 10.

There is a more general way, not necessarily linear, to structure a problem involving functional dependence. It allows for feedback between clusters. It is a network system of which a hierarchy is a special case. This more general structure is discussed in Chapter 8.

Setting priorities in a hierarchy requires that we perform measurement throughout the structure. We must then synthesize these measurements to obtain priorities for the bottom level alternatives. Perhaps the most significant aspect of the AHP is its use of ratio scales. They are special kinds of numbers that can be multiplied down a hierarchy and still define a resulting ratio scale. No other kind of derived scales have this property. Ratio scales and hierarchies are well suited to be together.

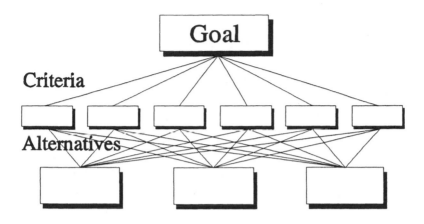

Figure 4-1. *A three level hierarchy.*

What kinds of hierarchies are there and how should they be structured to meet certain needs? How do we synthesize priorities in a hierarchy and what is the measure of consistency in a hierarchic structure? These are some of the questions we need to deal with in this chapter. Hundreds of examples of hierarchies in application are illustrated in the collection known as the Hierarchon [3].

2. Reasons for Hierarchies

What is the main purpose of arranging goals, attributes, issues, and stakeholders in a hierarchy? Most problems arise because we do not know the internal dynamics of a system in enough detail to identify cause-and-effect relationships. If we were able to do so, the problem could be reduced to one of social engineering, as we would know at what points in the system intervention is necessary to bring about the desired objective. The crucial contribution of the AHP is that it enables us to make practical decisions based on a "precausal" understanding - namely, on our feelings and judgments about the relative impact of one variable on another.

In sum, when constructing hierarchies one must include enough relevant detail to depict the problem as thoroughly as possible. Consider the environment surrounding the problem. Identify the issues or attributes that one feels contribute to the solution. Identify the participants associated with the problem. Arranging the goals, attributes, issues, and stakeholders in a hierarchy serves three purposes: It provides an overall view of the complex relationships inherent in the situation; it captures the spread of influence from the more important and general criteria to the less important ones; and it permits the decision maker to assess whether he or she is comparing issues of the same order of magnitude in weight or impact on the solution.

A hierarchy is said to be *complete* when the elements in a level are evaluated in terms of all the elements in the level above. Otherwise, it is said to be *incomplete*, and hence, an element in a given level does not have to function as a criterion for all the elements in the level below. Thus a hierarchy can be divided into subhierarchies sharing only a common topmost element. Further, a decision maker can insert or eliminate levels and elements as necessary to clarify the task of setting priorities or to sharpen the focus on one or more parts of the system. Elements that are of less immediate interest can be represented in general terms at the higher levels of the hierarchy and elements critical to the problem at hand can be developed in greater depth and specificity.

In addition to identifying within a hierarchic structure the major factors that influence the outcome of a decision, we need a way to decide whether these factors have equal effects on the outcome or whether some of them are dominant and others so insignificant they can be ignored. This is accomplished through the process of priority setting. The task of setting priorities requires that the criteria, the subcriteria, the properties or features of the alternatives being compared, and the alternatives themselves be gradually layered in the hierarchy so that the elements in each level are comparable among themselves in relation to the elements of the next higher level. Now the priorities are set for the elements in each level several times - once with respect to each criterion of the upper level. These in turn are prioritized with respect to the elements of the next higher level and so on. Finally a weighting process is used to obtain overall priorities. This is done by coming down the hierarchy and weighting the priorities measured in a level with respect to a criterion in the next higher level by multiplying by the weight of that criterion. The weighted priorities can then be added for each element in the level to obtain its overall or global priority.

The elements being compared should be clustered into homogeneous groups of five to nine so they can be meaningfully (greater consistency) compared with respect to elements in the next higher level. If they are not homogeneous, thus, if the disparity between them is great, they should belong to different levels. For example, we cannot make a precise comparison between two jobs whose performances differ in difficulty by a factor of 100 because our judgment would be subject to significant error. Instead, we first group simple jobs into a cluster and compare the cluster with a job one order of magnitude more difficult to perform than a simple job. We then compare the jobs in the cluster among themselves according to difficulty of performance. When we compare the results of the two comparisons processes, we obtain a net comparison of a simple job with the more difficult one.

Alternatively, the elements are placed in separate gradually increasing homogeneous groups or clusters with a common pivot (the largest element of the previous cluster) used as the smallest element of the next cluster. The clustering is successively refined through the prioritization which reveals those elements that are too small or too large when compared with the other homogeneous elements and must be moved to another cluster.

To avoid making large errors, we must carry out this

process of clustering. By forming hierarchically arranged clusters of like elements - simple jobs in this case - we can efficiently complete the process of comparing the simple with the very complex. Similarly, to compare small stones with boulders or atoms with stars, we must intervene between them several levels of objects of slightly different magnitude to make the transition and comparison possible.

The only restriction on the hierarchic arrangement of elements is that any element in one level must be capable of being related to some elements in the next higher level, which serves as a criterion for assessing the relative impact of elements in the level below.

Alternatives may be disparate or nonhomogeneous with one or several of them much larger or smaller than others with respect to a criterion. In that case, it is pointless to use dummy alternatives of intermediate sizes to link their comparisons. One only compares the largest homogeneous ones and distributes the weight of the criterion among them. If there is only a single such largest alternative, one simply assigns it the total weight of the criterion. The smaller homogeneous elements are assigned the value zero.

We also note that when a criterion occurs in ranges of intensity and not simply as a point, one sets priorities on the intensities, rescales the weight of the criterion by the relative number of alternatives and compares the alternatives with respect to the relevant range of intensities.

Finally, after judgments have been made on the impact of all the elements, and priorities have been computed for the hierarchy as a whole, the less important elements can be dropped from further consideration because of their relatively small impact on the overall objective.

Advantages of Hierarchies
(1) Hierarchical representation of a system can be used to describe how changes in priority at upper levels affect the priority of

elements in lower levels.

(2) They give great detail of information on the structure and function of a system in the lower levels and provide an overview of the actors and their purposes in the upper levels. constraints on the elements in a level are best represented in the next higher level to ensure that they are satisfied. For example, nature may be regarded as an actor whose objectives are the use of certain material and subject to certain laws as constraints.

(3) Natural systems assembled hierarchically, i.e. through modular construction and final assembly of modules, evolve much more efficiently than those assembled as a whole.

(4) They are stable and flexible; stable in that small changes have small effect and flexible in that additions to a well-structured hierarchy do not disrupt the performance.

Rationality

We can now define *rationality* in the AHP as:

- Focussing on the goal of solving the problem;
- Knowing enough about a problem to develop a thorough structure of relations and influences;
- Having enough knowledge and experience and access to knowledge and experience of others to assess the priority of influence and dominance (importance, preference or likelihood to the goal as appropriate) among the relations in the structure;
- Allowing for differences in opinion with an ability to develop a best compromise.

Top Down and Bottom Up Evaluation Process

In hierarchic structures we represent higher order goals to maintain a context for the decision. It is this context that shapes and influences the judgments both in absolute and relative measurement. The decision making context is made explicit in the AHP. It is context that determines the relative importance of the intensities we use to rate the alternatives in absolute measurement.

For example, if one develops rating intensities for job performance and uses them to judge employees on that single job, the intensities would receive different relative values from job to job. For all jobs, dependability may be an important criterion. Yet the relative values assigned to extremely dependable and very dependable would be different if one is rating soldiers responsible for pressing the nuclear button or rating waiters in a restaurant. In the first case the distinction is very high, but not in the second. In relative measurement, it has been demonstrated in many examples that, context creates nonlinearity in the paired comparison judgments which are then reflected in the derived ratio scale. Consider alternatives in which some are much more preferred than others. Among the less preferred ones, an alternative may be strongly preferred to another although there is only a slight difference in quality. On the other hand, among the highly preferred ones, one alternative may be preferred only slightly or moderately over another, even though their differences may be much greater. We note that in either case the importance of a criterion is derived with respect to the goal independently of the alternatives.

To choose among several bridge designs, a top down process would reveal safety to be very important. If all the bridges meet safety standards but one exceeds it somewhat, paired comparisons may still show the relative values of the bridges on safety to be about the same, and in hierarchic composition, safety would not play an important role in resolving differences among the bridges. Its presence is like adding a positive constant to all the rankings. However, safety would be a decisive factor if some bridges fall below the standards and one is better.

To improve understanding of context, hence the quality of the decision, one may run through evaluations by first going down from the goal and then again going up by first comparing the alternatives with respect to the criteria. This is particularly useful in absolute measurement to enable one to make the necessary adjustments in the intensities by refining them, to make them adequate to distinguish among the alternatives.

In the top down process the number and type of alternatives is open and one attempts to find a best choice from what is available at the time. In the bottom up process the alternatives are known, generally exhaustive and one wants to choose a best one or allocate resources among them.

3. Description of Hierarchies - Structural, Functional

We have already encountered examples of hierarchies in Chapter 1. We need to describe the types and functions of hierarchies in general terms. There are several kinds of hierarchies, the simplest of which are dominance hierarchies which descend like an inverted tree with the boss at the root, followed by successive levels of bossing. Another kind are holarchies which are essentially dominance hierarchies with feedback. Chinese box (or modular) hierarchies grow in size from the simplest elements or components (the inner boxes) to larger and larger aggregates (the outer boxes). In biology, neogenetic hierarchies are of interest because they have successive newly emerging top levels through evolution. We shall concentrate our attention on dominance hierarchies. Even if the structure of a system is characterized by a network of a high dimension of complexity, when it is analyzed according to function and purpose, it often takes on the simple form of a dominance hierarchy with descending levels of decreasing importance.

What interests us here is to provide a way for analyzing the impacts of different levels, representing subsystems, of a system, characterized as a hierarchy, on the entire hierarchy and conversely. the theory also enables us to study the stability of a hierarchy to perturbations in both structure and function.

Hierarchies can be divided into two kinds: structural and functional. In structural hierarchies, complex systems are structured into their constituent parts in descending order according to structural properties such as size shape, color or age. A structural hierarchy of the universe would descend from galaxies to constellations to solar systems to planets, and so on, down to atoms, nuclei, protons, and neutrons. Structural hierarchies relate closely to the way our brains analyze complexity by breaking down the objects perceived by our senses into clusters, subclusters, and still smaller clusters.

In contrast, functional hierarchies decompose complex systems into their constituent parts according to their essential relationships. A conflict over school busing to achieve integration can be structured into a cluster of major stakeholders (majority and minority communities, city officials, board of education, federal government); a cluster of stakeholders' objectives (education for children, retention of power, and the like); and alternative outcomes (complete, partial or no busing). Such functional hierarchies help people to steer a system toward a desired goal - like conflict resolution, efficient performance, or overall happiness. For the purposes of this book, functional hierarchies are the only kind that need to be considered.

Each set of elements in a functional hierarchy occupies a level of the hierarchy. The top level, called the *focus*, consists of only one elements: the broad, overall objective or goal. Subsequent levels may each have several elements, although their number is usually small - between five and nine.

Because a hierarchy represents a model of how the brain analyzes complexity, the hierarchy must be flexible enough to deal with that complexity. The levels of a hierarchy interconnect like layers of cell tissue to form an organic whole that serves a certain function. A spiraling effect is noticeable when we move from the focus by expanding the hierarchy to the level of simple elements. The expansion may be continued to the level of elements of minutest concern. Chapter 6 illustrates the flexibility of hierarchies with a variety of examples.

One's approach to constructing a hierarchy depends on the kind of decision to be made. If it is a matter of choosing among alternatives, we could start from the bottom level by listing the alternatives. The next level would consist of the criteria for judging the alternatives. And the top level would be a single element, the focus or overall purpose, in terms of which the criteria can be compared according to the importance of their contribution.

The basic problem with a hierarchy is to seek understanding at the highest levels from interactions of the various levels of the hierarchy rather than directly from the elements of the levels. Rigorous methods for structuring systems into hierarchies are gradually emerging in the natural and social sciences and in particular, in general systems theory as it relates to the planning and design of social systems.

Direct confrontation of the large and the small is avoided in nature through the use of a hierarchical linkage. Conceptually, the simplest hierarchy is linear, rising form one level of elements to an adjacent level. For example, in a manufacturing operation there is a level of workers dominated by a level of supervisors, dominated by a level of managers, on to vice presidents and the president. A nonlinear hierarchy as in Chapter 8 would be one with circular arrangements so that an upper level might be dominated by a lower level as well as being in a dominance position (e.g. in case of flow of information).

Each element of a hierarchy may belong functionally to several other different hierarchies. A spoon may be arranged with other spoons of different sizes in one hierarchy or with knives and forks in a second hierarchy. For example, it may be a controlling component in a level of one hierarchy or it may simply be an unfolding of higher or lower order functions in another hierarchy.

Two General Structures of Hierarchies
1) Generic Hierarchy for Forward Planning
    The levels of the hierarchy successively descend from the goal down to:
  • Time Horizons
  • Uncontrollable Environmental Constraints
  • Risk Scenarios

- Controllable Systemic Constraints
- Overall Objectives of the Systems
- Stakeholders
- Stakeholder Objectives (Separate for each)
- Stakeholder Policies (Separate for each)
- Exploratory Scenarios (Outcomes)
- Composite or Logical Scenario (Outcome)

Most prediction problems are of this kind. Contingency Planning policies must be devised to deal with unexpected occurrences and exploratory scenarios are included to allow for such a possibility. The exploratory scenarios are what each stakeholder would pursue if alone with no other stakeholders around.

(2) The Backward Planning Hierarchy
The levels of this hierarchy successively descend from the goal of choosing a best outcome to:
- Anticipatory Scenarios
- Problems and Opportunities
- Actors and Coalitions
- Actor Objectives
- Actor Policies
- Particular Control Policies of a particular actor to Influence the Outcome

Most decision problems are of this kind. Planning involves testing the impact of the high priority policies in the bottom level. These policies are added to the policies of that particular actor in the forward process which results in a second forward process hierarchy. The iterations are repeated [5] to close the gap between the dominant contrast scenarios (or composite scenario) of the forward process and the anticipatory scenarios of the backward process.

4. How to Structure a Hierarchy

Other than through an effort to define an idea in a particular way to obtain agreement on what it means, no object, phenomenon, or experience has a unique meaning of its own. Meaning depends on the disposition of the observer and on prior knowledge, state of mind and conditioning. The mind has a variety of "filters", perspectives and needs to view things. To a blind person, a human being is what that person can feel and hear. One cannot describe to the blind features which relate to vision in a way that can be understood without eyes. Without an electron microscope, viruses would be hypothetical; without a telescope, all stars look about the same. It is often said that when a person visits a land of strangers all people look alike. Only after prolonged familiarity does one perceive distinctions.

To construct a hierarchy one needs creative thinking, recollection, association, memory, other people's perspectives, and one also needs to learn in the process of construction. Otherwise few ideas present themselves and that which comes to mind may not be what one needs or is looking for. There is no escaping the fact that a dictionary of hierarchies is essential to enrich one's thinking. No one knows everything about a decision problem. We need to think, debate and revise until we are satisfied and can use what we have to persuade other interested parties.

In practice there is no set procedure for generating the objectives, criteria, and activities to be included in a hierarchy or even a more general system. It is a matter of what objectives we choose to decompose the complexity of that system. One facet of this approach is to assume the independence of an upper part or cluster of the hierarchy from the functions of all its lower parts. The structure of hierarchies is multilinear and proceeds downward from the most general and less controllable (goals, objectives, criteria, subcriteria) to the more concrete and controllable factors terminating in the level of alternatives. A useful criterion to check the validity of a hierarchy is to determine if the elements of an upper level can be used as common attributes to compare the elements in the level immediately below with each other.

One usually studies the literature for enrichment of ideas, and often by working with others, goes through a free wheeling brainstorming session to list all concepts relevant to the problem without regard to relation or order. One attempts to keep in mind the ultimate goal to be identified at the top of the hierarchy; the sub-objectives immediately below; the forces constraining the actors still below that. This dominates a level of the actors themselves, which in turn dominates a level of objectives followed by a level of policies which is then followed by a level of the various possible outcomes (scenarios). This is the natural form that planning and conflict hierarchies take. When designing a physical system, the policies can be replaced by methods of construction. This needs to be followed by several intermediate levels culminating in alternative systems. Considerable criticism and revision may be required before a well-defined hierarchy is formulated.

There is sufficient similarity between problems that one is not always faced with a completely new task in structuring a hierarchy. In a sense the task for the experienced becomes one of identifying the different classes of problems which arise in life systems. There is such a variety of these that the challenge is to become versed with the ideas and concepts which people, living within such a system, encounter. This requires intelligence, patience, and the ability to interact with others to benefit from their understanding and experience.

A valuable observation about the hierarchical approach to problem solving is that the functional representation of a system may differ from person to person, but people tend to agree on the bottom level of alternative actions to be taken and the level above it. In constructing a hierarchy upwards, it is paritcularly helpful to ask: can these elements be compared with respect to each element in the level above?

5. Extending Rank Order to a Hierarchy

The AHP is used to arrange the elements in comparable magnitudes from the very large to the very small in levels of the hierarchy. After performing comparisons of the elements in each level, it synthesizes the relative magnitudes in the entire hierarchy to make it possible to compare and rank all the stimuli in all levels.

The top element or goal of the hierarchy, whatever its absolute magnitude g, when compared with itself yields a ratio of $g/g = 1$. From then on the comparison process decomposes this derived unit among the elements in each succeeding level. Let us examine the kind of numbers obtained in this operation.

At each level of the hierarchy, the total priorities derived must reflect an appropriate distribution of the unit value of the goal among the elements of that level. For example, all the elements of the second level must be compared according to how much of the goal each accounts for. Their resulting priorities, w_1, w_2, ..., w_n must sum to unity. These priorities are unique to within a positive multiplicative constant and hence belong to an underlying ratio scale. They become unique through normalization. The resulting derived vector reflects the portion of the decomposition of unity which each element receives. For the third level elements let us assume that the priorities with respect to the n criteria of the second level are given in the following columns:

$$\begin{bmatrix} w_{11} & w_{12} & \cdots & w_{1n} \\ w_{21} & w_{22} & \cdots & w_{2n} \\ \vdots & \vdots & & \vdots \\ w_{m1} & w_{m2} & \cdots & w_{mn} \end{bmatrix}$$

Each column belongs to a different ratio scale, i.e. each scale has a different constant multiplier that is positive. Thus we may write

$w_{ij} = a_j x_{ij}$, $j = 1, \ldots, n$ for all i. For each scale, a_j transforms the x_{ij} reading on that scale, derived with respect to the jth criterion in the second level, to w_{ij}.

Hierarchic composition with the w_{ij} scales yields

$$\sum_{j=1}^{n} w_j w_{ij}, \quad i = 1, \ldots, m$$

In a hierarchy, dependence only occurs from level to level and the elements in a level are also independent. In that case hierarchic composition is a special case of network dominance composition and leads to an additive function from one level to the next. Multiple levels of the hierarchy give rise to a multilinear form that is non-linear and in general does not behave as an additive linear function.

We have seen that the principal eigenvector represents the relative dominance or rank of each element in the paired comparison matrix A. When the judgments are consistent each power of A is a constant multiple of A. Hence it is sufficient to normalize the row sums of A to derive the principal eigenvector which gives the relative priorities or ranks of the elements. When A is inconsistent, one must consider the mean of corresponding components obtained as the normalized row sums of every power of A. The result is again the principal eigenvector of A.

The overall ranks of the alternatives in a decision are derived through a generalization of the principal eigenvector of a single pairwise comparison matrix. We refer to the method of deriving these ranks as the Hierarchic Composition Principle. In Chapter 8, it will be shown that this principle is in fact a theorem and a special case of a graph theoretic network structure with dependencies and feedback represented by the supermatrix. In all three cases of a single matrix of judgments, of the matrix of a hierarchy, and of the supermatrix of a network, the matrix is raised to infinite powers to capture all transitivities and multiple influences leading to a vector of relative weights or priorities.

In graph theoretic terms, a hierarchy is a directed graph

from the goal to the bottom level. The levels of the hierarchy are the vertices of a path that connects the top goal to the level of alternatives. In addition, each of these vertices is itself a strongly connected subgraph. The directed graph gives rise to the supermatrix which represents the reachability of any vertex from any other vertex of the hierarchy according to dominance comparison.

It will be shown in Chapter 8 that the limit of the supermatrix of a hierarchy exists because it is column stochastic, irreducible, and imprimitive. In fact this limit is equal to the matrix raised to a power, one less than its order. In the distributive mode of the AHP, the alternatives are simply normalized with respect to a criterion before multiplying by the weight of that criterion. We have:

Theorem 4.1 (The Distributive Hierarchic Composition Principle): *Given a hierarchy H in which the alternatives are ranked by the distributive mode, and given its corresponding supermatrix A of order n, the ranks of the alternatives with respect to the goal are uniquely given in the corresponding positions of the first column of* $\lim_{k \to \infty} A^k$.

When the normalized weights are divided by the priority of the highest rated among them for each criterion (called the ideal for that criterion), we have for an $n \times n$ supermatrix A:

Corollary (The Ideal Hierarchic Composition Principle): Given a hierarchy H in which the alternatives are ranked by the ideal mode and given its supermatrix A of order n, the ranks of the alternatives are uniquely given in the corresponding positions of the first column of A^{n-1}.

6. Balance Between Structure and Composition Rule

It is sometimes suggested that additive weighting may be inadequate to capture legitimate expectations and that some other way is the better approach. But one can show that no method of synthesis is adequate by itself to capture every kind of expectation unless it is linked to a modifiable structure in breadth and depth to yield the appropriate, sufficiently complex, mathematical form.

It is by a combination of structure and a method of synthesis that gives rise to a dense numerical outcome that one can come arbitrarily close to any desired (expected) outcome. Here is an example of the inadequacy of additive synthesis which then becomes adequate by augmenting the structure.

Consider the problem of two criteria (English and typing) and three secretaries who apply for a job. The first is good at English and poor at typing, the second is good at typing and poor at English and the third is balanced between the two. Assume that the two criteria are equally weighted and that the weighting of the secretaries with respect to the two criteria when normalized to unity is as follows:

Secretary	Criterion 1(.5)	Criterion 2(.5)
A	.111	.615
B	.278	.231
C	.611	.154

Although Secretary B is not fully dominated by either A or C, and is thought to have greater balance with respect to both criteria taken together, he or she cannot come out as the best alternative using linear (additive) weighting. It is easy to show that for no choice of α and β with $\alpha \geq 0$, $\alpha + \beta = 1$ is $.287\alpha + .231\beta >$ $.111\alpha + .615\beta$ or $> .611 \alpha + .154\beta$. Yet if we add a third criterion of "balance," secretary B can become the winner.

Take another example. Suppose in fact B is the winner as

shown below.

	$\alpha=.5$	$\beta=.5$	Composite
A	1	10	5.5
B	6	6	6
C	10	1	5.5

Let us now change the judgments slightly in the second row and obtain,

	$\alpha=.5$	$\beta=.5$	Composite
A	1	10	5.5
B	5	5	5
C	10	1	5.5

so that B is now a loser. Because B shows greater balance, it may be desired to keep him or her as the winner which cannot be done by linear weighting. However, he or she can come out the winner by using a special kind of function known as a quasi concave weighting function. But in practice it is not easy to find a unique form for such a function. One can always construct counterexamples to any weighting scheme by showing that it is inadequate to meet legitimate expectations.

The AHP deals with this concern by adopting one composition rule that is general and applies equally to dependence and independence situations but provides the flexibility to change the structure of the problem to include the necessary criteria to capture expectations. The judgment process would favor those alternatives that have high priority under these criteria. In this manner one can deal with a situation in which the desired mathematical structure becomes a part of the overall evaluation.

7. Hierarchic Composition and Sensitivity Analysis

A useful concern in any theory based on measurement is to hypothetically make both small and large perturbations in the measurements and note their effect on the outcome. The general query is how sensitive or how stable is the outcome (the rank of a best alternative, or the ratio of the different alternatives) to changes in the various factors included in the hierarchy. In particular, how stable is it to changes in the priorities of the criteria in the second level of the hierarchy?

In the AHP, the theoretical basis for sensitivity analysis in a hierarchy is simple to perform. The outcome of a hierarchy is the product of matrices whose columns are priority vectors.

Let H be a complete hierarchy with h levels. Let B_k be the priority matrix of the kth level, $k = 2, ..., h$. If W' is the global priority vector of the pth level with respect to some element z in the (p-1)st level, then the priority vector W of the qth level ($p < q$) with respect to z is given by the multilinear form,

$$W = B_q B_{q-1}...B_{p+1} W'.$$

Thus, the global priority vector of the lowest level with respect to the goal is given by,

$$W = B_h B_{h-1}...B_2 W'.$$

In general, $W' = 1$. The sensitivity of the bottom level alternatives with respect to changes in the weights of elements in any level can be studied by means of this multilinear form.

8. Additive and Multiplicative Composition

The theory of section 6 leads one to consider one and only one way for hierarchic composition and that is by weighting and adding. However, it does occur to one to inquire whether raising the weights of the alternatives to the powers of their corresponding criteria and multiplying the results for each alternative may not also yield a valid ranking.

Some have gone further and suggested that combining scales in multicriteria decisions is a matter of taste rather than a compelling scientific concern, as we believe it should be, as suggested by the supermatrix approach. A. Easton [2] has suggested that there is an infinity of rules for combining scores of alternatives and they lead to different rankings. Some of these rules are safe and some are daring.

Alternatives that receive the same score are equally meritorious. For every choice rule there is a corresponding mathematical map. (The map would have one curve for each discrete value of the figure-of-merit.) For example, if the rule calls for computing the weighted arithmetic mean of criteria scores for an alternative, the underlying indifference map (for criteria pairs) is a set of negatively sloped straight lines. (The slope of the lines depends on the criteria weights.) If the rule calls for the weighted geometric means, the underlying indifference map is a set of hyperbolas. If the rule calls for the weighted quadratic mean of scores, the map consists of a set of quarter-arcs of circles or ellipses, depending on the relative criteria weights.

According to Easton, the degree and curvature of the underlying indifference curves provides the critical clue to the inner logics of the various rules. The greater the curvature, the greater the "safety" or "daring" of the rule for alternatives with a high degree of profile scatter in their criterion score-sets. Rules with indifference curves which bend away from the origin are the most conservative; rules with curves that bend toward the origin, the most "daring." Thus the arithmetic mean is indifferent and the geometric mean is conservative. Let us consider an example illustrating additive and multiplicative composition.

School Selection Example

We shall illustrate the two approaches with a well known example. Three high schools, A, B, and C, were analyzed from the standpoint of the author's son according to their desirability. Six dependent characteristics were selected for the comparison -- learning, friends, school life, vocational training, college preparation, and music classes. The pairwise matrices were as shown in Tables 4.1 and 4.2.

Table 4.1. Comparison of characteristics with respect to overall satisfaction with school

	Learning	Friends	School life	Vocational training	College Preparation	Music classes
Learning	1	4	3	1	3	4
Friends	1/4	1	7	3	1/5	1
School life	1/3	1/7	1	1/5	1/5	1/6
Vocational training	1	1/3	5	1	1	1/3
College preparation	1/3	5	5	1	1	3
Music classes	1/4	1	6	3	1/3	1

The priority vector of this matrix is given by (0.32, 0.14, 0.03, 0.13, 0.24, 0.14)

$$\lambda_{max} = 7.49$$
$$C.I. = 0.30$$
$$C.R. = 0.24$$

Table 4.2 Comparison of schools with respect to the six characteristics

	Learning				Friends				School life		
A	1	1/3	1/2	A	1	1	1	A	1	5	1
B	3	1	3	B	1	1	1	B	1/5	1	1/5
C	2	1/3	1	C	1	1	1	C	1	5	1

$\lambda_{max} = 3.05$ $\lambda_{max} = 3.00$ $\lambda_{max} = 3.00$
C.I. = 0.025   C.I. = 0   C.I. = 0
C.R. = 0.04   C.R. = 0   C.R. = 0

	Vocational training				College preparation				Music classes		
A	1	9	7	A	1	1/2	1	A	1	6	4
B	1/9	1	1/5	B	2	1	2	B	1/6	1	1/3
C	1/7	5	1	C	1	1/2	1	C	1/4	3	1

$\lambda_{max} = 3.21$ $\lambda_{max} = 3.21$ $\lambda_{max} = 3.05$
C.I. = 0.105   C.I. = 0   C.I. = 0.025
C.R. = 0.18   C.R. = 0   C.R. = 0.04

The priorities of each of these matrices are (0.16, 0.59, 0.25), (0.33, 0.33, 0.33), (0.45, 0.09, 0.46), (0.77, 0.05, 0.17), (0.25, 0.50, 0.25), and (0.69, 0.09, 0.22), respectively

The Additive Approach

If it is desired to choose the more unique and elitist of the schools so that the more alike schools are less desirable, then we use the distributive mode to obtain an outcome as in Table 4.3a.

Table 4.3a. Distributive Mode

(Normalization: Dividing each entry by the total in its column)

	L	F	SL	VT	CP	MC	Composite Impact of Schools
A	.16	.33	.45	.77	.25	.69	.37
B	.59	.33	.09	.05	.50	.09	.38
C	.25	.33	.46	.17	.25	.22	.25

If on the other hand, we want the best school no matter what other schools there are, we use the ideal mode to obtain:

Table 4.3b. Ideal Mode
(Dividing each entry by the maximum value in its column)

	L	F	SL	VT	CP	MC	Composite Impact of Schools	Normalized
A	.27	1	.98	1	.50	1	.65	.34
B	1	1	.20	.07	1	.13	.73	.39
C	.42	1	1	.22	.50	.32	.50	.27

The son, in seeking the optimal school, discovered that A and B were close and went to school A because it had almost the same rank as school B, yet school B was a private school charging a large sum for tuition, and school A was free. We have a conflict between a son and his mother; the first preferred school A, and the second school B, but neither took money into consideration as important. Although the inconsistency for the second level is high, the decision to choose A was taken anyway despite large inconsistency.

Multiplicative Weighting [4]
    Let us now look at an alternative way of synthesizing priorities. Instead of multiplying the normalized scales by the priority of their governing criterion, each value is raised to a power equal to the priority of that criterion; and instead of adding the results for synthesis, they are multiplied and the resulting vector is then normalized by dividing by the sum.
    The additive and multiplicative approaches can be related through the logarithmic law of Weber-Fechner. However, that law is assumed to apply in general and not just to homogeneous elements arranged in a hierarchic structure. Because of limitations on the ability of the mind to compare widely disparate elements,

accuracy may be lost in this process.

In the absolute mode of the AHP, the intensity ratings of the alternatives can be raised to the power of their criteria and multiplied to obtain an overall ranking. The logarithm of the outcome is the same as taking the logarithms of the intensitites and weighting them by the priorities of the corresponding criteria and then adding them. This approach can only be applied to a hierarchy of a goal, criteria, and alternatives. Beyond this, one must use additive composition to obtain meaningful results. Similarly, in relative measurement, one may take the logarithm of the relative values of the alternatives and multiply them by the priorities of the corresponding criteria and add. In the following application of multiplicative composition to the school example, we do not need to take logarithms because of the equivalent ranking results.

Applying the Multiplicative Approach

If we raise the priority of the elements of the distributive mode in each column to the power of the priority of the corresponding criterion and multiply the results, we obtain Table 4.4 and the priorities on the right:

Table 4.4. The priorities of the schools raised to the power of the corresponding criteria

						Product	Normalization of Product
.556	.857	.976	.967	.717	.949	.306	.35
.845	.857	.930	.677	.847	.714	.326	.37
.642	.857	.977	.974	.717	.809	.248	.28

The two approaches lead to the same decision, although the resulting priorities are somewhat but not markedly different in this particular problem.

Additive composition is more appropriate for computing the

relative portion that a part is of the whole. If we divide an object into four equal parts and each of these in turn into four equal parts, each of the latter is 1/16 of the total. This is obtained by multiplying 1/4 × 1/4 and not by raising 1/4 to the power of 1/4.

9. Multilinear Forms and Tensors [1]

There is an important formal area of mathematics where hierarchic decision-making and physics meet. It has to do with the representation of ratio scales as products of vectors in the various levels of the hierarchy. These transformations give rise to multilinear forms which correspond to multiplication (weighting) and summation (composition) of measurements on different attributes. Operating on measurement can be the process of weighting and adding to obtain a single number as one obtains in the AHP or in a physics formula.

A multilinear or a p-linear form on p vector spaces $E_1, \ldots, E_p$ defined over the same field K, is a mapping f of $E_1, \ldots, E_p$ into K such that if we fix all vectors except those of E_i, we obtain a linear form on E_i. When the vector spaces $E_1, \ldots, E_p$ are identical (e.g., when the measurements belong to the same basic scale), we can form the tensor product $f \otimes g$ of a mapping f of a p form and a mapping g of a q form. It is the (p + q) form defined by:

$$(f \otimes g)(v_1, \ldots, v_p, v_{p+1}, \ldots, v_{p+q}) = f(v_1, \ldots, v_p) \cdot g(v_{p+1}, \ldots, v_{p+q})$$

This product is associative and distributive with respect to the sum and also associative with respect to exterior multiplication. The tensor product of p forms that are linear is a p-linear form:

$$(f_1 \otimes \cdots \otimes f_p)(v_1, \ldots, v_p) = f_1(v_1) \ldots f_p(v_p)$$

Consider a p-linear form on E of dimension n related to a

basis e_i, and let $f(e_i, ..., e_i) = t_{i...i}$. Let $v_k = \sum_i x_k^i e_k^i$. Linearity enables us to write:

$$f(v_1, ..., v_p) = \sum_{i_1, ..., i_p} x_1^{i_1} x_2^{i_2} \cdots x_p^{i_p} \, t_{i_1} \cdots t_{i_p}.$$

Consider a change of basis defined by $u_j = \sum_i a_j^i e_i$. Let

$$T_{j_1}, ..., T_{j_p} = f(u_{j_1}, ..., u_{j_p}) = \sum_{i_1, ..., i_p} a_{j_1}^{i_1} \cdots a_{j_p}^{i_p} \, t_{i_1} \cdots t_{i_p}.$$

This transformation is a generalization of the formula for a linear form called a covariant vector and justifies the name of a covariant tensor of order p of the p-form. Here we have a natural way to see that the tensor calculus on a finite dimensional vector space can be characterized as a multilinear form on a product of identical spaces. A polynomial in one or more variables can be written as a multilinear form in which a variable raised to a power is expressed as a product of that variable as many times as its power. In this sense, multilinear forms are more general and have wider applicability than polynomials. It is known that polynomials can be used to approximate any continuous function on a closed interval as closely as desired. Multilinear forms generalize on this concept to many dimensional spaces for approximating functions that may not be continuous, such as in the measurement and composition of catastrophic events with respect to several criteria [6].

10. Paired Comparison of a Large Number of Alternatives

There are two ways to derive a scale for a large number of alternatives of a decision through clustering. The first is to divide them into clusters of a small number of elements in each and compare the elements in the first cluster according to a given criterion. Then take its highest priority element, include it in the second cluster, and compare these. One then divides the priorities of all the elements in the second cluster by the weight of the common element and multiplies by the weight of that element in the first cluster. Finally one eliminates the common element in that cluster (see example in b. below) from the second cluster, combines the two clusters and renormalizes the weights of all the elements. The process is then continued by including the highest priority element in another cluster and repeating. In this manner one derives a scale for all the elements for each criterion. If it is desired to repeat the process by using an average priority instead of the highest priority element one can derive a second set of priorities. One can then take the arithmetic average of the two sets. This method is useful when the elements are disparate and must be compared in homogeneous groupings.

An alternative and more efficient approach, particularly useful when all the elements are homogeneous, is to compare the elements in the various clusters in which they are grouped. One then takes the highest priority element from each cluster and forms new clusters of a small number of elements in each and compares the elements in each new cluster. Again one takes the highest priority elements, forms new clusters and compares the elements. The process is repeated until there is a single cluster whose elements are compared among themselves. A process of weighting is then applied from the top down. All the elements in an immediately lower level cluster are weighted by the priority of the highest priority element taken from it to form the adjacent higher level cluster. This is continued on downward to the original clusters. The elements in all these clusters can then be pooled and their priorities normalized.

The second procedure requires structural adjustment by multiplying the weights of the elements of a cluster in each level by the relative number of elements in the cluster to the total number of elements in all the clusters in that level. In this manner the effect of having a larger number of elements in one cluster than in another (and hence the relative priority of each element is smaller) is restored to what it should be. This is independent of how many elements there are in that cluster.

11. Structural Adjustment of Priorities

a - Rescaling criteria weights by the relative number of alternatives under each.

The process of structural adjustment may be necessary when for example not all the alternatives in the bottom level of a hierarchy are compared with respect to all the elements in the level immediately above. The typical case in an incomplete hierarchy is that the criteria do not share the same subcriteria among them but each has its own subcriteria whose number may be different. In that case the weight of a high priority criterion is diluted by being distributed among many subcriteria as compared with the weight of a lower priority criterion with fewer subcriteria.

If all the alternatives are evaluated in terms of all the subcriteria each gets its proportionate share of the distribution of the unit value of the goal through all the subcriteria. However, if not all the subcriteria are used to evaluate every alternative, then the distribution of the value would not be proportionate due to the variation in the number of subcriteria used under each criterion. To equalize the distribution, the priority of each criterion is multiplied by the relative number of its own subcriteria to the total number of subcriteria in that level. The resulting weights of the criteria are then normalized to unity and used to weight the subcriteria. In that case the effect of a different number of subcriteria is equally distributed among the subcriteria.

In this manner each alternative, when evaluated in terms of only a subset of the subcriteria gets its share of the total. The process of structural adjustment is incorporated in the software Expert Choice (EC).

Structural adjustment is automatically used in absolute measurement were one to always use the ideal mode for the intensities because the number of intensities differs from one criterion to another. All absolute measurement in EC is made with the ideal mode in order to conform with the requirement of rank preservation in that mode.

b - Decomposition: How to overcome limits on the number of elements being compared.

Assume that a computer program allows one to compare no more than 7 elements at a time, how would we deal with a situation involving eight or more elements? Let the elements be x_1, x_2, ..., x_n where n is large. Let us divide the elements into comparison sets as follows:

> We place in the first set the elements x_1, x_2, ..., x_7;
> we place in the second set the elements x_7, x_8, ..., x_{13};
> where x_7 is common to both sets;
> we place in the third set the elements x_{13}, x_{14}, ..., x_{20};
> where x_{13} is common to both sets, and so on.

We compare the first set, and derive the normalized set of priorities w_1, w_2, ..., w_7. We compare the second set and derive the priorities $\overline{w}_7$, w_8, ..., w_{13}. Similarly we derive the priorities $\overline{w}_{13}$, w_{14}, ..., w_{20} for the third set and so on. We then divide the priorities in the second set by $\overline{w}_7$ and in the third set by $\overline{w}_{13}$ respectively, etc. Then we multiply the priorities of the second set by w_7, eliminate x_7 from the second set and normalize the remaining priorities by dividing by their sum obtaining $W_2 = (w_8/\overline{w}_7) + ... + (w_{13}/\overline{w}_7)$. We also multiply the elements in the third set by $w_{13}/\overline{w}_7$ eliminate x_{13} from that set and normalize by dividing by the sum of the weights of the remaining elements and so on.

Finally we introduce artificial nodes each of which branches into one of the sets of elements. We assign the first node the weight $1/(1+W_1+W_2+...+W_k)$ and assign the ith node the weight $W_i/(1+W_1+W_2+...+W_k)$ where $(k+1)$ is the number of sets into which the elements are divided. In this manner we obtain a relative comparison of all the elements which can be combined to obtain a relative scale by multiplying the weight of each element by the corresponding weight of the artificial parent node. Such a decomposition can be made for each of the criteria with respect to which the comparisons are made. In each case, the artificial nodes with their weights may be inserted under the appropriate criterion. In the end, hierarchic composition would lead to the desired synthesis.

An Example

Suppose we have 9 criteria for choosing a car. After identifying these criteria, we arbitrarily divide them into two sets: A with 4 elements and B with 5 elements. We choose an element from A such as Price, and include it in B. We use this common element as our link between A and B. It is best to choose an important element from A so that when making comparisons in B that element represents a sufficiently significant factor that makes the comparisons easier. Assume that the paired comparisons in A and B yield the priorities shown in Figure 4-2. Here A and B are assigned the respective proportion of the total number of criteria under each.

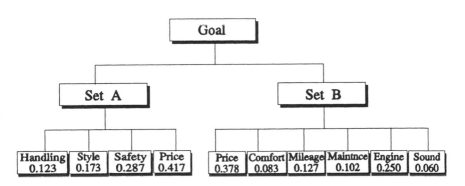

Figure 4-2. *Weights of criteria.*

Price, the common element, has a different global weight in A than in B. Our task is to make Price in B have the same global weight as it does in A so that the priority of, for example, Mileage vs. Safety will be in the proper ratio.

Now eliminate price from B and add the priorities of the elements in both A and B then divide the priorities in each set by the total. Add the resulting priorities of the elements in each set, and assign the value to the node above it that represents the set to which it belongs. Obtain, to within rounding off, the results shown in Figure 4-3.

Figure 4-3. *Relative weights of clusters and criteria.*

12. Exclusiveness and Independence

In probability theory the notions of mutually exclusive events (any two events cannot materialize simultaneously) and independent events (the occurrence of one event does not impact the occurrence of another) are central. The latter is defined based on the concept of conditional probability. The probability of an event B conditioned to the occurrence of another event A is by definition the ratio of the probability of the simultaneous occurrence of the events and the probability of the conditional event A. By definition, two events are independent if the conditional probability of one, given the other, is equal to the probability of the first. Also the probability of an event compounded by independent events is the product of their probabilities. The concept of conditional probability is the basis of Bayes theorem. Independence, however, does not mean the same thing in all contexts. For example, in Utility Theory, elaborate lottery exercises are performed to test for criteria independence. Each case relies on subjectivity and judgment about what things affect others and by how much. Independence is a general concept that needs to be specified in each theory where it is used.

In the AHP, whenever one asks the question of dominance between a pair of elements with respect to a property, one attempts to capture how much of that property is in one but not in the other element, even if the two elements overlap. The result is to give a relative value of the property in both despite overlap. By adding over the elements one obtains the sum of the relative presence of the property in all the elements. Thus independence in AHP is captured in the comparison. When the elements are dependent, one asks the question: how much more does one element depend on the other with respect to the property? For example, how much more does the steel industry depend on the electric industry for its energy than does the aluminum industry? When there is dependence among the elements, the AHP supermatrix approach is applied to establish priorities. Paired comparisons allow one to make such distinctions not inherent in attaching scale values to elements one at a time. Because independence in AHP is not defined the same as in probability theory, it is possible as proved in Chapter 8, and without the concept of conditional probability, that the basic result of Bayes theorem follows from a supermatrix model.

13. Double Counting

Double or multiple counting is the occurrence or use of the weight of a criterion more than once in the weighting of the alternatives, thus biasing (loading) the outcome in favor of that criterion, which is an undesirable outcome. Double counting is a concern of probability theory and could take place when one assumes that two events are mutually exclusive (a set theoretic concept) when they are not. Two events may be independent and not be mutually exclusive. Mutual exclusiveness implies order of occurrence. Criteria in the AHP are not mutually exclusive but that does not imply that they are dependent. As pointed out earlier, the concept of independence does not apply here. As a result, exclusiveness and independence are used interchangeably in the AHP.

Double counting may be attributed to inadvertent or erroneous representation of the criteria. More likely it is due to confusion in the structure of a decision by listing a criterion more than once in different guises.

An effective way to deal with double counting mentioned to me by my colleague Ernest Foreman is to list the objectives of a decision which are usually few and whose independence is easier to track. The criteria are then listed to satisfy the objectives. For example to choose a best car, the size of the car can in fact make two contributions, one to the objective of comfort and the other to the objective of safety and may thus be listed under both objectives. Here it is clear that size is interpreted in two different ways. It also highlights the need for carefully describing the meaning and contribution ascribed to each element represented in the hierarchy thus avoiding a habitual superficial use of criteria to rank alternatives without complete accounting of the influences and their consequences. Compiling a thorough description of the elements of the hierarchy and noting how they are perceived to affect each other in terms of the objectives of the decision would help prevent the occurrence of double counting.

14. The Consistency of a Hierarchy

The consistency of a hierarchy is obtained by first taking sums of products of each consistency index C.I., with the composite priority of its criterion. Then the ratio is formed of this number with the sums of the products of the random consistency index for that order matrix with the composite priority of its criterion. In general the ratio should be in the neighborhood of 0.10 in order not to cause concern for needed improvements in the judgments.

Let n_j, $j = 1, 2, ..., h$, be the number of elements in the jth level of the hierarchy. Let w_{ij} be the composite weight of the ith criterion of the jth level, and let $\mu_{i,j+1}$ be the consistency index of all elements in the $(j+1)^{st}$ level compared with respect to the ith criterion of the jth level.

The consistency index of a hierarchy is defined by,

$$C_H = \sum_{j=1}^{h} \sum_{i=1}^{n_{i,j+1}} w_{ij}\mu_{i,j+1}$$

where $w_{ij} = 1$ for $j = 1$, and $n_{i,j+1}$ is the number of elements of the $(j+1)^{st}$ level with respect to the ith criterion of the jth level.

References

1. Boutelop, J., 1967, L'Algebre Lineaire, Presses Universitaires de France, Paris.

2. Easton, A., 1973, "One-of-a-Kind Decisions Involving Weighted Multiple Objectives and Disparate Alternatives", Multiple Criteria Decision Making, University of South Carolina, South Carolin Press Columbia, South Carolina.

3. Saaty, T.L., 1993, "The Hierarchon", RWS Publications, 4922 Elsworth Ave, Pittsburgh, PA 15213.

4. Saaty, T.L., 1988, "A Note on Multiplicative Operations in the Analytic Hierarchy Process", in: Reprints of the First International Symposium on the Analytic Hierarchy Process, Tianjin University, Tianjin, China.

5. Saaty, T.L. and K.P. Kearns, 1985, "Analytic Planning - The Organization of Systems", International Series in Modern Applied Mathematics and Computer Science 7, Oxford, England, Pergamon Press.

6. Saaty, T.L., 1990, "How to Make a Decision: The Analytic Hierarchy Process", European Journal of Operational Research 48, 9-26.

CHAPTER FIVE

RANK PRESERVATION AND REVERSAL

1. Introduction

In its simplest form decision making involves ranking alternatives in terms of criteria or attributes of the alternatives. Adding (deleting) alternatives to (from) the set may not introduce new or eliminate old attributes yet the rank of the existing set may change due to the number of alternatives or to the actual measurements of the alternatives, neither of which is an attribute of any alternative.

There are two schools of thought about decision making. One school maintains through an axiom that new alternatives that introduce no additional attributes should not cause rank reversal as that would violate rationality. The same procedure is used to rank alternatives in all situations. The other school maintains that the effect of other alternatives on the old rank depends on whether the decision maker's preference is influenced or not by the number and measurement of these alternatives. One procedure is used to preserve rank and another to allow it to change.

Assume that an individual has expressed preference among a set of alternatives, and that as a result, he or she has developed a ranking for them. Can and should that individual's preferences and the resulting rank order of the alternatives be affected if alternatives are added to or deleted from the set? There has been a long and unresolved debate on the subject among the practitioners of utility theory.

Early developers of utility theory axiomatically determined

that introducing irrelevant alternatives should not cause rank reversal [11]. But, perhaps because it is difficult to be precise about what is irrelevant, most practitioners feel that there should be no rank reversal whatever the new alternatives may be. They claim that an informed person would not let it happen if only the right kind of responses were elicited.

Articles by both economists and behaviorists have shown (mostly through experiments) that preference and rank reversals do in fact take place in practice [6, 7, 12, 17]. These authors state that the outcomes of the experiments often contradict the assumption of preference theory (and utility theory) that preference order should not be affected by introducing new alternatives. As we shall see below, if one forces order preservation on the subjects in the experiments, one obtains unnatural and arbitrary rankings. A theory that always preserves rank cannot at the same time allow for rank reversal because it would contradict its own assumptions.

The Analytic Hierarchy Process (AHP) is a theory of ranking of alternatives based on ratio scales and not on interval scales as in utility theory. It elicits judgments in the form of paired comparisons and allows for rank reversals through the operation of normalization in its distributive mode. Normalization is concerned with a tally of the number of alternatives, which is not an attribute of any single alternative. It is also concerned with the rating value or priority of each alternative. Again, this value itself is not an attribute of that alternative but some measurement made on the alternative in a particular problem. Both number and rating cannot be ignored in ranking alternatives. They have an effect on how alternatives are perceived in contrast with other alternatives with which they are compared.

Some users of the AHP have heard about the problem of rank reversal and may have assumed that there is some proven principle about it that needs to be upheld in making decisions. We show that a robust theory must allow rank reversal when appropriate, and not allow it when inappropriate. In the next sections, we will give examples from the literature about rank reversal, and illustrate how the AHP modes of measurement deal with the rank preservation and reversal issues.

2. Examples of Rank Reversal From the Utility Literature

In multicriteria decision making, it is safe to say that for every condition one may wish to impose to prevent an irrelevant alternative from causing rank reversal one can find a real life example that shows rank reversal to be reasonable and proper. Although rank reversals do not occur often, the very possibility of their occurrence has substantial logical implications about the methodology used to make decisions and whether it accounts for them or not. We recall that in science and in mathematics counterexamples can have profound effect on the validity of the assumptions we make.

There are two types of papers written on preference and rank reversals. One is by economists and behaviorists who use experiments to demonstrate the occurrence of rank reversal and speculate on the reasons why it happens. The other is by operations researchers and utility theorists who construct specific quantitative examples showing that it can occur. We discuss both types with a degree of brevity.

In 1990, Tversky et. al. [17] wrote a paper "The Causes of Preference Reversal" immediately drawing attention to the phenomenon in the title of their paper. They attempt to ascribe its occurrence to various phenomena. In the end they conclude that preference reversal "cannot be adequately explained by violations of independence, the reduction axiom, or transitivity." They say that its "primary cause is the failure of procedure invariance" which means one is stuck with one kind of procedure - precisely the point of this chapter.

In 1979, Grether and Plott [6] published a paper with the title "Economic Theory of Choice and the Preference Reversal Phenomenon". In it they describe experiments they performed in which preference reversal occurred. In their conclusions section they say "The preference reversal phenomenon which is inconsistent with the traditional statement of preference theory remains. ... No alternative theory currently available appears to be capable of covering the same extremely broad range of phenomena. ... Preference theory is circular and/or without empirical content."

In 1982, Pommerehne, Schneider and Zwiefel [12] elaborated further on Grether and Plott's experiments. In their concluding remarks, they say "Even when the subjects are exposed to strong incentives for making motivated, rational decisions, the phenomenon of preference reversal does not vanish. ... The argument calls for moving outside the framework of expected utility theory." Then they mention Prospect Theory as an alternative but say that Hershey and Shoemaker [7] found serious reservations concerning its generality.

Now let us look at some particular examples of rank reversal under varying hypotheses due to decision theory practitioners, other theoreticians, and experimentalists.

Adding Copies of an Alternative

A condition assumed in many individual choice models is regularity. Simply stated it says that the choice probability of any alternative cannot be altered by increasing or decreasing the number of alternatives of a choice set. Regularity has to do with rank preservation and there are examples where it is violated. R. Corbin and A. Marley [2] provide an example that, "concerns a lady in a small town, who wishes to buy a hat. She enters the only hat store in town, and finds two hats, A and B, that she likes equally well, and so might be considered equally likely to buy. However, now suppose that the sales clerk discovers a third hat, A_1, identical to A. Then the lady may well choose hat B for sure (rather than risk the possibility of seeing someone wearing a hat just like hers), a result that contradicts regularity." The authors could as well have written that the lady first preferred A to B but on learning about A_1, preferred B to A.

If the lady making the choice lived in a distant city where a copy of hat A is not likely to be worn in her city, her preference for A is not likely to change on seeing copies of A. Thus depending on who makes the choice we are faced with two situations. In the first, the best alternative does not depend on what other alternatives there are, as in buying a car or a computer, and in the second it does.

If a copy can convincingly cause rank reversal and a near copy also can, then a series of perturbations leading to some far off alternative also can give rise to rank reversal as the example below shows. It is easy to see this by considering alternatives A_j rated with relative values on equally weighted criteria C_i. Here the alternative $A_{3.1}$ is a copy of A_3 and $A_{3.2}$, $A_{3.3}$, $A_{3.4}$ and $A_{3.5}$ are each a perturbation of the preceding one, producing changes in rank and in weight. Each column is normalized, weighted and the rows summed.

	C_1 (.25)	C_2 (.25)	C_3 (.25)	C_4 (.25)	Rank	Weight	
A_1	1	9	1	3	3	.320	
A_2	9	1	9	1	2	.336	(1)
A_3	8	1	4	5	1	.344	

	C_1	C_2	C_3	C_4	Rank	Weight	
A_1	1	9	1	3	1	.265	
A_2	9	1	9	1	2	.250	(2)
A_3	8	1	4	5	3	.243	
$A_{3.1}$	8	1	4	5	3	.243	

	C_1	C_2	C_3	C_4	Rank	Weight	
A_1	1	9	1	3	1	.264	
A_2	9	1	9	1	2	.247	(3)
A_3	8	1	4	5	3	.246	
$A_{3.2}$	7	1	5	5	4	.243	

	C_1	C_2	C_3	C_4	Rank	Weight	
A_1	1	9	1	3	1	.264	
A_2	9	1	9	1	3	.245	(4)
A_3	8	1	4	5	4	.243	
$A_{3.3}$	6	1	6	5	2	.248	

	C_1	C_2	C_3	C_4	Rank	Weight	
A_1	1	9	1	3	1	.264	
A_2	9	1	9	1	4	.244	(5)
A_3	8	1	4	5	3	.245	
$A_{3.4}$	5	1	7	5	2	.248	

	C_1	C_2	C_3	C_4	Rank	Weight	
A_1	1	9	1	3	1	.264	
A_2	9	1	9	1	4	.243	(6)
A_3	8	1	4	5	2	.246	
$A_{3.5}$	4	1	8	5	2	.246	

Number and Quality of Alternatives (Perturbations of Near Copies)

E. Forman [4] gives the following example that illustrates the effect of the number and quality of alternatives introduced. At a company, Susan excels over Jack in every quality except computer skills, where he is much needed and thus he is overall preferred to Susan. When the company hires John, who also has computer skills but is not as good as Jack, Susan becomes the preferred employee and there is reversal in Jack and Susan's rank. One can see that if one additional computer literate employee is not sufficient to reverse Jack and Susan's rank, surely when enough people are hired with computer skills, at some point such rank reversal would happen.

Intransitivity and Rank Reversal

Robin Hogarth [8] gives the following example to illustrate the effect of intransitivity on rank and how a low priority alternative can become dominant.   Assume that of many possibilities the higher quality brand is chosen at the supermarket if its price is not more than 5 cents higher, otherwise the cheaper brand is chosen.

Brand	Price	Quality
X	60 cents	High
Y	55 cents	Medium
Z	50 cents	Low

In a comparison between X and Y, one would prefer X; between Y and Z, one would choose Y; however, a comparison between X and Z leads to the choice of Z. In other words, the apparently sensible heuristic that considers both price and quality implies an inconsistent ordering of one's preferences over the three brands. Actually if paired comparisons are used to rank the brands one would see the problem in a different light, relating to the degree of inconsistency and strength of relative preference.

Irrelevant (Phantom) Alternatives

P.H. Farquhar, K.M. Freeman, and A.R. Pratkanis [5] in their experiments on phantom alternatives observe that their findings, "violate the basic axioms of classical choice theory." Marketing literature has many examples of consumer preference rank reversals. An example used by my colleagues in the classroom is the case of a product that sells for $300, but is considered too expensive by customers and is less preferred than one that sells for $150. A strategy that is often implemented is to introduce a product similar to the $300 one, but priced much higher, e.g., $1,000. It is well documented that the formerly most expensive $300 product then looks like a much better value and is now preferred. Another example deals with the introduction of a phantom alternative that might be priced slightly lower but is not actually available for purchase because it is "out of stock." The consumer will perceive the existing alternative as an overpriced one despite its better quality and will select a cheaper one that is also available. It is asserted by these practitioners that normative utility theory (and we might add absolute measurement) fail to account for such behavior.

Irrelevant (Decoy) Alternatives

T. Tyszka [18] has done empirical work to support the hypothesis that there are no irrelevant alternatives in multicriteria decisions. His experiments deal with ordinal preferences. In a typical experiment, he gave subjects choices among pairs or triplets of alternatives already ordered with respect to the attributes. They were to choose the most preferred. An irrelevant alternative was introduced in the set preserving the old order, and they were again asked to select the most preferred alternative. The individuals used different decision rules to choose among pairs than among triplets. Two conclusions drawn from his detailed experiments are:

1 - People selected the best one among the nondominated alternatives and,

2 - They avoided choosing dominated alternatives even on a single criterion.

Thus for example, if it occurred that the new alternative dominated some other alternative that was chosen on the first pass because it was dominant on several but not all the criteria, that alternative was no longer the favored one! The subjects would have to be forced to comply with rank preservation.

Huber, Payne, and Puto [10] and Huber and Puto [9] provide empirical evidence on the systematic violation of regularity in choice sets with three alternatives. The choice alternatives are described on two attributes for which "more is better" on each attribute. They define a decoy as an asymmetrically dominated alternative in the choice set. They show that the presence of a decoy in the choice set increases the probability of choosing the target alternative close to it. One is familiar with the example of a sales pamphlet that has an attractive and well priced item that one is told is out of stock. One can often infer that it is placed in the pamphlet as a decoy to induce one to buy another similar item that is available in abundance. This surprising result violates the regularity principle in a predictable direction without imposing any apparent constraints on the choice process. This enhancement of the target's choice probability has been called the attraction effect, although no conclusive explanation for this phenomenon has appeared in the literature.

Displacement of Preferences and Intransitivities

An example contradicting the axiom [11] "if an alternative is nonoptimal, it cannot be made optimal by adding a new alternative to the problem" is due to Zeleny [19].   The following table of lotteries with two possible outcomes gives the payoffs with probabilities p_1 and p_2, corresponding to five alternatives A_i.

Table 5.1 Lotteries with two possible outcomes

	p_1	$p_2 = (1-p_1)$
A_1	4	2
A_2	6	4
A_3	4	3
A_4	6	0
A_5	3 1/3	3 1/3

Consider the alternatives A_1 and A_2 only. A_2 dominates A_1 for all possible combinations of outcomes because
$$4 p_1 + 2(1 - p_1) < 6 p_1 + 4(1-p_1).$$
A_3 and A_4 dominate each other for different values of p_1 and are equal at $p_1 = .6$.
A_3 dominates A_4 for $0 \le p_1 < .6$ and A_4 dominates A_3 for $.6 < p_1 \le 1$.
If p_1 is chosen at random, A_3 is the winner 60% of the time and would be chosen over A_4. Consider now A_3, A_4 and A_5. A_5 is independent of p_1 because it gets the same return from p_2. However A_5 and A_3 dominate each other for different values of p_1 between 0 and .6. Thus A_3 is no long dominant 60% of the time

which makes A_4 which is dominant 40% of the time and is independent of A_5 the optimal alternative!

Switching

Switching studied by Bell [1] is a phenomenon of choosing among gambles A and B by assessing their utility on a utility function, determining their respective probability and then computing their expected values. But the utility of a gambling prospect depends on the wealth level of an individual which can affect the preferred gamble. In the utility paradigm the dependence of the prospect on the wealth level has been ignored until recently [16]. Maintaining preference for one of the gambles holds if and only if the utility function is a polynomial exponential function. Another example involving switching is provided by A. Makhija and appears in [13].

3. The Distributive and Ideal Modes of the AHP

We now briefly discuss the various forms of performing multicriteria ranking by assuming the independence of the criteria from alternatives and also the independence of the criteria and the alternatives among themselves. (The general form of the AHP, known as the supermatrix approach, not discussed here, deals with these two kinds of dependence.) In the AHP, adding alternatives never gives rise to rank reversal with respect to a single criterion. The AHP can also preserve rank under multiple criteria by dividing by the weight of the highest ranked alternative after normalization in its ideal mode. Before we developed the ideal mode, rank preservation was assured by using absolute measurement, known as the ratings procedure. Ratings involves developing scales of intensities for each of the criteria through paired comparisons, establishing a priority rating for each alternative on these intensities, weighting by the priority of the corresponding criterion, and summing over the criteria. However, examples and discussion in the literature highlighted the fact that one should be able to preserve rank when necessary even with relative measurement. The Distributive mode of the AHP includes the effect of number and rating of alternatives when needed. However, the AHP was also extended to include the Ideal mode (dividing by the priority of the highest rated alternative for each criterion) which preserves rank with respect to dominated (and hence irrelevant) alternatives. Both reversal and nonreversal are essential in decision making and need to be considered in practice. Such practice for the AHP is implemented through the software package Expert Choice which incorporates the Distributive and Ideal modes plus the Absolute Measurement or Ratings mode.

The overall weight of the ith alternative in the rank preserving Absolute Measurement mode in which alternatives are rated one at a time is given by the Absolute Mode:

$$w_i = \sum_{j=1}^{m} w_{ij} x_j \qquad (1)$$

where x_j, $j=1,\ldots,m$, is the weight of the jth criterion and w_{ij} is the rating of the ith alternative for that criterion. If the alternatives are independent of each other, this weight can only change if there is a change in m or in x_j.

In relative measurement, the weight of the ith alternative after normalization is given by the Distributive Mode:

$$w_i = \sum_{j=1}^{m} w_{ij} \left(x_j / \sum_{i=1}^{n} w_{ij} \right) \qquad (2)$$

or after standardization to the ideal value by the Ideal Mode:

$$w_i = \sum_{j=1}^{m} w_{ij} x_j / \max_i w_{ij} = \sum_{j=1}^{m} w_{ij} (x_j / \sum_{i=1}^{n} w_{ij}) / (\max_i w_{ij} / \sum_{i=1}^{n} w_{ij}) \quad (3)$$

giving the same result with or without normalization. The ideal mode is used only when other alternatives have no relevance to making a best choice. As indicated in (2), normalization of the priorities of the alternatives can be interpreted as a process of rescaling or revising the weight of each criterion. When an alternative is added, for example, that weight is additionally affected by an extra term w_{ij}, in which case we would for example

have $w_i = \sum_{j=1}^{m} w_{ij}(x_j / \sum_{i=1}^{n+1} w_{ij})$. Briefly then, normalization

implies the dependence of the final ranking on the number of alternatives and on their relative measurement with respect to each other. Each time a new alternative is introduced, the overall rank of the alternatives for the several criteria can change because a new measurement is added. Two examples are given in section 4 that demonstrate the compelling need for normalization in certain decisions.

There are decision problems in which the main concern is to choose the best alternative <u>independently</u> of what other alternatives may come to light after the initial ranking. In other problems, as we have seen, the best alternative may <u>depend</u> on what other alternatives are added. This new factor may cause the choice to shift to a formerly less desirable alternative. Thus the presence of another alternative requires the decision maker to consider a criterion that is not a characteristic of the alternatives, but is related to their availability, concrete or hypothetical, as with phantoms. This is a form of <u>dependence</u> among the alternatives. Another type of decision involving dependence may not relate to choosing the best alternative, but to the best ordering and proportionality among the alternatives. Dependence on other alternatives occurs in problems of scarcity, in resource allocation, and in planning where all the scenarios contribute a part to the planning exercise. In all these cases the distributive mode is used.

When there is dependence among the alternatives one must use the usual paired comparisons of alternatives together with normalization, called the distributive mode in the AHP. On the other hand, when the alternatives are independent, one must preserve the initial ranking from changing if irrelevant (low ranking) alternatives are added.

Two ways have been proposed for maintaining rank

preservation in relative measurement:

1 - The ratio scale ideal mode approach: Here one divides the relative weights of all the alternatives by the weight of the highest ranked alternative for each criterion. Adding a new alternative requires that it be compared only with the highest ranking one. Adding an alternative that ranks lowest on all the criteria would not affect the ranks of the other alternatives. Adding a higher ranking alternative on some criterion would become the ideal and could cause change in the other ranks. However, such an occurrence is admissible. For example, it does not contradict the axioms of utility theory. But it is prohibited for new alternatives that are dominated on all the criteria.

2 - The interval scale ideal approach: Interval scale values are obtained by converting the weight w of an alternative with respect to a criterion to $\dfrac{w - w_{min}}{w_{max} - w_{min}}$ where w_{min} and w_{max} are the priority weights of the minimum and maximum ranked alternatives respectively. One introduces a hypothetical ideal alternative with which all added alternatives are compared. Here a new alternative, whether relevant or irrelevant cannot affect the ranks of other alternatives. This approach creates the concern that we now have a forced attempt to always preserve rank even when there are examples of both relevant and irrelevant alternatives that give rise to rank reversal outside the traditional requirement for a change in the criteria or their weights. Also, by converting to interval scales for the alternatives, one would no longer be able to form ratios of the ranks. Without such ratios one would have difficulty making direct use of this ranking through proportionate resource allocation or benefit-cost analysis. Ratio Scales uniquely enable one to study interdependence by accumulating weights

through dominance analysis as in the supermatrix approach of the AHP [14].

Note that both of the foregoing approaches yield similar rankings and both can use the hypothetical alternative. But the second is an undesirable departure from ratio scales.

4. Distributive and Ideal Modes: Examples and Experiments

Here are two examples of rank preservation and reversal in relative measurement.

Rank Preservation with the Ideal Mode - Introducing Irrelevant Alternatives

If we add many copies of an "irrelevant" or in better words, "dominated" alternative C (total Cs are 20) in a problem involving two equally weighted criteria, Efficiency and Cost, we have for example for paired comparisons using the AHP 1-9 scale, rounded off to two decimal places:

Efficiency (.5)

	A	B	C	C	C	...	C	Norm	Ideal
A	1	3	4	4	4	...	4	.16	1
B	1/3	1	4/3	4/3	4/3	...	4/3	.05	.33
C	1/4	3/4	1	1	1	...	1	.04	.25
C	1/4	3/4	1	1	1	...	1	.04	.25
⋮	⋮	⋮	⋮	⋮	⋮		⋮	⋮	⋮
C	1/4	3/4	1	1	1	...	1	.04	.25

Cost (.5)

	A	B	C	C	C	...	C	Norm	Ideal
A	1	1/2	4	4	4	...	4	.13	.50
B	2	1	8	8	8	...	8	.25	1
C	1/4	1/8	1	1	1	...	1	.03	.13
C	1/4	3/4	1	1	1	...	1	.04	.25
C	1/4	1/8	1	1	1	...	1	.03	.13
C	1/4	1/8	1	1	1	...	1	.03	.13
⋮	⋮	⋮	⋮	⋮	⋮		⋮	⋮	⋮
C	1/4	1/8	1	1	1	...	1	.03	.13

The Distributive mode gives: A=.145, B=.150, C=.040, or, normalized, A = .43, B = .45, C = .12, and adding copies of the irrelevant (dominated) alternative C will eventually, like the proverbial "straw that broke the camel's back," cause rank reversal as we have just seen.

The Ideal mode gives: A=.75, B=.68, C=.19, and there is no rank reversal regardless of how many copies of C are added.

Rank Reversal with the Ideal Mode Introducing a Relevant (Phantom-like) Alternative

Again we begin with A and B as above. We have:

Efficiency (.5)   Cost (.5)

	A	B	Norm	Ideal
A	1	3	.75	1
B	1/3	1	.25	.33

	A	B	Norm	Ideal
A	1	2	.67	1
B	1/2	1	.33	.5

and the Distributive mode gives A = .71 and B = .29 while the Ideal mode gives A = 1.00 and B = .42 (or normalized again A = .71, B = .29).

Now, if we add C that is a relevant alternative under efficiency, because it dominates both A and B we obtain:

Efficiency (.5)   Cost (.5)

	A	B	C	Norm	Ideal
A	1	3	1/2	.3	.50
B	1/3	1	1/6	.1	.17
C	2	6	1	.6	1

	A	B	C	Norm	Ideal
A	1	1/2	4	.31	.50
B	2	1	8	.62	1
C	1/4	1/8	1	.08	.13

Here with the Distributive mode A = .30, B = .36 and C = .34 and with the Ideal mode A = .50, B =.59, and C = .57 which when normalized becomes: A = .30, B = .36, and C = .34. There is rank reversal with both the Distributive and the Ideal modes because C is dominant with respect to efficiency.

An experiment involving 64,000 hierarchies with random assignment of priorities to criteria and to alternatives was conducted to test the number of times the best choice obtained by normalizing, or by dividing by the maximum (the Ideal case) or by converting to utilities coincided with each other (Tables 5.2-5.4 below). It turns out that all three methods yield the same answer nearly all the time. We have included three tables to show the comparisons. Each number indicates the total coincidences of the best choice out of 1000 experiments with the indicated number of criteria and alternatives. For example the first entry 988 in Table 5.2 below gives the number of times out of 1000 trials that the best alternative chosen was the same when the distributive and the ideal modes were used. We note that if one excludes the distinctions on uniqueness introduced by copies, for most decisions it does not matter which mode one uses to rank the alternatives. The same kind of experiment was performed to note the coincidence of the 1st and 2nd ranked alternatives. A similar type of conclusion was obtained for the three methods when no copies were involved [15].

Table 5.2 Distributive vs. Ideal

| | \multicolumn{8}{c}{no. of alternatives} |||||||| |
no. of criteria	2	3	4	5	6	7	8	9
2	988	965	954	949	958	951	954	940
3	967	952	934	944	926	927	938	932
4	973	948	901	904	916	912	927	901
5	974	924	920	911	902	880	901	910
6	951	921	906	914	897	906	889	911
7	953	919	893	901	900	903	903	900
8	957	927	913	865	908	879	892	897
9	972	910	916	881	882	875	889	916

Table 5.3 Distributive vs. Utilities

no. of criteria	2	3	4	5	6	7	8	9
	no. of alternatives							
2	859	877	882	903	918	923	913	917
3	830	849	855	871	873	875	897	893
4	841	832	795	823	860	854	878	863
5	801	817	832	831	835	831	849	880
6	791	796	798	829	826	837	840	857
7	790	793	794	806	824	848	839	847
8	803	813	806	781	833	803	840	853
9	808	785	812	795	813	801	845	868

Table 5.4 Utilities vs. Ideal

no. of criteria	2	3	4	5	6	7	8	9
	no. of alternatives							
2	871	906	920	947	949	959	955	967
3	855	891	906	916	931	936	949	949
4	862	877	881	902	931	915	939	946
5	821	874	890	899	907	926	923	941
6	830	850	869	892	907	914	925	925
7	825	855	869	886	906	924	916	923
8	836	867	875	879	910	890	928	932
9	826	859	870	886	902	895	924	928

5. Conclusion

The AHP has been extended so that with relative measurement rank is preserved when desired by using the ideal mode, and allowed to reverse as necessary by using the distributive mode. We have seen abundant examples from the literature that indicate the need for both.

References

1. Bell, D.E., 1988, "One Switch Utility Functions and A Measure of Risk," Management Science 34/12, 1416-1424.

2. Corbin, R. and A.A.J. Marley, 1974, "Random Utility Models with Equality: An apparent, but Not Actual, Generalization of Random Utility Models", Journal of Mathematical Psychology 11, 274-293.

3. Expert Choice Software, produced by Expert Choice, Inc., 4922 Ellsworth Avenue, Pittsburgh, PA.

4. Forman, E.H., 1992, "Multicriteria Prioritization in Open and Closed Systems", George Washington University, forthcoming.

5. Freeman, K.M., A.R. Pratkanis, and P.H. Farquhar, 1990, "Phantoms As Psychological Motivation: Evidence for Compliance and Reactance Processes", University of California, Santa Cruz, and Carnegie Mellon University, Pittsburgh.

6. Grether, D.M. and C.R. Plott, 1979, "Economic Theory of Choice and the Preference Reversal Phenomenon", The American Economic Review 69/4, 623-638.

7. Hershey, J.C. and P.J.H. Shoemaker, 1980, "Prospect Theory's Reflection Hypothesis: A Critical Examination", Organization of Behavioral Human Performances 25, 395-418.

8. Hogarth, R., 1987, Judgment and Choice, John Wiley and Sons, New York.

9. Huber, J., and C. Puto, "Market Boundaries and Product Choice: Illustrating Attraction and Substitution Effects", Journal of Consumer Research, 10, 31-44

10. Huber, J., J.W. Payne and C. Puto, "Adding Asymmetrically Dominated Alternatives: Violations of Regularity and the Similarity Hypotheses", Journal of Consumer Research 9, 90-98.

11. Luce, R.D. and H. Raiffa, 1957, "Games and Decisions", Wiley, New York.

12. Pommerehne, W.W., F. Schneider and P. Zweifel, 1982, "Economic Theory of Choice and the Preference Reversal Phenomenon: A Reexamination", The American Economic Review 72/3, 569-574.

13. Saaty, T.L., 1991, "Rank and the Controversy About the Axioms of Utility Theory, A Comparison of AHP and MAUT", University of Pittsburgh, Pittsburgh, PA.

14. Saaty, T.L., 1993, "Fundamentals of the AHP", RWS Publications, Pittsburgh, PA.

15. Saaty, T.L. and L.G. Vargas, 1993, "Experiments of Rank Preservation and Reversal in Relative Measurement", Mathematical and Computer Modelling 17/4-5, 13-18.

16. Seidenfeld, T, M.J. Schervish and J.B. Kadane, 1991, "Shared Preferences and State-Dependent Utilities, Management Science 37/12, 1575-1589.

17. Tversky, A., P. Slovic and D. Kahneman, 1990, "The Causes of Preference Reversal", The American Economic Review 80/1, 204-215.

18. Tyszka, Tadeusz, 1983, "Human Decision Making" Edited by Lennart Sjoberg, Tadeusz Tyszka and James A. Wise.

19. Zeleny, M., , 1982, Multiple Criteria Decision Making, McGraw Hill, New York.

CHAPTER SIX

APPLICATIONS

1. Introduction

There are numerous areas of application of the AHP. In general, decision making involves the following kinds of concerns:

- Planning;
- Generating a Set of Alternatives;
- Setting Priorities;
- Choosing a Best Policy after Finding a Set of Alternatives;
- Allocating Resources;
- Determining Requirements;
- Predicting Outcomes;
- Designing Systems;
- Measuring Performance;
- Insuring the Stability of a System;
- Optimizing; and
- Resolving Conflict.

In all of these areas it is crucial that we have the capability to predict the outcomes to ensure that our decision survives the pressures and conflicts it may encounter later on. Otherwise a presumably good decision in the present may not appear that way in the short, mid or long terms. The hierarchic structure of the AHP allows us to incorporate the forces a decision might encounter.

A number of applications have appeared in the literature in

each of these areas. Some are articles in journals. Others are books. For example I have co-authored three books in applications of the AHP: one on planning, one on conflict resolution and one on prediction and forecasting. I have co-authored a book on general applications of the AHP by setting priorities and co-edited one on its application to design and in science and technology.

Often the structure of the AHP is extended from one of simply making a best choice to a more complex construct where the alternatives are based on benefits and costs. Here one constructs two hierarchies. One is for the benefits where one answers the question: which alternative yields the greater benefits. The other is for the costs where one answers the question of which alternative incurs the greater costs. After synthesis, one forms the benefit to cost ratio for each alternative and reflects the alternative with the largest ratio. Sometimes one can perform marginal analysis by arranging the costs in increasing order forming the ratio of the benefits to the costs of the least cost alternative and then successively taking ratios of the differences of the benefits of the next alternative from the previous one to the difference in their costs. If the difference in the benefits is negative one eliminates that alternative. The alternative with the largest marginal ratio is chosen.

A second kind of concern in the AHP is with the risk of what is likely to happen. One way to deal with risk is to introduce scenarios and determine their likelihood and also the likelihood of their effects. In addition, one can introduce risk separately in benefit and cost hierarchies. In such hierarchies one must answer the question: which is more likely to be a greater benefit of a certain cause or, correspondingly, which is more likely to be a higher cost?

A third area of AHP applications is resource allocation. Here one must make optimal allocations of one or of several limited resources to a set of activities. There are several possibilities for such an allocation. For example one may wish to completely implement a few of those that give the highest benefit to cost ratio, or allocate a certain minimal amount to most or all of them. We shall only illustrate a few of these applications in this chapter.

2. Benefits and Costs

Costs are pains and losses of all sorts - economic, physical, psychological and social.

Benefits are gains and advantages of all sorts - economic, physical, psychological and social.

Generally these two assessments cannot be combined. They are like the Yin and Yang, opposing each other. Not even philosophers have been able to find a single hierarchy to include them simultaneously. The prick of a pin cannot be regarded as a low form of pleasure, unless one is a masochist. When costs are committed in advance, they compete with other benefits in importance and are used with them to make best choices. In that case, for example, cost would be considered as low cost in comparing the alternatives.

Benefit Cost Analysis

To make a decision by considering benefits and costs, one must first answer the question:

In this problem, do the benefits justify the costs?

If they do, then either the benefits are much more important than the costs and the decision is based simply on benefits, or both the benefits and costs should be considered. Then two hierarchies are used for the purpose and the choice made by forming ratios from them. One asks which is most beneficial and which is most costly?

If they do not, then the costs must determine the least costly alternative. If costs are committed to make a best choice, then one can include them in the same hierarchy as the benefits. Otherwise, two hierarchies are used. Putting costs in the same hierarchy, one asks in comparing the alternatives, which one do I prefer with respect to this cost?

Here are four examples with their accompanying figures of benefit and costs hierarchies and the benefit/cost ratios formed from the outcome: the first (Figures 6-1a and 6-1b) for purchasing word processing equipment, with direct benefits and costs and with marginal analysis. We do the same for the second (Figures 6-2a and 6-2b) for checking on the mix of power generation method. In marginal analysis the costs are arranged in ascending order and ratios of differences of successive benefits and costs are formed. When the difference of the benefits is negative, that alternative is eliminated from consideration. The third example (Figures 6-3a and 6-3b) has to do with whether to build or not to build a refinery in East Java, Indonesia. The final example (Figures 6-4a and 6-4b) is without numbers and has to do with keeping or giving up a cat kept as a pet by one of my students.

Choosing Word Processing Equipment

Benefits Hierarchy

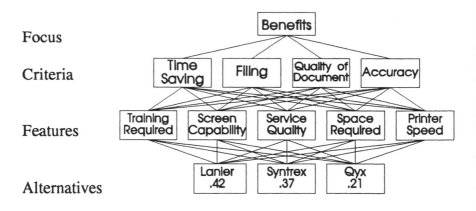

Figure 6-1a - *Benefits for choosing word processing equipment*

Cost Hierarchy

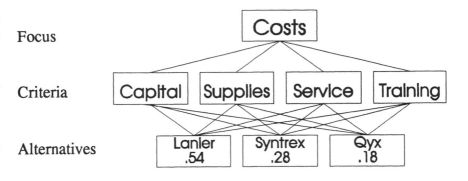

Figure 6-1b - *Costs of choosing word processing equipment*

Benefit/Cost Preference Ratios

Lanier	Syntrex	Qyx
$\frac{.42}{.54} = 0.78$	$\frac{.37}{.28} = 1.32$	$\frac{.21}{.18} = 1.17$

Marginal benefit to cost ratios are obtained by arranging the costs in increasing order and forming the ratios of the differences $(b_{i+1} - b_i)/(c_{i+1} - c_i)$, buying with the ratio of the smallest costs. We have $.21/.18 = 1.17$, $(.37-.21)/(.28-.18) = 1.60$ and $(.42-.37)/(.54-.28) = .19$ and again the Syntrex is the best choice.

Benefit/Cost ratios with wide time horizons are used when one wants to select one of several projects for initial investment. Marginal analysis is used when additional resources are to be allocated above and beyond the initial investment to obtain more benefit. The following example may clarify this idea further.

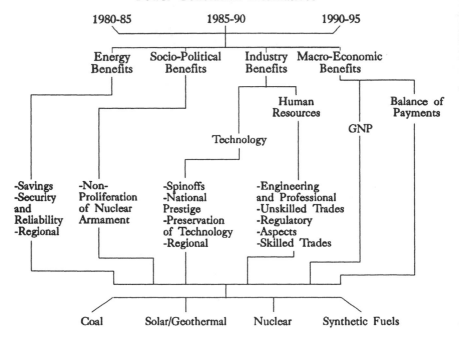

Figure 6-2a - *Power Generation Alternatives: Benefits Hierarchy*

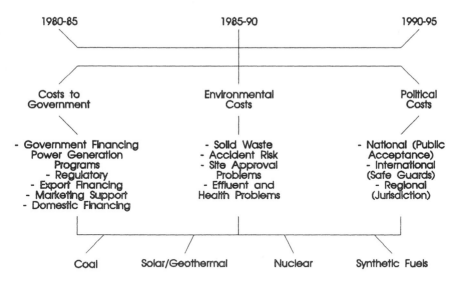

Figure 6-2b - *Power Generation Alternatives: Costs Hierarchy*

Combining Benefits and Costs

	Benefits	Costs	Benefits/Costs	Marginal Benefits/Costs
Coal	.137	.152	.901	.901
Solar/Geothermal	.169	.216	.782	----
Nuclear	.288	.210	1.371	2.603
Synthetic Fuels	.406	.432	.940	.532

The marginals are given by:
.137/.152 = .909, (.288-.137)/(.210-.152)=2.603,
(.169-.288)/(.216-.210) which is negative and is deleted as a potential option and (.406-.288)/(.432-.210)=.532.

Here the nuclear option is preferred in both columns.

Figure 6-3a - *Benefits of locating a refinery in an agricultural area in East Java, Indonesia*

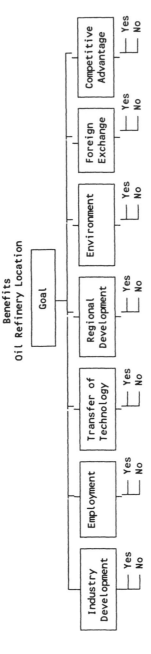

Sorted details for sorted synthesis of leaf nodes with respect to GOAL

Level 1		Level 2					Synthesis	
Environment	= 0.277	No = 0.221		Yes = 0.055			Yes	(0.487)
Regional Development	= 0.254	No = 0.076		Yes = 0.178			No	(0.513)
Employment	= 0.250	No = 0.150		Yes = 0.100				
Foreign Exchange	= 0.095	No = 0.029		Yes = 0.067				
Industry Development	= 0.056	No = 0.017		Yes = 0.039				
Competitive Advantage	= 0.038	No = 0.011		Yes = 0.027				
Transfer of Technology	= 0.030	No = 0.009		Yes = 0.021				

Figure 6-3b - *Costs of Locating a Refinery in a Agricultural Area in East Java, Indonesia*

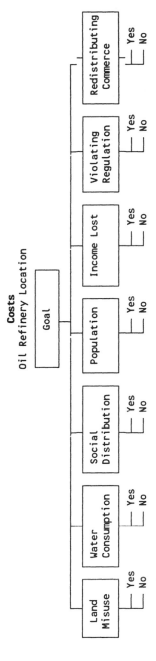

Sorted details for sorted synthesis of leaf nodes with respect to GOAL

Level 1		Level 2	
Violating Regulations	= 0.387	No = 0.116	Yes = 0.271
Water Consumption	= 0.191	No = 0.076	Yes = 0.115
Social Distribution	= 0.164	No = 0.074	Yes = 0.076
Land Misuse	= 0.104	No = 0.021	Yes = 0.084
Income Lost	= 0.069	No = 0.049	Yes = 0.021
Redistributing Commerce	= 0.043	No = 0.006	Yes = 0.037
Population	= 0.041	No = 0.016	Yes = 0.025

Synthesis
Yes **(0.641)**
No **(0.359)**

$$\frac{Benefits}{Costs}$$

$$Yes: \frac{0.487}{0.641} = .760 \quad No: \frac{0.513}{0.359} = 1.429$$

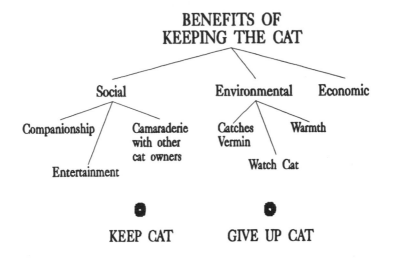

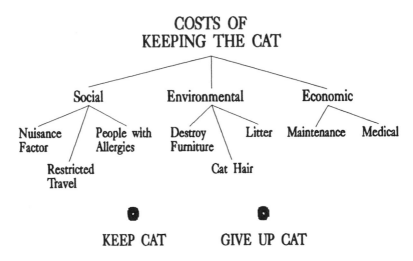

Figures 6-4a and 6-4b - *Benefits and Costs Hierarchies For Keeping the Cat*

Benefit/Cost Analysis with Absolute Measurement

The same principles applied to carry out benefit-cost analysis with relative measurement carry over to absolute measurement. One must construct two hierarchies, one representing ratings according to benefits and another according to costs. To rate the alternatives in the costs hierarchy one must answer the question about which costs more. The benefit/cost ratios themselves belong to a ratio scale and can be used to make resource allocation.

In the case of evaluating bids with a large number of bidders, the bidder can be rated by absolute measurement according to their merit and the result divided by the relative values of their estimated costs to determine the overall value of each bidder.

3. Resource Allocation

There are three types of allocation problems for a resource pool of total amount X.

(1) *Total funding* If we start with new projects which must be completed in the allocation period, we calculate their benefits b_i and costs c_i and relabel them so that we can identify the projects according to the relation

$$b_1/c_1 \geq b_2/c_2 \geq \cdots \geq b_n/c_n$$

and allocate the resource in decreasing order until it is depleted.

(2) *Partial funding* In case several projects must be started and monitored over several allocation periods, one allocates according to

$$\sum_{i=1}^{n} (b_i/c_i)x_i = \max$$

subject to

$$\sum_{i=1}^{n} x_i = X$$

$$0 \le x_i \le R_i/X$$

R_i = required amount of resource of activity i

Thus we do not support a project which gets less than the relative value of its cost to the total resource available.

(3) For projects that are already in progress one may allocate according to their remaining (marginal) priority to cost ratio.

For a full discussion of resource allocation, see Bennett and Saaty [1]. Spreadsheet software often has optimizing utilities included with the software, as in the case of Excel's Q-Solver or Lotus 1-2-3's What's Best available as a separate package. One uses Expert Choice priorities in these programs to do optimization and then resource allocation.

4. The AHP and Expected Value Theory

Consider the following example of a standard method used in decision theory to make a best choice based on expected value theory. It illustrates how to use expected return to invest money in three time periods. The investments will require varying sums of money in each of the three years, but the total amount to be invested is $65 for each of three investment plans considered here. We have:

	Y1	Y2	Y3	
P1:	40	10	15	P = Plan
P2:	30	15	20	Y = Year
P3:	30	25	10	

We will assume that the interest rate for the three years is 5% per year. Thus, in effect we will be using the reciprocals of 1.05, its square and cube or multiply by 0.95, 0.91 and 0.87 respectively, as the weighting factors for the three years. Which plan should we choose?

The expected value approach yields:

$$E(P1) = 40 \times 0.95 + 10 \times 0.91 + 15 \times 0.87 = 60.15$$
$$E(P2) = 30 \times 0.95 + 15 \times 0.91 + 20 \times 0.87 = 59.55$$
$$E(P3) = 30 \times 0.95 + 25 \times 0.91 + 10 \times 0.87 = 59.95$$

The first alternative would be the best choice.

Suppose that instead of doing it this way, we wish to see how the expected value idea works if we use ratios instead of absolute numbers. We do this because the AHP uses ratios (although in a different way) and we wish to find the relationship between the two approaches.

Our first matrix of paired comparisons would use the first column to construct the paired comparisons. We have:

$$\begin{bmatrix} 40/40 & 40/30 & 40/30 \\ 30/40 & 30/30 & 30/30 \\ 30/40 & 30/30 & 30/30 \end{bmatrix}$$

and the scale of relative values derived from this consistent reciprocal matrix is obtained by normalizing any of its columns. We have:

$$40/100$$
$$30/100$$
$$30/100$$

which is simply the original first column normalized.

Similarly for the second and third columns, yielding:

	Y1	Y2	Y3
P1:	40/100	10/50	15/45
P2:	30/100	15/50	20/45
P3:	30/100	25/50	10/45

Notice, for example, that previously the (P3,Y1) element was 30 and the (P3,Y2) element was 25 and the latter was smaller than the former, whereas now we have 30/100 and 25/50, respectively, and the opposite is true. In other words, we no longer can calculate expected values in the same way from the normalized numbers as we did prior to normalization. Why did this happen? Because it violated the stringent conditions that the weight of the alternatives be measured in the same dollar unit for all the years and column normalization in this special case of using the same scale throughout destroys the relationship between row elements.

What must one then do to choose the best alternative if she were to apply normalization? After one has normalized the columns to unity, the criteria must be rescaled to preserve the dollar relationship between the row elements as follows:

$$
\begin{aligned}
E(P1) &= 40/100 \times 100 \times 0.95 \\
&+ 10/50 \times 50 \times 0.91 \\
&+ 15/45 \times 45 \times 0.87 = 60.15 \\
E(P2) &= 30/100 \times 100 \times 0.95 \\
&+ 15/50 \times 50 \times 0.91 \\
&+ 20/45 \times 45 \times 0.87 = 59.55 \\
E(P3) &= 30/100 \times 100 \times 0.95 \\
&+ 25/50 \times 50 \times 0.91 \\
&+ 10/45 \times 45 \times 0.87 = 59.95
\end{aligned}
$$

Note that these operations do not alter the final answer. We continue by dividing each term by the sum of the column sums, $100 + 50 + 45 = 195$, which is the sum of all the elements in the matrix. We obtain:

$E(P1) = 40/100 \ (100/195 \times 0.95)$
$\qquad + \ 10/50 \quad (\ 50/195 \times 0.91)$
$\qquad + \ 15/45 \quad (\ 45/195 \times 0.87) = 60.15/195$
$E(P1) = 30/100 \ (100/195 \times 0.95)$
$\qquad + \ 15/50 \quad (\ 50/195 \times 0.91)$
$\qquad + \ 20/45 \quad (\ 45/195 \times 0.87) = 59.55/195$
$E(P1) = 30/100 \ (100/195 \times 0.95)$
$\qquad + \ 25/50 \quad (\ 50/195 \times 0.91)$
$\qquad + \ 10/45 \quad (\ 45/195 \times 0.87) = 59.95/195$

It is clear that all the operations we have carried out so far are legitimate and give the same answer as calculating expected values on unnormalized entries. In addition we have learned something important. With normalization, when the same unit of measurement is used throughout, the criteria weights must be rescaled proportionately by multiplying each weight by the ratio of the column sum under it to the total sum of the elements in the matrix. Thus, even if the criteria are considered to be independent from the alternatives, their weights depend on the measurements of the alternatives given under them. This is an example of structural dependence.

Let us summarize. If we have a matrix of data using the same scale in the background and are given the normalized columns of that matrix, we would be unable to reconstruct the highly interrelated matrix of coefficients without knowledge of rescaling factors. If on the other hand there is no scale relationship between the columns of the matrix, it would not make sense to simply divide the elements in each column by some number such as the sum of the elements in that column and then obtain the weighted sums of each row. The procedure would be quite arbitrary. What one must do is to interpret the data represented by each column according to relative importance to a decision maker so that the alternatives under each criterion are pairwise compared according to the fundamental scale. This procedure leads to a set of vectors which belong to the same ratio scale. Only in that case can they be combined by using the weights of the criteria. There is no need to rescale the criteria because there is no scale relationship that one would be required to preserve as an initial constraint of the problem.

5. Risk in the AHP

Treatment for a Heart Problem

In the following example concerning the type of treatment for a heart problem, three hierarchies are used; one for benefits, one for costs and one for risks. In the benefits hierarchy (Figure 6-5a) one answers the question what yields the greatest benefit, in the costs hierarchy (Figure 6-5b) what incurs the greatest pain or costs, and in the risks hierarchy (Figure 6-5c) what has the greatest risk. When the composite results are obtained for the alternatives, one divides the benefits by the product of the costs and risks and selects the highest ranked alternative. Combining the results is justified because the product and quotient of ratio scales is again a ratio scale.

Heart Problem

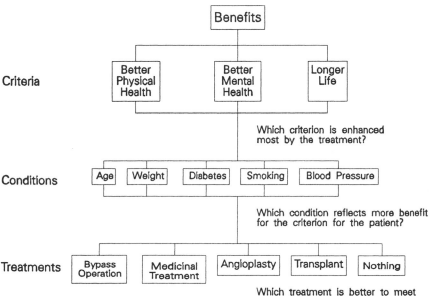

Figure 6-5a - *Heart Problem: Benefits Hierarchy*

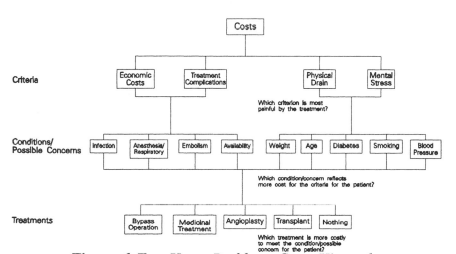

Figure 6-5b - *Heart Problem: Costs Hierarchy*

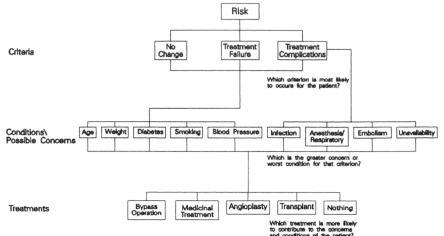

Figure 6-5c - *Heart Problem - Risk Hierarchy*

6. Measuring Dependence Between Activities; Input-Output Application to the Sudan

We illustrate how to deal with dependence between the elements of the same cluster (inner dependence) with an application we made in the design of a transport system for the Sudan. The outcome of this analysis was an input-output table which parallels what econometricians do.

Input-output matrices in economics are obtained in general as follows. Given N sectors (of an economy) $A_1, A_2, ..., A_N$, and given a matrix S whose s_{ij} entry indicates the output from sector i which becomes an input to sector j. The net output from sector i to final (consumer) demand we denote by Y_j. We have

$$\sum_{i=1}^{N} s_{ij} = S_j \text{ total intermediate output of sector } j$$

(domestic needs from other sectors)

$$S_j + Y_j = O_j \text{ total output of sector } j$$

The technological coefficients are obtained as follows

$$\frac{s_{ij}}{S_j + Y_j} = w_{ij} \text{(contribution of sector } i \text{ to produce a unit of}$$

output j)

$$\frac{s_{ij}}{S_j + Y_j} = \frac{s_{ij}}{S_j} \cdot \frac{S_j}{S_j + Y_j} = \frac{s_{ij} S_j}{S_j O_j}$$

To obtain the matrix of technological coefficients by the AHP we must estimate s_{ij}/S_j and S_j/O_j. Let us see what these represent. $S_j/(S_j + Y_j)$ represents the proportion of the total output of sector j allocated to domestic consumption. The total output is estimated, for $j = 1, \ldots, N$, by means of the AHP by asking the following question: How strong is one sector compared to another when allocating outputs to domestic needs? If this question cannot be answered directly, domestic needs may be hierarchically decomposed into production, demand, labor, capital, and cost. These sectors are prioritized separately with respect to each criterion. After prioritizing these criteria according to their impact on production, composition is used to obtain an overall measure of importance for the sectors. Let us denote the estimates of (S_j/O_j) by x_j.

Again s_{ij}/S_j represents the proportion of the total intermediate output from sector i allocated to sector j. We have $\sum_{i=1}^{N} s_{ij}/S_j = 1$. We construct a matrix of pairwise comparisons among the sectors as they relate to sector i. We answer the following question. How strong is the dependence of one sector in comparison with another in receiving output from sector j? The result is a matrix of pairwise comparisons which yields a column eigenvector of weights. When this is done for each sector we obtain a matrix W whose columns are these eigenvectors.

Finally, we take the product elementwise of each column of the matrix W with the column vector $x = (x_1, x_2, \ldots, x_N)$ to obtain the estimates of the technological coefficients, i.e., the input-output matrix.

The most important fact we have to take into consideration when the matrix of technological coefficients is estimated by means of the hierarchical approach, is the proportion of total intermediate outputs for each sector in relation to the total output. This proportion was estimated in this example by extensive study of the literature on the Sudanese economy available at the time [9].

The Sudan is considered mainly as an agricultural country. At the time the econometric models were constructed (1973) and the input-output analysis was done, the data used were from the year 1961. The major problem of the Sudan was the lack of an adequate transport system.

We considered the following six sectors.

(1) Agriculture (AGR)
(2) Public utilities (PU)
(3) Manufacturing and mining (M&M)
(4) Transportation and distribution (T&D)
(5) Construction (CONS)
(6) Services (SERV)

To make the same order of magnitude comparison with Agriculture and Transportation (another major activity), the other sectors were grouped into an aggregate. We have

$$
\text{Aggregate (AGG)} \left\{
\begin{array}{l}
\textit{Public utilities} \\
\textit{Manufacturing and mining} \\
\textit{Construction} \\
\textit{Services}
\end{array}
\right.
$$

The question to be asked to form the matrices of pairwise comparisons is: Given two sectors, i and j, which sector allocates more of its outputs to satisfy domestic needs (total intermediate outputs)? We first compare the elements in the aggregate, then separately compare the aggregate with agriculture and transport and use the resulting weight of the aggregate to compose the relevant weights from the four sectors in the aggregate itself. To save space we have not written out justifications of the judgments, which are available in a separate study.

	Satisfaction of domestic needs	PU	M&M	CONS	SERV	Eigenvector
AGG:	PU	1	1/2	1/2	1/3	0.1272
	M&M	2	1	1	1	0.2804
	CONS	2	1	1	1	0.2804
	SERV	3	1	1	1	0.3120

$\lambda_{max} = 4.02$,   C.I. = 0.007,   C.R. = 0.007

Satisfaction of domestic needs	AGR	T&D	AGG	Eigenvector
AGR	1	1/2	2	0.3108
T&D	2	1	2	0.4934
AGG	1/2	1/2	1	0.1948

$\lambda_{max} = 3.05$,   C.I. = 0.025,   C.R. = 0.04

We have for the relative importance of the sectors:

Sectors	Final Weights $S_i/(S_i + Y_i)$	Estimates of $Y_i/(S_i + Y_i)$
1	0.3108	0.6892
2	0.0248	0.9752
3	0.0546	0.9454
4	0.4934	0.5066
5	0.0546	0.9454
6	0.0608	0.9392

Now we identify the relationships among the sectors. They are given by the rows of the following table.

I.O.	AGR	PU	M&M	T&D	CONS	SERV
AGR	X		X	X	X	
PU	X		X	X		X
M&M	X			X	X	X
T&D	X	X	X		X	X
CONS						X
SERV		X	X	X	X	X

Given a certain sector i we ask: for any two sectors, h and k, to which sector are more products from sector i allocated? The following treatments answer this question for each sector.

Agriculture

The main crop in the Sudan is cotton. Cotton is exported and also allocated to the manufacturing sector. Thus agriculture, transportation and distribution, and construction do not receive a large amount of agricultural products. A new aggregate is formed. (Note that only four sectors are considered under agriculture.)

$$\text{Aggregate} \atop (AGG) \left\{ \begin{array}{l} \textit{Agriculture} \\ \textit{Transport and distribution} \\ \textit{Construction} \end{array} \right.$$

As we pointed out above, the Sudan lacks adequate transportation. We aggregated the two sectors which do not consume substantial quantities from agriculture, AGR and T&D, because, although the main crop after cotton is wheat, the agricultural sector allocates most of its output (i.e., wood) to construction. Transportation is developed by means of loans from Arab oil countries and the World Bank. Thus, we also aggregated agriculture and transportation to form a subaggregate.

Input from agriculture	AGR	T&D	Eigenvector
SUBAGG: AGR	1	9	0.9000
T&D	1/9	1	0.1000

λ_{max} = 2.0,   C.I. = 0.0,   C.R. = 0.0

Input from agriculture	SUBAGG	CONS	Eigenvector
AGG: SUBAGG	1	1/9	0.1000
CONS	9	1	0.9000

λ_{max} = 2.0,   C.I. = 0.0,   C.R. = 0.0

Input from agriculture	AGG	M&M	Eigenvector
AGG	1	1/3	0.25
M&M	3	1	0.75

λ_{max} = 2.0,   C.I. = 0.0,   C.R. = 0.0

Sectors	Final weights
1	0.0225
2	0.0000
3	0.7500
4	0.0025
5	0.2250
6	0.0000

Note: The weights of AGR and T&D are obtained as follows.

$$\begin{array}{c} AGR \\ T\&D \end{array} \begin{bmatrix} 0.9 \\ 0.1 \end{bmatrix} \times (0.1) \times (0.25) = \begin{bmatrix} 0.0225 \\ 0.0025 \end{bmatrix}$$

The weight of construction is obtained by multiplying (0.9) by (0.25) = 0.225.

Public Utilities

Input from PU	AGR	M&M	T&D	SERV	Eigenvector
AGR	1	1/9	1/7	1/5	0.0410
M&M	9	1	2	5	0.5242
T&D	7	1/2	1	3	0.3030
SERV	5	1/5	1/3	1	0.1318

$\lambda_{max} = 4.12$,   C.I. = 0.04,   C.R. = 0.04

Manufacturing and Mining

Input from M&M	AGR	T&D	CONS	SERV	Eigenvector
AGR	1	1/2	1/9	1	0.0758
T&D	2	1	1/5	3	0.1628
CONS	9	5	1	9	0.6941
SERV	1	1/3	1/9	1	0.0681

$\lambda_{max} = 4.03$,   C.I. = 0.01,   C.R. = 0.01

Transportation and Distribution

Input from T&D	AGR	PU	M&M	CONS	SERV	Eigenvector
AGR	1	1/3	1/2	1/2	7	0.1400
PU	3	1	1	2	9	0.3434
M&M	2	1	1	1	7	0.2596
CONS	2	1/2	1	1	7	0.2260
SERV	1/7	1/9	1/7	1/7	1	0.0310

$\lambda_{max} = 5.11$,   C.I. = 0.03,   C.R. = 0.03

Construction

Construction only gives its products to services. Thus we associate the value 1 with services.

Services in the Sudan are very poor. We have assumed that the allocation of service outputs to services, and to construction, are so negligible that these two could be aggregated. We have

$$Aggregate(AGG) \begin{cases} Construction \\ Services \end{cases}$$

Input from services		CONS	SERV	Eigenvector
AGG:	CONS	1	9	0.9000
	SERV	1/9	1	0.1000
	λ_{max} = 2.0,	C.I. = 0.0,	C.R. = 0.0	

Services

Input from Services	PU	M&M	T&D	AGG	Eigenvector
PU	1	1/2	1/2	3	0.1930
M&M	2	1	1	5	0.3680
T&D	2	1	1	5	0.3680
AGG	1/3	1/5	1/5	1	0.0704
	λ_{max} = 4.004,		C.I. = 0.001,	C.R. = 0.001	

The weights of construction and services are obtained by multiplying 0.0704, the weight of the aggregate, by 0.9 and 0.1, respectively.

Sectors	Final weights
1	0.0000
2	0.1930
3	0.3680
4	0.3680
5	0.0634
6	0.0070

The matrix whose rows are the foregoing eigenvectors gives the distribution of total intermediate outputs to the sectors. It is given by the following table.

	Producers						
Shares →	↓	AGR	PU	M&M	T&D	CONS	SERV
of the total	AGR	0.0225	0	0.7500	0.0025	0.2250	0
intermediate	PU	0.0410	0	0.5242	0.3030	0	0.1318
outputs	M&M	0.0750	0	0	0.1628	0.6841	0.0681
	T&D	0.1400	0.3434	0.2596	0	0.2260	0.0310
	CONS	0	0	0	0	0	1
	SERV	0	0.1939	0.3683	0.3683	0.0634	0.0070

At the beginning we computed how strongly the sectors allocate outputs to domestic needs. The vector of weights was

$$
\begin{matrix}
AGR \\
PU \\
M\&M \\
T\&D \\
CONS \\
SERV
\end{matrix}
\begin{bmatrix}
0.3108 \\
0.0248 \\
0.0546 \\
0.4934 \\
0.0546 \\
0.0608
\end{bmatrix}
$$

Thus we multiply each column of the above matrix by this vector (element-wise multiplication), e.g., for the first column we have

$$
\begin{bmatrix}
0.0225 \times 0.3108 \\
0.0410 \times 0.0248 \\
0.0750 \times 0.0546 \\
0.1400 \times 0.0546 \\
0 \quad \times 0.0546 \\
0 \quad \times 0.0608
\end{bmatrix}
=
\begin{bmatrix}
0.0070 \\
0.0009 \\
0.0041 \\
0.0691 \\
0 \\
0
\end{bmatrix}
$$

The weighted matrix is then given by:

	AGR	PU	M&M	T&D	CONS	SERV
AGR	0.0070	0	0.2331	0.0008	0.0699	0
PU	0.0009	0	0.0130	0.0075	0	0.0033
M&M	0.0041	0	0	0.0089	0.0379	0.0037
T&D	0.0691	0.1694	0.1281	0	0.1115	0.0153
CONS	0	0	0	0	0	0.0546
SERV	0	0.0117	0.0117	0.0224	0.0039	0.0004

If we compare this matrix with the following input-output matrix obtained by traditional methods, we see that there are very minor differences.

	AGR	PU	M&M	T&D	CONS	SERV
AGR	0.00737	0	0.21953	0.00042	0.06721	0
PU	0.00024	0	0.01159	0.00618	0	0.00283
M&M	0.00393	0	0	0.00857	0.04216	0.00322
T&D	0.06993	0.14536	0.12574	0	0.09879	0.00641
CONS	0	0	0	0	0	0.05402
SERV	0	0.01030	0.02549	0.02422	0.00520	0.00021

The factors involved in this problem were purely economic. This suggests extending this type of analysis to study social systems and particularly to introduce social factors in the resource allocation problem (a problem briefly mentioned by V. Leontief, the founder of input-output analysis) when the activities are inter-related.

8. On Forecasting Economic Recoveries: The Case of the U.S. Economy in 1992

Introduction

By convention, the U.S. economy is typically judged to be in a recession if the change in real gross national product (GNP) is negative for two consecutive quarters. (Increasingly, an alternative measure of U.S. aggregate economic activity is being used by the U.S. Department of Commerce: namely, gross domestic product, which nets out international factor payments and receipts, but we will continue to cite GNP patterns in this section for historical purposes; currently, real GNP is running slightly higher than real GDP.) Analogously, a rebound or end of a recessionary period may be suggested whenever two consecutive quarters of positive GNP growth occurs. Such rules of thumb are perhaps convenient indicators of cyclical variation, but they lack the ability to convey a general sense of decline or improvement in economic conditions. The National Bureau of Economic Research (NBER) has by consensus been given the responsibility for dating the actual turning points in the U.S. economic cycle. It arrives at its assessments by utilizing a variety of economic indicators, in addition to changes in real GNP [6].

Additionally, the severity of a recession as well as the strength of a recovery should be measured by both the cycle's amplitude and duration. With regard to its most recent cyclical phase, for example, the U.S. economy peaked in the third quarter of 1990, and then proceeded to fall in terms of real GNP for the next two quarters at an annual rate of 2.7%. Since the second quarter of 1991, however, the economy has technically been expanding, growing at an annual rate of about 1.4% from the first quarter of 1991 through the first quarter of 1992. Data that became available for the second quarter [4] suggested no change in this average growth figure, though the second quarter results were, in fact, significantly below the first quarter expansion rate. Nevertheless, if the NBER eventually dates the most recent cyclical trough as 1991's first quarter (as many now apparently believe it should [3]), its initial phase must already be judged the weakest in recent history, as indicated by the following data for the first four quarters of the three previous expansions (using the NBER dates for the previous troughs):

RECENT ECONOMIC EXPANSIONS
REAL GNP GROWTH
(average annual rates)

Trough	Nov. 1970	March 1975	Nov. 1982
1st Four Qrtrs.	5.0%	7.2%	6.2%

Moreover, other general economic indicators performed sluggishly: most importantly, total employment failed to grow appreciably during this putative expansion, unlike the three previous ones, which ranged between 4% and 6% for the same number of months following the trough (about 15 months).

It needs to be emphasized that much of this information was unavailable to us when we convened in late-December 1991/early

January 1992 to engage in an exercise aimed at forecasting the trough of the current cycle. At that point, we were not impressed that a 1.2% rate of real GNP growth from the first quarter 1991 to the third quarter 1991 (the latest data available) signified an economic expansion, especially when coupled with other economic data being reported at that time. When we reconvened in May 1992 to review our previous assessment and to engage in an exercise aimed at forecasting the strength of the eventual recovery, the annual rate of real GNP growth through the fourth quarter of 1991 (the latest then available) had actually weakened to 0.9%. The rate of real GNP growth between the last quarter of 1991 and the first quarter of 1992 subsequently rose to 2.9% on an annual basis, only to decelerate again in the second quarter to something of the order of 1.4% [4]. This information was not available to us in early May, though other negative economic portents certainly were.

The foregoing provides the context for the forecasting exercises of December 1991 and May 1992 which are quite instructive. Ultimately, we leave it to the NBER to provide the date from which the economic recovery began. Ensuing events will also disclose the eventual strength of that recovery. Our judgment in December 1991 was that a meaningful turning point in the current cycle was still a number of quarters in the future. Our further judgment in May 1992 was that the strength of the eventual recovery was likely to be quite weak when compared to previous expansions, owing chiefly to the "braking" influence of major structural changes taking place in the domestic and global economies.

Traditional approaches to resolving the forecasting problem are constrained by underlying assumptions about the structure of the economy and the impact of historical data on the projection of relevant economic variables. In particular, they have not proved useful in predicting changes in the current state of economic stagnancy because of their failure to account for structural changes acting as moderating influences on economic performance.

The Model

Our approach was to address two critical issues germane to forecasting the timing and strength of the recovery. The first concern is the need to incorporate into the forecasting exercise the sequence of global events of the past two and a half years. These events are forging a restructuring of global resources and institutional arrangements. The second issue is the need to think through the ways in which such restructuring acts as a moderating influence on the performance of the key macroeconomic variables most proximately connected to the U.S. economic cycle. Our exercise had two objectives. The first was to predict the timing of a sustained turnaround in the economy, as measured by a composite of relevant economic variables, including real GNP. The second was to provide an estimate of the strength of the recovery.

The Process

In the first stage, the object was to forecast the most likely date of a turnaround. Instead of establishing a single goal, we used the bottom level alternatives to create a feedback cycle resulting in a special case of a feedback network known as a holarchy. There, instead of the single goal, one uses the entire set of elements in the bottom level to make the comparisons of the second level elements in parallel with how it is done between levels in a hierarchy. The result of the comparisons in a holarchy is a cycle whose net effects are derived by limiting operations on the initial matrix of derived weights.

The top level of our exercise consists of the factors representing the forces or major influences driving the economy. These forces are grouped into two categories: "conventional adjustment" and "economic restructuring." Both of these categories are decomposed into subfactors represented in the second level of the holarchy. The third level consists of time periods in which the recovery can occur. Figure 6-6 provides a schematic layout of the holarchy used to forecast the timing of the economic turnaround.

In the second stage, the goal is to forecast the strength of the recovery. Here, we used a standard format for the hierarchy, beginning with the primary factors of conventional adjustment and economic restructuring. Figure 6-7 is a standard hierarchy, and provides a representation of the factors affecting the strength of the recovery.

Conventional adjustment assumes a status quo with regard to the system of causes and consequences in the economy. The presumption is that the underlying structure of the economy is stationary. Forecasting is possible within acceptable ranges of error. This is achieved by tracing the existing network of stimulus/response patterns initiated by a perturbation in a fundamental parameter of the economy. In our view, conventional adjustment can formally be divided into six macroeconomic subfactors that occupy the second level: consumer spending, investment spending, exports, indicators of confidence in the economy, fiscal policy, and monetary policy. We recognized that these subfactors are in some instances interdependent.

Viewed independently, for example, a lowering of interest rates by the Federal Reserve should induce portfolio rebalancing throughout the economy. In turn, this should reduce the cost of capital to firms and stimulate investment. Simultaneously, it should reduce financial costs to households and increase their disposable incomes. Any resulting increase in disposable income stimulates consumption and at the margin has a positive impact on employment and GNP. However, all of this assumes that the linkages of the economy are in place and are well understood.

Recent events in the global economy will exert fundamental changes in the way the U.S. economy will operate for the next several years and beyond by inducing an economic restructuring. The Gulf War, the demise of centrally planned economies in eastern Europe and the former Soviet Union, the integration of western Europe, the emergence of newly industrialized economies, and the quickening integration of financial sectors throughout the world are all events which suggest an economic structure that is not stationary but is undergoing dramatic change. Prudent recognition of these facts suggests that patience and monitoring of events are appropriate guidelines for public policy.

With regard to the nature of the current economic restructuring, we specifically recognized the transformation of the financial sector, the reduction in the defense-based component of the economy, and the changing global competitive position of the U.S. economy as subfactors also in the second level.

Changes in the domestic economic environment induced by these factors affect the economy in ways that are not well understood and are too complex to pursue in this forum. We summarized these effects by estimating the impact of each subfactor on the expected length of time prior to a turnaround as well as their impact on the relative strength of the ensuing expansion.

With respect to the timing of the turnaround, we considered four possible time periods of adjustment in the third level of the holarchy: 3 months, 6 months, 1 year, and 2 or more years, dated from late December 1991.

The strength of the expansion was categorized in May 1992 according to ranges of average real GNP growth. We considered the following possible outcomes: very strong (5.5% to 6.5%), strong (4.5% to 5.5%), moderate (3.0% to 4.5%), and weak (2.0% to 3.0%). These ranges represent annualized measures of percentage change in real gross national product for the first two years of the recovery. While the ranges are somewhat arbitrary, they generally reflect actual experiences during various post World War II cyclical expansions.

The judgments with regard to the identification of factors as well as the comparisons of relative impact and strength of factors were conducted by colleagues who coauthored this section. They assumed the role of representative "experts". Obviously, the outcomes are heavily dependent on the quality of those judgments. The first exercise (timing of the turnaround) was conducted during the third week of December, 1991 and refined during first week of January, 1992. The estimation of the strength of the recovery was conducted during the second week of May, 1992.

Tables 6.1 through 6.6 provide the associated matrices of relative comparisons as well as a limiting and completed supermatrix.

When the judgments were made, the AHP produced the following results. First, a meaningful turnaround in the economy would likely require an additional ten to eleven months, occurring during the fourth quarter of 1992. This forecast is derived from weights generated in the first column of the limiting matrix in Table 6.6, coupled with the mid-points of the alternate time periods (so as to provide unbiased estimates):

.224 x 1.5 + .151 x 4.5 + .201 x 9 + .424 x 18 = 10.45 months from late December 1991/early January 1992.

Tables 6.7 through 6.10 provide the comparison matrices for prediction of the expected strength of the recovery, once underway. The summary finding is that the recovery will be "moderate" (using our range definition), resulting in an annual percentage change in real gross national product of about 3.5%. This finding is documented in Table 6.10.

Conclusion

In addition to presenting the somewhat contrarian view that a meaningful turnaround in the present economic cycle is still some months in the future, we concluded that the initial period of recovery will not be strong. In this connection, it is interesting to place this forecasted rate of recovery in an historical context by comparing the evidence on percentage changes in real GNP for the first two years (first eight quarters) of five recent expansions; namely, those spanning the periods: 2/1961-12/1969; 11/1970-11/1973; 3/1975-1/1980; 7/1980-7/1981; and 11/1982-7/1990. Setting aside the short recovery of 7/1980-7/1981 (with an average growth rate of only 2.98%), the range of percentage changes in real GNP for the first two years of these expansions is 5.73% to 6.37%. Our forecast suggests that the next U.S. economic recovery will be substantially less strong than those of the past three decades. We concluded that this is fundamentally attributable to the dramatic restructuring of important sectors of the global economy. The restructuring process, moreover, also is acting to postpone the time period during which the expansion will actually begin. Most importantly, we concluded that since these structural constraints cannot be adequately addressed through the use of commonly applied forecasting techniques, a more robust approach (AHP) is necessary in order to capture these influences.

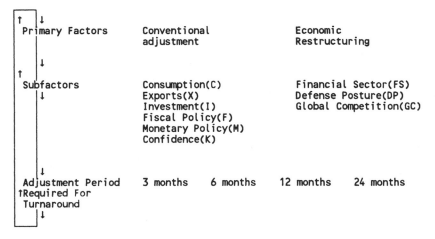

Figure 6-6 *The U.S. holarchy of factors to forecast a turnaround in the U.S. economic stagnation*

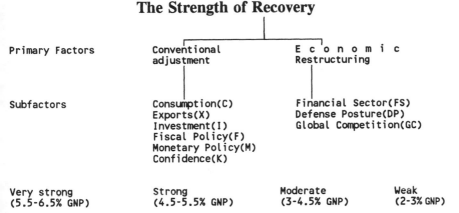

Figure 6-7 *Strength of recovery hierarchy*

Table 6.1 Matrices for subfactor importance relative to primary factors influencing the Timing of Recovery

Panel A: Which subfactor has the greater potential to influence Conventional Adjustment and how strongly?

		C	E	I	K	Vector F	M	Weights
Consumption	(C)	1	7	5	1/5	1/2	1/5	0.118
Exports	(E)	1/7	1	1/5	1/5	1/5	1/7	0.029
Investment	(I)	1/5	5	1	1/5	1/3	1/5	0.058
Confidence	(K)	5	5	5	1	5	1	0.334
Fiscal Policy	(F)	2	5	3	1/5	1	1/5	0.118
Monetary Policy	(M)	5	7	5	1	5	1	0.343

Table 6.2 Matrices for relative influence of subfactors on periods of adjustment (months) (Conventional Adjustment)

Panel B: Which subfactor has the greater potential to influence Economic Restructuring and how strongly?

		Vector FS	DP	GC	Weights
Financial Sector	(FS)	1	3	3	0.584
Defense Posture	(DS)	1/3	1	3	0.281
Global Competition	(GC)	1/3	1/3	1	0.135

TABLE 6.3 Matrices for relative influence of subfactors on periods of adjustment (months) (Economic Restructuring)

For each panel below, which time period is more likely to indicate a turnaround if the relevant factor is the sole driving force?

Panel A: Relative importance of targeted time periods for consumption to drive a turnaround

	3	6	12	24	Vec. Wts.
3 months	1	1/5	1/7	1/7	.043
6 months	5	1	1/5	1/5	.113
12 months	7	5	1	1/3	.310
24 months	7	5	3	1	.534

Panel B: Relative importance of targeted time periods for exports to drive a turnaround

	3	6	12	24	Vec. Wts.
3 months	1	1	1/5	1/5	.083
6 months	1	1	1/5	1/5	.083
12 months	5	5	1	1	.417
24 months	5	5	1	1	.417

Panel C: Relative importance of targeted time periods for investment to drive a turnaround

	3	6	12	24	Vec. Wts.
3 months	1	1	1/5	1/5	.078
6 months	1	1	1/5	1/5	.078
12 months	5	5	1	1/3	.305
24 months	5	5	3	1	.538

Panel D: Relative importance of targeted time periods for fiscal policy to drive a turnaround

	3	6	12	24	Vec. Wts.
3 months	1	1	1/3	1/5	.099
6 months	1	1	1/5	1/5	.087
12 months	3	5	1	1	.382
24 months	5	5	1	1	.432

Panel E: Relative importance of targeted time periods for monetary policy to drive a turnaround

	3	6	12	24	Vec. Wts.
3 months	1	5	7	7	.605
6 months	1/5	1	5	7	.262
12 months	1/7	1/5	1	1/5	.042
24 months	1/7	1/7	5	1	.091

Panel F: Expected time for a change of confidence indicators of consumer and investor activity to support a turnaround in the economy

	3	6	12	24	Vec. Wts.
3 months	1	3	5	5	.517
6 months	1/3	1	5	5	.305
12 months	1/5	1/5	1	5	.124
24 months	1/5	1/5	1/5	1	.054

TABLE 6.4 Most likely factor to dominate during a specified time period

For each panel below, which time period is more likely to indicate a turnaround if the relevant factor is the sole driving force?

Panel A: Most likely length of time for restructuring of financial system to support a turnaround

	3	6	12	24	Vec. Wts.
3 months	1	1/3	1/5	1/7	.049
6 months	3	1	1/5	1/7	.085
12 months	5	5	1	1/5	.236
24 months	7	7	5	1	.630

Panel B: Most likely time required for defense readjustment to affect a turnaround in economy

	3	6	12	24	Vec. Wts.
3 months	1	1/3	1/5	1/7	.049
6 months	3	1	1/5	1/7	.085
12 months	5	5	1	1/5	.236
24 months	7	7	5	1	.630

Panel C: Most Likely time required for an adjustment to global competition can affect a turnaround in economy

	3	6	12	24	Vec. Wts.
3 months	1	1	1/3	1/5	.089
6 months	1	1	1/3	1/5	.089
12 months	3	3	1	1/5	.208
24 months	5	5	5	1	.613

Which factor is more likely to produce a turnaround during the specified time period?

Conventional Adjustment --> CA
Restructuring --> R

Panel A : 3 Months

	CA	R	Vec. Wts.
CA	1	5	.833
R	1/5	1	.167

Panel B : 6 Months

	CA	R	Vec. Wts.
CA	1	5	.833
R	1/5	1	.167

Panel C : 1 Year

	CA	R	Vec. Wts.
CA	1	1	.500
R	1	1	.500

Panel D : 2 Years

	CA	R	Vec. Wts.
CA	1	1/5	.167
R	5	1	.833

Note to Tables 6.5 and 6.6

Now we group all the derived vector weights as columns in the appropriate positions of a matrix of mutual influences known as the supermatrix. For example, the first vector we derived from the matrix of subfactors of conventional adjustment is placed in the first column next to the six subfactors and under conventional adjustment. The factors are listed systematically so that the right vectors are listed to indicate the impact of the relevant factors on the left on the factors at the top. The supermatrix, being stochastic (with columns adding to one) is then raised to limiting powers to capture all the interactions and obtain the steady state outcome in which all columns within each block of factors are the same. We are particularly interested in the two identical columns at the bottom left corner of the matrix of Table 6.8. Either one is given by (0.224, 0.141, 0.201, 0.424).

To obtain the forecast we multiply each value by the midpoint of its corresponding time interval and add (as one does when evaluating expected values). We have

.224 × 1.5 + .151 × 4.5 + .201 × 9 + .424 × 18 = 10.54

months from Jan. 1.

Note that at times the resulting supermatrix may not be stochastic which would then require weighting each cluster of factors as it impacts another cluster at the top.

TABLE 6.5 The Completed Supermatrix

	Conven. Adjust	Economic. Restruc.	Consum.	Exports	Invest.	Confid.	Fiscal Policy	Monet. Policy	Financ. Sector	Defense Posture	Global Compet.	3 mo.	6 mo.	1 yr.	≥ 2 years
Conven. Adjust	0.0	0.0	0.0	0.0	0.0	0.0	0.0	0.0	0.0	0.0	0.0	0.833	0.833	0.500	0.167
Economic. Restru.	0.0	0.0	0.0	0.0	0.0	0.0	0.0	0.0	0.0	0.0	0.0	0.167	0.167	0.500	0.833
Consum.	0.118	0.0	0.0	0.0	0.0	0.0	0.0	0.0	0.0	0.0	0.0	0.0	0.0	0.0	0.0
Exports	0.029	0.0	0.0	0.0	0.0	0.0	0.0	0.0	0.0	0.0	0.0	0.0	0.0	0.0	0.0
Invest.	0.058	0.0	0.0	0.0	0.0	0.0	0.0	0.0	0.0	0.0	0.0	0.0	0.0	0.0	0.0
Confid.	0.334	0.0	0.0	0.0	0.0	0.0	0.0	0.0	0.0	0.0	0.0	0.0	0.0	0.0	0.0
Fiscal Policy	0.118	0.0	0.0	0.0	0.0	0.0	0.0	0.0	0.0	0.0	0.0	0.0	0.0	0.0	0.0
Monetary Policy	0.343	0.0	0.0	0.0	0.0	0.0	0.0	0.0	0.0	0.0	0.0	0.0	0.0	0.0	0.0
Financ. Sector	0.0	0.584	0.0	0.0	0.0	0.0	0.0	0.0	0.0	0.0	0.0	0.0	0.0	0.0	0.0
Defense Posture	0.0	0.281	0.0	0.0	0.0	0.0	0.0	0.0	0.0	0.0	0.0	0.0	0.0	0.0	0.0
Global Compet.	0.0	0.135	0.0	0.0	0.0	0.0	0.0	0.0	0.0	0.0	0.0	0.0	0.0	0.0	0.0
3 months	0.0	0.0	0.043	0.083	0.073	0.517	0.099	0.605	0.049	0.049	0.089	0.0	0.0	0.0	0.0
6 months	0.0	0.0	0.113	0.083	0.073	0.305	0.086	0.262	0.085	0.085	0.089	0.0	0.0	0.0	0.0
1 year	0.0	0.0	0.310	0.417	0.305	0.124	0.383	0.042	0.236	0.236	0.209	0.0	0.0	0.0	0.0
≥ 2 years	0.0	0.0	0.534	0.417	0.539	0.054	0.432	0.091	0.630	0.630	0.613	0.0	0.0	0.0	0.0

TABLE 6.6 The Limiting Supermatrix

	Conven. Adjust	Economic. Restruc.	Consum.	Exports	Invest.	Confid.	Fiscal Policy	Monet. Policy	Financ. Sector	Defense Posture	Global Compet.	3 mo.	6 mo.	1 yr.	≥ 2 years
Conven. Adjust	0.0	0.0	0.484	0.484	0.484	0.484	0.484	0.484	0.484	0.484	0.484	0.0	0.0	0.0	0.0
Economic. Restru.	0.0	0.0	0.516	0.516	0.516	0.516	0.516	0.516	0.516	0.516	0.516	0.0	0.0	0.0	0.0
Consum.	0.0	0.0	0.0	0.0	0.0	0.0	0.0	0.0	0.0	0.0	0.0	0.057	0.057	0.057	0.057
Exports	0.0	0.0	0.0	0.0	0.0	0.0	0.0	0.0	0.0	0.0	0.0	0.014	0.014	0.014	0.014
Invest.	0.0	0.0	0.0	0.0	0.0	0.0	0.0	0.0	0.0	0.0	0.0	0.028	0.028	0.028	0.028
Confid.	0.0	0.0	0.0	0.0	0.0	0.0	0.0	0.0	0.0	0.0	0.0	0.162	0.162	0.162	0.162
Fiscal Policy	0.0	0.0	0.0	0.0	0.0	0.0	0.0	0.0	0.0	0.0	0.0	0.057	0.057	0.057	0.057
Monetary Policy	0.0	0.0	0.0	0.0	0.0	0.0	0.0	0.0	0.0	0.0	0.0	0.166	0.166	0.166	0.166
Financ. Sector	0.0	0.0	0.0	0.0	0.0	0.0	0.0	0.0	0.0	0.0	0.0	0.301	0.301	0.301	0.301
Defense Posture	0.0	0.0	0.0	0.0	0.0	0.0	0.0	0.0	0.0	0.0	0.0	0.145	0.145	0.145	0.145
Global Compet.	0.0	0.0	0.0	0.0	0.0	0.0	0.0	0.0	0.0	0.0	0.0	0.070	0.070	0.070	0.070
3 months	0.224	0.224	0.0	0.0	0.0	0.0	0.0	0.0	0.0	0.0	0.0	0.0	0.0	0.0	0.0
6 months	0.151	0.151	0.0	0.0	0.0	0.0	0.0	0.0	0.0	0.0	0.0	0.0	0.0	0.0	0.0
1 year	0.201	0.201	0.0	0.0	0.0	0.0	0.0	0.0	0.0	0.0	0.0	0.0	0.0	0.0	0.0
≥ 2 years	0.424	0.424	0.0	0.0	0.0	0.0	0.0	0.0	0.0	0.0	0.0	0.0	0.0	0.0	0.0

TABLE 6.7 Matrices for Primary and Subfactors for Strength of Recovery

Panel A: Which primary factor will be more influential in determining the Strength of the Recovery?

	CA	R	Vector Weights
Conventional Adjustment (CA)	1	1/5	.167
Restructuring (R)	5	1	.833

Panel B: Which subfactor is more important in influencing Conventional Adjustment?

		C	E	I	K	F	M	Vector Weights
Consumption	(C)	1	7	3	1	7	3	0.317
Exports	(E)	1/7	1	1/5	1/5	1	1/5	0.037
Investment	(I)	1/3	5	1	1/3	1/3	1/5	0.099
Confidence	(K)	1	5	3	1	7	3	0.305
Fiscal Policy	(F)	1/7	1	3	1/7	1	1/7	0.035
Monetary Policy	(M)	1/3	7	5	1/3	7	1	0.207

CI = 0.071

Panel C: Which subfactor is more important in influencing Economic Restructuring?

		FS	DP	GC	Vector Weights
Financial Sector	(FS)	1	1/5	1/3	0.105
Defense Posture	(DS)	5	1	3	0.637
Global Competition	(GC)	3	1/3	1	0.258

CI = 0.037

TABLE 6.8 Matrices for relative influence of subfactors on Strength of Recovery (Conventional Adjustment)

For each panel below, which intensity is more likely to obtain if the designated factor drives the recovery?

Panel A: Relative likelihood of the strength of recovery if consumption drives the expansion.

	V	S	M	W	Vec. Wts.
Very Strong (V)	1	1	5	7	.423
Strong (S)	1	1	5	7	.423
Moderate (M)	1/5	1/5	1	3	.104
Weak (W)	1/7	1/7	1/3	1	.051

CI = 0.028

Panel B: Relative likelihood of the strength of recovery if exports drives the expansion.

	V	S	M	W	Vec. Wts.
Very Strong (V)	1	1	1/3	1/5	.095
Strong (S)	1	1	1/3	1/5	.095
Moderate (M)	3	3	1	1/3	.249
Weak (W)	5	5	3	1	.560

CI = 0.016

Panel C: Relative likelihood of the strength of recovery if investment drives the expansion.

	V	S	M	W	Vec. Wts.
Very Strong (V)	1	1	1/3	2	.182
Strong (S)	1	1	1/3	2	.182
Moderate (M)	3	3	1	6	.545
Weak (W)	1/2	1/2	1/6	1	.091

CI = 0.0

Panel D: Relative likelihood of the strength of recovery if confidence drives the expansion.

	V	S	M	W	Vec. Wts.
Very Strong (V)	1	1	3	5	.376
Strong (S)	1	1	3	5	.376
Moderate (M)	1/3	1/3	1	7	.193
Weak (W)	1/5	1/5	1/7	1	.054

CI = 0.101

Panel E: Relative likelihood of the strength of recovery if fiscal policy drives the expansion.

		V	S	M	W	Vec. Wts.
Very Strong	(V)	1	1	1/5	1	.125
Strong	(S)	1	1	1/5	1	.125
Moderate	(M)	5	5	1	5	.625
Weak	(W)	1	1	1/5	1	.125

CI = 0.0

TABLE 6.9 Matrices for relative influence of subfactors on Strength of Recovery (Restructuring)

For each panel below, which intensity is more likely to obtain if the designated factor drives the recovery?

Panel A : Relative likelihood of the strength of recovery if financial sector drives the expansion.

		V	S	M	W	Vec. Wts.
Very Strong	(V)	1	1	1/3	1/5	.095
Strong	(S)	1	1	1/3	1/5	.095
Moderate	(M)	3	3	1	1/3	.249
Weak	(W)	5	5	3	1	.560

CI = 0.016

Panel C : Relative likelihood of the strength of recovery if global competition drives the expansion.

		V	S	M	W	Vec. Wts
Very Strong	(V)	1	1	1/3	1/5	.101
Strong	(S)	1	1	1/3	1/5	.101
Moderate	(M)	3	3	1	1	.348
Weak	(W)	5	5	1	1	.449

CI = 0.012

Panel F: Relative likelihood of the strength of recovery if monetary policy drives the expansion.

		V	S	M	W	Vec. Wts.
Very Strong	(V)	1	1	1/5	1/3	.084
Strong	(S)	1	1	1/5	1/3	.084
Moderate	(M)	5	5	1	7	.649
Weak	(W)	3	3	1/7	1	.183

CI = 0.101

Panel B: Relative likelihood of the strength of recovery if defense posture drives the expansion.

		V	S	M	W	Vec. Wts.
Very Strong	(V)	1	1/3	1/5	1/7	.055
Strong	(S)	3	1	1/3	1/5	.118
Moderate	(M)	5	3	1	1/3	.262
Weak	(W)	7	5	3	1	.565

CI = 0.044

Table 6.10 Overall results for Strength of Recovery

% GNP Growth

Very strong	(5.5-6.5)	0.108
Strong	(4.5-5.5)	0.141
Moderate	(3-4.5)	0.290
Weak	(2-3)	0.461

% GNP Recovery Rate*   3.6

*% GNP Recovery rate calculated using the relative strength of conventional adjustment and restructuring in Table 6.5 Panel A each used to multiply midpoints of % GNP Growth and then summed.

8. Power of the AHP in Estimation

Three people, A, B, and C compared the consumption of liquids in the United States. We give the judgments and their average:

	Coffee	Wine	Tea	Beer	Soft Drinks	Milk	Water
Coffee	1,1,1	5,9,7	7,2,7	2,4,5	1/3,3,3	2,1,3	1/7,1/3,1/3
Wine		1,1,1	1,1/8,2	1/5,1/5,1/5	1/7,1/7,1/5	1/5,1/8,1	1/7,1/7,1/7
Tea			1,1,1	1/6,3,1/3	1/5,1,1/3	1/6,1/4,1/2	1/9,1/3,1/7
Beer				1,1,1	1/4,2,1/5	1/3,1/5,1	1/5,1/4,1/7
Soft Dr					1,1,1	1/2,1/5,2	1/4,1/3,1
Milk						1,1,1	1/3,1/2,9
Water							1,1,1

	Coffee	Wine	Tea	Beer	Soft Drinks	Milk	Water
Coffee	1	7	5	4	2	3	1/3
Wine		1	1/5	1/5	1/7	1/7	1/9
Tea			1	1/4	1/3	1/2	1/7
Beer				1	1/3	1/2	1/5
Soft Drinks					1	3	1/3
Milk						1	1/7
Water							1

	Actual	A	B	C	Average of A,B,C	Group
Coffee	.20	.13	.19	.25	.19	.22
Wine	.01	.03	.02	.04	.03	.02
Tea	.04	.02	.10	.03	.05	.05
Beer	.12	.08	.07	.07	.07	.06
Soft Drinks	.18	.17	.07	.18	.14	.13
Milk	.14	.15	.25	.06	.15	.09
Water	.30	.42	.30	.37	.36	.42
λ_{max}		7.82	7.62	7.77		7.56

If we allow 2 quarts of water a day, we can derive the amount of consumption of the others from it. It should be emphasized that the individuals did not have access to the actual consumption figures until after the completion of the exercise. In all cases the closeness of the results was impressive and the consistency acceptable.

It is interesting to note that a group may not do better than an individual if some of them are more articulate than others and in addition have strong biases. It is best that they be allowed to speak briefly without forcing the vote their way. Generally, people should be encouraged to stick to their feelings unless they get a convincing and over-riding reason from the others to change their beliefs. Fair democratic kind of interaction has often led to excellent results better than what individuals could do.

How Long Do Animals Live?

We now derive an estimate of the relative life span of the following animals:

            Horse Dog Cow Cat   Man Guinea Pig

Actual Life Span: 30   9   26   8   100   6
Normalized Value: .168 .050 .145 .045 .558 .034

Direct guesses by three individuals produced the following results:

	Years	Normalized	Years	Normalized	Years	Normalized
Horse	18	.069	30	.157	34	.166
Dog	25	.095	15	.079	15	.073
Cow	60	.229	30	.157	31	.151
Cat	20	.076	12	.063	18	.088
Man	135	.515	100	.524	100	.488
Guinea Pig	4	.015	4	.021	7	.034

The first individual then filled out the following two comparison matrices:

Liberal Comparison

	Horse	Dog	Cow	Cat	Man	Guinea Pig	Eigenvector
Horse	1	5	4	6	-	9	.237
Dog	-	1	-	-	-	7	.056
Cow	-	4	1	5	-	8	.136
Cat	-	2	-	1	-	6	.063
Man	6	5	6	5	1	9	.489
Guinea Pig	-	-	-	-	-	1	.019

$\lambda_{max} - 7.14$, $(\lambda_{max}-n)/(n-1) = .028$

Conservative Comparison

	Horse	Dog	Cow	Cat	Man	Guinea Pig	Eigenvector
Horse	1	2	1	-	-	3	.118
Dog	-	1	2	2	-	2	.124
Cow	-	-	1	-	-	2	.077
Cat	2	-	2	1	-	3	.127
Man	5	5	7	5	1	7	.506
Guinea Pig	-	-	-	-	-	1	.047

$\lambda_{max} = 6.38$, $(\lambda_{max}-n)/(n-1) = .075$

Dashes in the matrix represent reciprocals of the elements in the transpose position; i.e., $a_{ji} = 1/a_{ij}$.

An individual attempted to estimate the relative kilowatt hours of electricity consumed by each of the following home appliances by comparing it with the others.

	Range	Refrig- erator	T.V. Color	Dish- washer	T.V. B&W	Iron	Radio	Hair- dryer	Eigen- vector	Actual
Range	1	3	6	3	7	7	9	9	.362	.348
Refig- erator	1/3	1	4	5	5	5	7	9	.252	.215
T.V.- Color	1/6	1/4	1	1	1/2	4	4	8	.088	.148
Dish- washer	1/3	1/5	1	1	2	3	9	9	.118	.107
T.V.- B&W	1/7	1/5	2	1/2	1	3	3	7	.083	.101
Iron	1/7	1/5	1/4	1/3	1/3	1	4	9	.053	.042
Radio	1/9	1/7	1/9	1/4	1/3	1/4	1	7	.030	.025
Hair- Dryer	1/9	1/9	1/8	1/9	1/7	1/9	1/7	1	.014	.003

Here is another estimate of the amount of protein per unit weight in the following foodstuffs: A = Steak; B = Potatoes; C = Apples; D = Soybean; E = Whole Wheat Bread; F = Tasty Cakes; G = Fish.

	A	B	C	D	E	F	G	Eigenvector	Actual
A	1	7	9	6	5	6	2	.389	.366
B	1/7	1	5	1/3	1/5	1/4	1/7	.039	.037
C	1/9	1/5	1	1/5	1/7	3	1/9	.018	.000
D	1/6	3	5	1	1/2	1/3	1/5	.065	.070
E	1/5	5	7	2	1	2	1/4	.119	.108
F	1/6	4	1/3	3	1/2	1	1/5	.083	.093
G	1/2	7	9	5	4	5	1	.287	.324

References

1. Bennett, J.P. and Saaty, T.L., "Knapsack Allocation of Multiple Resources in Benefit-Cost Analysis By Way of the Analytic Hierarchy Process." Mathl. Comput. Modelling, Vol 17, No. 4/5, 1993

2. Blair, A., R. Nachtmann, and T.L. Saaty, 1993, "Incorporating Expert Judgment in Economic Forecasts: The Case of the U.S. Economy in 1992", to appear.

3. Greenhouse, S., "A Blip or a Dip?", New York Times, July 7, 1992.

4. Greenhouse, S., "Economy's Growth in Second Quarter Was a Slight 1.4%", New York Times, July 31, 1992.

5. Hall, T.E., Business Cycles - The Nature and Causes of Economic Fluctuation, Praeger, New York, 1990.

6. Hoshey, R.D., Jr., "Good Riddance to Recession?", New York Times, June 18, 1992.

7. Saaty, T.L. Multicriteria Decision Making: The Analytic Hierarchy Process, RWS Publications, Pittsburgh, PA, 1990.

8. Saaty, T.L. and L.G. Vargas, Prediction, Projection and Forecasting, Kluwer Academic, Boston, 1991.

9. Saaty, T.L. and L.G. Vargas, "A Note on Estimating Technological Coefficients by Hierarchical Measurement," Socio-Econ. Plan. Sci., Vol. 13, No. 6, 333-336, 1979.

10. Sorkin, A.L., Monetary and Fiscal Policy and Business Cycles in the Modern Era, Lexington Books, Lexington, MA, 1988.

11. U.S. Department of Commerce, Survey of Current Business, various issues.

12. Council of Economic Advisors, Economic Report of the President, January 1992.

CHAPTER
SEVEN

GROUP DECISION MAKING AND CONFLICT RESOLUTION

1. Introduction

Sometimes one cannot influence individual decision making because individuals have established structures for making their decisions. However, one may have something useful to say to a group to increase their ability to work together and arrive at a generally accepted answer. Since a group does not usually have a single voice it is necessary to combine the judgments to get the final priorities of the group. Some conditions for group cooperation can be a consequence of the method used rather than the result of general philosophical suggestions. The latter are likely to seem arbitrary and may often be forgotten. If the rules are part of the method and if the method is natural and understandable, then people are more willing to accept its recommendations in the group decision process. Nature has not designed into social interaction a successful group process that coincides with what an individual who puts his/her thoughts and experiences together does to make a decision. But we can learn from what the individual does to derive consistent principles for a group. A group may work together seeking agreement through persuasion or by vote. But there are also cases of people at large holding different opinions that need to be canvassed and statistically analyzed.

People must feel comfortable in interpreting what happens as if the process were within themselves. A group decision process that does not derive meaningfully and harmoniously from individual decision making is unlikely to succeed. It must have continuity and improve on the thoughts and practices of individuals. Otherwise people would reject it because it is alien to their own system.

Normative rules and proposals should be used in group decisions only if absolutely necessary. They should facilitate the process and should help to arrive at an acceptable outcome when seen from the different points of view of the individuals. They should generalize from individual to group decisions. The group process should be an easy and effective generalization and synthesis of what the various members of the group would do on their own. Furthermore, they must be able to assess and justify what went on when the group is no longer together.

Conflicting parties are unlikely to make a habit of getting together. Any kind of theoretical question or technical concern in group decisions must be settled and meaningfully so, while the group is together. Once the group is adjourned, it is no longer convenient to pose the questions because groups cannot meet continuously, unlike individuals who can do so by switching the mind to the question. Thus the composition of a group, the frequency of meetings and its mode of operation are central concerns in group decision making. There is even greater complexity when one considers the members within each group and the number of groups. Some form of conflict resolution must be reached both between the individuals in each group and between the groups.

One of the first questions to answer is how to assess the consistency of group judgments. More generally, how should one judge the consistency of the outcome of conflict resolution with the judgments and expectations of its member groups. How consistent is the outcome with the judgments and expectations of each individual. If it is not possible to relate the larger concerns to the individual, decision making and conflict resolution become unique situations offering little hope for learning about how to deal with other situations. But if there is a way to make the lateral connection then the challenge is to find it, and use it.

To resolve a conflict, each party must know well its own assessment of the situation and what its demands and priorities are. Group decision making requires an ordering of priorities that is not easily susceptible to change when new factors come to light. It should be possible to rate alternatives as if they are independent by presenting them one at a time in order to exact higher returns through negotiation. However, when the members of the opposing group analyze the concessions they are offered, they are likely to link them to each other as a package. They will assume dependence among the alternatives because they do not have the same standards as the other side so they could rate alternatives one at a time to see their individual merit. Because the outcome of relative measurement in a hierarchy differs from the outcome obtained through absolute measurement, conflict resolution needs a way to reconcile rankings obtained by the two methods.

In conflict resolution, the party accepting concessions may at times assume an adversarial role, stand its ground, and declare that its priorities are set in advance and cannot be influenced by unimportant concessions the other side makes even though these are the only concessions available. Thus while these concessions appear dominated and unimportant (irrelevant to the receiver), they are important to the giver who wants to show the opponent that his ranking should be affected by them. The idea that only explicit information should lead to change in the ranking priorities because it introduces criteria is inadequate in conflict resolution. The object of the parties should be to change each other's preferences through negotiation. With many concessions it is no longer possible to show how new information is created or priorities changed. In this case each side would like to show that the number of concessions it makes and their relation to the other side's demands should affect the importance ranking by the other side of its own demands.

Thus one must realize the central importance and

inevitability of the two side's views in a conflict. Depending on whose point of view it is, one side wants to stand fast on what it considers as irrelevant concessions and the other would like to show that what it has is indeed relevant. On the other hand, in cooperative conflicts the parties would work closer together to gain understanding of what is possible without resorting to polemics and deception. These are the easier situations to handle. If we learn to resolve win/lose conflicts, we would find situations with potential win/win outcome easier to deal with.

2. Group Judgment, A Technical Discussion [6]

In group decision making, aggregation of the preference rankings of individuals into a consensus ranking is the most important problem. Consensus is a process of general agreement on public issues. The question remains as to how many individuals must agree in order to carry the group. A decision for a group can be dictated by one or several people from within or outside the group or by partial or total participation by the group. When the decision is made through participation, there are at least three known types of consensus - spontaneous, emergent and manipulated. Spontaneous consensus is exhibited in traditional communities, with very few public issues, who change their view as a collective entity. Emergent consensus happens only in nontraditional societies which are relatively secular and urbanized. After all points of view have been considered, each individual weighs and judges the ideas and then draws a rational conclusion. Crystallization of these judgments forms the public opinion. If the emergent majority is sufficiently forceful, the minorities would adopt its view and emergent consensus would arise with the viewpoint of the majority. Manipulated consensus exists in societies in which emergent consensus can theoretically occur, but general agreement depends on who controls the means or power of persuasion. The last two types of consensus generally prevail in modern societies. We discuss ways to amalgamate or synthesize group judgments and thereby obtain a public judgment. A basic notion underlying these types of consensus, which is practical throughout the world, is that human wisdom is worthy of aggregation to reach a decision.

In the AHP, two fundamentally different approaches are used to synthesize group judgments. One of them is deterministic and the other statistical or stochastic. The participating individuals may be geographically close enough together to engage in extended discussion so that all empirical data and theoretical ratiocination are considered or they may be dispersed without the possibility of discussing the issue. When a small group of individuals work closely together - interacting and influencing each other, the deterministic approach is appropriate. We synthesize their judgments mathematically. When a large number of geographically scattered individuals provide the judgments, inconsistency (variation) between individuals is much more important than the inconsistency of a single one of them. Thus we need a statistical procedure to deal with variation among several people to surface a single value for the weights of the alternatives.

In both situations, one may examine how to divide the judges into homogeneous subgroups with significant sub-group differences. Judgment matrices are obtained for each group in cases where the groups are significantly different from each other. Otherwise a single judgment matrix is developed for the judgments of all the individuals.

In the close group decision process, the problem is to find a mathematical method for aggregating the information articulated by its members to determine what weight is most reasonable on the basis of the varying weights assigned by members of the group. The problem of amalgamating total information in the group has been studied in detail by Indrani Basak [4].

In psychophysical comparisons, where one may not physically feel the attributes, order of presentation of the attributes plays an important role in quantification of the responses. For example, in a taste-testing experiment of similar kind of soft drinks, the order of presentation makes a difference in the responses. In an experiment to evaluate the intensity of small electric shocks, one's response is strongly modified by the first shock. In the statistical approach, these variations can be accounted for by a proper model. Again Basak has provided a statistical method to accommodate the order effects in the prioritization of the alternatives, with a method to test the existence of the effect of the order of presentation. She also shows how to obtain priority weights after eliminating order effects.

3. The Deterministic Approach

In the literature of the AHP, one needs to distinguish between the deterministic and the statistical approaches to synthesize group judgments.

In this section we discuss the deterministic approach. Here one can combine: 1) the judgments, 2) the eigenvectors or 3) the synthesized overall priorities. The latter can be regarded as an eigenvector of a matrix of comparisons of the alternatives with respect to the goal. Whatever rules we use to combine eigenvectors we also apply here. In the pairwise comparison matrix $A = ((a_{ij}))$; $i,j = 1,2,...,n$, the reciprocal condition $a_{ij}.a_{ji} = 1$ is necessary because of the underlying mathematical justification. It derives the relative priority weights using the assumption that one can observe the preferences with certainty and the only uncertainty lies in the elicitation of these preferences which give rise to the inconsistency condition $a_{ij}.a_{jk} \neq a_{ik}$. Suppose we have a group of people, each of whom has a different judgment (and reciprocal) in comparing two alternatives. What rank should we use to combine the judgments for one alternative over the other? The object would be to also apply the rank to the reciprocal judgments. The two single member outcomes should be reciprocals of one another. When equal importance is given to voters in a group, Aczel & Saaty [1] published a result which incorporated and extended Saaty's derivation of the geometric mean as the proper way for synthesizing the judgments.

Let the function $f(x_1, x_2, ..., x_n)$ for synthesizing the judgments given by n judges, satisfy the following :

(i) *Separability condition* (S):

$$f(x_1, x_2,...,x_n) = g(x_1) \circ g(x_2) \circ ... \circ g(x_n)$$

for all $x_1, x_2,...,x_n$ in an interval P of positive numbers, where g is a function mapping P onto a proper interval J and $\circ$ is a continuous, associative and cancellative operation.

[(S) means that the influences of the individual judgments can be separated as above.]

(ii) *Unanimity condition* (U):

$$f(x, x,...,x) = x \text{ for all } x \text{ in } P.$$

[(U) means that if all individuals give the same judgment x, that judgment should also be the synthesized judgment.]

(iii) *Homogeneity condition* (H):

$$f(ux_1, ux_2,...,ux_n) = uf(x_1, x_2,...,x_n) \text{ where } u > 0$$

and x_k, ux_k (k=1,2,...,n) are all in P.

[For ratio judgments (H) means that if all individuals judge a ratio u times as large as another ratio, then the synthesized judgment should also be u times as large.]

(iv) *Power conditions* (P_p) :

$$f(x_1^P, x_2^P,...,x_n^P) = f^P(x_1, x_2,...,x_n)$$

[(P_2) for example means that if the kth individual judges the length of a side of a square to be x_k, the synthesized judgment on the area of that square will be given by the square of the synthesized judgment on the length of its side.]

Special case ($R=P_{-1}$):

$$f(1/x_1, 1/x_2,...,1/x_n) = 1/f(x_1, x_2,...,x_n)$$

[(R) is of particular importance in ratio judgments. It means that the synthesized value of the reciprocal of the individual judgments should be the reciprocal of the synthesized value of the original judgments.]

Aczel and Saaty [1] proved the following theorem:

Theorem 7.1 *The general separable (S) synthesizing functions satisfying the unanimity (U) and homogeneity (H) conditions are the geometric mean and the root-mean-power.* If moreover the reciprocal property (R) is assumed even for a single n-tuple $(x_1, x_2,...,x_n)$ of the judgments of n individuals, where not all x_k are equal, then only the geometric mean satisfies all the above conditions.

However, in any rational consensus, those who know more should, accordingly, influence the consensus more strongly than those who are less knowledgeable. Some people are clearly wiser and more sensible in such matters than others, others may be more powerful and their opinions should be given appropriately greater weight. For such unequal importance of voters not all g's in (S) are the same function. In place of (S), the weighted separability property (WS) is now:

$$f(x_1, x_2,...,x_n) = g_1(x_1) \circ g_2(x_2) \circ ... \circ g_n(x_n)$$

[(WS) implies that not all judging individuals have the same weight when the judgments are synthesized and the different influences are reflected in the different functions $g_1, g_2,...,g_n$.)]

In this situation, Aczel and Alsina [2] proved the following theorem:

Theorem 7.2 *The general weighted-separable (WS) synthesizing functions with the unanimity (U) and homogeneity (H) properties are the weighted geometric mean* $f(x_1, x_2, \cdots, x_n) = x_1^{q_1} x_2^{q_2} \cdots x_n^{q_n}$ *and the weighted root-mean-powers* $f(x_1, x_2, \cdots, x_n) = \sqrt[\gamma]{q_1 x_1^{\gamma} + q_2 x_2^{\gamma} \cdots + q_n x_n^{\gamma}}$, *where* $q_1 + q_2 + ... + q_n = 1$, $q_k > 0$ $(k=1,2,...,n)$, $\gamma \neq 0$, *but otherwise* $q_1, q_2,...,q_n, \gamma$ *are arbitrary constants.*

If f also has the reciprocal property (R) and for a single set of entries $(x_1, x_2, \ldots, x_n)$ of judgments of n individuals, where not all x_k are equal, then *only the weighted geometric mean* applies.

We give the following theorem which is an explicit statement of the synthesis problem that follows from the previous results, and applies to the second and third cases of the deterministic approach:

Theorem 7.3 *If* $x_1^{(i)}, \ldots, x_n^{(i)}$ $i=1, \ldots, m$ *are rankings of n alternatives by m independent judges and if a_i is the importance of judge i developed from a hierarchy for evaluating the judges, then* $\left(\prod_{i=1}^{m} x_1^{a_i} \right)^{1/m}, \ldots, \left(\prod_{i=1}^{m} x_n^{a_i} \right)^{1/m}$ *are the combined ranks of the alternatives for the m judges.*

The power or priority of judge *i* is simply a replication of the judgment of that judge (as if there are as many other judges as indicated by his/her power a_i), which implies multiplying his/her ratio by itself a_i times, and the result follows.

4. The Statistical Approach

When one obtains pairwise comparison judgments one can look at it statistically as observations coming from a true but unknown population of judgment values. By collecting information on the comparison values one is interested in estimating some parameters of that population. This approach is in harmony with the philosophy of the statistical approach which is different from the deterministic approach.

In the statistical approach to the AHP, one needs to consider the problem of how to separate judgments into homogeneous subgroups with significant differences between these subgroups. Individual judgments within a homogeneous subgroup can be synthesized using maximum likelihood estimates to give a single answer for that subgroup [3,4,5,6].

If the subgroups conflict with each other, then what do we do? One might note that consensus within each subgroup is arrived at in a formally identical manner. In this situation, if there is a forceful majority subgroup one possibility is to follow the rule that the majority wins. Alternatively, one can aggregate judgments of the homogeneous subgroups weighted by the importance of these subgroups to surface an opinion for the entire group. AHP conflict resolution methodology discussed later can also be considered for this case.

For a large number of geographically dispersed people, the statistical approach is the one more likely to be needed. It is assumed that the group as a whole has true preference parameters to be estimated by multiple paired comparison input matrices. The difference between existing statistical methods and the method shown here is that in the former, individuals express their judgments as preferred / not preferred / tied [7,8]. In the AHP further information is elicited on how far apart the alternatives are perceived to be by the judges. Since the AHP is in principle based upon the elicitation of ratio information, the corresponding statistical estimation method utilizes a multiplicative model with input data errors given in the following perturbation form:

$$a_{ij} = \frac{\pi_i}{\pi_j} \epsilon_{ij} \tag{1}$$

where the error ϵ_{ij} has some continuous distribution. Therefore the probability that ϵ_{ij} is equal to 1 (so that pairwise preferences a_{ij} are error-free) is equal to zero. This means that preferences subject to error are well suited for statistical analysis. In fact, the score a_{ij} assigned by a judge to the alternative T_i over the alternative T_j is thought of as the product of two components. The first, π_i/π_j is the average preference of T_i over T_j in the decision making body to which the judge belongs. The second, ϵ_{ij}, represents the deviation of a_{ij} from this average preference. The set of scale values π_1, π_2, ..., π_n is derived leaving the unsystematic (random) chance deviations to the error ϵ_{ij}. Since the errors can have a continuous distribution, ϵ_{ij} and ϵ_{ji} also have continuous distributions. Therefore the probability that the product $\epsilon_{ij} \epsilon_{ji}$ is equal to 1 (so that the matrix A is reciprocal, $a_{ij} a_{ji} = 1$) is equal to zero. Thus, if all the off diagonal entries are collected and synthesized, the pairwise comparison matrix will not be reciprocal.

In (1), one would expect the statistical distribution of ϵ_{ij} to be such that the probability density of ϵ_{ij} has a maximum at $\epsilon_{ij} = 1$ (in order to have an error-free estimate with maximum probability) and/or the expected value of ϵ_{ij} to be equal to one (in order to have the expected value of the observed preference ratios equal to the true preference ratios). These two requirements contradict each other and cannot be satisfied simultaneously in (1). If ϵ_{ij} has a maximum at 1 then the distribution of ϵ_{ij} on the positive real line must be skew-symmetric and therefore its mean or expected value cannot be attained at 1. One must choose between the foregoing two properties. It would not be correct to apply the statistical approach in the setting of the deterministic paradigm, because none of these two properties is satisfied. In the deterministic approach, only $n(n-1)/2$ entries of the paired comparison matrix are observed and it is assumed that the comparison matrix is reciprocal. Under this restriction, the corresponding statistical approach fails to have these two properties. The reasons are :

Result 1. Let X be a continuous and reciprocally symmetric random variable. If the expected value $E(X^k)$ (k any real number) exists, $E(X^{-k})$ also exists and $E(X^k) = E(X^{-k}) \geq 1$. For $k \neq 0$, $E(X^k) = E(X^{-k}) > 1$.

Result 2. Let $f(x)$ be a differentiable and reciprocally symmetric probability density function. Then $f'(1) = -f(1)$ and $f(x)$ has no maximum at $x = 1$.

For the proof of results 1 and 2 see Remark 5 and 9 of Fichtner

(1983) respectively.

In the statistical approach, the reciprocal constraint must be satisfied in the true (parameter values) preference ratios. One may find it analytically easier and more tractable to collect both the entries a_{ij} and a_{ji}. This is mainly due to the fact that one allows for errors represented by ϵ_{ij} in (1) without coupling ϵ_{ji} and ϵ_{ij}. In that case one finds it convenient to use the maximum likelihood procedure. Also, in this approach it is not necessary for each single individual to provide all the entries of the paired comparison matrix to estimate the priority weights. While there is a maximum of $n(n-1)/2$ entries to be collected, only a minimum of $n-1$ comparisons are required to establish ratios between n entities. The redundancy in questioning however provides more information and the resulting relative priorities would be less sensitive to judgment errors. In a decision-making committee, this approach allows for the possibility of incomplete judgments where some members may abstain from giving their opinions.

Consider a typical situation in a certain level of the hierarchy. Suppose n elements T_1, T_2, ... ,T_n are compared pairwise by a number of individuals in a decision-making committee. Let π_i be the priority weight of T_i, $\pi_i \geq 0$ and $\sum \pi_i = 1$ (ensuring determinacy). For a particular T_i and T_j, $i \neq j$, the preference of T_i over T_j is given by N independent judges. For the purpose of independence of the observations we assume that each judge gives a judgment on just one preference requiring a total of $Nn(n-1)$ judges. In fact, we can do better than that. Each individual may give judgments on pairs with no common elements; for example (T_1,T_2) and (T_3,T_4). This procedure guarantees the independence of observations, but entails the implicit assumption that individual differences among the judges are unsystematic and can be ignored. Following the model described in (1) we have

$$a_{ijk} = \frac{\pi_i}{\pi_j} \epsilon_{ijk} . \tag{2}$$

Only one set of scale values $\pi_1, \pi_2, ..., \pi_n$ will be derived to represent the population of the judges leaving the unsystematic individual differences to the error values ϵ_{ijk}. In (2) the ϵ_{ijk} are assumed to be independent and do not depend on the π_i. As before, ϵ_{ijk} cannot have both the properties that ϵ_{ijk} has a mode at $\epsilon_{ijk} = 1$ and expected value equal to unity. Let us, for example, choose the property that the expected value $E[\epsilon_{ijk}]$ be equal to one. Assume that the ϵ_{ijk} are identically distributed according to Gamma (ρ,ρ) since these are positive random variables with expectation unity and the choice of the Gamma distribution for judgment matrices have been shown by Vargas [14] to be appropriate. One can use this assumption if the data fit the Gamma (ρ,ρ) distribution. Here ρ is treated as a parameter and is estimated jointly with the parameters $\pi = (\pi_1, \pi_2, ..., \pi_n)$. We observe that the estimation of priority weights $\pi_1, \pi_2, ..., \pi_n$ does not depend on ρ. On the other hand, the estimate of ρ depends on the priority weights. The maximum likelihood estimates of $\pi_1, \pi_2, ..., \pi_s$ can be used to obtain the maximum likelihood estimate r of ρ [6].

5. Resolution of Retributive Conflicts [11,13]

Gains as Benefits and Costs

There are two types of conflict resolution. We call the first kind *constructive*. It is what is conventionally treated in the so-called rational approach to conflict resolution. Each party identifies its demands and it is assumed that a way can be found to satisfy both parties' demands fairly. Fairly here means that each party forms a ratio of its benefits to those of the opponent and attempts to satisfy its own needs at least as much as its perceived evaluation of the opponent's benefits because the values may be interpreted differently by the two sides. The tug of war by each can end up in equalizing the ratio to unity. It is inadvisable for either party to give up too early. Cooperative conflicts are a special case of this general approach since both sides can work together to find the most productive outcome for both of them (or for all of them if there are more than two).

In this case negotiations begin with each party setting down what it expects to get. The negotiations may either result in getting that much, or changing the outcome so that both sides receive more, or often, less than their expectations because there is not enough to go around. The parties begin by offering some concessions from a larger set of concessions which they maintain secretly. An offer is evaluated in terms of the benefits of the counter-offer received and may be withdrawn if not reciprocated adequately.

The second kind of conflict is *retributive* with one or both parties harboring ill will towards the other. The idea is particularly relevant in long drawn-out conflicts which in the end fester and create almost ineradicable resentments. Here a party may be willing to give up much of its demands if misfortune can be brought to its opponent through some means, including justice as dispensed by the court system. Should the enemy die, they may forgive and forget, or sometimes they may be resentful because they have not extracted their pound of flesh.

The Allies' demand for unconditional surrender in World War II is an example. The object was to annihilate a hated opponent. If some German general had taken over and impaled Hitler in a vengeful way like the Italian patriots did to Mussolini, the end of the war with Germany may have come earlier. Until today there is resentment that Hitler, by eliminating himself, cheated those who wanted to deal him justice.

In Saudi Arabia the justice system allows a murderer to negotiate for his life with the surviving members of the family by paying them a large sum of money; hence cost to the defendant is turned into a material benefit to the plaintiff. The family members may reject this and demand his life. Finally, terrorists work to extract benefits by making the costs to their opponent sufficiently high to induce him to trade off such pains by offering them some benefits.

Most conflicts are easier to solve if they are nipped in the bud early. If they are delayed, the parties often become frustrated and angry and get to believe there is malice and dirty work that is prolonging their pain. This rankling increases the grievance, not only by insisting on unreasonable terms, but also by a hidden desire to inflict pain on the opponent to even things out. This hidden desire does not surface in the emotional way it developed because of the demand that people appear rational and interested in maximizing their own gain, rather than concentrating on incurring losses to the opponent. To love one's enemy and bless him becomes increasingly more difficult as time lapses and people start doing mean things to each other. The parties could become malicious and apply themselves persistently to hurt each other. Our world is not so civilized as to rule out this possibility and its frequency. While earlier a party would have been willing to settle for its benefits, now in an implicit way that party wishes to get even with the opponent by causing him pain. In this case gain to a party is a combination (or product) of its benefits and its opponent's costs, pains or losses. This loss component meets emotional needs. Sometimes it can be bought off with additional benefits, but not always. The opponents suspect everything, including rationality, even when in principle it is supposedly serving the interests of both sides.

Thus in negotiations, each party not only calculates the incremental benefits it gets, but also the costs to its opponent. The more of either, the greater is the gain. Gain is the product of the benefits to the party and the costs (whose aim may also be long-run benefits) to the opponent. Each side must calculate what it estimates to be the opponent's gain as a product of benefits to the opponent and costs to itself and make sure that the ratio of its gain to the opponent's gain which it considers as a loss is greater than unity or not less than what the opponent is perceived to get. Thus each party is concerned with maximizing its gains via its benefits and the costs to the opponent and also by negotiating to increase this gain and decrease its loss (which is the gain to the opponent). When several concessions are considered simultaneously, sums of the products of benefits and costs must be taken. We have the following ratios for the two parties A and B:

A's
ratio $=$ $\dfrac{\text{gain to A}}{\text{A's perception of gain to B}}$

(as perceived by A)

$=$ $\dfrac{\Sigma \text{ A's benefits x B's costs}}{\Sigma \text{ B's benefits x A's costs}}$

(where Σ is the sum taken over all concessions by B in the numerator and by A in the denominator)

$=$ $\dfrac{\text{gain to A}}{\text{loss to A}}$

A's *perceived* ratio for B is the reciprocal of the above.

B's
ratio $=$ $\dfrac{\text{gain to B}}{\text{B's perception of gain to A}}$

(as perceived by B)

$=$ $\dfrac{\Sigma \text{ B's benefits x A's costs}}{\Sigma \text{ A's benefits x B's costs}}$

(where Σ is the sum taken over all concessions by A in the numerator and by B in the denominator)

$=$ $\dfrac{\text{gain to B}}{\text{loss to B}}$

B's *perceived* ratio for A is the reciprocal of the above.

If each of the ratios is perceived by the corresponding party to be less than unity, the problem is to alter these perceptions so that both parties think that they are equally treated. By looking at its own ratio and the opponent's perceived ratio, that party will argue as follows: "Look what I am giving up. He gets high benefits and the costs to me are very high. He should be happy. On the other hand, look at what he is offering me. My benefits are low and the costs to him are very low. It is not a fair deal. He is not hurt enough by what he is offering me."

Note that constructive conflict resolution is a special case of retributive conflict resolution whereby the costs to the opponent are assigned a unit value. Each party assumes that the opponent is paying the full cost and concentrates on maximizing his own benefits. He cannot incur any further costs on the opponent.

In many instances where the parties feel that an essential part of the conflict arises from their disparity in relative power, it would be appropriate to weight the ratio of each party by its proportion of perceived power computed for both from appropriate hierarchies of influence as has been done in many examples. In that case, to equalize the two expressions becomes a more difficult task. By accepting guaranteed concessions, the weaker party may become stronger and its perceived power may change accordingly. It is exactly because of such possible changes that some long-standing conflicts should not be negotiated as a one-shot affair, but dealt with in terms of short, medium and long-range objectives.

A mediator works with each party to evaluate the priority of what it says it is giving up and what it is receiving based on its declared values (benefits and costs). He or she then attempts to obtain convergence in a way which shows each party that the outcome is fair - i.e., that both their ratios are close. The mediator must substitute each party's perception of benefits and costs to the other by what he knows about the other party's values, avoiding exaggerations and distortions.

Unilateral concessions are actions taken by a single party evaluated in terms of their benefits to the acting party and their costs to that party. By forming the ratio of benefits to costs, those actions would be evaluated by the party to determine whether it is to its advantage to make such concessions.

Bilateral concessions are taken by both parties and may be evaluated in terms of their benefits to the party and the costs to the opponent. To make a trade-off they are compared with what it is estimated that the opponent would get. There are two outcomes, one for the party and one for the opponent. Concessions are sought to both obtain a certain level of gains to each side and also attain a fair ratio for both.

Multilateral concessions are based on comparisons made when there are several parties. In this case we use for each party the sum of the relative benefits times the relative costs for that party with every other party.

Conflict Resolution as a Multi-Criteria Process

The complexity of negotiating conflicts is attributable to the fact that it is a multiobjective, multicriteria decision problem involving many intangible goals, criteria and alternatives. It cannot be reasoned one factor at a time and then implemented by putting the pieces together. Doing one thing in one place affects things everywhere else. Our usual method of logical reasoning generates linear chains of syllogisms. It is better suited for simple problems which deal with one factor at a time. It is not very effective in application to a complex problem involving many factors without having to make numerous assumptions which in the end give rise to a solution best characterized as a good guess. Often the reason why such a solution is acceptable to one side but not to the other is because no collaborative reasoning can be adequately factored into the solution. This lack may also be the reason why the people in diplomacy and political science find it difficult to apply formal models to resolve conflicts.

What is needed here is a multicriteria decision approach that enables one to deal with the complexity as a whole, incorporating judgments and making trade-offs for all the parties involved with their participation in the process. Examples are given in my book with J. Alexander on conflict resolution [13].

The power of a nation cannot be ignored in conflict resolution. That power is what it and the rest of the world perceive its capabilities to be. To judge the relative power of nations we need to identify a set of factors that any nation assumes to be important. The relative power is then developed by first setting priorities on the factors followed by paired comparisons of the influence of the nations being considered. The synthesized result is a relative index of power for these nations.

The stability of the outcome of a conflict depends on the overall behavior of the parties and not just on the payoffs resulting from the strategies of the particular conflict. When the resolution of a conflict derives its principles simply from the local conditions of that conflict, it is possible and likely that in the global context with its many interactions, the outcome would not make sense, nor would the rationality ascribed to the payoffs of the local conflict. Rationality applied in a narrow sense needs to be moderated or modified according to the larger context of global rationality. This is done by examining the relative merits, strengths and weaknesses of the parties, not just in that conflict, but in general. The ability and willingness to take and give are deduced from the large to the small and not vice versa - otherwise the outcome would appear to be incongruous and would not be honored.

We must involve the parties and, if they are unwilling to participate, then conjecture effectively best and worst scenarios for them and the outcome of confrontation resulting from these scenarios. We need to also look at the capabilities and history of the parties beyond the existing conflict, something which none of the quantitative theories of conflict resolution has taken into account so far.

To diminish negative feelings towards an opponent, the opponent must visibly take actions to improve expectations. Continued frustration in expectations increases hostility. One way to diminish frustration is to genuinely express good feelings and intentions towards the opponent. Another is to take unilateral actions indicating one's good intentions. Still a third is for the two sides to work together on some project which benefits both or benefits a third party to which the two sides are committed. Visits, contacts, and improved socialization are useful ways to decrease suspicion through exposure.

The difficulty with scientific, formal or technological problem solving is that it puts the greatest faith in the expert's understanding of the problem. Strategic analysis of conflicts is only one sociological way to look at things and is colored by the perceptions of the analysts who formalize them.

The Decomposition of Issues

What we must do is to unfold the complexity of conflicts as perceived by all sorts of thinking people. We then need to use our scientific approach to deal with them by first breaking them down into steps surmised to be essential in conflict resolution together with the dilemmas or anomalies associated with them. Factors that should be considered are cultural, social and psychological. We need to distinguish between types of conflicts and types of dispositions of the actors involved. We also need to develop different ways to assist in conflict resolution at each stage and then also as a whole. These steps may first be decoupled for better understanding and then brought together for a total solution. The origin of the conflict should be actually a part of the formulation of the problem together with a background on the parties, their needs and requirements and how willing they are to solve the problem. The formulation should also mention the means the parties are likely to follow to obtain resolution, and how likely they are to implement it and stick with the outcome. Only then may we really believe that we have an operationally useful approach to conflict resolution.

The process requires decomposing complexity according to different points of view, providing value judgments as to the importance of the factors involved in this decomposition, and then bringing together the different decompositions and judgments into a single overall framework, and finally synthesizing the diversity in a unified but rich and comprehensive understanding. This understanding can then be used to search for ways to narrow the differences and accelerate the process of conflict resolution, having employed the thinking and judgments of the same individuals or groups charged with the responsibility for action.

Comparing Apples and Oranges - Trading Off Intangibles

We use the Analytic Hierarchy Process to make the assessment of how much one set of concessions, some of which may be intangible, is worth against another set, often with the help of a negotiator.

Alternatives for negotiation have been observed in the literature to include the following categories:

1. Things: Territory, Money, Property
2. Concessions and recognition of rights
3. Weapon agreements
4. Trade and other material exchange
5. Ideological designs
6. Human rights and democracy
7. Cease bad propaganda
8. Compete successfully and enviably
9. Openness for movement
10. Share wealth and knowledge
11. Cultural exchange
12. Integrity and honesty in dealings
13. Motives for making policies and taking actions
14. Threats

It is important to note that incomplete information plays an important role in conflict resolution. One must use whatever information is available and keep revising the outcome with the arrival of new information.

An important factor in conflict resolution is that each party's conception of value is usually different. To align their value systems the parties may be able to find something which they agree on as a common frame of reference for making trade-offs. Alternatively, a mediator is invited to interrogate the parties and come to an understanding of worth between them.   Such understanding is much more difficult to accomplish when there are several parties, each of whom may be reluctant to reveal anything about its values, for then the opponent may decide to ask for more.   The less known the values and possessions of a party the more room that party has to negotiate and to offer concessions. Even divulging information to a negotiator can be done piecemeal so that it would not be easy to infer how much is available for exchange.

If one party is short on useful concessions to make in order to get concessions from the other, it can instead make credible threats to force the other side to make available more concessions for negotiation.   It can also offer future concessions and extended cooperation. If one side holds back alternatives that the other side thinks should be in the negotiation set, the other side can refuse to negotiate or it must force the opponent with threats and sanctions to bring them into the set.   Finally, it could offer such attractive concessions to cause the opponent to relax his tight hold. Conflicts do get resolved or forgotten. They get resolved by the threat of the use of force, by mediation, arbitration or by negotiation.

6. A Lesson From Conflict Resolution

The benefit/cost framework of AHP in conflict resolution indicates that unless B can offer benefits to A to exchange for concessions it wants or unless it has threats that can incur valuable costs to A, A would not be willing to make concessions. The real situation strongly suggests that to avoid the use of force in society we need many more bodies for mediation and arbitration than we have.

7. Group Decision Making

Consensus is not always the best way to obtain a group decision. Sometimes the group can establish a hierarchy to judge the relative power or knowledge of the individual making the judgments. Include such criteria as experience, power, political favors, wealth, fame, and the ability to threaten disruption or withhold participation. Compare the individuals for their relative influence using consensus or structured debate.

A set of priorities can be obtained from the power hierarchy of Figure 7-1 which is used to weight the individuals' results after they independently evaluate the decision hierarchy. The issues should first be debated by the group.

• The outcome is one weighted by power and merit rather than one obtained through consensus. The relative power of the participants may shift as the issues change.

Power Hierarchy for
Best Ranking of Experts

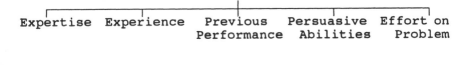

Figure 7-1 *A Hierarchy to judge the judges*

One reason why people in power may not immediately accept decision making methods like the AHP may be their fear that bringing other opinions into a decision would diminish their power. If such people are in control of the resulting situation, the others in the group may need to collect allies to apply pressure to force them to participate.

Structural and Judgment Synthesis Issues

1) Group at large with many individuals: use statistical integration of judgments.
2) Group that is small but cannot get together: use questionnaire shown in Figure 7-2.
3) Group that gets together to reach agreements: structure hierarchy together and seek consensus on judgments; allow adequate time for debate; engage everybody.
   A) When the group consists of experts: all form hierarchy but each works out assessment.
      a) Use geometric mean of outcome if all judges are equally important.
      b) Use weighted geometric mean by creating a hierarchy as above to prioritize judges if they are not equally important.
   B) When the group consists of tyros: combine judgments in each comparison using the geometric mean.
4) When the group has a conflict problem, use AHP approach to conflict resolution.

Questionnaire Example

Compare X and Y		X over Y				or	Y over X			
		Extreme	Very Strong	Strong	Moderate	Equal	Moderate	Strong	Very Strong	Extreme
1990 -2000	After 2000									

Figure 7-2 *Sample Questionnaire (one for each judgment)*

Political and Psychological Issues

1 -   Do homework before meeting and use it to brief audience on issues and hierarchy.
2 -   AHP is not a tool for an isolated application, but a process that has ongoing validity and usefulness.
3 -   When an individual or faction seeks to dominate ask for other people to participate, or break group into smaller groups.
4 -   There may be hidden agendas, political commitments, or reluctance to participate.
5 -   One party may insist on including alternatives to serve its own purpose, add criteria to cover its own concerns; or exaggerate and distort preferences. Use referees to decide if it is justified or an intentional distortion.
6 -   Disagreements and conflicts may show up strongly in the meeting. To help cope, summarize conclusions, clarify, bring new information and have more discussion.
7 -   When an impasse occurs it may be because of lack of a rich enough framework for compromise. Diversify participants and expand the hierarchy.
8 -   If the knowledge of participants is narrowly specialized in their own areas, let the different parties provide judgments for their part of the hierarchy.
9 -   If there is not enough time to complete the work in one session, hold several briefer sessions in a relaxed environment.
10 - If there are too many people for satisfactory discussion and interaction, divide into smaller groups. This also helps to control bias.
11 - If the decision group does not have enough knowledge of the subject, invite briefings by knowledgeable people.
12 - When there is too much knowledge and information, cut through excessive detail by summarizing the essential facts.
13 - If people are impatient with other people's discussion, break up into groups for individualized clarifications. Summarize

positions and take a straw vote.
14 - If people are inattentive and preoccupied with other matters, but later demand to be told what they missed, ask them what they think more often.

References

1.   Aczel, J. and Saaty, T. L., 1983, "Procedures for Synthesizing Ratio Judgments", Journal of Mathematical Psychology 27, pp. 93-102.

2.   Aczel, J. and Alsina, C., 1986, "On synthesis of judgments", Socio-Econ. Planning Sci., 20, pp. 333-339.

3.   Basak, I., 1988, "When to combine judgments and when not to in Analytic Hierarchy Process : A New Method", Mathematical Comput. Modelling 24, pp. 1-14.

4.   ----------, 1989, "Estimation of the multicriteria worths of the alternatives in a hierarchical structure of comparisons", Communications in Statistics - Theory and Methods 18/10, pp. 3719-3738.

5.   ----------, 1991, "Inference in pairwise comparison experiments based on ratio scales", Journal of Mathematical Psychology, forthcoming.

6.   ---------- and T.L. Saaty, 1993, "Group Decision Making Using the Analytic Hierarchy Process", Journal of Mathematical Modelling 17/415.

7. Bradley, R.A. and Terry, M.E., 1952, "Rank analysis of incomplete block designs I. The method of paired comparisons", Biometricka 39, pp. 324-345.

8. Davidson, R.R., 1970, "On extending the Bradley-Terry model to accommodate ties in paired comparisons experiments", Journal of the American Statistical Association 65, pp. 317-328.

9. Fichtner, J., 1983, "Some thoughts about the mathematics of the Analytic Hierarchy Process", Hochschula der Bundeswehr, Munich.

10. Lehrer, K. and Wagner, C., 1981, "Rational Consensus in Science and Society. A Philosophical and Mathematical Study", D. Reidel Publishing Company, Boston.

11. Saaty, T.L., 1986, "Resolution of Retributive Conflicts", in: Contributions of Technology to International Conflict Resolution. Ed. H. Chestnut. Pergamon Press.

12. -------------, 1990, The Analytic Hierarchy Process. RWS Publications, Pittsburgh.

13. ------------- and J. Alexander, 1989, Conflict Resolution - The Analytical Hierarchy Approach. Praeger Publishers, NY.

14. Vargas, L.G., 1982, "Reciprocal matrices with random coefficients", Mathematical Modelling 3, pp. 69-81.

CHAPTER EIGHT

SYSTEMIC INTERDEPENDENCE:
THE SUPERHIERARCHY AND
THE SUPERMATRIX

1. Structure in the AHP - Hierarchies and Networks

The AHP emphasizes the use of elaborate structures to represent a decision problem. The soundness of a decision is reflected at least as much by the richness and accuracy of the structure and relations in the structure, as it is in assigning and manipulating numbers according to some theory. In fact, a reasonable test of a method of measurement is how efficient and accurate it is when applied to elaborate structures. How well the mathematical operations generalize to cases of dependence within and between clusters of elements is a good test of whether the theory appears natural or forced. With its use of relative ratio scales and corresponding formal operations, the AHP is capable of incorporating all observed dependencies.

Figure 8-1 depicts the structural difference between the two frameworks of a hierarchy and a network.

A network can be used to identify relationships among components using one's own thoughts, relatively free of rules. It is especially suited for modeling dependence relations. Such a network approach makes it possible to represent and analyze interactions and also to synthesize their mutual effects by a single logical procedure. In a hierarchy, on the other hand, we have the outer dependence of the elements in a level on the elements in the level above. A loop means that there is inner dependence of elements within a component. In the network diagram shown below, interaction within a cluster is called inner dependence and interaction between clusters is called outer dependence. Inner dependence is analyzed with respect to the attributes of a dominating cluster linked to the given cluster. Formal definitions of the foregoing are found in Chapter 10. In a given problem there may be several networks associated with each of the criteria of a separate governing design hierarchy called the control hierarchy. Synthesizing interactions into different networks involves the use of priorities from the control hierarchy.

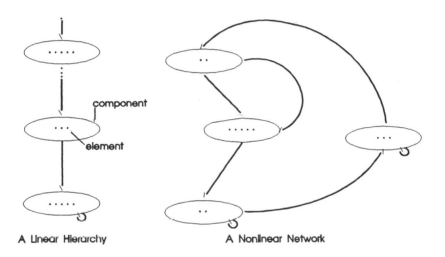

component

element

A Linear Hierarchy   A Nonlinear Network

(A) — (B)   means that A dominates B or that B depends on A.

Figure 8-1   *Structural Difference Between a Linear and a Nonlinear Network*

2. Networks and Dependence

Two familiar illustrations involving the analysis of dependence are W. Leontief's practical notion of input-output analysis among industries in the field of economics, and the dependence among events in probability theory. There are even more complex dependencies of stochastic processes found in Markov and Semi-Markov processes. All these are special attempts to deal with dependence.

The notion of dependence also occurs in utility theory where the idea of a lottery plays an important role. Here, Y is defined to be utility independent of Z when conditional preferences for lotteries on Y given $z \, \epsilon \, Z$ do not depend on the particular level of z. One theoretical objective when using utility theory is to derive a utility function, but the existence of such a function is conditioned by the independence of criteria from alternatives. In addition one ordinarily assumes that the criteria are independent among themselves and similarly for the alternatives.

How does one structure a decision problem with dependencies, derive priorities and make choices among interdependent attributes and alternatives?

The concept of independence requires a definition in terms of space and time. Two objects may be independent because they are far apart but they can depend on each other if they came closer. In addition there may be agents or transformations that cause weak dependence among things. If some events occur before other events, we may think that they are independent of them. This need not be the case if we were to think of time as a long cycle.

When compared in relative terms, all alternatives depend on each other according to how good one alternative is as compared to another with which it is compared. This is done either by directly comparing each alternative with every other, or by comparing it with just one alternative that has already been compared with the others. Dependence is a primitive concept that has two meanings.

1) *Outer dependence*, is the dependence of an alternative in a set of alternatives on an attribute in a set of attributes possessed by the alternatives. It is the degree or intensity with which that attribute is present in the alternative (one car has a lot of style and another little or no style). This intensity is either measured

relative to other alternatives or measured alone on a standard scale. In the end both results can be expressed in relative terms. The first is already relative and the second becomes relative after normalization. We shall not distinguish between these two possibly different derived results in our analysis of dependence.

Another form of outer dependence occurs in the opposite way. Which attribute of several is more salient in this alternative? We note that attributes derive from their objects and become mental abstractions only after the objects are experienced. Here, instead of setting priorities on attributes in relative terms by comparing them with other attributes on higher order criteria, one compares them with respect to each alternative. One way to justify such comparisons of criteria is to compare each of two criteria in an alternative by first taking the ratio of its presence in that alternative with its presence in an ideal or aggregate alternative. One then forms the ratio of these two ratios to obtain a relative comparison of the criteria in that alternative. It is important to note that people do this kind of thinking. For example, this apple is more red than it is tasty. Previous experience is involved in this process to develop a frame of reference. A child cannot make such comparisons.

2) *Inner dependence*, or the dependence of an alternative on another alternative, is the influence, contribution or impact of the second alternative on the first with respect to an attribute they have in common. For example, all industries depend on the electric industry for their lighting. The electric industry itself depends on the oil, coal and nuclear industries for raw material which in turn use electricity to produce their goods. An alternative may depend on another with respect to several attributes. A child depends on its family for physical and social care. Conversely, the family depends on the child for its self realization and for physical help in maintaining some order.

To study dependence in decision problems we need to know both the alternatives and the attributes and what depends on what; we call this *functional dependence*. Structural dependence is the precise way in which these elements are located and interconnected. Let us make some general observations about what we are looking for to cope with dependence. A mathematical model is limited by its structure: it can be linear or nonlinear, normative or descriptive, have or not have dependencies among the variables; and it is limited by what operations one needs to perform to derive useful results. A crucial property of a model is its adaptability to represent complex problems and its faithfulness to reflect the degree and variety of dependencies among the variables considered. Our understanding of the world depends on our ability to model it faithfully.

Figure 8-2, taken from the New York Times, Sunday, December 12, 1976, illustrates how dependence occurs naturally in the real world. In order to understand the net cause and effect in this messy system and how to control them we need to set priorities.

The Supermatrix - General Composition of Priorities

The structure of a hierarchy can be generalized to a network system. Consider a system which has been decomposed into N clusters or components $C_1, C_2, \ldots, C_N$. Let the elements in component C_k be denoted by $e_{k1}, e_{k2}, \ldots, e_{kn_k}$ where n_k is their number. Our earlier discussion of impact between adjacent levels of a hierarchy enables us to construct the following type of matrix of impact measurement between the elements in corresponding components. Here we assume that every pair of components interact. If this is not the case, then the corresponding entries in the matrix are zero.

The supermatrix plays a fundamental role in our subsequent development of priorities for systems. However, we first show how hierarchical composition may be derived by raising the supermatrix to powers.

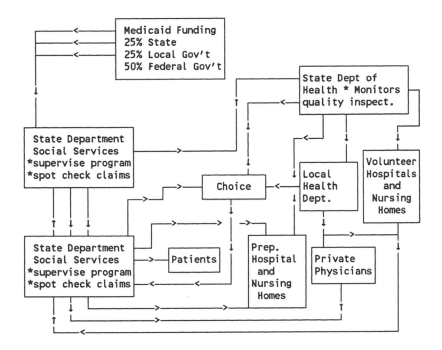

Figure 8-2 *The Health Care System*

The components of a system, and hence also the elements in these components, can interact along more than a single path. One component can, for example, interact indirectly with another by first influencing an intermediate component. The priorities of influence of a component of the system on another component may be measured over all the paths and cycles which connect them. Note that if elements in one component depend on the elements of another then we can also speak of dependence between the two components. However, two components may depend on each other due to the synergy of their elements without the elements themselves being directly dependent. For example, two industries may depend on each other's output without their machines depending on each other directly.

One could construct pairwise comparisons to measure the priority of all the elements in the system as if there were no clustering of the elements into components.   For example, we may be comparing industries and their impact on, or contribution to, every other industry.   However, clustering elements into components is what one does in practice because it is efficient.   It is also convenient to make pairwise comparison judgments on a small set of elements.   Thus we assume that we have the priority eigenvectors of the elements in a component with respect to the elements in another component (which may be the component itself).   When this comparison makes no sense we use zeros for the eigenvector.

The supermatrix corresponding to the interaction between the components of a system may be displayed as follows.

$$W = \begin{array}{c} \\ \\ C_1 \\ \\ \\ \\ C_2 \\ \\ \\ \vdots \\ \\ C_N \\ \\ \end{array} \begin{array}{c} e_{11} \\ e_{12} \\ \vdots \\ e_{1n_1} \\ e_{21} \\ e_{22} \\ \vdots \\ e_{2n_2} \\ \\ e_{N1} \\ e_{N2} \\ \vdots \\ e_{Nn_N} \end{array} \begin{bmatrix} \overset{\displaystyle C_1}{\overset{e_{11}e_{12}\ldots e_{1n_1}}{W_{11}}} & \overset{\displaystyle C_2}{\overset{e_{21}e_{22}\ldots e_{2n_2}}{W_{12}}} & \cdots & \overset{\displaystyle C_N}{\overset{e_{N1}e_{N2}\ldots e_{Nn_N}}{W_{1N}}} \\ W_{21} & W_{22} & \cdots & W_{2N} \\ \vdots & \vdots & \vdots\vdots\vdots & \vdots \\ W_{N1} & W_{N2} & \cdots & W_{NN} \end{bmatrix}$$

where the i,j block is given by,

$$W_{ij} = \begin{bmatrix} w_{i1}^{(j_1)} & w_{i1}^{(j_2)} & \cdots & w_{i1}^{(j_{n_j})} \\ w_{i2}^{(j_1)} & w_{i2}^{(j_2)} & \cdots & w_{i2}^{(j_{n_j})} \\ \vdots & \vdots & \vdots\vdots\vdots & \vdots \\ w_{in_i}^{(j_1)} & w_{in_i}^{(j_2)} & \cdots & w_{in_i}^{(j_{n_j})} \end{bmatrix}$$

each of whose columns is an eigenvector which represents the impact of all the elements in the ith component on each of the elements in the jth component.

The discussion of this chapter will focus on deriving limiting or steady state priorities from the supermatrix. It must first be reduced to a matrix each of whose columns sums to unity. Such a matrix is known as a *column stochastic* or simply, a *stochastic* matrix. If the matrix is stochastic, the limiting priorities will be obtained in three different ways, depending on the reducibility, primitivity, and cyclicity of that matrix. If the supermatrix is not stochastic, one must develop weights for the impact of the components on each of the components. Interaction in the supermatrix may be measured according to several different criteria. To display and relate the criteria, we need a separate *control hierarchy* that includes these criteria with their priorities. For each criterion, a different supermatrix of impacts is developed and in terms of that criterion the components are compared according to their relative impact on each other component, thus developing priorities to weight the block matrices of eigenvector columns under that component in the supermatrix. The resulting supermatrix would then be a stochastic matrix. Hereafter, whenever we refer to W we assume that it has been weighted to a stochastic matrix.

Analysis of priorities in a system can be thought of in terms of a control hierarchy with dependence among its bottom level alternatives arranged in clusters. Dependence can occur within the clusters and between them.

3. Impact and Absolute Priorities

We shall need the idea of an irreducible matrix in the theory developed below for priorities in a feedback system. Although it is defined elsewhere in the book, for completeness of the chapter we repeat it here.

Definition - A square matrix is *reducible* if it can be partitioned (by permutations) into the form

$$\begin{bmatrix} A_1 & 0 \\ A_2 & A_3 \end{bmatrix}$$

where A_1 and A_3 are square matrices and 0 is the zero matrix. Otherwise the matrix is said to be *irreducible*.

Theorem 8-1 *A square matrix A is either irreducible or can be reduced by a permutation of indices to a block diagonal matrix of irreducible matrices, and other block matrices, having the normal form*

$$\begin{bmatrix} A_1 & 0 & \cdots & 0 & 0 & \cdots & 0 \\ 0 & A_2 & \cdots & 0 & 0 & \cdots & 0 \\ \vdots & \vdots & & \vdots & \vdots & & \vdots \\ 0 & 0 & \cdots & A_k & 0 & \cdots & 0 \\ A_{k+1,1} & A_{k+2,2} & \cdots & A_{k+1,k} & A_{k+1} & \cdots & 0 \\ \vdots & \vdots & \cdots & \vdots & \vdots & \cdots & \vdots \\ A_{m1} & A_{m2} & \cdots & A_{mk} & A_{m,k+1} & \cdots & A_m \end{bmatrix}$$

Definition - A nonnegative irreducible matrix A is *primitive* if and only if there is an integer $m \geq 1$ such that $A^m > 0$. Otherwise it is called *imprimitive*.

The graph of a primitive matrix has a path of length $\geq m$ between any two vertices.

It is useful to mention the following facts.

Theorem 8-2 *A nonnegative matrix A is stochastic if and only if the vector (1, 1, ..., 1) is a solution of $xA = x$ where unity is the* *principal eigenvalue of A* [6].

Theorem 8-3 *An n by n matrix A is irreducible if and only if its directed graph is strongly connected.*

Theorem 8-4 *A connected graph is strongly connected if and only if every arc belongs to at least one cycle.*

Theorem 8-5 *A matrix A is reducible if and only if at least one of the principal minors of order n - 1 of the matrix $(\lambda_{max}I - A)$ is zero.*

Theorem 8-6 *If A is a nonnegative irreducible matrix of order n we have $(I+A)^{n-1} > 0$.*

(This says that if a graph is strongly connected and we add loops at every vertex the resulting matrix is primitive, i.e., any vertex is reachable from any other by a path of fixed length.)

Theorem 8-7 *A strongly connected graph (with $n \geq 2$ vertices) with vertex matrix A is primitive if and only if the greatest common divisor of the lengths of all simple cycles is unity.*

Theorem 8-8 *A primitive (column) stochastic matrix A has the property that $\lim A^k$ has identical columns w (the unique equilibrium probability vector) and hence $w = Aw$ has a unique solution; in addition, for any initial probability vector*

$$w^{(0)}(w_i^{(0)} \geq 0, \sum w_i^{(0)} = 1), \quad A^k w^{(0)} \to w.$$

This is the key theorem for calculating priorities when the matrix is primitive.

We are interested in two types of priorities. Those that give the influence or impact of one element on any other element in the system are known as the impact priorities. We are also interested in the absolute priority of any element regardless of which elements it influences. Generally we seek limiting values of these two kinds of priorities. Calculation of these priorities shows where existing trends might lead if there is no change in preference which affects the priorities. By experimenting with the process of modifying priorities and noting their limiting trends, we may be able to steer a system towards a more desired outcome.

Now for the formal definitions. If w_{ij} is the impact priority of the ith element on the jth element in the system then

$$w_{ij}^{(1)} = w_{ij}$$

$$w_{ij}^{(2)} = \sum_m w_{im} w_{mj}$$

$$w_{ij}^{(k+1)} = \sum_m w_{im} w_{mj}^{(k)}$$

$$w_{ij}^{(h+k)} = \sum_m w_{im}^{(h)} w_{mj}^{(k)}$$

The last expression is equivalent to $W^{h+k} = W^h W^k$.

The sum of the impact priorities along all possible paths from a given element gives the priority of that element. It is equivalent to raising the matrix W to powers.

Given that the initial priority of the ith element is $w_i^{(0)}$, we have the following absolute priority of the jth element in paths of length $k \neq 0$:

$$w_j^{(k)} = \sum_i w_i^{(0)} w_{ij}^{(k)}$$

The problem is to find the limiting impact priority (LIP) matrix W^∞ and the limiting absolute priority (LAP) vector w^∞ as $k \to \infty$. For a priority system we may also be interested in determining priorities for finite values of k. That does not present problems of existence as does the limiting case. Of particular interest is to determine when the LAP priority is independent of the initial priorities $w_i^{(0)}$. Such independence is called the *ergodicity* of the system.

The following is a classification of elements useful in characterizing a system. The reader may wish to go on to the actual discussion of existence and construction of LIP and LAP solutions.

The element j can be reached from the element i if for some integer $k \geq 1$, $w_{ij}^{(k)} > 0$ where $W^k = (w_{ij}^{(k)})$. Here W^k gives the k-reach of each element. A subset of elements C of a system is *closed* (opposite definition to that for Markov chains) if $w_{ij}^{(k)} = 0$ whenever i is in C and j is not in C. It follows that no element in C can be reached from any element not in C. The subset C is minimal if it contains no proper closed subset of elements. A set of elements which forms a minimal closed subset corresponds to an irreducible matrix. If the matrix of an entire system or subsystem is irreducible, the system or subsystem itself is called irreducible. A system is called decomposable if it has two or more closed sets.

If we *initially* start with the jth element for some fixed j and denote its first impact on itself in a path of length $k \geq 1$ by $f_j^{(k)}$, we have $f_j^{(1)} = w_{jj}^{(1)}$, $f_j^{(2)} = w_{jj}^{(2)} - f_j^{(1)} w_{jj}^{(1)} \ldots f_j^{(k)} = w_{jj}^{(k)} - f_j^{(1)} w_{jj}^{(k-1)} - \ldots - f_j^{(k-1)} w_{jj}^{(1)}$ and

$$f_j = \sum_{k=1}^{\infty} f_j^{(k)}$$

gives the cumulative impact of j on itself. The *mean* impact (of j on itself) is given by

$$u_j = \sum_{k=0}^{\infty} k f_j^{(k)}$$

According to priority influence we have (the new terms introduced below are essential, as we are not dealing with time transitions):

(1) If $f_j = 1$, j is called an *enduring* (recurrent) element. Thus an element is enduring if the sum of its impact priorities on

itself in a single step (by a loop) in two steps (through a cycle involving one other element), in three steps involving two other elements, etc. is equal to unity.   (2)   If $f_j < 1$, j is called *transitory* (transient).   An element j that is either enduring or transitory is called *cyclic* (periodic) with cyclicity c if u_j has values c, $2c$, $3c$,.... where c is the greatest integer *greater than* unity with this property ($w_{ij}^{(k)} = 0$ where k is not divisible by c).   An enduring element j for which u_j is infinite is called *fading* (null).   An enduring element j that is neither cyclic nor fading (i.e., $u_j < \infty$) is called *sustaining* (ergodic).

For either a transitory or a fading element j, $w_{ij}(k) \to 0$ for every i.   If one element in an irreducible subsystem is cyclic with cyclicity c, all the elements in that subsystem are cyclic with cyclicity c.   It is known that if j is a sustaining element, then as $k \to \infty$, $w_{jj}^{(k)} \to 1/u_j$; j is a fading element if this number is zero and sustaining if it is positive.   Either all the elements of an irreducible subsystem are all transitory or all enduring and the system itself is called transitory or enduring, respectively.

The following expression always exists whether a system is irreducible or not.   In the former case its values are known and are as indicated

$$\lim_{m\to\infty} \sum_{k=0}^{m-1} w_{ij}^{(k)} = \begin{cases} 0 & \text{if } i \text{ and } j \text{ are transitory} \\ 1/u_j & \text{if } i \text{ and } j \text{ are enduring} \end{cases}$$

All finite systems of elements must have at least one sustaining element which generates a closed irreducible subset of elements.   Since the enduring elements of a finite system are all sustaining, the block (or component) thus generated is called sustaining.

If j is cyclic with cyclicity $c > 1$ then

$$w_{jj}^{(k)} = 0$$

if k is not a multiple of c and

$$w_{jj}^{(m)} \to c/u_j$$

as $m \to \infty$; $k = mc$, m positive and c the largest integer for which $k = mc$ holds.

Reducibility and primitivity play an important role in proving the existence of LIP and LAP. We now give a few basic facts relating these concepts.

A nonnegative irreducible matrix is primitive if it has a unique principal eigenvalue. If the matrix has another eigenvalue with the same modulus as the principal eigenvalue, it is called imprimitive.

If the principal eigenvalue has multiplicity greater than unity (equal to unity), but there are no other eigenvalues of the same modulus as the principal eigenvalue then the matrix is called proper (regular).

A primitive matrix is always regular and hence proper but not conversely, e.g., the identity matrix which has unity as an eigenvalue of multiplicity equal to the order of the matrix. A matrix is proper if and only if in the normal form, the isolated blocks are primitive. For a regular matrix the number of isolated blocks is unity.

We note that if all the entries of W are positive, we have a primitive matrix and the theorem on stochastic primitive matrices applies, both LIP and LAP exist. LIP and LAP are the same and are given by the solution of the eigenvalue problem $Ww = w$. Actually w is any column of $\lim_{k \to \infty} W^k$. The same result is true if W is a primitive matrix.

In general the nonnegative matrix W may have some zeros. In that case it is either an irreducible or a reducible matrix. If it is irreducible then it is either primitive in which case the above discussion applies, or it is imprimitive. In the latter case it has a number c of eigenvalues (called the index of imprimitivity) that are not equal to unity whose moduli are equal to unity. This number plays an important role in the solution of the general case from which we can also obtain the solution to this case. It is sufficient to point out that W, W^2,..., W^{c-1} are not all proper and multiples of these matrices tend toward repetition. The system is cyclic with cyclicity c.

The system is acyclic, cyclic, irreducible, reducible, depending on whether the corresponding matrix W is primitive, imprimitive, irreducible, reducible.

If W is nonnegative and reducible then it is reduced to the normal form. If the isolated blocks are primitive they are said to correspond to essential components and the residual matrices correspond to inessential components. The system is by definition called proper and LIP and LAP exist [6, p. 112].

When the column stochastic matrix is reducible its essential components drive the system. They are "sources" or impact-priority-diffusing components as compared with "sinks" or transition-probability-absorbing states of a Markov chain. In any diagram, except for loops, arrows initiate from and none terminate at such components.

The solution for LIP is given by

$$W^{\infty} \equiv \lim_{k \to \infty} W^k = \frac{(I-W)^{-1}\psi(1)}{\psi'(1)}$$

where $\psi(\lambda)$ is the minimum polynomial of W and $\psi'(\lambda)$ is its first derivative with respect to λ. Each column of W^{∞} is a characteristic vector of W corresponding to $\lambda_{max} = 1$. If $\lambda_{max} = 1$ is simple, i.e., W is regular, $\psi(\lambda)$ may be replaced by $\Delta(\lambda)$ the characteristic polynomial of W. To see this note that LIP exist if and only if W is regular. For a regular matrix we have:

$$\psi(\lambda) \equiv \prod_{i=1}^{k} (\lambda - \lambda_i)^{m_i}$$

for the minimum polynomial of W with $\lambda_i \neq \lambda_j$.

Since W is stochastic $\lambda_1 = 1$, $m_1 = 1$.

If
$$C(\lambda)=(\lambda I-W)^{-1}\psi(\lambda)$$

and the characteristic polynomial of W is

$$\Delta(\lambda) = \prod_{i=1}^{n}(\lambda-\lambda_i)^{n_i}$$

and if
$$B(\lambda)=(\lambda I-W)^{-1}\Delta(\lambda)$$

then by Sylvester's formula we have

$$W^\infty=\frac{C(1)}{\psi'(1)}=\frac{n_1 B^{(n_1-1)}(1)}{\Delta^{(n_1)}(1)}$$

with (n_1-1) and (n_1) indicating the order derivatives of B and Δ, respectively.

Also, if W is fully regular then

$$W^\infty=\frac{B(1)}{\Delta'(1)}=\frac{\Delta(1)}{\Delta'(1)}(I-W)^{-1}$$

LAPs exist and are independent of the initial priorities, if and only if, W is fully regular. They are positive, if and only if, W is acyclic.

LAPs are obtained as

$$w^\infty = W^\infty w^{(0)},$$

if W is proper, and as the eigenvector solution of

$$Ww^\infty = w^\infty,$$

if W is regular.

One can show that the blocks of W^∞ corresponding to essential components are positive and that those corresponding to priority impacts from essential to inessential components are also positive. Only impacts from inessential to inessential or from inessential to essential components are zero.

Finally, if not all isolated blocks are primitive then each has an index of imprimitivity as we pointed out earlier. We consider the least common multiple of these which is the cyclicity c of the system. Using the powers of W, LIP is given by

$$\tilde{W} = \frac{1}{c}(I+W+\cdots W^{c-1})\ (W^c)^\infty$$

$$= \frac{1}{c}(I-W^c)\ (1-W)^{-1}(W^c)^\infty$$

and LAP is given by

$$w = \tilde{W}w^{(0)}$$

Both $\tilde{W}$ and w are called the mean LIP and mean LAP, respectively.

If there is a single isolated block, then the mean LAP priorities are independent of the initial priorities and are uniquely determined by the solution of $Ww = w$, which is precisely the case of an irreducible imprimitive system.

Summary of Cases of Supermatrix

1) If all entries of the stochastic matrix W are positive or if W is primitive both LIP and LAP exist and are the same. They are given by any column of W^∞.

2) If W is irreducible (its directed graph is strongly connected and hence a path exists between any two nodes) and

   a) Primitive: The only eigenvalue of W of modules 1 is 1, $\lim W^k$ exists and is positive. Its columns are identical and each denoted by w. It is the unique limiting vector of W such that $Ww = w$

   b) Imprimitive: LIP, given by $\lim W^k$ do not exist. W is cyclic with cyclicity c equal to the number of isolated blocks. LAP are obtained from $Ww = w$.

3) If W is reducible and its isolated blocks are irreducible and *primitive* (checked by putting in normal form)

   a) LIP is given by $W^\infty \equiv (I - W)^{-1} \dfrac{\psi(1)}{\psi'(1)}$ if $\lambda_{max} = 1$ is not simple and $\psi(\lambda)$ is the minimum polynomial of W;

   $$W^\infty \equiv (I - W)^{-1} \frac{\Delta(1)}{\Delta'(1)} \quad \text{if } \lambda_{max} = 1 \text{ is simple, } \Delta(\lambda) \text{ is the characteristic polynomial of } W.$$

   b) LAP is given by $W^\infty w^{(0)}$ if $\lambda_{max} = 1$, is not simple (isolated blocks primitive) $w^{(0)}$ is an initial vector,
   $W(W^\infty w^{(0)})$ if $\lambda_{max} = 1$, is simple (one isolated block)

4) If W is reducible and its isolated blocks are *imprimitive* assume that each has an index of imprimitivity (the number of eigenvalues of each block not equal to one whose moduli are equal to one). Take c the least common multiple of these.

Mean LIP is given by $\bar{W} = \dfrac{1}{c}(I - W^c)(I - W)^{-1}(W^c)^\infty$ and mean LAP is given by $\bar{W} w^{(0)}$.

How do we determine when a matrix is reducible or irreducible, primitive or imprimitive, cyclic or acyclic? For AHP purposes each cluster is assigned the vertex of a directed graph [12, appendix]. Arrows are then drawn from a vertex to all those vertices that are dominated by that vertex according to influence in the network. Now we can associate a vertex-vertex matrix B with this graph. The entries of B are zero or one depending on whether there is an arrow leading from the vertex to the left of the matrix to a vertex at the top.

We use B to study reducibility, primitivity and cyclicity of the supermatrix associated with a network. To test its irreducibility we simply check to see if $(I+B)^{n-1} > 0$ where n is the order of B. Otherwise it is reducible. Alternatively B is reducible if and only if at least one of the principal minors of order (n-1) of $(\lambda_{max}I-B)$ is zero.

To determine if B is primitive we must find some power m such that $B^m > 0$. A computer can be used to check this by raising B to powers and noting if all its entries become positive. If they do not, we do not have a conclusive proof because m may be very large, but this is a practical check without performing complex calculations. Otherwise the matrix is imprimitive. To determine the cyclicity c one successively calculates the limiting expression for mean LIP $\tilde{W}$ for values of c from one on to c no greater than the order of the matrix B and adopts the smallest value of c and $\tilde{W}$ for which that expression converges.

4. The Supermatrix of a Hierarchy and the Validity of Hierarchic Independence

In general, the supermatrix of a hierarchy has the following form

$$W = \begin{bmatrix} 0 & 0 & 0 & \cdot & \cdot & & 0 & 0 \\ W_{21} & 0 & 0 & \cdot & \cdot & \cdot & 0 & 0 \\ 0 & W_{32} & 0 & \cdot & \cdot & \cdot & 0 & 0 \\ \cdot & \cdot & \cdot & \cdot & \cdot & \cdot & \cdot & \cdot \\ \cdot & \cdot & \cdot & \cdot & \cdot & \cdot & \cdot & \cdot \\ \cdot & \cdot & \cdot & \cdot & \cdot & W_{n-1,n-2} & \cdot & \cdot \\ 0 & 0 & 0 & \cdot & \cdot & \cdot & W_{n,n-1} & I \end{bmatrix}$$

This matrix has the stable form

$$W^k = \begin{bmatrix} 0 & 0 & \cdots & 0 & 0 & 0 \\ 0 & 0 & \cdots & 0 & 0 & 0 \\ \vdots & \vdots & \vdots\vdots\vdots & \vdots & \vdots & \vdots \\ 0 & 0 & \cdots & 0 & 0 & 0 \\ W_{n,n-1}W_{n-1,n-2}\cdots W_{32}W_{21} & W_{n,n-1}W_{n-1,n-2}\cdots W_{32} & \cdots & W_{n,n-1}W_{n-1,n-2} & W_{n,n-1} & I \end{bmatrix}$$

for all $k \geq n\text{-}1$. Each coefficient in the last row gives the composite priority impact of the last component on each of the remaining components.   Note that the outcome of hierarchic composition appears in the $(n,1)$ position as the impact of the nth part of an absorbing state in a Markov chain. It is a component of elements which diffuse or are a source of priority impacts. The essence of the above is summarized by the *Principle of Hierarchical Composition* given as a theorem:

Theorem 8-9 *The composite vector of a hierarchy of n levels is the entry in the (n,1) position of $W^{k\text{-}1}$, $k \geq n\text{-}1$.*

Proof The supermatrix of a hierarchy is reducible, imprimitive and   acyclic.   The   limiting   priorities   are   obtained   from

$\tilde{W} = \dfrac{1}{c}(I-W)(I-W^c)^{-1}(W^c)^\infty$ where $c=1$. The result is simply W^∞.

Inner Dependence of the Criteria in a Hierarchy

Consider a three level hierarchy with a goal, criteria and alternatives. Assume that the criteria are dependent among themselves. The supermatrix representation is given by:

$$W = \begin{pmatrix} 0 & 0 & 0 \\ X & Y & 0 \\ 0 & Z & I \end{pmatrix}$$

where X is the column vector of priorities of the criteria with respect to the goal, Y is the matrix of column eigenvectors of interdependence among the criteria, and Z is the matrix of column eigenvectors of the alternatives with respect to each criterion. W is a column stochastic matrix obtained by appropriate weighting of the matrices corresponding to interactions between levels.

The kth power of W that captures rank dominance along paths of length k is given by:

$$W^k = \begin{pmatrix} 0 & 0 & 0 \\ Y^{k-1}X & Y^k & 0 \\ Z\sum_{i=0}^{n-2} Y^iX & Z\sum_{i=0}^{n-1} Y^i & I \end{pmatrix}$$

and the priorities are obtained from the limit of W^k as k tends to infinity. We have:

$$W^\infty = \begin{pmatrix} 0 & 0 & 0 \\ 0 & 0 & 0 \\ Z(I-Y)^{-1}X & Z(I-Y)^{-1} & I \end{pmatrix}$$

Note that if $Y=0$, and hence the criteria are independent among themselves, the weights of the alternatives are given by ZX, the result of the additive model obtained by hierarchic composition. Also when Y is not zero, but is a small perturbation in a neighborhood of the null matrix, the additive model would be a good representation of the limiting priorities and hierarchic composition is still valid. It is only when Y is a large perturbation away from zero that the supermatrix solution should be used. In general, unless there are strong dependencies among the criteria, the additive model is an adequate estimate of the priorities in a hierarchy. Otherwise, the criteria should be redefined to ensure the independence of the new set.

To test for the mutual independence of the criteria, one proceeds as follows. Construct a zero-one matrix of criteria against criteria using the number one to signify dependence of one criterion on another, and zero otherwise. A criterion need not depend on itself, as for example, an industry may not use its own output. For each column (criterion) of this matrix construct a pairwise comparison matrix only for the dependent criteria, derive an eigenvector and augment it with zeros for the excluded criteria. If a column is all zeros, then assign a zero vector. The question in the comparison would be: For a given criterion, which of two criteria depends more on that criterion?

5. The Consistency of a System

Let $|C_k^-|$ be the number of elements of C_k^-, and let $w_{(k)(h)}$ be the priority of the impact of the hth component on the kth component, i.e. $w_{(k)(h)} = w_{(k)}(C_h)$ or $w_{(k)} : C_h\, w_{(k)(h)}$.

If we label the components of a system along lines similar to those we followed for a hierarchy, and denote by w_{jk} the limiting priority of the jth element in the kth component, we have

$$C_S = \sum_{k=1}^{s} \sum_{j=1}^{n_t} w_{jk} \sum_{h=1}^{|C_i^-|} w_{(k)(h)} \mu_k(j,h)$$

where $\mu_k(j,h)$ is the consistency index of the pairwise comparison matrix of the elements in the kth component with respect to the jth element in the hth component. [See revision sec. 4, Appendix]

6. Priorities in Systems with Outer and Inner Dependence

Every system has a purpose that arises out of how that system is designed. A television set has the purpose of producing good pictures and good sound. Behind this purpose there are higher order purposes such as economy and efficiency of operation, reliability and so on. The performance of each part is evaluated in terms of how these factors are incorporated in its design so that the system has some redundancy. For example, its components should be located in some optimal way and it should have little or no undesirable side effects such as radiation, heat and interference with other systems in the house. These higher order purposes are usually incorporated by choosing the appropriate material and by manufacturing the parts in a certain way. They are then located in the network in the best way to fulfill their function to satisfy all the higher order purposes which we might call supercriteria. It will be seen below that in setting priorities in systems with feedback, these higher order criteria and their priorities play an important role.

Outer Dependence

The simplest example of outer dependence is between two components encountered in the last section of Chapter 1. One consists of m independent alternatives which depend on the other of n independent criteria. The other component containing the criteria in turn depends on the alternatives. As usual, vectors of priorities are derived for the alternatives in terms of each of the criteria. These vectors can be arranged in an m by n matrix A which represents the influence of the criteria on the alternatives. Similarly vectors of priorities for the criteria with respect to the alternatives are derived and arranged as columns of an n by m matrix B. The two matrices are incorporated as blocks of an $n+m$ by $n+m$ supermatrix. This matrix represents the impact of the elements of the two components C_1 and C_2 of criteria and alternatives respectively on the elements themselves of the two components C_1 and C_2. There are four block matrices in the supermatrix of interactions. The diagonal blocks represent the impact of the elements of each component on themselves and has zero values. The off diagonal blocks A and B represent the interaction (C_2, C_1) and (C_1, C_2), respectively. The supermatrix has the form

$$\begin{array}{cc} & C_1\ C_2 \\ \begin{array}{c} C_1 \\ C_2 \end{array} & \begin{pmatrix} 0 & B \\ A & 0 \end{pmatrix} \end{array}$$

This matrix is irreducible because the two components are enduring (or recurrent) [11]. It is also column stochastic because the columns of A and B are normalized eigenvectors and hence sum to unity. By raising the supermatrix to powers one captures the dominance among the elements over all the paths and cycles in the network in a limiting matrix. In this matrix, the columns in the A block position become identical and thus any one of them yields the limiting priorities of the alternatives in component C_2. Similarly, the columns in the B block position are identical and any one of them yields the limiting priorities of the criteria in component C_1.

Inner Dependence

An example of inner dependence is illustrated in family-life, where housekeeping responsibilities and other duties are shared, creating dependencies undertaken by the different members with various degrees of leadership and performance to satisfy the needs of the family. The fact that the father may be the president of the United States would not matter very much to his standing in his family. He must still fulfill his family obligations.

For the inner dependence between elements in a component, we must develop the diagonal blocks of the supermatrix in a similar manner. As in the industry example, we ask which of a pair of elements contributes more to one of the elements with respect to that supercriterion of the control hierarchy.

Remarks:

1) The ideal mode is used in the supermatrix when the criteria do not depend on the alternatives and when, as in a hierarchy, it is desired to choose the best alternative regardless of what other alternatives (how many and of what quality measurement) there are. When the ideal mode is used, the alternatives can be ranked separately after the limiting results for the criteria are obtained from the supermatrix.

2) Assume that one is faced with ranking a set of alternatives twice with respect to two independent sets of criteria and no common goal, how should one combine the two outcomes? One can use the elementwise product of the two outcomes as a way to smooth one ranking with the other. More generally, one can use the geometric mean to combine n different rankings of a set of alternatives made by the same individual. If several people are involved, a weighted outcome is derived with the aid of a hierarchy used to compare the judges. This situation is analogous to combining the rankings of several judges to form a consistent matrix whose entries are simply the ratios of the rankings of the alternatives by each judge. If the judges have weights, the result would be to take the product of their rankings, each raised to a power equal to the priority of the corresponding judge.

The Control or Superhierarchy

Now let us describe again the process of generating priorities for a general system with outer and inner dependence. In simple terms, there are three categories of components in this system. A source component (for example of criteria) with no arc entering that component (there may be several such components);

intermediate components (of subcriteria) with arcs entering and others exiting (flow in such components may repeat if they belong to cycles); and an end or sink component (of alternatives) with arcs only entering and none exiting. A supermatrix for the several components is defined as before. The block matrices of eigenvectors as A and B discussed earlier are determined and inserted in the appropriate position in the supermatrix to indicate interaction between the elements of their respective components. In positions where there is no interaction, a zero block matrix is introduced. The diagonal block matrices correspond to the interaction of a component with itself. Often, these are zero except when the component is a sink in which case it is the identity matrix. Thus for example, in the supermatrix corresponding to a hierarchy, the nonzero blocks occupy the subdiagonal positions. Everywhere else there are zeros except for an identity matrix in the last row and column block. That position corresponds to the elements of the last level in the sink component.

There may be several nonzero blocks under a component. The sum of the entries in each column can be an integer equal to the number of nonzero blocks since the column in each block is a normalized eigenvector. To transform the supermatrix to a stochastic matrix, we must set priorities on the components themselves as they influence each column component. To do this we need to use the criteria of the control (or design) hierarchy in which the third level or more generally last level elements are these components of the supermatrix. The top level supergoal of this control hierarchy referred to as the *superhierarchy*, is the satisfactory functioning of the system. In the second level are supercriteria mentioned earlier. To ensure this satisfactory functioning, the supercriteria may be economy, reliability, replaceability, usability; or in another case economic, environmental, and social factors, and so on. We first obtain their priorities in the usual hierarchical way.

Some or all of the components in the bottom level may influence themselves (inner dependence) as would be known from the arcs of the network. For each supercriterion of the control hierarchy, inner dependence eigenvectors are derived for the components of the supermatrix as they impact each component. Each of these vectors is used to weight the blocks of matrices of the supermatrix in the column corresponding to the dependent component. As a result of this weighting the supermatrix becomes stochastic and the existence of a limiting matrix and corresponding priorities depend on the irreducibility of this matrix.

For each supercriterion, we obtain different weighting for the components in the supermatrix. The limiting priorities derived from each supermatrix are weighted by the importance of the supercriterion with respect to which the priorities of the components are determined and the results are added. Thus every element in the limiting supermatrix is multiplied by the single priority number of the supercriterion and the supermatrices are added to obtain a single composite supermatrix. The outcome is the overall outer dependence priorities in the network.

Remark One can imagine a problem in which there is an infinite sequence of nested feedback problems. The outcome of each of these problems provides the limiting weights (as in the case of the weights of a control hierarchy) to synthesize the outcome of several supermatrices. The combined weights of these is again used to synthesize the limiting impacts of the supermatrices of the next problem. The components of each problem serve as supercriteria for that problem.

7. How to Use Lotus 1-2-3 for Outer Dependence

In this section we describe the steps to follow in using Lotus 1-2-3 to set up the supermatrix and calculate the limiting priorities.

1. Enter Lotus 1-2-3.
2. Fill in the matrix.

3. Press / (and a menu will appear).
4. Select DATA (Press D),
   then MATRIX (Press M),
   then MULTIPLY (Press M).
5. The computer will ask you to enter the First Range to Multiply.
   - Put the cursor in the first cell of the matrix using the arrow keys.
   - Press .(period) to fix the first part of the range.
   - Use the arrow keys to block the entire matrix.
   - When you are finished Press Enter.
   You have now blocked the first matrix.
6. The computer will now ask you to enter the Second Range to Multiply.
   - Do as in Step 5 by reblocking the same matrix. You have now blocked the second matrix in the product calculation.
7. The computer will now ask to select the Output Range.
   - Position the cursor below the original matrix leaving at least one blank row and Press Enter.
   - The product of the two matrices now appears.
8. Repeat Steps 3 through 6. When you have to select the second range to multiply, first press Escape, then blockout the product matrix.
9. From then on, all one does is Press /,D,M,M, Enter, Enter, and Enter until the desired accuracy is reached. This result is realized when all the columns of each block of the product matrix are the same.

Note: The process leads to a single increment of power for each cycle. To speed the process, multiply the product matrix by itself repeatedly. In the end, stop if you want even powers or multiply the result by the original matrix for an odd power result.

8. Examples

Example 1 - Predicting Performance in Throwing Darts [7]

In a dart throwing exercise by three individuals, an attempt was made to predict the outcome, which was later validated by actually throwing darts. Six factors were used to determine the relative dart-throwing abilities of the actors. The short term factors are: mental condition, physical condition; the long term factors are: mental skill, physical skill; and the environmental factors are: visual ability, audio ability. Only four of the six criteria were compared for their contribution to each one of them; the two left out belong to the same category to which the dependent criterion belongs and it was thought to be meaningless to compare their effect on themselves. Zeros were entered in the supermatrix for these criteria. One obtains the following supermatrix followed by its resulting limiting matrix whose identical columns in this case correspond to the solution of the eigenvalue problem $Aw=w$. For computational purposes it is easy to raise the matrix to powers.

	Mental Condition	Physical Condition	Mental Skill	Physical Skill	Visual Factor	Audio Factor
Mental Condition	0	0	.429	.100	.450	.445
Physical Condition	0	0	.072	.400	.050	.056
Mental Skill	.375	.072	0	0	.429	.438
Physical Skill	.125	.429	0	0	.072	.063
Visual Factor	.100	.063	.167	.072	0	0
Audio Factor	.400	.438	.334	.429	0	0

	Mental Condition	Physical Condition	Mental Skill	Physical Skill	Visual Factor	Audio Factor
Mental Condition	.276	.276	.276	.276	.276	.276
Physical Condition	.079	.079	.079	.079	.079	.079
Mental Skill	.248	.248	.248	.248	.248	.248
Physical Skill	.079	.079	.079	.079	.079	.079
Visual Factor	.069	.069	.069	.069	.069	.069
Audio Factor	.257	.257	.257	.257	.257	.257

The individuals were then compared in pairs against each of the six factors. Hierarchic composition with the priority of the factors given by any column of the second matrix above yielded .268, .164, and .568 for their respective success priorities at throwing darts. In fact when they actually did throw darts each doing so 130 times, their normalized relative bulls eye scores were .26, .23 and .51 which are close to the relative predicted values. They attributed the lack of an even higher accuracy to their inability to compare the criteria with greater confidence because of the hurried exercise.

Example 2 - Sports prediction [5,9]

In addition to business applications, dependence can be used to evaluate the performance of sporting events. For instance, AHP has been used by students of the author who describe here what they did to predict which NBA (National Basketball Association) team would win the championship in 1991. In order to construct an accurate model the following influencing factors were considered: offense, defense, team statistics, and others (i.e. injuries, home court advantage and star players). The interaction of these components is shown in Figure 8-3. The supermatrix was then raised to powers to achieve a steady state. The results after normalization are shown in Table 8.1.

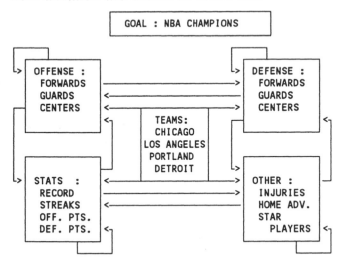

Figure 8-3 *Evaluating Four NBA Contenders*

We need to determine how important each factor (Offense, Defense, Team Stats, Other, Teams) is relative to the others with one particular factor in mind. For example, we compare the team factors with respect to Offense. An example of our thought process for this decision proceeds as follows: a team's offensive potential influenced its offensive productivity strongly; the next most important factor affecting a team's offense was star players and injuries (Other factors); following this, a team was influenced by its record and current streak; lastly, a teams' offense was influenced by its defense. The numbers representing these factors are used in the paired comparisons.

Here the effect of the components on each component were calculated and the corresponding blocks of the supermatrix were multiplied by these weights to obtain a stochastic supermatrix. This matrix is then raised to powers to obtain the following steady state result:

Table 8.1 Relative Priority of Teams

Chicago	0.305
Los Angeles	0.262
Portland	0.250
Detroit	0.183

Chicago won against Los Angeles in the final.

Another sports example is the Hockey Stanley Cup Playoffs of 1991, in which the last series of hockey games were considered from which the national champion is determined.

This problem can be approached in four ways. It can be structured as a hierarchy, a holarchy, a straight network or a network/hierarchy combination. Each of these methods indicated that the Pittsburgh Penguins would be the Stanley Cup Champions (which they were) but each was arrived at in a different way. The network model reflects the factors affecting the outcome (Figure 8-4) and the summary results of the four approaches is shown in Table 8.2.

Table 8.2 Summary Results in NHL Competition

	Hierarchy Eight Teams	Holarchy Without Injuries	Holarchy With Injuries	Straight Network	Network Hierarchy Combination
Pittsburgh	0.145	0.326	0.289	0.073	0.257
Edmonton	0.144	0.206	0.216	0.066	0.249
Boston	0.136	0.281	0.294	0.068	0.248
Minnesota	0.103	0.187	0.201	0.067	0.246
St. Louis	0.135				
Montreal	0.133				
LA	0.118				
Washington	0.086				

Normalized Semifinalists :

	Hierarchy	Holarchy Without Injuries	Holarchy With Injuries	Straight Network	Network Hierarchy Combination	Average
Pittsburgh	0.275	0.326	0.289	0.266	0.257	0.283
Edmonton	0.273	0.206	0.216	0.241	0.249	0.237
Boston	0.258	0.281	0.294	0.248	0.248	0.266
Minnesota	0.195	0.187	0.201	0.245	0.246	0.215

1991 STANLEY CUP PLAYOFFS NETWORK

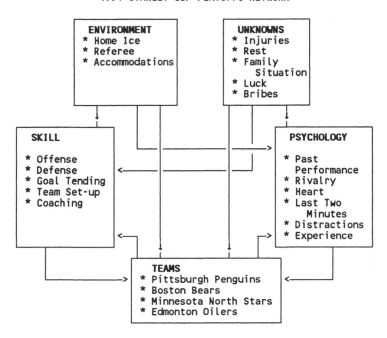

Figure 8-4 *1991 NHL Playoffs*

Example 3 - Choosing Fuel Alternatives for Cars [2]

Consider the problem of choosing, in the next decade, between fuel alternatives for motor cars from a list of leading alternative fuels. This problem can be viewed in two ways. One is to do a cost benefits analysis of the competing alternatives and determine which is best after evaluating them in light of various criteria. The result would tell us what the optimal choice might be. Another way to view the problem is to look at the various actors and forces that shape the outcome and see how they interact with each other to influence that outcome. The result would be used to predict what would be chosen rather than what would be the best choice. With the many competing actors and forces interacting with each other, the problem is a good example of a system formulation. To save on detail the network of Figure 8-5 gives a sketch of the various elements of the problem. To weight the components, we have the control hierarchy of Figure 8-6. The three factors of level two of this hierarchy are Environmental, Economic and Social impacts.

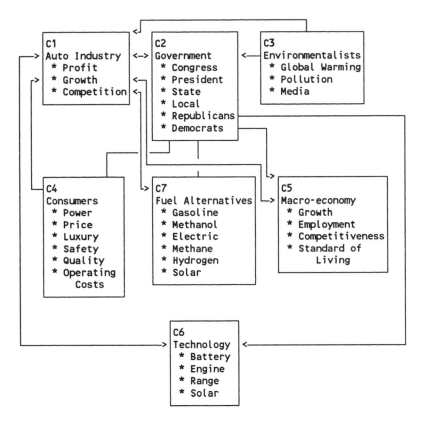

Figure 8-5 *Network*

Optimum Function of System

| Environmental | Economic | Social |

Figure 8-6 *Control Hierarchy*

The synthesized dependence priorities of the components with respect to the three criteria of the control hierarchy are shown in Table 8.3 below.

Table 8.3 The Component Weights Matrix

	AI	G	E	C	ME	T	FA
Automobile Industry	0.000	0.216	0.353	0.469	0.433	1.000	1.000
Government	0.416	0.000	0.647	0.000	0.000	0.000	0.000
Environment- alists	0.000	0.000	0.000	0.000	0.000	0.000	0.000
Consumers	0.000	0.362	0.000	0.000	0.000	0.000	0.000
Macro-Economy	0.230	0.218	0.000	0.000	0.000	0.000	0.000
Technology	0.205	0.118	0.000	0.000	0.000	0.000	0.000
Fuel Alternatives	0.149	0.176	0.000	0.000	0.000	0.000	0.000

Each column vector was used to weight the eigenvectors in the corresponding blocks of the supermatrix shown in Table 8.5. The resulting stochastic supermatrix was then raised to limiting powers (not shown here). The priorities for the various fuels were obtained from that matrix and are shown here in Table 8.3.

Table 8.4 Fuel Alternative Results

Relative Fuel Alternative Weights	
Gasoline	0.13759
Methanol	0.20030
Electric	0.21533
Methane	0.21946
Hydrogen	0.10497
Solar	0.12235

Table 8.5 Entry Key

Auto Industry -	Profit	AIP
	Growth	AIG
	Competition	AIC
Government	Congress	GC
	President	GP
	State	GS
	Local	GL
	Republican	GR
	Democrat	GD
Environmentalists	Global Warming	EGW
	Pollution	EP
	Media	EM
Consumers	Power	CPw
	Price	CPr
	Luxury	CL
	Safety	CS
	Quality	CQ
	Operating Costs	COC
Macro-Economy	Growth	MEG
	Employment	MEE
	Competitive	MEC
	Standard of Living	MESL
Technology	Battery	TB
	Range	TR
	Engine	TE
	Solar	TS
Fuel Alternatives	Gasoline	FAG
	Methanol	FAMl
	Electric	FAE
	Methane	FAMe
	Hydrogen	FAH
	Solar	FAS

Table 8.6

	AIP	AIG	AIC	GC	GP	GS	GL	GR	GD	EGW	EP	EM	CPw	CPr	...
AIP	.000	.000	.000	.075	.075	.075	.128	.582	.072	.111	.111	.157	.091	.091	...
AIG	.000	.000	.000	.696	.696	.696	.595	.309	.649	.111	.111	.249	.091	.091	...
AIC	.000	.000	.000	.229	.229	.229	.276	.109	.279	.778	.778	.594	.818	.818	...
GC	.150	.198	.360	.000	.000	.000	.000	.000	.000	.334	.235	.381	.310	.441	...
GP	.212	.161	.114	.000	.000	.000	.000	.000	.000	.334	.261	.348	.119	.188	...
GS	.130	.108	.099	.000	.000	.000	.000	.000	.000	.154	.304	.157	.310	.129	...
GL	.079	.065	.099	.000	.000	.000	.000	.000	.000	.042	.043	.097	.069	.063	...
GR	.376	.419	.296	.000	.000	.000	.000	.000	.000	.060	.070	.059	.096	.090	...
GD	.053	.049	.032	.000	.000	.000	.000	.000	.000	.075	.082	.059	.096	.090	...
EGW	.000	.000	.000	.000	.000	.000	.000	.000	.000	.000	.000	.000	.000	.000	...
EP	.000	.000	.000	.000	.000	.000	.000	.000	.000	.000	.000	.000	.000	.000	...
EM	.000	.000	.000	.000	.000	.000	.000	.000	.000	.000	.000	.000	.000	.000	...
CPW	.000	.000	.000	.047	.047	.047	.047	.047	.047	.000	.000	.000	.000	.000	...
CPr	.000	.000	.000	.212	.212	.212	.212	.212	.212	.000	.000	.000	.000	.000	...
CL	.000	.000	.000	.047	.047	.047	.047	.047	.047	.000	.000	.000	.000	.000	...
CS	.000	.000	.000	.445	.445	.445	.445	.445	.445	.000	.000	.000	.000	.000	...
CQ	.000	.000	.000	.173	.173	.173	.173	.173	.173	.000	.000	.000	.000	.000	...
COC	.000	.000	.000	.075	.075	.075	.075	.075	.075	.000	.000	.000	.000	.000	...
MEG	.504	.635	.125	.189	.321	.531	.579	.658	.296	.000	.000	.000	.000	.000	...
MEE	.096	.079	.125	.642	.453	.350	.328	.136	.614	.000	.000	.000	.000	.000	...
MEC	.347	.079	.625	.047	.083	.046	.047	.075	.045	.000	.000	.000	.000	.000	...
MESL	.053	.207	.125	.122	.143	.074	.047	.131	.045	.000	.000	.000	.000	.000	...
TB	.346	.250	.096	.313	.313	.308	.268	.313	.250	.000	.000	.000	.000	.000	...
TR	.424	.250	.190	.313	.313	.308	.268	.313	.250	.000	.000	.000	.000	.000	...
TE	.181	.250	.643	.313	.313	.308	.268	.313	.250	.000	.000	.000	.000	.000	...
TS	.049	.250	.071	.063	.063	.077	.143	.063	.250	.000	.000	.000	.000	.000	...
FAG	.404	.167	.167	.044	.049	.036	.047	.049	.036	.000	.000	.000	.000	.000	...
FAMl	.174	.167	.167	.262	.254	.180	.084	.281	.180	.000	.000	.000	.000	.000	...
FAE	.174	.167	.167	.262	.254	.352	.447	.159	.352	.000	.000	.000	.000	.000	...
FAMe	.174	.167	.167	.262	.254	.248	.091	.370	.248	.000	.000	.000	.000	.000	...
FAH	.041	.167	.167	.067	.079	.074	.143	.053	.074	.000	.000	.000	.000	.000	...
FAS	.033	.167	.167	.104	.110	.109	.209	.087	.109	.000	.000	.000	.000	.000	...

Table 8.6 (continued)

	CL	CS	CQ	COC	MEG	MEE	MEC	MESL	TB	TR	TE	TS	FAG
AIP	.091	.091	.091	.091	.218	.226	.109	.167	.333	.400	.200	.200	.333 ...
AIG	.091	.091	.091	.091	.630	.674	.163	.167	.333	.200	.117	.117	.333 ...
AIC	.818	.818	.818	.818	.151	.101	.729	.167	.333	.400	.683	.683	.333 ...
GC	.369	.441	.369	.180	.217	.275	.200	.275	.000	.000	.000	.000	.000 ...
GP	.215	.188	.215	.138	.302	.241	.272	.241	.000	.000	.000	.000	.000 ...
GS	.144	.129	.144	.433	.089	.087	.106	.087	.000	.000	.000	.000	.000 ...
GL	.072	.063	.072	.177	.057	.188	.067	.188	.000	.000	.000	.000	.000 ...
GR	.100	.090	.100	.036	.283	.156	.297	.156	.000	.000	.000	.000	.000 ...
GD	.100	.090	.100	.036	.053	.053	.058	.053	.000	.000	.000	.000	.000 ...
EGW	.000	.000	.000	.000	.000	.000	.000	.000	.000	.000	.000	.000	.000 ...
EP	.000	.000	.000	.000	.000	.000	.000	.000	.000	.000	.000	.000	.000 ...
EM	.000	.000	.000	.000	.000	.000	.000	.000	.000	.000	.000	.000	.000 ...
CPW	.000	.000	.000	.000	.000	.000	.000	.000	.000	.000	.000	.000	.000 ...
CPr	.000	.000	.000	.000	.000	.000	.000	.000	.000	.000	.000	.000	.000 ...
CL	.000	.000	.000	.000	.000	.000	.000	.000	.000	.000	.000	.000	.000 ...
CS	.000	.000	.000	.000	.000	.000	.000	.000	.000	.000	.000	.000	.000 ...
CQ	.000	.000	.000	.000	.000	.000	.000	.000	.000	.000	.000	.000	.000 ...
COC	.000	.000	.000	.000	.000	.000	.000	.000	.000	.000	.000	.000	.000 ...
MEG	.000	.000	.000	.000	.000	.000	.000	.000	.000	.000	.000	.000	.000 ...
MEE	.000	.000	.000	.000	.000	.000	.000	.000	.000	.000	.000	.000	.000 ...
MEC	.000	.000	.000	.000	.000	.000	.000	.000	.000	.000	.000	.000	.000 ...
MESL	.000	.000	.000	.000	.000	.000	.000	.000	.000	.000	.000	.000	.000 ...
TB	.000	.000	.000	.000	.000	.000	.000	.000	.000	.000	.000	.000	.000 ...
TR	.000	.000	.000	.000	.000	.000	.000	.000	.000	.000	.000	.000	.000 ...
TE	.000	.000	.000	.000	.000	.000	.000	.000	.000	.000	.000	.000	.000 ...
TS	.000	.000	.000	.000	.000	.000	.000	.000	.000	.000	.000	.000	.000 ...
FAG	.000	.000	.000	.000	.000	.000	.000	.000	.000	.000	.000	.000	.000 ...
FAMl	.000	.000	.000	.000	.000	.000	.000	.000	.000	.000	.000	.000	.000 ...
FAE	.000	.000	.000	.000	.000	.000	.000	.000	.000	.000	.000	.000	.000 ...
FAMe	.000	.000	.000	.000	.000	.000	.000	.000	.000	.000	.000	.000	.000 ...
FAH	.000	.000	.000	.000	.000	.000	.000	.000	.000	.000	.000	.000	.000 ...
FAS	.000	.000	.00	.000	.000	.000	.000	.000	.000	.000	.000	.000	.000 ...

Table 8.6 (continued)

	FAMl	FAE	FAMe	FAH	FAS
AIP	.333	.333	.333	.333	.333
AIG	.333	.333	.333	.333	.333
AIC	.333	.333	.333	.333	.333
GC	.000	.000	.000	.000	.000
GP	.000	.000	.000	.000	.000
GS	.000	.000	.000	.000	.000
GL	.000	.000	.000	.000	.000
GR	.000	.000	.000	.000	.000
GD	.000	.000	.000	.000	.000
EGW	.000	.000	.000	.000	.000
EP	.000	.000	.000	.000	.000
EM	.000	.000	.000	.000	.000
CPw	.000	.000	.000	.000	.000
CPr	.000	.000	.000	.000	.000
CL	.000	.000	.000	.000	.000
CS	.000	.000	.000	.000	.000
CQ	.000	.000	.000	.000	.000
COC	.000	.000	.000	.000	.000
MEG	.000	.000	.000	.000	.000
MEE	.000	.000	.000	.000	.000
MEC	.000	.000	.000	.000	.000
MESL	.000	.000	.000	.000	.000
TB	.000	.000	.000	.000	.000
TR	.000	.000	.000	.000	.000
TE	.000	.000	.000	.000	.000
TS	.000	.000	.000	.000	.000
FAG	.000	.000	.000	.000	.000
FAMl	.000	.000	.000	.000	.000
FAE	.000	.000	.000	.000	.000
FAMe	.000	.000	.000	.000	.000
FAH	.000	.000	.000	.000	.000
FAS	.000	.000	.000	.000	.000

Example 4 - Predicting the Market for Microcomputer CPUs

The CPU (Central Processing Unit) is the heart of the microcomputer today. We will predict the manufacturer that will dominate the market for the next five years by using information from the current literature [1].

There are three majors factors that determine the future of the CPU market -- Economic, Reputation, and Social. The importance of these factors is prioritized in the usual way and included in the superhierarchy part of Figure 8-7.

The economic factor is the most important because the majority of users are in the business or educational fields and are sensitive to the economic factor of price. Most people consider buying a computer as an investment and expect to get return in the future.

Reputation is the second factor. Even though most of the users are price sensitive, they tend to think of computer usage in the long run and are affected by the reputation of who makes the computer and its parts. Big manufacturers have a significant effect on the consumer's buying decision. Finally, we have the social factor of computers, what one's friends are using. It has the least priority.

For each factor, there are six criteria that are critical to the outcome of CPU-market prediction-- Technology, Research & Development, Price, Popularity, User, and Manufacturer. These factors are inner dependent as indicated in Figure 8-7.

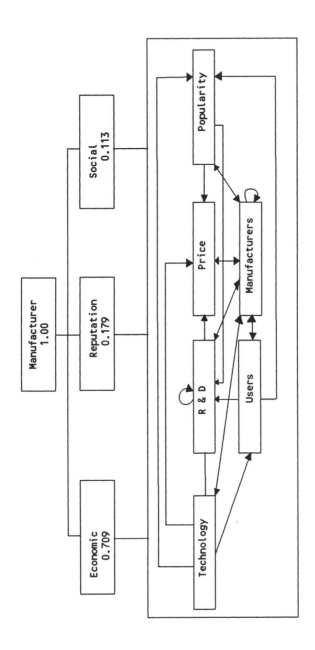

Again, an arrow from A to B means that A dominates, impacts, or contributes to B.

Figure 8-7 *Market Interaction.*

Users will choose to buy a computer which has a suitable technology and reasonable price. They can upgrade the computer without changing the major part of the system. Popularity of software is the other concern. Even though a computer is cheap and has high capability, if it is not supported by good software, users will not buy it. Moreover, the price of a computer is somewhat high. The reputation of CPU manufacturers is also crucial to ensure the reliability of the computer. Finally, users themselves are another factor in the buying decision. To share data, they prefer to buy a computer that is compatible with their friends' system.

CPU manufacturers play a major role in deciding on the current and future technology (Research & Development). They also have the power to determine the CPU price. Moreover, the relation between CPU manufacturers and companies would affect the popularity of the computer. Satisfied users tend to be loyal to the manufacturers they use to back up the high cost they pay for a computer system. Finally, competition among CPU manufacturers would affect the market. The question is who will dominate the CPU market for microcomputers in the next five years?

Current technology is also crucial for the next generation of CPU. New innovation will make computer design simpler, resulting in lower costs and lower prices. It will stimulate demand and result in greater popularity of microcomputers.

Research and development(R&D) plays an important role in the future of the microcomputer and CPU market and will affect CPU manufacturers' cost structure in the long run. It is critical for CPU manufacturers in planning their long-term strategies.

Although price is an essential buying factor for users, it does not affect the decision directly. On the other hand, users prefer to pay more money for a more expensive high performance system if that system is popular in the user market. Since a major manufacturing cost for a microcomputer is CPU cost, price is included in the model.

Finally, popularity would accelerate the sale, netting great profit to microcomputer companies. They would invest more in R&D. Moreover, the more companies build computers, the less would be the manufacturing cost because of the learning effect.

Tables 8.6a-8.6c give the column eigenvectors of matrices for the economic, reputation and social impacts respectively of the six factors on each other factor with which they interact according to Figure 8-7. What an element impacts is shown by its column entries in the supermatrix. What an element is impacted by is shown by its row entries.

Table 8.7a Weights Matrix for Economic

	Technology	R & D	Price	Popularity	Users	Manufacturers
Technology	0	.633	0	0	0	.041
R & D	.485	.197	.339	.125	.092	.067
Price	.251	.050	0	.796	.314	.235
Popularity	.173	0	0	0	.531	.167
Users	.062	0	0	0	0	.456
Manufacturers	.030	.120	.661	.079	.063	.034
Totals	1	1	1	1	1	1

Table 8.7b Weights Matrix for Reputation

	Technology	R & D	Price	Popularity	Users	Manufacturers
Technology	0	.595	0	0	0	.464
R & D	.506	.107	.344	.067	.050	.030
Price	.038	.049	0	.272	.621	.039
Popularity	.262	0	0	0	.094	.260
Users	.131	0	0	0	0	.128
Manufacturers	.063	.249	.656	.661	.235	.080
Totals	1	1	1	1	1	1

Table 8.7c Weights Matrix for Social

	Technology	R & D	Price	Popularity	Users	Manufacturers
Technology	0	.488	0	0	0	.364
R & D	.098	.373	.677	.194	.104	.077
Price	.562	.053	0	.743	.646	.132
Popularity	.090	0	0	0	.204	.039
Users	.199	0	0	0	0	.024
Manufacturers	.051	.086	.323	.063	.045	.363
Totals	1	1	1	1	1	1

Finally, there are five major innovators in the current CPU chip market-- Intel, Motorola, Advanced Micro Devices (AMD), Cyrix, and Chips and Technologies (C&T).   Intel is the leader in this field.   The company initially produced the chip for IBM. After the market boom, Intel provided the chip to IBM clone microcomputer manufacturers.   During the past five years, the other chip makers have developed their own Intel compatible CPU.

AMD was the first company to make the 80386 compatible chip.   AMD offers a variety of flexible products, including the 386SXL-25 microprocessor, a low-power device compatible with Intel's 80386SL that runs at 25-Mhz, 25 percent faster than Intel's 20-Mhz chip.   In addition, AMD offers a 40 Mhz version of the CPU, while Intel's 386 line tops out at 33 Mhz.   The success of the AMD chip has spurred the company's recovery from multimillion-dollar losses; according to industry observers, it is now reporting steady sale increases.   The price of the CPU has been decreasing dramatically because of high competition.   Intel has tried to protect its market share by developing a new generation, the CPU: 80486, P5(80586), and P6(80686).   But Intel will face strong competition.

Another chip manufacturer offering chips geared toward increased systems integration is C&T, of San Jose, California.

C&T has advocated integration. It offers "multimedia solutions" such as SuperState programmable circuits. These circuits are included in the company's Super386 clone chips, which it created without incorporating Intel designs. The SuperState circuits allow computer manufacturers to customize processors with features such as I/O (Input-Output) enhancements or software accelerators. C&T claims that with SuperState circuits, OEMs (Original Equipment Manufacturing) have more flexibility with software and hardware configurations. C&T design contrasts with Intel's design which uses a hardware approach to problems. Moreover, C&T offers a wider breadth of products than Intel. The company contends that C&T's Super386 family of products, with its systems logic, 32-bit software and price/performance, is a better microprocessor than Intel's 486SX.

Cyrix has announced that it could make an 80486 compatible chip, the CX486SLC, at a very cheap price. Its CPU is pin compatible with Intel's 386SX but has Intel's 80486SX like architecture. Moreover, in June 1992, Cyrix debuted its 32-bit 486 CPU. Cyrix plans to provide its new 25 MHz CX486DLC and its CX87DLC math coprocessor, available together to PC makers for only $119. The package with a 33 MHz or a 40MHz version of the 486 chip is priced at $159 and $199, respectively. The CX486DLC chip is similar to the CX486SLC processor that the company introduced in April 1992, but it has a full 32-bit design. Like the first iteration, it includes a 1K-byte of cache, rather than the 8K-byte cache on Intel's 486SX. Moreover, the CPU, which is pin compatible with the 386DX, offers 486SX-like performance, and will sell for $99 at 25 MHz, $119 at 33MHz and $159 at 40MHz.

In contrast, Intels 25MHz and 33MHz 486DX chips list for $406. Cyrix claims that its DLC, coupled with the math coprocessor, will give them competition. So far, systems makers that have adopted the 486SLC-- including Zeos International Inc., Wyse Technology, MicroSlate Inc., and PC Brands-- find Cyrix's 32-bit chip appealing. Moreover, Cyrix is also considering selling its new 32-bit 486DLC processor directly to PC users in much the same way Intel sells its OverDrive chips.

Motorola is the other major CPU manufacturer. Instead of producing X86 Intel compatible CPU, Motorola designs its own CPU. Though competition in the personal computer (PC) is less direct, still, the rivalry continues. As the two leading CISC (complex instruction set computer) processors, comparisons between the Intel 80486 and the Motorola 68040 are inevitable. In many ways the two are well matched. Each was constrained to be user-mode compatible with its forerunners. Each provides an integer unit, floating-point compatible with its memory-management system, and 8K bytes of cache on-chip. Each consumes 1.2 million transistors, and each initially runs at 25 MHz. In addition to technological comparison, Motorola provides the CPU for Apple Computer Inc. to produce the Macintosh computer, so successful in the educational market. Moreover, IBM is planning to join Motorola to develop a new generation CPU for future microcomputers.

Since there are five major CPU specialized companies as described above in the current market, we must prioritize them with respect to each of the six criteria; Technology, R&D, Price, Popularity, Users, and Manufacturers and also among themselves for each of the three major factors with which we began. The eigenvectors of the paired comparison are entered in the appropriate blocks of the three super matrices given below.

Tables 8.8 & 8.9 Entry Key

Technology	T
R & D	R
Price	PR
Popularity	PO
Users	U
Manufacturers -	
Motorola	MM
Cyrix	MCY
C & T	MCT
Intel	MI
AMD	MA

Table 8.8a Unweighted Supermatrix for Economic

	T	R	PR	PO	U	MM	MCY	MCT	MI	MA
T	.000	.633	.000	.000	.000	.041	.041	.041	.041	.041
R	.485	.197	.339	.125	.092	.067	.067	.067	.067	.067
PR	.250	.050	.000	.796	.314	.235	.235	.235	.235	.235
PO	.173	.000	.000	.000	.531	.167	.167	.167	.167	.167
U	.062	.000	.000	.000	.000	.456	.456	.456	.456	.456
MM	.426	.509	.141	.333	.213	.518	.061	.314	.065	.065
MCY	.041	.098	.384	.081	.342	.067	.561	.055	.252	.132
MCT	.059	.032	.040	.027	.025	.121	.035	.293	.036	.036
MI	.382	.287	.168	.442	.208	.253	.220	.309	.515	.252
MA	.093	.073	.266	.117	.212	.040	.124	.030	.132	.515

Table 8.8b Unweighted Supermatrix for Reputation

	T	R	PR	PO	U	MM	MCY	MCT	MI	MA
T	.000	.595	.000	.000	.000	.464	.464	.464	.464	.464
R	.506	.107	.344	.067	.050	.030	.030	.030	.030	.030
PR	.038	.049	.000	.272	.621	.039	.039	.039	.039	.039
PO	.262	.000	.000	.000	.094	.260	.260	.260	.260	.260
U	.131	.000	.000	.000	.000	.128	.128	.128	.128	.128
MM	.250	.519	.065	.257	.492	.510	.058	.294	.062	.067
MCY	.062	.064	.252	.126	.289	.079	.552	.051	.243	.125
MCT	.118	.131	.036	.030	.122	.131	.035	.328	.039	.040
MI	.537	.250	.515	.525	.061	.239	.221	.300	.521	.244
MA	.033	.035	.132	.062	.036	.041	.134	.028	.135	.525

Table 8.8c - Unweighted Supermatrix for Social

	T	R	PR	PO	U	MM	MCY	MCT	MI	MA
T	.000	.488	.000	.000	.000	.364	.364	.364	.364	.364
R	.098	.373	.677	.194	.104	.077	.077	.077	.077	.077
PR	.562	.053	.000	.743	.646	.132	.132	.132	.132	.132
PO	.090	.000	.000	.000	.204	.039	.039	.039	.039	.039
U	.199	.000	.000	.000	.000	.024	.024	.024	.024	.024
MM	.496	.463	.513	.337	.416	.514	.060	.214	.173	.088
MCY	.036	.106	.129	.082	.245	.097	.536	.052	.171	.145
MCT	.070	.034	.261	.034	.047	.043	.033	.516	.036	.034
MI	.264	.321	.033	.421	.088	.276	.257	.167	.454	.368
MA	.134	.077	.063	.126	.204	.070	.114	.051	.166	.365

The matrices in Tables 8.8a-8.8c can be classified into four blocks. Different questions are asked for each block to derive the eigenvectors. We ask: given a particular criterion, which of the other criteria has the greatest impact on it with respect to a particular factor -- economic, reputation, and social -- for the upper-left corner block? The same question is used for the upper-right block but the same numbers are assigned to all columns in this block because the CPU manufacturers are in the same environment and tend to prioritize the criteria in the same way. Since there are no subcriteria in both upper-left and upper-right corners, the eigenvectors must be the same as those in Table 7. The assumption can be changed if we think that different manufacturers prioritize the criteria differently. In this case, we have to ask the same question as we ask for the upper-right block of every manufacturer. For the third block located in the lower-left hand corner we ask: which manufacturer is the most important with respect to a particular criterion -- Technology, R&D, Price, Popularity, and Users. We do this once for each supermatrix relative to its corresponding factor: economic, reputation, social. For the fourth block in the lower-right corner, the question to ask is, for a particular manufacturer, which manufacturer poses the greatest concern to that manufacturer.

The matrices in Tables 8.8a-8.8c must be weighted so that the sum of each column is equal to one. The weighted matrix is obtained by weighting each subcolumn in a block corresponding to the number in the weights matrix (Tables 8.7a-8.7c) for each factor. The resulting matrices are shown in Tables 8.9a-8.9c.

Table 8.9a - Weighted Supermatrix for Economic

	T	R	PR	PO	U	MM	MCY	MCT	MI	MA
T	.00000	.63300	.00000	.00000	.00000	.04100	.04100	.04100	.04100	.04100
R	.48499	.19700	.33966	.12500	.09200	.06703	.06700	.06700	.06700	.06700
PR	.24999	.05012	.00000	.79600	.31400	.23500	.23500	.23500	.23500	.23500
PO	.17299	.00000	.00000	.00000	.53100	.16700	.16700	.16700	.16700	.16700
U	.06200	.00000	.00000	.00000	.00000	.45600	.45597	.45597	.45597	.45597
MM	.01278	.04608	.09320	.02631	.01342	.01761	.00207	.01068	.00221	.00221
MCY	.00123	.01176	.25382	.00640	.02155	.00228	.01907	.00187	.00857	.00449
MCT	.00177	.00384	.02644	.00213	.00158	.00411	.00119	.00996	.00125	.00125
MI	.01146	.04944	.11105	.03492	.01310	.00860	.00748	.01051	.01751	.00857
MA	.00279	.00876	.17583	.00924	.01336	.00136	.00422	.00102	.00449	.01751
Total	1	1	1	1	1	1	1	1	1	1

Table 8.9b - Weighted Supermatrix for Reputation

	T	R	PR	PO	U	MM	MCY	MCT	MI	MA
T	.00000	.59500	.00000	.00000	.00000	.46300	.46300	.46300	.46300	.46300
R	.50600	.10700	.34400	.06700	.05000	.03000	.03000	.03000	.03000	.03000
PR	.03800	.04925	.00000	.27200	.62100	.03900	.03900	.03900	.03900	.03900
PO	.26200	.00000	.00000	.00000	.09400	.26000	.26000	.26000	.26000	.26000
U	.13100	.00000	.00000	.00000	.00000	.12800	.12800	.12800	.12800	.12800
MM	.01575	.12923	.04264	.16988	.11562	.04080	.00464	.02352	.00496	.00536
MCY	.00391	.01594	.16531	.08329	.06791	.00632	.04416	.00408	.01944	.01000
MCT	.00743	.03262	.02362	.01983	.02867	.01048	.00280	.02616	.00312	.00320
MI	.03383	.06225	.33784	.34703	.01434	.01912	.01768	.02400	.04168	.01952
MA	.00208	.00872	.08659	.04098	.00846	.00328	.01072	.00204	.01080	.04192
Total	1	1	1	1	1	1	1	1	1	1

Table 8.9c - Weighted Supermatrix for Social

	T	R	PR	PO	U	MM	MCY	MCT	MI	MA
T	.00000	.48791	.00000	.00000	.00000	.36400	.36400	.36400	.36400	.36400
R	.09800	.37300	.67732	.19400	.10500	.07700	.07700	.07700	.07700	.07700
PR	.56200	.05300	.00000	.74300	.64600	.13200	.13200	.13200	.13200	.13200
PO	.09000	.00000	.00000	.00000	.20400	.03900	.03900	.03900	.03900	.03900
U	.19900	.00000	.00000	.00000	.00000	.02400	.02400	.02400	.02400	.02400
MM	.02530	.03982	.16570	.02123	.01872	.18658	.02178	.07768	.06280	.03194
MCY	.00184	.00912	.04167	.00517	.01103	.03521	.19457	.01888	.06207	.05264
MCT	.00357	.00292	.08430	.00214	.00212	.01661	.01298	.18831	.01407	.01334
MI	.01346	.02761	.01066	.02652	.00396	.10019	.09329	.06062	.16480	.13358
MA	.00683	.00662	.02035	.00794	.00918	.02541	.04138	.01851	.06026	.13250
Total	1	1	1	1	1	1	1	1	1	1

After weighting, each matrix is raised to powers to obtain the steady state solution shown in Tables 8.10a-8.10c. Each supermatrix is then multiplied by the priority of its factor from the superhierarchy and the three results are added to give the combined result shown in Table 8.11.

Table 8.10a - Steady State Supermatrix for Economic

	T	R	PR	PO	U	MM	MCY	MCT	MI	MA
T	.15215	.15215	.15215	.15215	.15215	.15215	.15215	.15215	.15215	.15215
R	.22771	.22771	.22771	.22771	.22771	.22771	.22771	.22771	.22771	.22771
PR	.21489	.21489	.21489	.21489	.21489	.21489	.21489	.21489	.21489	.21489
PO	.11128	.11128	.11128	.11128	.11128	.11128	.11128	.11128	.11128	.11128
U	.09854	.09854	.09854	.09854	.09854	.09854	.09854	.09854	.09854	.09854
MM	.03779	.03779	.03779	.03779	.03779	.03779	.03779	.03779	.03779	.03779
MCY	.06210	.06210	.06210	.06210	.06210	.06210	.06210	.06210	.06210	.06210
MCT	.00763	.00763	.00763	.00763	.00763	.00763	.00763	.00763	.00763	.00763
MI	.04406	.04406	.04406	.04406	.04406	.04406	.04406	.04406	.04406	.04406
MA	.04383	.04383	.04383	.04383	.04383	.04383	.04383	.04383	.04383	.04383
Total	1	1	1	1	1	1	1	1	1	1

Table 8.10b - Steady State Supermatrix for Reputation

	T	R	PR	PO	U	MM	MCY	MCT	MI	MA
T	.23761	.23761	.23761	.23761	.23761	.23761	.23761	.23761	.23761	.23761
R	.19783	.19783	.19783	.19783	.19783	.19783	.19783	.19783	.19783	.19783
PR	.10568	.10568	.10568	.10568	.10568	.10568	.10568	.10568	.10568	.10568
PO	.13563	.13563	.13563	.13563	.13563	.13563	.13563	.13563	.13563	.13563
U	.06428	.06428	.06428	.06428	.06428	.06428	.06428	.06428	.06428	.06428
MM	.06833	.06833	.06833	.06833	.06833	.06833	.06833	.06833	.06833	.06833
MCY	.04194	.04194	.04194	.04194	.04194	.04194	.04194	.04194	.04194	.04194
MCT	.01694	.01694	.01694	.01694	.01694	.01694	.01694	.01694	.01694	.01694
MI	.11154	.11154	.11154	.11154	.11154	.11154	.11154	.11154	.11154	.11154
MA	.02024	.02024	.02024	.02024	.02024	.02024	.02024	.02024	.02024	.02024
Total	1	1	1	1	1	1	1	1	1	1

Table 8.10c - Steady State Supermatrix for Social

	T	R	PR	PO	U	MM	MCY	MCT	MI	MA
T	.21479	.21479	.21479	.21479	.21479	.21479	.21479	.21479	.21479	.21479
R	.30883	.30883	.30883	.30883	.30883	.30883	.30883	.30883	.30883	.30883
PR	.21726	.21726	.21726	.21726	.21726	.21726	.21726	.21726	.21726	.21726
PO	.03578	.03578	.03578	.03578	.03578	.03578	.03578	.03578	.03578	.03578
U	.04697	.04697	.04697	.04697	.04697	.04697	.04697	.04697	.04697	.04697
MM	.07460	.07460	.07460	.07460	.07460	.07460	.07460	.07460	.07460	.07460
MCY	.02369	.02369	.02369	.02369	.02369	.02369	.02369	.02369	.02369	.02369
MCT	.02760	.02760	.02760	.02760	.02760	.02760	.02760	.02760	.02760	.02760
MI	.03400	.03400	.03400	.03400	.03400	.03400	.03400	.03400	.03400	.03400
MA	.01624	.01624	.01624	.01624	.01624	.01624	.01624	.01624	.01624	.01624
Total	1	1	1	1	1	1	1	1	1	1

We obtain for the manufacturers the following normalized priorities:

Table 8.11 Final Prediction.

Manufacturers

MOTOROLA	CYRIX	C & T	INTEL	AMD
.23	.26	.06	.27	.18

It should be noted that the outcome for C&T seems to be lower than one might expect.

At present, Intel continues as the leader in the CPU market. Simultaneously, Cyrix is investing heavily in R&D to produce Intel's X86 compatible and has aggressively cut the CPU price to gain a market share.   Motorola is trying to protect itself by redesigning its CPU to support Apple Computer to gain a larger market share in the business sector. AMD is also busy upgrading its product to the 80486 compatible version. The company plans to launch a new 80486 compatible chip in December 1992. Moreover, C&T is trying to gain microcomputer manufacturer support. So far, only Epson computer has begun to use C&T's super 386 in its product.

The final outcome shows that Intel will continue to dominate the CPU market for microcomputers for the next five years. The result is not surprising. However, it has not been clear that Cyrix will rank second in this market. Since there are many factors and criteria to determine who is going to win, it is difficult to predict the future outcome from the current situation directly. The supermatrix condenses the current situation and the interaction among the criteria.

Example 4 References

1. Computer Shopper, June 1992 p569.
2. Government Computer News, May 27 1991 v10 n11 p64(1).
3. Microprocessor Report, April 18 1990 v4 n7 p16(2).

4. Microprocessor Report, October 17 1990 v4 n18 p3(1).
5. Microprocessor Report, February 6 1991 v5 n2 p3(3).
6. PC Week, November 11 1991 v8 n45 pS27(2).
7. PC Week, June 8 1992 v9 n23 p33,38.

9. The Supermatrix and Bayes Theorem [13]

Bayes theory [3,8] has contributed greatly to decision making by providing a paradigm with which information, encoded in the form of probabilities, is updated. It is based on the assumption that decisions involving uncertainty can only be made with the help of information about the environment in which the decision is made. The vehicle by means of which Bayes theory updates information is Bayes theorem. It is a statement in conditional probabilities relating causes or states of nature to outcomes, the results of experiments used to uncover those causes. It revises or maps the prior probabilities of causes into posterior probabilities by using the outcome of an experiment. Prior probabilities are obtained either subjectively or empirically by sampling the frequency of occurrence of a cause in a population. Posterior probabilities are those based on the prior probabilities, and on both the outcome of the experiment and on the observed reliability of that experiment.

In medical diagnostics the symptoms (effects) of a probable disease (cause) are usually many and not always independent. The real situation is that there are multiple effects that depend on each other in such a way that an experiment to understand one symptom (effect) may bias the results of another experiment on other symptoms. In the case of two symptoms for example, an experiment performed on one symptom may be affected by a prior experiment on the other symptom. In addition, data may not be available on both effects together and on their result from a given cause. Charniak and McDermott [4, p.464] write:

"... to use Bayesian statistics the way we have, one

must make very strong assumptions about the independence of symptoms, and the independence of symptoms given diseases. "

Consider the example of an individual who needs both liver and heart transplants. A condition of the liver can affect the heart and hence it may not be known whether the cause of the illness is a disease of the liver alone or of both the liver and the heart. Bayes theory is inadequate to solve such problems. Doctors at Presbyterian Hospital, of the University of Pittsburgh, a center for organ transplantations, perform procedures that give rise to such questions.

We now provide a framework for dealing with statistical decisions with such dependencies. We show that this framework includes Bayes Theory as a special case. To do this we need to introduce concepts related to Markov processes and column stochastic matrices. These concepts have a natural setting in decision making involving priorities and dependencies. That setting is a simple generalization of decisions involving independent causes and effects which use hierarchic structures.

In the context of Bayes theory, the AHP can be used to link prior probabilities and the probabilities of the outcomes from an experiment. Consider a hierarchy consisting of three levels: the goal, the states of nature (Θ) and the outcomes of the experiment (**X**). Let $P(\Theta)$ be the column vector of prior probabilities and let $P(\Theta)$ coincide with the priorities of the states of nature under the goal in the hierarchy. Let $P(\mathbf{X}|\Theta)$ be the matrix of likelihoods, and let it coincide with the priorities of the outcomes according to the states of nature. Hierarchic composition yields priorities of the outcomes in the form:

$$P(X) = P(X|\Theta) \, P(\Theta).$$

This form coincides with the probabilities of the outcomes as obtained under probability rules. What we need in this framework is a way to represent the dependence of causes on outcomes and generalize it to the case of dependence of outcomes on other outcomes. In its simplest form, this type of dependence involves inversion of a hierarchy (turning it upside-down) and evaluating states of nature in terms of outcomes, precisely the reverse of what we have just done in synthesizing the impact of outcomes in terms of states of nature.

Bayes Theorem, A Special Case of the Independence of Effects

Consider the network of Figure 8-8 consisting of four nodes. Let $P_1 = P(L_1)$ be the column vector of impacts of G_1 on the node L_1, let $P_{21} = P(L_2|L_1)$ be the column stochastic matrix of impacts of the node L_1 on the node L_2, let $P_{12} = P(L_1|L_2)$ be the column stochastic matrix of impacts of the elements of L_2 on the elements of L_1, and let $P_2 = P(L_2)$ be the column vector of impacts of G_2 on L_2.

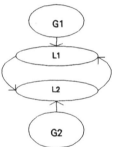

Figure 8-8 *The Bayes Loop*

The supermatrix corresponding to this feedback network is given by:

$$W = \begin{array}{c} \\ L_1 \\ L_2 \\ G_1 \\ G_2 \end{array} \begin{array}{cccc} L_1 & L_2 & G_1 & G_2 \\ \begin{bmatrix} 0 & P_{12} & P_1 & 0 \\ P_{21} & 0 & 0 & P_2 \\ 0 & 0 & 0 & 0 \\ 0 & 0 & 0 & 0 \end{bmatrix} \end{array} \qquad (1)$$

Theorem 8-10 *Given W, there exist two unique vectors $\overline{a}$ and $\overline{b}$ that satisfy:*

$$P_{12}\,\overline{b} = \overline{a} \qquad and \qquad P_{21}\,\overline{a} = \overline{b}. \qquad (2)$$

Proof For a column stochastic reducible matrix W, the limiting impact priorities [6, 10] are given by:

$$W^\infty = (I - W)^{-1}\psi(1)/\psi'(1) = \frac{\psi(1)}{\psi'(1)}\sum_{k=0}^{\infty} W^k, \quad |W| < 1 \qquad (3)$$

where $\Psi(\lambda)$ is the minimum polynomial of W and $\Psi'(\lambda)$ is its first derivative with respect to λ.

We decompose the sum on the right into odd powers:

$$W^{2k+1} = \begin{bmatrix} 0 & P_{12}[P_{21}P_{12}]^k & [P_{12}P_{21}]^kP_1 & 0 \\ P_{21}[P_{12}P_{21}]^k & 0 & 0 & [P_{21}P_{12}]^kP_2 \\ 0 & 0 & 0 & 0 \\ 0 & 0 & 0 & 0 \end{bmatrix}$$

and even powers:

$$W^{2k} = \begin{bmatrix} [P_{12}P_{21}]^k & 0 & 0 & [P_{12}P_{21}]^kP_{12}P_2 \\ 0 & [P_{21}P_{12}]^k & [P_{21}P_{12}]^kP_{21}P_1 & 0 \\ 0 & 0 & 0 & 0 \\ 0 & 0 & 0 & 0 \end{bmatrix}$$

from which we obtain:

$$W^\infty = \frac{\psi(1)}{\psi'(1)}\sum_{k=0}^{\infty}(W^{2k+1}+W^{2k}) = \frac{1}{2}\begin{bmatrix} A & P_{12}B & AP_1 & AP_{12}P_2 \\ P_{21}A & B & BP_{21}P_1 & BP_2 \\ 0 & 0 & 0 & 0 \\ 0 & 0 & 0 & 0 \end{bmatrix} \qquad (4)$$

where $\quad A = \displaystyle\sum_{k=0}^{\infty} [P_{12}P_{21}]^k \quad and \quad B = \displaystyle\sum_{k=0}^{\infty} [P_{21}P_{12}]^k$

The stochasticity of W implies that the columns of W^∞ are identical [6]. It follows that all columns of A and of B are identical. This implies that if $e_n^T = (1, \ldots, 1)$ and $e_m^T = (1, \ldots, 1)$ are row vectors of dimension n and m, respectively, then:

$$A = \bar{a}e_n^T, \qquad and \qquad B = \bar{b}e_m^T$$

where $\bar{a} = (a_1, \ldots, a_n)^T$ and $\bar{b} = (b_1, \ldots, b_m)^T$. To show that $\bar{a}$ and $\bar{b}$ satisfy (2), we equate the first column of A to the first column of $P_{12}B$, and also the first column of $P_{21}A$ to the first column of B. This yields:

$$P_{12}\,\bar{b} = \bar{a} \qquad and \qquad P_{21}\,\bar{a} = \bar{b}.$$

By construction both vectors are unique.   ∎

Note that the system of equations (2), can be represented as an eigenvalue problem in the following form:

$$\begin{bmatrix} 0 & P_{12} \\ P_{21} & 0 \end{bmatrix} \begin{bmatrix} \bar{a} \\ \bar{b} \end{bmatrix} = \begin{bmatrix} \bar{a} \\ \bar{b} \end{bmatrix} \tag{5}$$

We rewrite (5) in the form:

$$\begin{bmatrix} 0 & P_{12} \\ P_{21} & 0 \end{bmatrix} \begin{bmatrix} \Delta A & 0 \\ 0 & \Delta B \end{bmatrix} \begin{bmatrix} e_n \\ e_m \end{bmatrix} = \begin{bmatrix} \Delta A & 0 \\ 0 & \Delta B \end{bmatrix} \begin{bmatrix} e_n \\ e_m \end{bmatrix} \tag{6}$$

where

$$\Delta A = \begin{bmatrix} a_1 & \ldots & 0 \\ & \ddots & \\ 0 & \ldots & a_n \end{bmatrix}, \quad \Delta B = \begin{bmatrix} b_1 & \ldots & 0 \\ & \ddots & \\ 0 & \ldots & b_m \end{bmatrix}, \quad \bar{a} = \Delta A\, e_n \quad and \quad \bar{b} = \Delta B\, e_m$$

or

$$\begin{bmatrix} 0 & P_{12}(\Delta B) \\ P_{21}(\Delta A) & 0 \end{bmatrix} \begin{bmatrix} e_n \\ e_m \end{bmatrix} = \begin{bmatrix} \Delta A & 0 \\ 0 & \Delta B \end{bmatrix} \begin{bmatrix} e_n \\ e_m \end{bmatrix} \tag{7}$$

If we multiply both sides of (7) by

$$\begin{bmatrix} \Delta A & 0 \\ 0 & \Delta B \end{bmatrix}^{-1}$$

we have:

$$\begin{bmatrix} (\Delta A)^{-1} & 0 \\ 0 & (\Delta B)^{-1} \end{bmatrix} \begin{bmatrix} 0 & P_{12}(\Delta B) \\ P_{21}(\Delta A) & 0 \end{bmatrix} \begin{bmatrix} e_n \\ e_m \end{bmatrix} = \begin{bmatrix} e_n \\ e_m \end{bmatrix}$$

or

$$\begin{bmatrix} 0 & (\Delta A)^{-1}P_{12}(\Delta B) \\ (\Delta B)^{-1}P_{21}(\Delta A) & 0 \end{bmatrix} \begin{bmatrix} e_n \\ e_m \end{bmatrix} = \begin{bmatrix} e_n \\ e_m \end{bmatrix} \tag{8}$$

Theorem 8-11 *A necessary and sufficient condition for (5) to have a solution is that:*

$$P_{12} = (\Delta A)P_{21}^{T}(\Delta B)^{-1} \tag{9}$$

Proof (Necessity) If for some Q_{12}, (5) is true, i.e.,

$$\begin{bmatrix} 0 & Q_{12} \\ P_{21} & 0 \end{bmatrix} \begin{bmatrix} \bar{a} \\ \bar{b} \end{bmatrix} = \begin{bmatrix} \bar{a} \\ \bar{b} \end{bmatrix} \tag{10}$$

but (9) is false, i.e.,

$$Q_{12}^{T} \neq (\Delta B)^{-1}P_{21}(\Delta A)$$

then

$$(\Delta B)Q_{12}^T \neq P_{21}(\Delta A)$$

Multiplying by e_n on both sides we have:

$$(\Delta B)Q_{12}^T e_n \neq P_{21}(\Delta A)e_n \tag{11}$$

Substituting $Q_{12}^T e_n = e_m$ in (11), we obtain:

$$P_{21}(\Delta A)e_n \neq (\Delta B)e_m$$

or

$$P_{21}\overline{a} \neq \overline{b}$$

contradicting (5).

(Sufficiency) If (9) is true, then on multiplying both sides on the right by $(\Delta B)e_m$ we obtain:

$$P_{12}\overline{b} = (\Delta A)P_{21}^T e_m$$

or

$$P_{12}(\Delta B)e_m = (\Delta A)P_{21}^T e_m$$

Similarly, transposing (9) and multiplying both sides on the left by ΔB, and on the right by e_n we obtain:

$$(\Delta B)P_{12}^T e_n = P_{21}(\Delta A)e_n$$

From

$$\begin{pmatrix} 0 & P_{21}^T \\ P_{12}^T & 0 \end{pmatrix}\begin{pmatrix} e_n \\ e_m \end{pmatrix} = \begin{pmatrix} e_n \\ e_m \end{pmatrix} \tag{12}$$

we have:

$$P_{12}\overline{b} = (\Delta A)e_n = \overline{a}$$

$$P_{21}\overline{a} = (\Delta B)e_m = \overline{b}$$

and (5) is true. ∎

Assume now that $L_1 \equiv \theta = \{\theta_1, \theta_2, ..., \theta_n\}$ is the space of states of nature (e.g., consequences of actions), and let $L_2 \equiv X = \{x_1, x_2, ..., x_m\}$ be the sample space from which observations are drawn at random. Let $P_{12} \equiv P(\theta|X) = (P[\theta_i|X=x_j])$ be the $n \times m$ column stochastic matrix of posterior probabilities, let $P_{21} \equiv P(X|\theta) = (P[X=x_j|\theta_i])$ be the $m \times n$ column stochastic matrix of likelihoods, and let $P_1 \equiv P(\theta)$ be the $n \times 1$ vector of prior probabilities.

Theorem 8-12 *Given W, if $P(X) \equiv P_2 = P(X|\theta)P(\theta)$, then:*
$$P(\theta|X)P(X) = P(\theta) \tag{13}$$

Proof From Theorem 8-10 we have $\overline{a} = P(\theta)$, and from (2) we have $P(X) = \overline{b}$, and the result obtains. ∎

Let

$$\Delta P(\theta) = \begin{pmatrix} P(\theta_1) & 0 & \cdots & 0 \\ \vdots & \vdots & \ddots & \vdots \\ 0 & 0 & \cdots & P(\theta_n) \end{pmatrix} \quad and \quad \Delta P(X) = \begin{pmatrix} P(X=x_1) & 0 & \cdots \\ \vdots & \vdots & \ddots \\ 0 & 0 & \cdots \end{pmatrix}$$

Theorem 8-13 *Given W, if $P(X) \equiv P_2 = P(X|\theta)P(\theta)$ then:*
$$P(\theta|X) = \Delta P(\theta)P(X|\theta)^T \Delta P(X)^{-1} \tag{14}$$

Proof From Theorem 8-10 we must also have $P(\theta|X)P(X) = P(\theta)$ yielding (5), and (14) follows from Theorem 8-11. ∎

Equation (14) is the matrix form of Bayes' theorem:

$$P(\theta_i|X=x_j) = \frac{P(X=x_j|\theta_i)P(\theta_i)}{P(X=x_j)} = \frac{P(X=x_j|\theta_i)P(\theta_i)}{\sum_{j=1}^{m} P(X=x_j|\theta_i)P(\theta_i)}$$

As with Bayes' theorem, the foregoing easily generalizes to the case of hierarchical priors.

Note that the assumption $P(X) = P(X|\theta)P(\theta)$ is a consequence of the definition of conditional probability:

$$P(X|\theta) \equiv \frac{P(X \cap \theta)}{P(\theta)}.$$

on which Bayes' theorem is based, in contrast to Theorem 8-10 which follows from the network model used to represent interactions among nodes, and hence, is independent of the idea of conditional probability.

Simple Example

Consider the following problem which appeared in the Economist, July 4, 1992, p. 74: If a test to detect a disease, whose prevalence is 1/1,000, has a false-positive rate of 5%, what is the chance that a person found to have a positive result actually has the disease, assuming that one knows nothing about the person's symptoms? The supermatrix is given by:

	D	NoD	+	−	G_1	G_2
Disease (D)	0	0	$P(\theta_1|x_1)$	$P(\theta_1|x_2)$	.001	0
NoDisease (NoD)	0	0	$P(\theta_2|x_1)$	$P(\theta_2|x_2)$	.999	0
Positive (+)	.95	.05	0	0	0	.0509
Negative(−)	.05	.95	0	0	0	.9491
G_1	0	0	0	0	0	0
G_2	0	0	0	0	0	0

$W = $ (matrix above)

where

$$P(X|\theta)P(\theta) = \begin{bmatrix} .95 & .05 \\ .05 & .95 \end{bmatrix} \begin{bmatrix} .001 \\ .999 \end{bmatrix} = \begin{bmatrix} .0509 \\ .9491 \end{bmatrix}.$$

To compute the probability that a person with a positive test actually has the disease we must find the matrix $P(\theta|X)$. The (1,1) entry of this matrix would be the desired result. We have:

$$P(\theta|X) = \overset{\Delta P(\theta)}{\begin{bmatrix} .001 & 0 \\ 0 & .999 \end{bmatrix}} \overset{P(X\&\theta)^T}{\begin{bmatrix} .95 & .05 \\ .05 & .95 \end{bmatrix}} \overset{\Delta P(X)^{-1}}{\begin{bmatrix} 1/.0509 & 0 \\ 0 & 1/.9491 \end{bmatrix}} = \begin{bmatrix} .01866 & .00005 \\ .98134 & .99995 \end{bmatrix}$$

and the desired probability is equal to 0.01866.

The powers of the supermatrix W with the (1,2) block $P(\theta|X)$ converge to the limiting probabilities given by the prior probability vector augmented with the probability vector of outcomes from the experiment:

		D	NoD	+	−	G_1	G_2
	Disease (D)	0.0005	0.0005	0.0005	0.0005	0.0005	0.0005
	NoDisease (NoD)	0.4995	0.4995	0.4995	0.4995	0.4995	0.4995
W =	Positive (+)	0.02545	0.02545	0.02545	0.02545	0.02545	0.02545
	Negative(−)	0.47455	0.47455	0.47455	0.47455	0.47455	0.47455
	G_1	0	0	0	0	0	0
	G_2	0	0	0	0	0	0

This combined vector is normalized to unity so that the matrix is column stochastic.

Beyond Bayes Theorem

The foregoing formulation can be extended to more general situations. Consider two non-mutually exclusive symptoms of a disease (D): a heart symptom (H), and a liver symptom (L). Assume that among the people who have the heart symptom, 5 percent have a negative result from a test (H-) when they have the disease, and 5 percent have a positive result from a test (H+) when they do not have the disease. For the population affected by the liver symptom, for those who have the disease, the probabilities of obtaining positive and negative results from a test are the same as for the heart symptom. If an individual has positive (negative) results from the test, does he have (not have) the disease if he has both symptoms?

This problem can be analyzed as two separate Bayes problems, with <u>contradictory conclusions</u>. Let us see how. The supermatrix of this problem is given by:

$$
W = \begin{array}{c} \\ \Theta \\ Heart \\ Liver \\ H+- \\ L+- \end{array}
\left[\begin{array}{c|cccc}
 & \Theta & H \quad L \quad H\pm \quad L\pm \\
\hline
0 & P_1 \quad Q_1 \quad P_{12} \quad Q_{12} \\
0 & 0 \quad 0 \quad 0 \quad 0 \\
0 & 0 \quad 0 \quad 0 \quad 0 \\
\alpha P_{21} & 0 \quad 0 \quad 0 \quad 0 \\
(1-\alpha)Q_{21} & 0 \quad 0 \quad 0 \quad 0
\end{array}\right]
$$

where Θ = {Disease, No Disease}, P_1 and Q_1 are the prior probabilities of having the disease or not having the disease with the heart symptom and with the liver symptom respectively (see below); α is the relative importance of the results of the people with the heart symptom versus the people with the liver symptom. The other blocks of W are given by:

$$
P_{21} = Q_{21} = \begin{bmatrix} 0.95 & 0.05 \\ 0.05 & 0.95 \end{bmatrix}
$$

$$
P_{12} = \begin{bmatrix} 0.0187 & 0.00005 \\ 0.9813 & 0.99995 \end{bmatrix} \quad and \quad Q_{12} = \begin{bmatrix} 0.6786 & 0.0058 \\ 0.3214 & 0.9942 \end{bmatrix}.
$$

P_{12} and Q_{12} are the posterior probabilities corresponding to the

likelihoods P_{21} and Q_{21}, for the priors P_1 and Q_1, respectively.
Note that if the results of the test with the heart symptom are used,
the chance of having the disease is 1.87 percent in contrast with
67.86 percent if the liver symptom is considered. This provides
inconclusive evidence about the disease.

For $\alpha = 0.5$, we have:

		D	NoD	H	L	H+	H−	L+	L−
	Disease	0	0	0.001	0.1	0.0187	0.0001	0.6786	0.0058
	NoDisease	0	0	0.999	0.9	0.9813	0.9999	0.3214	0.9945
	Heart	0	0	0	0	0	0	0	0
$W =$	Liver	0	0	0	0	0	0	0	0
	H+	0.475	0.025	0	0	0	0	0	0
	H−	0.025	0.475	0	0	0	0	0	0
	L+	0.475	0.025	0	0	0	0	0	0
	L−	0.025	0.475	0	0	0	0	0	0

Because W is reducible and periodic with period 2, W^∞ is given
by:

$$W^\infty = \frac{1}{2} (I + W) \lim_{n \to \infty} \left(W^2\right)^n$$

and we obtain:

$$W^\infty = \begin{pmatrix} 0.0073 \\ 0.2427 \\ 0 \\ 0 \\ 0.0287 \\ 0.3463 \\ 0.0287 \\ 0.3463 \end{pmatrix} \begin{pmatrix} 1 & 1 & 1 & 1 & 1 & 1 & 1 & 1 \end{pmatrix} = w^\infty e^T$$

Once normalized to unity, the first two components of w^∞ on the right correspond to the prior probabilities; the fifth and sixth components correspond to $P(H+)$ and $P(H-)$, respectively, and the seventh and eighth components correspond to $P(L+)$ and $P(L-)$, respectively.

In general, W^∞ is given by:

$$W^\infty = \frac{1}{2} \begin{pmatrix} I & P_1 & Q_1 & P_{12} & Q_{12} \\ 0 & I & 0 & 0 & 0 \\ 0 & 0 & I & 0 & 0 \\ \alpha P_{21} & 0 & 0 & I & 0 \\ (1-\alpha)Q_{21} & 0 & 0 & 0 & I \end{pmatrix} \begin{pmatrix} A^\infty & 0 & 0 & 0 & 0 \\ 0 & 0 & 0 & 0 & 0 \\ 0 & 0 & 0 & 0 & 0 \\ 0 & P_{21}B^\infty P_1 & P_{21}B^\infty Q_1 & P_{21}B^\infty P_{12} & P_{21}B^\infty Q_{12} \\ 0 & Q_{21}C^\infty P_1 & Q_{21}C^\infty Q_1 & Q_{21}C^\infty P_{12} & Q_{21}C^\infty Q_{12} \end{pmatrix}$$

where

$$A^\infty = \lim_{n \to \infty} \left[\alpha P_{12}P_{21} + (1-\alpha)Q_{12}Q_{21} \right]^n, \ B^\infty = \alpha A^\infty, \ and \ C^\infty = (1-\alpha)A^\infty.$$

Hence, the limiting probabilities corresponding to {Disease} and {NoDisease} are given by A^∞. Note, that for $\alpha=1$, A^∞ yields the principal eigenvector of $P_{12}P_{21}$ that are the corresponding probabilities of {Disease} and {NoDisease}. For $\alpha=0$, the results correspond to the liver test. The limiting probabilities of the states of nature {Disease, NoDisease} are given by the normalized values of the first two components of w^∞. They are given in Table 8.12

as a function of α.

Table 8.12 Probabilities of the States of Nature as a function of α

α	P[D]		P[D|+]	P[D|-]
0	0.1		0.6786	0.0058
0.2	0.062	0.5587	0.0035	
0.4	0.0382		0.4301	0.0021
0.5	0.0293		0.3645	0.0016
0.6	0.0219		0.2985	0.0012
0.8	0.01		0.1610	0.0005
1.0	0.001	0.0187	0.0001	

If $\alpha = 0$, the liver symptom drives the outcome, while if $\alpha = 1$ the heart symptom does so. For $\alpha = 0.5$, the probability of having the disease is equal to 0.0293 which yields the posterior probability $P[D|+] = 0.3645$.

Assume that there is interaction between the two symptoms. For example, for the heart-liver problem under study, suppose that when the test is positive with the liver symptom, it is also positive in 100 percent of the cases with the heart symptom. Also assume that when the test is negative with the liver symptom, it is also negative in 100 percent of the cases when the person has the heart symptom. What is the probability that the individual has the disease?

The supermatrix of this problem is given by:

$$
W = \begin{array}{c} \\ \Theta \\ Heart \\ Liver \\ H\pm \\ L\pm \end{array}
\begin{array}{c} \Theta \\ \left[\begin{array}{c} 0 \\ 0 \\ 0 \\ \alpha P_{21} \\ (1-\alpha)Q_{21} \end{array} \right. \end{array}
\begin{array}{cccc} H & L & H\pm & L\pm \\ P_1 & Q_1 & P_{12} & \beta Q_{12} \\ 0 & 0 & 0 & 0 \\ 0 & 0 & 0 & 0 \\ 0 & 0 & 0 & (1-\beta)R_{12} \\ 0 & 0 & 0 & 0 \end{array}
\left. \begin{array}{c} \\ \\ \\ \\ \end{array} \right]
$$

where β is a normalization constant that represents the relative importance of the contribution Q_{12} corresponding to the results from the test with the liver symptom to Θ versus the relative

contribution $R_{12} = \begin{bmatrix} 1 & 0 \\ 0 & 1 \end{bmatrix}$ to the results from the test with the

heart symptom. Varying the values of α and β from 0 to 1, we obtain the results of Table 8.13. Note that $\alpha=1$ indicates that the liver test result does not contribute to the limiting probabilities. The previous example is obtained by setting $\beta=1$.

Table 8.13 Probabilities of the States of Nature as a function of α and β

	P[D]				
β	**0**	**0.2**	**0.4**	**0.6**	**0.81**
α					
0	0.0010	0.01	0.0219	0.0382	0.0620
0.2	0.0010	0.008	0.0167	0.0278	0.0422
0.062					
0.4	0.0010	0.0061	0.0121	0.0192	0.0278
0.0382					
0.6	0.0010	0.0043	0.008	0.0121	0.0167
0.0219					
0.8	0.0010	0.0026	0.0043	0.0061	0.008
0.01					
1.0	0.0010	0.0010	0.0010	0.0010	0.0010
0.0010					

Note for example that for $\alpha=0.2$ and $\beta=0.4$, P[D]=0.0278, and hence P[D | +] = 0.352 which is significant.

This example illustrates that the supermatrix provides a general procedure for dealing with more complicated diagnostic situations than the single loop approach of Bayes theory in which each test is analyzed separately and the judgment of an expert is needed to infer their significance. Such judgment can now be explicitly based on the results of dependence. It is useful to note (as we have also been told by medical practitioners) that not taking into account dependencies among tests can lead to wrong conclusions about how to treat a disease.

We have shown how to derive Bayes theorem from a process of establishing priorities of influence in a network of interactions with dependencies. More significantly, we have illustrated how to use the network process in diagnosing a disease where there is dependence among the symptoms. Many decision problems require interpretations that allow for dependence of the kind described in this section.

References

1. Ahunai, Somphote, 1992, "Case Report : The prediction of CPU Market", submitted to T.L. Saaty, coursework.

2. Bennett, E.J., 1991, "Alternative Fuels For Automobiles", University of Pittsburgh.

3. Berger, J.O., 1985, Statistical Decision Theory and Bayesian Analysis, Springer-Verlag.

4. Charniak, E. and D. McDermott, 1985, Introduction to Artificial Intelligence, Addison-Wesley.

5. Duffy, T.P. and A.M. Stuart, 1991, "AHP Techniques as Tools for Prediction: The 1991 Stanley Cup Playoffs, University of Pittsburgh.

6. Gantmacher, F.R., 1959, Matrix Theory, John Wiley, New York.

7. Hauser, D., M. Baker, and M. Ogawa, 1991, "Prediction Modeling: AHP and Darts", University of Pittsburgh.

8. Howson C. and P. Urbach, 1989, Scientific Reasoning: The Bayesian Approach, Open Court, La Salle, Illinois.

9. Rabin, A. and T. Simpson, 1991, "Predicting the 1991 NBA Championships", University of Pittsburgh.

10. Saaty, T.L., 1981, "Priorities in Systems with Feedback," The International Journal of Systems, Measurement and Decisions 1, 24-38.

11. Saaty, T.L. and M. Takizawa, 1986, "Dependence and Independence : From Linear Hierarchies to Nonlinear Networks," European Journal of Operational Research 26/2, 229-237.

12. Saaty, T.L., 1990, The Analytic Hierarchy Process, RWS Publications, Pittsburgh.

13. Saaty, T.L. and L.G. Vargas, 1993, "Diagnosis with Dependent Systems: Bayes Theorem Derived from the Analytic Hierarchy Process", to appear.

CHAPTER NINE

HIGHLIGHTS AND CRITICAL POINTS IN THE
THEORY AND APPLICATION
OF THE ANALYTIC HIERARCHY PROCESS

1. Introduction

This chapter summarizes what has been said before and involves further comments and explanations that may be helpful to the reader. The Analytic Hierarchy Process (AHP) is a theory of measurement concerned with deriving dominance priorities from paired comparisons of homogeneous elements with respect to a common criterion or attribute. Such measurement can be extended to nonhomogeneous elements through "clustering." In a multicriteria setting, the AHP can be used to scale elements in a hierarchy (feedforward) structure with mutually independent elements in each level, or in a network (feedforward-feedback) system of components allowing for dependence within and between components. Thus a hierarchy is a special case of the more general system formulation, the network. Applications of the AHP have included parallel hierarchies (one for benefits and one for costs), and solitary hierarchies (projected and idealized planning, resource allocation). More complex applications of the AHP include the case of an infinite number of elements (via Fredholm integral operators), and the modelling of neural firing and its synthesis described in Chapter 13.

Because of its widespread use, the AHP has been repeatedly put under the microscope and every aspect has been examined, questioned, and explained [11]. Scholarly criticism and inquiry is a healthy process for a new theory. Replies to individual queries have appeared in the literature, and the theory has been extended over the years. This chapter provides a more detailed account of some of the basic technical and behavioral aspects of the subject.

A number of applications of the AHP have been published in the literature. In a recent book, "The Silverlake Project", by IBM [3], the subject occupies an entire chapter in which it is said, "AHP is an extraordinarily powerful decision-making tool. It brings structure to decision making, yet it's flexible...". The AHP contributed to IBM producing the best-selling computer, the AS/400 which led to their winning the Malcolm Baldrige National Quality Award. In another application to household population forecasts, Cook, Falchi, and Mariano used the AHP to evaluate the impacts of cross-sectional variables which cannot be explicitly captured in a time-series approach [7]. J. F. Bard used the AHP to rank Pareto-optimal solutions for selecting automation options [2]. R. P. Hamalainen used the AHP to structure and set priorities on alternative methods of power generation in Finland by working with members of the parliament of that nation [13]. Golden, Wasil, and Harker edited a book with a dozen applications of AHP in project selection, the electric utility industry, the federal government, and others in medicine, politics, engineering and business [12]. In 1977 this author won an award from the Institute of Management Sciences on an application of the AHP in transport planning in the Sudan [19,20]. Numerous applications of the AHP have been made in industry and government by using the software package Expert Choice. The proceedings of the First International Symposium on AHP held in Tianjin, China include a few of several hundred applications (estimated by a member of the Academy of Sciences of China) of the AHP by the government of China [18]. The Xerox Corporation has institutionalized use of the AHP in their strategic decision making. It is also used by the Departments of Defense and of Energy in Washington. A recent bibliography of the AHP is included in the back of this book.

Special issues of various journals have been dedicated to the AHP; two by Socio-Economic Planning Sciences [35,36], two by

Mathematical Modelling [15,16], and one by the European Journal of Operational Research [10]. Since 1989, a semiannual journal called AHP and Decision Making has been published by the Science Press in Beijing, China. A special issue of the Communications of the Operations Research Society of Japan is about the AHP [9]. Nearly twenty books and translations have appeared on the subject in several languages including Chinese, Japanese, Indonesian, French, German, Russian and Portuguese. Several software packages implementing AHP have been reviewed in a recent issue of the Journal of Multi-Criteria Decision Analysis [6]. There was a Second International Symposium on AHP in Pittsburgh in 1991 with proceedings [17]. Also, two survey articles have appeared on the subject [37,38]. This chapter includes five sections to analyze the foundations and questions raised about the AHP together with our explanation why the theory is as it is today: 1.) Structure in the AHP - Hierarchies and Networks, 2.) Scales of Measurement, 3.) Judgments, Consistency and the Eigenvector, 4.) Synthesis, and 5.) Normative - Descriptive.

2. Structure in the AHP - Hierarchies and Networks

The AHP emphasizes the use of elaborate structures to represent a decision problem. The soundness of a decision is reflected at least as much by the richness and accuracy of the structure and relations in the structure, as it is in assigning and manipulating numbers according to some theory. In fact, a reasonable test of the efficiency of a mathematical theory is how well it can deal with elaborate structures without undue condensing and alteration of that structure to make it possible to perform its manipulations. How well the mathematical operations generalize to cases of dependence within and between clusters of elements is the acid test as to whether the theory seems natural or contrived. With its use of relative ratio scales and corresponding formal operations, the AHP is capable of incorporating all observed dependencies.

A hierarchy is a structure used to represent the simplest type of functional dependence of one level or component of a system on another in a sequential manner. It is also a convenient way to decompose a complex problem in search of cause-effect explanations in steps which form a linear chain. One result of this approach is to assume the independence of an upper part or cluster of the hierarchy from the functions of all its lower parts. The structure of hierarchies is linear and proceeds downward from the most general and less controllable (goals, objectives, criteria, subcriteria) to the more concrete and controllable factors terminating in the level of alternatives. A useful criterion to check the validity of a hierarchy is to determine if the elements of an upper level can be used as common attributes to compare the elements in the level immediately below with each other. There are two general types of hierarchies that arise in planning. One is the forward process hierarchy which descends from the goal to time horizons. This is then followed successively by levels of various types of factors in decreasing generality and uncontrollability. Environmental, political, social, actors, actor objectives, actor policies, and so on down to a level of contrast scenarios are factors from which a composite scenario is derived with the measurement approach of the AHP. The other is the backward process hierarchy. It descends from the goal of choosing a best outcome, to feasible and desired anticipatory scenarios, to problems and opportunities facing the future. This can be followed by a level of actors who control the problems and opportunities, followed by a level of their objectives and one of their policies, down to a level of the most likely policies of a particular actor to influence the other actors. Planning involves testing the effect of the high priority policies for some actor in a second forward process hierarchy to close the gap between the dominant contrast scenarios (or composite scenario) of the forward process and the anticipatory scenarios of the backward process. The iterations are repeated.

Hierarchic structures are fundamental to planning and to the analysis of risk. The AHP has been documented for and used extensively in planning [25]. One cannot do planning without considering risk and uncertainty, and therefore risk and uncertainty have also been addressed in the literature [27,22]. One way to deal with risk is to construct three hierarchies, one for benefits, one for costs and one for risk whose results are used to appropriately weight the benefit to costs ratios. Concern with risk is represented in the hierarchy through scenarios expressing uncertainty to be faced, through benefits and costs of risky operations and through criteria indicating both uncertain and risky outcomes. Sensitivity analysis is used to test the effect of risky factors on the outcome.

3. Scales of Measurement

Since there do not exist numerical units applicable in all domains, scales need to be generated to solve problems according to specific goals. Despite this dilemma, traditional methods continue to use homogeneous linear scales with a unit. It is this issue, however, which substantially differentiates AHP from these approaches. Prior to this millennium, there were very few scales of measurement, if any, and negative numbers had not been formalized. Yet it is incorrect to assume that decisions made in the past were inferior because of the lack of scales of measurement. All people share a mental ability to perform the more general approach of relative measurement to capture priorities without systematic organization of the elements of the decision. The AHP organizes and quantifies this very process of thinking.

Decision making involves making tradeoffs reflected through arithmetic operations on the weights used to represent judgments. The type of arithmetic performed on these weights is a major concern in multicriteria problems since the freedom to add and multiply measurements does not always exist. For example, one cannot meaningfully multiply two readings on the Fahrenheit scale. In this quest one is faced with the question of what kinds of numerical scales there are. Widely known scales include ordinal (invariant under strictly monotone increasing transformations), interval (invariant under positive linear transformations), ratio (invariant under positive similarity transformations), and absolute (invariant under the identity transformation) scales. A decision theory needs to justify the way it elicits judgments, converts them to numbers, and produces an overall answer that belongs to one of these scales. Additionally, the outcome of the calculation must remain in the same scale or change continuously if the structure of the decision were to be extended or perturbed. What scale admits such flexibility?

Ratio and Interval Scales

Since ordinal scales cannot be added or multiplied, we need to examine interval and ratio scales as candidate scales for decision making.

Interval scales have the form $ax + b$ with $a > 0$, $b \neq 0$. When $b = 0$, we have a ratio scale. In terms of perturbations of b, the two scales are related. One can add or subtract interval scale numbers but not multiply or divide them. Ratio scales permit manipulation with respect to all four arithmetic operations keeping subtraction appropriately positive.

Throughout the hierarchic structure, the AHP elicits judgments in the form of absolute numbers and derives the ranks on a ratio scale of priorities. These interim scales are weighted to produce commensurate ratio scales that can later be added to obtain an overall ranking of the alternatives. There are no scaling constants for the criteria in the AHP with indeterminate scale affiliation as there is in other theories using interval scales [14]. As in the temperature example, interval scale numbers cannot be used to weight interval scale numbers. When the alternatives rated on an interval scale in one decision become criteria for the alternatives of a new decision also measured on an interval scale, it is a puzzle how one abandons the old calculations and begins new calculations to make things compatible. This is a weakness of interval scales in decision making. An example of this occurrence is when policy alternatives of one decision become criteria to judge consequences of policies as new alternatives. To use such an approach to derive weights for the consequences, different technical and philosophical procedures are needed to avoid multiplication of the two interval scale results! With ratio scales, one weights the ratios from the consequences by the priority ratios of the criteria, which is what one would do anyway continuing the previous composition operations of weighting and adding.

Consider a person given a choice between paying $1 with an assurance of a $10 return, or paying $2 to get a $15 return. No gambles are involved in this transaction and one would reason 15 - 2 = 13 is more than 10 - 1 = 9 and chooses to pay $2. It would not be correct to form the ratios 15/2 = 7.5 and 10/1 = 10. This transaction should not be determined by benefit/cost ratios, but by differences. So when does one use benefit cost ratios? Answer: when dealing with two different ratio scales (for example, when the rewards are gambles). Then there is one ratio scale for the reward and one for the gamble, and the choice should be based on benefit/cost ratios. The benefit belongs to a different scale than the cost represented by the gamble taken to earn it. Two different ratio scales cannot be added or subtracted -- only multiplied or divided. However, the resulting ratios now belong to the same scale among themselves and all four operations can be performed on them again. According to the criterion of maximizing expected value, gambling $1 to gain $10 is preferred to gambling $2 to gain $15 if the probability of getting $10 is less than 1/6. As the risk decreases (the probability of getting $10 converges to 1) one should again turn to differences and the gamble with the greater difference should be taken. However, generally speaking, under risk one should use ratios.

Absolute and Relative Scales

Abstractly, absolute measurement is the comparison of some value on a scale with the unit value of the scale. The task is to define the meaning of a unit before using it to construct the scale. This is rarely adequate in practice. Sometimes a range is first given and the unit is suitably defined without ascribing deeper meaning to the operation. In essence a unit is arbitrary but needs consensus for its adoption.

A major philosophical difference between the AHP and theories based on absolute measurement is that the latter require units of measurement to tradeoff weights for the criteria or attributes. For example, for characteristics such as style and color, one must have an existing scale to measure style, and another for color. Further, some means to trade off a unit of one against a unit of the other is required. In the AHP, relative measurement does not tradeoff units in the same way, because measurement ascends from paired comparisons to derive (rather than assume) a scale.

Measurements of phenomena on an absolute scale serve as surrogates, indicators, or stimuli to the mind educated about the significance of the magnitude of the number, in terms of the goals and understanding of an individual. For a group, its members would have to agree on how measurements are to be interpreted to lend credence to an objective acceptance. Thus measurements have no intrinsic significance apart from the people who use them. Significance itself can be represented in the form of priorities with respect to a hierarchy of objectives. These priorities need not behave linearly or monotonically or even correspond to the original numbers. To the blind, the comparison of two alternatives according to visual brightness is impossible, thus an absolute scale for such comparison is valueless. But this person may be able to feel or judge brightness by comparing the heat or electric intensity generated by the light, which has a meaning. Hence, it is imperative to understand how to transform absolute measurements to priorities to take advantage of both qualitative and quantitative information.

Relative measurement of alternatives introduces two additional properties unrecognized by absolute measurement approaches. These properties are the number of alternatives and the portion of the total that an alternative has for each criterion (which cannot be inserted as criteria in the traditional way that new information is incorporated). Both of these properties change when an alternative is added or deleted, in some cases causing rank reversal.

Two types of relative scales are encountered in multicriteria decisions. One is obtained by directly converting absolute numbers to relative numbers as for example by dividing by their sum, known as normalization. The other is in the form of priorities derived from comparisons of elements relative to a common attribute or from comparison of numbers associated with them. The comparison of homogeneous elements, which fall within an order of magnitude, is made in terms of the dominance of one element over another. This relationship is expressed as the number of times the more preferred entity is preferred to the less preferred entity. The latter serves as the unit of comparison. Comparisons expressing individual preferences are an innate ability of the mind. Measurement on an absolute scale simply complies with the mechanics of associating a reading with its object. What the numbers mean is not and cannot be designed into the scale. Note that absolute measurement applies to elements one at a time. Relative measurement is based on comparing elements in multiples. Without priorities to interpret and quantify information, one would need to create an infinite number of different homogeneous measurement scales with a unit, one for each of the infinite number of properties known and would still need a way to interpret and combine the resulting information in order to make a decision. Additionally, one cannot reduce ethics, religion, happiness, politics, and society into fixed units as some theories do by converting to dollars in an attempt to unify all measurements into some absolute scale with a unit. In constructing priorities, consideration of how science generates and processes measurement should be taken. When priorities are derived from ratios of measurements, they must give back their measurements as they do in the AHP. Otherwise, setting priorities would itself be a contrived number crunching process.

Tangibles and Intangibles

We note that it is not meaningful to take numbers on the same absolute scale used to measure alternatives for different criteria, normalize them for each criterion and then weight and synthesize and achieve the same rank results. While it is true that a set of numbers such as dollars can be normalized to develop a relative score, it does not follow that normalizing such numbers with respect to several criteria and weighting by the priorities of the criteria and adding yields the same (correct) result that would be obtained by weighting the numbers before normalization and then adding. The reason is that the mapping from absolute to relative numbers is many to one ($2/1 = 4/2 = 8/4 = 2000/1000,...$). The elements whose absolute measurements are 8 and 4 do not fall in the same cluster as those whose absolute measurements are 2000 and 1000. This is how the AHP distinguishes between magnitudes before ratios are formed. It is not possible to recover the original set. Thus to use absolute numbers directly in the AHP for a priority scale, all those absolute measurements with respect to a single scale must first be composed with respect to their several criteria. This leads to a single composite criterion representing all the tangible criteria measured on that unit. The same process is repeated if other units are used. It is only then that tangibles and intangibles are combined in a hierarchic framework. Alternatively, all tangible criteria may be treated as intangibles in the hierarchy without using their unit directly but benefiting from the measurements to carefully make paired comparisons on a priority scale. Only then can they be normalized to combine with tangible criteria on a relative scale.

The transformation of absolute numbers to relative numbers

has little influence over how meaning is assigned to generate priorities on a relative scale whose ratios may not be the same as those of the corresponding absolute numbers. Priorities should not be combined with measurements unless they coincide with them, in which case no difficulties arise. However priorities based on information from different scales are a generalization that requires comparison of the criteria with respect to a higher criterion. For emphasis, note that after absolute numbers are converted to priorities, one cannot take the final scale and treat it arithmetically as if it is still the original scale of absolute numbers.

Suppose we wished to determine the best of three vacation sites A, B, C relative to travel cost and lodging costs as shown in Table 9.1.

Table 9.1 Choosing the best vacation site.

Criteria Alternatives	C_1 Travel Cost (\$)	C_2 Lodging Cost (\$)
A	50	200
B	100	170
C	150	230
	300	600

The overall costs are given by:

$$\text{Cost A} = 50 + 200 = 250 \text{ (minimum)}$$
$$\text{Cost B} = 100 + 170 = 270 \qquad\qquad (1)$$
$$\text{Cost C} = 150 + 230 = 380 \text{ (maximum)}$$

and thus A would be the preferred site (minimized cost).

The same problem can be studied with a hierarchic interpretation using a relative scale. Upon multiplication and division of the costs of the alternatives for each criterion by the total costs for that criterion and addition we obtain:

$$\text{Cost A} = 300 \times \left(\frac{50}{300}\right) + 600 \times \left(\frac{200}{600}\right);$$

$$\text{Cost B} = 300 \times \left(\frac{100}{300}\right) + 600 \times \left(\frac{170}{600}\right); \qquad (2)$$

$$\text{Cost C} = 300 \times \left(\frac{150}{300}\right) + 600 \times \left(\frac{230}{600}\right).$$

which yields the same results as (1). The criteria derived their importance from the alternatives because dollars have the same priority for both criteria. However, this is not always true for any unit and any criterion. The quantities 300 and 600 can be used to determine the relative priorities of the criteria C_1 and C_2 (the ratio of 300 to 600 is 1 to 2, ½ to 1 or .333 to .667). If we compare these with respect to the goal of selecting the best vacation site, we have:

Table 9.2 Relative priority of the costs

Goal	C_1	C_2	Priorities
C_1	1	½	.333
C_2	2	1	.667

For comparison of A, B, and C with respect to each criterion, use the ratios of the quantities in (2) for the costs which are the relative values. When A is compared with B relative to travel one has $\frac{50}{300} \div \frac{100}{300} = \frac{1}{2}$ and so on. For each criterion the following matrices arise:

Table 9.3 Relative priorities of the sites

C_1	A	B	C	Pri.
A	1	1/2	1/3	.167
B	2	1	2/3	.333
C	3	3/2	1	.500

C_2	A	B	C	Pri.
A	1	2/1.7	2/2.3	.333
B	1.7/2	1	1.7/2.3	.283
C	2.3/2	2.3/1.73	1	.383

Weighting by the corresponding criteria priorities and adding yields:

$$\text{Cost A} = .333 \times .167 + .667 \times .333 = .278 \text{ (minimum)}$$

$$\text{Cost B} = .333 \text{ x } .333 + .667 \text{ x } .283 = .300 \qquad (3)$$
$$\text{Cost C} = .333 \text{ x } .500 + .667 \text{ x } .383 = .422 \text{ (maximum)}$$

which is the same as (1) and (2). Thus the costs obtained by additive hierarchic composition lead to the same solution as an appropriate analysis of the original data.

For elements of the same order of magnitude (homogeneous), the paired comparison judgments in the matrices may be approximated by values from the scale 1-9 based on perception. This is useful when there are no known numerical values to form the ratios. In such a case, the matrices of the above example are as in Table 9.4.

Table 9.4 Relative priorities of sites using the AHP scale

C_1	A	B	C	Priorities		C_2	A	B	C	Priorities
A	1	1/2	1/3	.163		A	1	1	1	.333
B	2	1	1/2	.297		B	1	1	1	.333
C	3	2	1	.540		C	1	1	1	.333

$$\text{Cost A} = .333 \text{ x } .163 + .667 \text{ x } .333 = .276 \text{ (minimum)}$$
$$\text{Cost B} = .333 \text{ x } .297 + .667 \text{ x } .333 = .321 \qquad (4)$$
$$\text{Cost C} = .333 \text{ x } .540 + .667 \text{ x } .333 = .402 \text{ (maximum)}$$

and A is again the preferred alternative. The approximation using a 1-9 scale could lead to a different choice than the best one, but there would be no need to approximate if exact numbers are known. However in general one needs to compare the dollar values according to the importance of their magnitudes. The numerical differences between them may not be an adequate indicator of significance to the decision maker.

The example demonstrates that when the criteria weights are described in terms of the unit of measurement of the alternatives, the arithmetic operations of the AHP can be used to duplicate with relative numbers the answers one gets with absolute numbers. Yet that is not the purpose of the AHP. The priorities associated with numbers may not vary linearly or monotonically with those numbers. In fact for each problem the priorities would satisfy the needs of that problem according to the judgments of the involved individual or group.

Suppose we have three foods and their content measured in milligrams for the two criteria, vitamin X and vitamin Y. The importance of the criteria is no longer determined by the total or average milligram content of the alternatives as before, but rather by the needs of the body for that vitamin to remain healthy. It may be harmful to get an excessive amount of one vitamin but healthy to get such an amount from the other. We must establish priorities by comparing the criteria with respect to healthful contribution, and the alternatives' milligram content for their positive contribution to meet body needs.   The actual measurements and their totals cannot determine the single best food to eat in small quantities.

How to Combine Tangibles with Intangibles

Assume that a family is considering buying a house and there are three houses to consider. Four factors dominate their thinking: the price of the house, the remodeling costs, the size of the house as reflected by its footage and the style of the house which is an intangible. They have looked at three houses with data shown below on the quantifiables:

Choosing the Best House

	Price ($1000)	Remodeling Costs ($300)	Size (sq.ft.)	Style
A	200	150	3000	Colonial
B	300	50	2000	Ranch
C	500	100	5500	Split Level

First we normalize for each of the quantifiable factors. Then we must normalize the factors measured with respect to a single scale.

Choosing the Best House

	Price (1000/1300)	Remodeling Costs (300/1300)	Size (sq.ft.)	Style
A	200/1000	150/300	3000	Colonial
B	300/1000	50/300	2000	Ranch
C	500/1000	100/300	5500	Split Level

Next we combine the factors with a common scale. We have:

Choosing the Best House

Economic Factors (combining Price and Remodeling Cost)	Size	Style
A 350/1300	3000/10500	Colonial
B 350/1300	2000/10500	Ranch
C 600/1300	5500/10500	Split Level

Next we establish priorities for the factors through paired comparisons. The resulting priorities are used to weight the normalized values of the alternatives as they are given here. Alternatively, and better, we can perform paired comparisons on them first and then weight them. The former approach would be probably used by a disinterested party for whom the dollar costs are simply numbers of no personal significance, although they might have substantially different significance to the family. To treat dollars (or any other scale measurements) directly without comparisons can yield misleading results. In this example, tangible and intangible factors had to be compared. Their priorities are used to weight the priorities of the altneratives. These priorities are obtained by converting measurements to priorities directly through normalization (seldom justified) or by interpreting their relative importance through judgment (essential where no measurements are possible).

There are two other cases to consider. The first is when gambles and expected values are involved between factors measured on the same scale which are then combined accordingly into a single factor for that scale. The other may involve relations between subfactors from a common scale and intangible factors. The subfactors must be normalized with the other subfactors as above and then combined with the intangibles accordingly. The other subfactors from the given scale would be combined into a single scale factor as above and one proceeds in the usual way to complete the prioritization process.

Priority Scales

Priority scales (which are derived ratio scales) are essential in multicriteria decisions. One may be tempted to use readings from existing scales, but a single ordinary scale may not be unique. For example, temperature can be measured either with a mercury or an alcohol thermometer and both readings belong to an interval scale. Even when only mercury is used there can be different calibrations, such as the Fahrenheit and Celsius scales with different size units. Different numbers are produced for measurements with different scales. Measurements from different scales cannot be combined because they are not commensurate. In the AHP, all such measurements are transformed into a uniform priority scale based on the judged importance or preference for different readings as they affect our objectives. The goal has a priority scale to measure the criteria. Each criterion in turn has a priority scale to measure the alternatives. When the priority of the criteria is used to weight the priorities of that alternative with respect to each of those criteria, and the sum then taken, the result is the priority of the alternative with respect to the goal and the measurements of the alternatives define a scale for measuring them in terms of the goal.

Physics and mathematics extend some one-dimensional absolute measurements to multiple dimensions such as areas, volumes, and measurement in higher dimensions. There are two ways to convert these measurements to relative numbers. The first is to compare areas (or volumes) with other areas (or volumes) directly. The second is to use logarithms which enable one to compose higher dimensional measurements by adding corresponding one dimensional measurements, instead of multiplying them. (This kind of transformation was discovered by Fechner to be in use by the mind to respond to stimuli measured on an absolute scale [23].) Numbers associated with areas, volumes, or even lengths can be suspect. A blanket whose total area is known to be adequate but is full of holes would not be a suitable cover. A farmer can grow crops on a narrow elongated strip of land, that would be useless to a tennis player who needs an area of the same magnitude with prescribed dimensions, to play tennis. Readings on the same scale may have opposite interpretations in different settings. Freezing and boiling are both good for preserving food, mid temperatures undesirable, whereas the opposite applies to human comfort. While it is helpful to have numerical measurements, interpretation differs from problem to problem. Priorities are needed to determine what numbers imply about the underlying situation. Higher dimensions have properties not reflected in the arithmetic of composing lower dimensional measurements and must be compared as they are on these properties to create meaningful priorities.

Observations made about numerical measurements as stimuli to be interpreted apply equally to probabilities generated directly or through Bayes Theorem from posterior to prior by complex and laborious calculations. Probabilities are not esoteric numbers that have deeper meaning than other numbers used as stimuli. The supermatrix formulation of the AHP implies Bayes Theorem, thus making probabilities part of the AHP priority framework.   The outcome of probability computations have different implications in the mind of a decision maker about what they mean depending on how high or how low the probabilities are.   Traditional expected value reasoning is not the only way nor always the best way to apply to every decision.   Playing with probabilities is often a numbers game because of the fascination generated in some academic minds due to the intricacies of thought involved in the calculations and not because the significance of the probabilities in a decision is an automatic consequence of the numerical probability.

4. Decision Making and Number Crunching

Decision making requires the use of numbers and scales. What numbers to choose to represent judgments, what scales to derive from them and what are admissible operations on the scales are an important concern.   Let us begin with an example.

To supply large quantities of food to the hungry population of a poor country, the most practical type of food had to be chosen.   The decision was based on the attributes of low cost, high calories and compact volume of the food.   The alternative foods were ranked according to cost per unit, number of calories per unit, and volume per unit.   A major problem was whether it is meaningful and possible to combine these different scales to get a ranking for the foods with respect to all the attributes.   It is clear that it is both meaningful and possible if one of the foods is best in all categories.   This observation lures one to believe that there must be a way to manipulate the scales to obtain an overall ranking.   But, the solution to the problem is beyond simple arithmetic operations on scales.   This is the case even if we were to assign relative importance per unit to cost, calories and volume with the intention of weighting the measurement of each food by the corresponding weight.   The weighted values for that food would then be added with respect to all the criteria. Such a ranking of the foods, to determine the best one overall to ship, would be meaningless because we would be combining different kinds of numbers that have no intrinsic meaning. The difficulty is compounded if a fourth criterion, without a known way of measurement, like how digestible the food is, were to be included.

Decision making based on scale manipulations is mere number crunching. It is the process of taking a variety of numbers and running them through arithmetic procedures that yield a new set of numbers. These numbers are thought to have more meaning than the original collection.

A theory for decision making should facilitate creativity in seeking, selecting from, and successively modifying the many criteria and alternatives that come to mind which have bearing on the goal of the decision. It also needs a way to elicit judgments and scale them uniquely. It must have a valid procedure to combine the scale values to arrive at a unique decision.

Expectations, Scales, and Manipulations

One might argue that the whole process of decision making is so unstructured and so amorphous, involving as it does objectives, criteria, subcriteria and alternatives, that it is no use trying to be precise. In addition, there are no definite criteria that can be used to judge what is the best answer. Simon [33,34] for example, has proposed that people practice satisficing by continued search, until a certain "aspiration level" is reached. He did not offer a formal procedure for making a decision, but speculated about its complexity. It is assumed of course that satisficing depends on experience, knowledge and some kind of updated enlightenment.

One is tempted to conclude that "participant satisfaction" is the main objective of decision making regardless of how the decision is made. Were this the case, multicriteria decision making would be a matter of using ingenuity to improvise numbers that please people. But different sets of arbitrary numbers are likely to produce different decisions, and we still need a theory to tell us how best to proceed. A group of people may be equally pleased with two different sets of numbers that contradict each other in what is recommended. If the object is to fulfill expectations, why not ask for them directly and save time and effort?

As far as the relevance of pleasing a decision maker who is participating in the judgment process, the outcome should arise from a sound theory based on his best judgments. It should not come from an attempt to anticipate and reproduce his guess as the outcome. This should be true of a normative theory that searches for a best answer according to some predetermined principle. A descriptive theory like the Analytic Hierarchy Process should help the decision maker explore, honestly and without oversimplification, the complexity of the decision. He should be able to express his judgments according to intensity of preference, and also derive a solution that clearly and rigorously captures these intensities according to magnitude. In this learning process he finds that he accepts the answer rationally. He feels comfortable with it because it is all based on his perceptions.

Misuse of Normalization

Among the various number crunching procedures the most pernicious is to assign judgments to the alternatives under a particular criterion. This is done by selecting numbers from some arbitrary set, and then normalizing the numbers (multiplying them by a constant that is the reciprocal of their sum). Generally the sets of numbers from which the judgments are assigned are different for each criterion. Still, the normalized sets now lie in the interval [0,1], no matter what scale they originally came from, and can be passed off to the uninitiated as comparable. The appealing part of this practice is that the numbers have an apparently uniform underlying structure, looking not unlike probabilities. Thus they go unchallenged by the decision maker and are then manipulated by the consultant or facilitator, who weights and adds them to find the most preferred alternative.

To see the weakness of this practice, suppose that the initial numbers assigned before normalization are ordinals, arbitrary numbers that preserve order but carry no information about differences or ratios of relative magnitudes. Then the resulting transformation (the normalization procedure) produces a new set of ordinals lying between zero and one. The only thing we can be sure of is that order is preserved. The operations of weighting and adding are not meaningful, because it is easy to produce different results by choosing different scales from which to draw the ordinals. By a judicious choice of these scales one can make an alternative that dominates the others on even one criterion, no matter how unimportant that criterion may be, have the largest value after weighting and adding, and thus come out as the most preferred. A method such as this cannot be trusted to lead to a valid decision. Ordinal scales do not work. So what other scales are there?

As we have seen, there are several examples of types of numerical scales and conditions they satisfy. Ordinal scales are invariant under strictly monotone increasing transformations. Interval scales are invariant under positive linear transformations. Ratio scales are invariant under positive similarity transformations. Absolute scales are invariant under the identity transformation. If they all lead to the same result it would not matter which we used and this distinction among scales would be superfluous.

As with ordinal scales, normalization cannot be applied to interval scales. Incidentally, both interval scales and ratio scales (to which normalization is applicable) present us with ambiguities with regard to uniqueness. For example, temperature can be measured with either a mercury or an alcohol thermometer, and both readings belong to an interval scale. Even when only mercury is used one can have different calibrations. Taking measurements from one scale leads to different answers than taking them from another. Besides there is the problem of intangible criteria and how to perform measurement. So how do we deal with such a diversity of scales? We cannot do it directly.

The Heart of the Matter

Let us take a simple example in which the same unit is used to perform the measurement (in this case, number of people) to see what insight it gives us.

Two trains (analogous to criteria) bring passengers (a passenger is the unit of measurement) to a station. Three buses (analogous to alternatives), A, B, and C pick up the passengers from each train as shown in Table 9.5.

Table 9.5 Number of passengers transported

	Bus A	Bus B	Bus C		Total passengers
From train 1:	40	10	10	—>	60
From train 2:	20	30	30	—>	80
Total passengers	60	40	40		140

The proportions of passengers on the buses from each train, are then computed. They are then multiplied by the proportion of passengers on the corresponding trains and added. We have Table 9.6:

Table 9.6 Proportion of passengers transported

	Bus A	Bus B	Bus C	Proportion of total passengers
From train 1:	2/3	1/6	1/6	3/7
From train 2:	1/4	3/8	3/8	4/7
Proportion of all passengers	6/14	4/14	4/14	

For example $2/3 \times 3/7 + 1/4 \times 4/7 = 6/14$. If we simply add the proportion of passengers on each bus (which is equivalent to weighting by .5 from each train), and normalize the total outcome for the three buses we get the wrong result. Thus we have Table 9.7:

Table 9.7 Incorrect normalization procedure

	Bus A	Bus B	Bus C	Total	Proportions
From train 1:	2/3	1/6	1/6	—> 1	-> .5
From train 2:	1/4	3/8	3/8	—> 1	-> .5
	---	---	---	---	
	11/12	13/24	13/24	2	
Proportion of all passengers	11/24	6.5/24	6.5/24	1	

For example $2/3 \times .5 + 1/4 \times .5 = 11/12 \times .5 = 11/24$. We conclude that the only meaningful operation is to perform weighting by criteria weights derived from the total number of passengers on each train. We cannot assign them arbitrary importance and still get meaningful results.

One more point before we draw another conclusion. The foregoing analysis was made possible because we dealt with proportions of the same unit of measurement: a passenger. When different units are used in the same decision problem, it is impossible to combine measurements using these different units into a meaningful overall answer. They must be transformed to measurements in terms of a more abstract unit that is common to all of them. It is our sense of importance, or priority, that we attach to them reflected through our knowledge and experience of the decision at hand. Numbers are one way to obtain indicators about a phenomenon for our thinking mind just as light and sound and temperature need to be sensed and their intensities interpreted through our senses. To us the world only has meaning through our collective awareness and needs to be discussed and debated to structure and act on decisions that lead to individual or commonly shared goals.

Do numbers have an objective meaning?

In his book <u>Counting & Measuring</u> (1887), the physician, physicist and mathematician Hermann von Helmholtz (1821-1894) concludes that the very concept of number is derived from experience. Only experience can tell us where the laws of arithmetic apply, and we cannot be sure a priori that they do apply in any given situation. Arithmetic fails to always correctly describe the result of combining liquids or gases by volumes.

2 volumes Hydrogen + 1 volume Oxygen = 1 volume Water
1 qt. Alcohol + 1 qt. Water = 1.8 qts. of Vodka, not 2

What do we think of when we speak of 1, 2, ..., 10 pounds or 1, 2, ... 10 tons of butter? When we think of one pound of butter we think of a rectangular package with four 1/4 pound sticks of butter. Then we also think of how many days it takes to spread it on toast. We also think of cholesterol and hardening of the arteries and of an acidic stomach. When we think of two pounds we think of more of the same. When we think of more we lose sight of meaning. A ton of butter may be a useful measure to order and distribute butter among the supermarkets of a chain in a city. Beyond that it has no special meaning.

A large sheep and a small one do not have the same amount of meat, thus even though one sheep plus one sheep is two sheep, it is not the number but the size of sheep that gives us the correct idea about the amount of meat. We need to distinguish between number and measurement. With number we determine how many things there are, with measurement we determine the magnitude or size of the objects. Two apples may be equal in size or one may be much larger. In many problems, magnitude is what is needed. In the past we were unable to measure relative magnitudes on every property. Now we can. In what sense is one plus one two? In reality we are told that two objects are the same if and only if they have the same molecules and occupy the same position in space and time. One to one correspondence is not always helpful. Magnitude with respect to a property is even more important. A mother with a one day old baby cannot be put in one to one correspondence with chairs or anything practical, yet we count them as two despite the extreme dependence of the child on the mother.

One may be inclined to think that scales of measurement are scientific discoveries that have an objectivity beyond the dimensions they are designed to measure. For example, our use of time devices convinces us that time is movement on a clock or a calendar. Length is a multiple of a foot or a meter. But on looking into the history of development of these instruments, one finds that they were invented for convenience and have evolved over a long period of time. Besides, we keep inventing new ways to measure time, length, mass and other dimensions. In addition, we become addicts in using these measurements. We invent ways to justify their use even when some other property may be the more important one such as politics not economics which cannot be measured in dollars.

Again, let us look at temperature. A temperature of 30° Fahrenheit is very cold to a person who has just walked in from a 90 degree outside temperature. If that person lives in a city in Alaska, a temperature of 30 degrees in February is balmy weather. To a person from the tropics 30 degrees and minus 30 degrees designate very cold and indistinguishable temperatures which one would not wish to encounter; both equally undesirable. Thus 30 degrees as an indicator of temperature signifies different things to different people. The indication on the thermometer has no significance in itself except in the meaning it conveys to the individual.

To repeat, if we want to make a decision involving a tradeoff among several properties measured on different scales, how do we combine these scales? One is measured in dollars, one in yards, one in pounds, one in seconds and one in IQ units. Besides, what do we do if there is more than one scale for some of them, like pounds and kilograms? Or for temperature measured on a Kelvin and a Fahrenheit scale? The first is a ratio scale and the second an interval scale. All numbers and scales are structured to create significance or priority in the context of a decision problem.

To connect the AHP with our earlier discussion of scaling

we offer the following illustration.   For most scales, the importance of the numbers is interpreted in a nonlinear way. For example student's numerical grades may range from zero to 100 but we assign them letter grades as follows: 0-50: F, 51-70: D, 71- 85: C, 86-92: B, 93-100: A.   The first observation is that the range for each letter grade is different.   The second is that the upper range is at a premium.   The higher the grade the fewer the students achieving it.   We can perform paired comparisons on the ranges designated by F, D, C, B, and A according to preference or excellence, obtaining normalized ratio scale values that reflect our sense of priority for these grades.

In situations of quality control where more and more effort is needed to attain the perfect grade the top range itself is stretched out and divided into intervals.   These are compared among themselves, obtaining a ranking which serves as a decimal refinement of the top range of the previous decomposition.

Mary Blocksma [4] lists a few dozen attributes for which measurements have been developed and are in common practice. They are :

Age, Extraordinary (carbon dating); Alcohol; Alcohol, Blood Levels; Annual Percentage Rate; Bar Codes; Barometric Pressure; Binoculars; Blood Pressure; Calcium; Calendar; Cans; Checks, Bank; Cholesterol; Cigarettes; Circles; Clothing Sizes; Comfort Index (Weather); Commercial Items; Compass; Computers; Consumer Price Index (CPI); Copyright Page; Crash Test Rating Index (CTRI); Currency (Notes); Distance, Nautical; Dow Jones Industrial Averages; Dwellings (Size); Earthquakes; Electricity; Engines (Horsepower); Exponents; Fabric Care; Fabric Widths; Fertilizers; Financial Indexes; Firewood; Food (Energy Value); Food Grading; Gas; Gasoline; Gold; Greenwich Mean Time; Gross National Product (GNP); Hats; Heart Rate (Pulse); Highways; Humidity; Insulation; ISBN Numbers; Land Measures; Latitude and Longitude; Length (Common Short); Light

Beer; Light Bulbs; Lumber; The Metric System; Microwave Ovens; Military Time; Motorcycles; Nails; Oil (Engine); Paper; Paper Clips; Pencils; Ph; Pins; Plywood; Points, Mortgage; Postal Rates; Precious Stones; Prefixes, Astronomical; Prefixes for the Minuscule; Prime Rate; Produce; Property (Legal Description); Radio Waves; Rain; Roman Numerals; Rubber Bands; Sandpaper; Screws and Bolts; Ships; Shoes; Snow; Social Security Numbers; Socks; Sodium (Salt); Soil, Garden; Sound; Staples; Steel Wool; Street Addresses; Sunscreen Lotion; Temperature; Tide Tables; Time; Time Units; Time Zones; Tires; Type; Universe (Distances); Vision; Vitamins and Minerals; Volume; Week; Weight; Wind; ZIP Codes.

But in everyday life we also deal with myriads of intangibles involved with behavior, politics, religion, sociology and economics, for which we have no measurement and which we need to assess directly.   How do we use information supplied quantitatively through numbers in the AHP? Our values vary from one situation to another. We do not have the same value for every problem. Low temperature is used to preserve food from bacteria, middle temperature not so good, high temperature again good as it boils bacteria.   For health and comfort it is the other way around, low temperature is poor, middle temperature is good and high temperature is poor.   There is no way to ensure that increasing values are always to our advantage or disadvantage, they can oscillate. We cannot use a single rule to judge the utility of all numbers. The way out of the dilemma of diverse scales and numbers is to interpret different ranges of numbers as different stimuli that are then prioritized by the individual interested in using them. These priorities which are applied to a diversity of numerical stimuli must come from the same underlying mental response scale, so they can be combined to derive a commensurate overall synthesis.

The procedures of turning all sorts of stimuli, including

numbers, into a unified system of priorities is what one does with the Analytic Hierarchy Process. We argue that there is a universal constructability of ratio scales. For any physical, nonphysical, real or imaginary property whose total absence can be discerned, it is possible to measure that property directly on a priority ratio scale. It is also possible to measure it indirectly by first constructing some numerical representation and then interpreting it on a priority ratio scale. Different people may arrive at different priority ratio scales reflecting their perceptions. There may not be consensus on the priorities. Thus the problem of unifying these perceptual scales — known as conflict resolution — becomes an area of particular research interest in the field of collective human values. We have written a book about conflict resolution through the AHP [5].

5. Objectivity

What does it mean to be objective? If all reality is a matter of interpreting stimuli and information according to our needs and goals, then it is meaningless to speak of universal objectivity. Facts, numbers and other stimuli are regarded by each person according to a certain purpose. Unless purpose and the experience behind it are identical for all people, it is futile to insist that they all look at a datum with the same sense of priority or urgency. What we need is to persuade each other of the usefulness for all concerned to see things from the standpoint of some interpretation. But that is a process of buying into an idea. We are all conditioned and biased by our family, environment, the teachers who teach us and the books we read. An aborigine who has never seen a car or a road, may be afraid of a car unveiled before him. After he gets over the initial fear of the unfamiliar object, he may later decide it is a place for sleeping. If the engine is started he may be afraid of the noise. As it persists, he may be emboldened to approach and think it is a place for cooking food (if he cooks his food). If it does not move, he never thinks of it as a vehicle for transportation.   Even if it moves, he may not be able to imagine the idea of transportation unless he has experienced it seriously before.   To him the idea "car" has no particular meaning.

We have learned this century from Russell and Whitehead and from Gödel that logic is not capable of answering every question by a "yes" or a "no". Some propositions are undecidable. We also know that intuition does not always work. For example, people asked if they think they could slip a mouse under a tight fitting wire around the circumference of a sphere like the earth, with that wire slightly slackened by increasing its length by one meter distributed homogeneously around, mostly say no.   The correct answer is yes.

If logic does not always work and intuition does not always work, what works? We believe that a multivalued logic with a closed set of rules applied to a well defined structure of a problem as we use the AHP works better if there is adequate information, a satisfactory structure and knowledgeable people to judge. There are situations though where it may not work if used improperly. In principle it should always work if it is treated as a process of learning.

According to Carl Jung,
> "The great decisions of human life have as a rule far more to do with the instincts and other mysterious unconscious factors than with conscious will and well-meaning reasonableness.   The shoe that fits one person pinches another; there is no recipe for living that suits all cases. Each of us carries his own life-form -- an indeterminate form which cannot be superseded by any other."

6. Types and Uses of Dominance In Making Comparisons

Dominance is the basic link between relations among qualities, and corresponding relations among magnitudes associated with these qualities. Dominance requires a relative criterion or goal in order for one entity to dominate another. Dominance precedes and is needed to derive utility. To determine dominance, the following question is asked: Which of each pair of given elements dominates the other, and how much more important (dominant) is it?

Although genetics plays an important part in shaping personalities and inclinations, humans need knowledge and experience to form ideas, feelings and preferences. In total, these are used to judge what is familiar, important, desired, or likely. Human memory is crucial to this process, however accurate or inaccurate it may be. When faced with choices, humans tend to silently ask: Do I like this? Is it what I want? Is it what I need? Is it important for this purpose? How important is the purpose itself?

There are different ways to ask the question of dominance in the AHP. Relative to conditions, one needs to ask which is more important; relative to opportunities, one needs to ask which is more preferred; relative to possibilities, one needs to ask which is more likely. In some problems the conditions arise in connection with space, matter, and energy. They offer distinctions between sizes, shapes, density, frequency, and others. Dominance applies in social, political, and behavioral areas. In fact, dominance is such an essential part of human thinking, that it is difficult to find where it is not used, except perhaps in the arts where one observes quietly. Even then some feelings tend to be dominant. Dominance is related to the stimulation and firing of neurons, and is how humans quantify the strength of response to diverse stimuli [29]. It is this firing that people try to verbalize in the form of judgment. In a decision some or all of the questions about importance, preference and likelihood may be involved. However, each would be applied to all the elements in a level of the hierarchy as it relates to the preceding level.

Dominance is useful in other areas that require measurement, such as in predicting the outcome of interactions of natural phenomena, or in predicting the outcome of decisions based on preferences. In passing, we note that to predict the outcome of competition, one does not need to answer questions involving utility, but the concept of dominance is natural for that purpose. The AHP has been used on numerous occasions to successfully predict the outcome of presidential elections, games, sports and other forms of competition. Given an outcome in the AHP, one asks: Which is more likely to be the cause of such an outcome and how important is this cause when compared with that cause? Conversely, given a cause one asks which is the more likely effect or outcome of this cause. Such questions can only be answered with respect to a criterion one has in mind. There are also problems involving natural conditions imposed on a decision. In all such problems, the outcome is not determined by the preference or utility of the judge, but by surmising the importance or dominance of the factor involved.

Dominance Among Criteria

It has been argued that one cannot assign importance weights to criteria without knowledge of the ranges of the particular alternatives. The vitamin example in which the need for vitamins is determined according to body needs (not its presence in foods to be chosen as alternatives) shows, that this is not a valid argument. People compare criteria most frequently without consulting the existing alternatives and their measurements. The weakness arises from focusing exclusively on the absolute measurement of alternatives one at a time, giving rise to the belief that it is the only way to do ranking. Consider an arithmetically illiterate person who is entirely unschooled in numbers, scales and arithmetic yet is a successful decision maker. Such an individual can say, without any knowledge about how to scale the alternatives, not only which alternative is more important on a criterion, but also which criterion is more important, and does it correctly, not accidentally. We believe that he does it by comparing them.

Note that people can correctly label one attribute as more important than another in an alternative. For example, one can say that a particular person is a better politician than a scientist. It can even be noted that this person is a much better politician than a scientist or that (s)he is about as good a politician as (s)he is a scientist. In the AHP criteria weights are often established with respect to a goal and independently from the alternatives. From the standpoint of absolute measurement, multiplying the relative weights of the alternatives by the weights of the criteria can be interpreted as a process of rescaling the criteria weights. This is analogous to the vitamin example where the ranges of the alternatives were irrelevant in deciding on the weights of the criteria. When the criteria derive their importance from the alternatives as if they are emergent properties of a particular set of alternatives, the AHP establishes their weights in terms of these alternatives. The first is a top down approach and the second is a bottom up approach. It is interesting to note that when alternatives are tied or nearly tied relative to the more important criteria, the less important criteria play a decisive role in ranking them.

Researchers have compared the use of dominance information with other forms of data such as proximity, profile, and conjoint. In making dominance comparisons, the question of what dominates what must be asked with regard to a third element, a property they have in common or a goal they serve. Shepard writes [31],

> Instead of giving "i dominates j" the geometrical interpretation "i falls beyond j in a particular direction," one can give it the alternative geometrical interpretation "i falls closer than j to a particular *ideal* point." These two interpretations become equivalent in the special case in which any ideal points move out sufficiently far beyond the periphery of the configuration of the remaining points.

He also says there is a connection between proximity and

dominance; for the first, closeness is taken between elements alone whereas in the second their closeness is related to an ideal.

Coombs [8] proposed that some combination of attributes is "ideal" to the decision maker who compares other elements in the decision with them as a frame of reference. The ideal as a standard helps to update what is important from experience and use it to evaluate the next choice to make (relative to what has been experienced and not to the ideal).

Experienced individuals gather and organize information (by repetition) about the impact of certain criteria in the satisfaction of a higher criterion or goal: the desired ideal. There are two models for interpreting how criteria are assessed as to importance. The first is the (w_i/w_j) model which assumes the elements in a paired comparison are measured in the mind on some inborn or acquired ratio scale and the ratios are then formed. To justify this, imagine the goal or criterion is divided according to the contributions of the criteria into ranges of degrees of fulfillment. These ranges cover such intensities as: negligible, moderate, strong, very strong, and extreme. A geometric scale is then used to assign values to the ranges and ratios are formed from these values.

The second is the $(w_i/w_j)/1$ model mentioned before in which the numerator is an absolute number, a multiple of the unit denominator. The goal is divided into ranges of perception, as in the fundamental scale of the AHP, as multiples of that unit, and a range is chosen and value assigned to the larger element as a multiple of that unit. Reciprocal comparison in the AHP is the tradeoff of one unit against another. This rationale explains how a person with no knowledge of actual weights, can hold a stone in each hand, and judge how many times heavier one is over the other. A person can also ably answer: How much more important is it for one to study than to do physical exercise to do well on a test? We said before that when there are absolute scales they do not automatically signify importance and must be interpreted in relative terms through comparisons. The ability to posit a criterion or goal in the mind, and make comparisons relative to that goal is what people do. Experience indicates that people can do this successfully and willingly without being coached. Schoemaker and Waid [30] have compared the validity of the results obtained through the AHP with those obtained by other methods and found that direct judgment comparisons give close results on their respective scales.

7. The Measurement of Inconsistency and The Principal Right Eigenvector

The AHP deals with consistency explicitly because in making paired comparisons, just as in thinking, people do not have the intrinsic logical ability to always be consistent. Thus if we can identify how serious this inconsistency is and where it can be improved, we can also improve the quality of a decision. In the AHP we both locate the inconsistency and suggest the optimal value to improve it. The suggested value or some value in that direction may be adopted if it is compatible with the overall understanding. The measurement of inconsistency and the derived scale must be structurally linked in order to determine the most inconsistent judgments. Otherwise a general measure of inconsistency given in statistical terms cannot be brought to focus on particular judgments as one can with the eigenvalue and the eigenvector.

The eigenvector is associated with the idea of dominance and consistency of judgments. It is the only way to capture inconsistency in the judgments [24]. The degree of inconsistency is measured by the deviation of the principal eigenvalue of the matrix of comparisons from the order of the matrix. We use the right eigenvector, and not the left, because in the paired comparisons the smaller of two elements serves as the unit and the larger element is given as a multiple of that unit. It is not possible to take the larger of two elements and ask what fraction of it is the smaller one without first using the latter to decompose the former.

Thus we can only say what dominates what. What is dominated has the reciprocal value. A dominance matrix also has a left eigenvector that measures "dominated" through the forced reciprocal relation. In principle one would like another left eigenvector that measures "dominated" directly by comparing the smaller element with the larger one, thus eliciting new kinds of information in the comparisons, but as just noted this is not possible. The principal left and right eigenvectors of any matrix are structurally linked. If the matrix is consistent, left and right eigenvectors are elementwise reciprocal. But this can also hold true in special cases when the matrix is inconsistent [26].

When the judgments are inconsistent, the need for the principal right eigenvector and for no other derived scale has been mathematically proved in two ways. The first uses a theorem in matrix theory which says that a small perturbation of a matrix leads to a small perturbation of its eigenvalues and left and right eigenvectors. The principal eigenvector setting obtained algebraically in the consistent case should go over to a principal eigenvector setting in the inconsistent case. The other way is that due to inconsistency, all powers of the matrix of judgments participate in determining the priority vector. When the contribution of each matrix, obtained by normalizing its row sums, is averaged over the vectors and on passing to the limit the principal right eigenvector is obtained [23]. Eigenvector ranking is arrived at deductively without additional assumptions as those made by least squares and logarithmic least squares methods which superimpose a criterion to minimize errors and derive ranks that do not relate to inconsistency and sometimes lead to different ranking which in the case of least squares may not be unique [21].

8. Synthesis

In multicriteria decision making, synthesis of the rankings of the alternatives with respect to the several criteria requires the use of mathematics. In the AHP hierarchic composition uses an additive multilinear function, a special case of the dependence approach of the supermatrix in which composition involves raising that matrix to infinite power leading to a highly nonlinear function. In a hierarchy dependence only occurs from level to level and the elements in a level are also independent. In that case hierarchic composition is a special case of network dominance composition and leads to an additive function from one level to the next. Multiple levels of the hierarchy give rise to a multilinear form (a tensor) that does not behave as an additive linear function, but is non-linear.

Another argument derives from the questionable belief that one can fix a structure to model a problem and adopt manipulations that satisfy some axioms. In the AHP more of the burden is placed on a comprehensive structure adjusted to incorporate new information and also new expectations about the priorities represented in terms of concrete criteria and subcriteria. It is not reasonable to think of computational operations as some kind of magic to capture every important nuance one would like to see come out. The outcome of the manipulations arising from paired comparisons in fact has far reaching mathematical properties. Depending on the breadth and depth of the hierarchy, a multilinear form can be used to come as close as desired to any preconceived underlying answer.

In the supermatrix approach, the limiting priorities are given by a general nonlinear form with an infinite number of terms each of which is an infinite product of linear variables. There can be no general functional form for the computations that captures all expectations. No matter how general a composition function one may adopt, there would always be examples calling for a still more general one to capture a higher order nonlinearity not captured by the existing method. At best we can derive multilinear forms that come arbitrarily closely to any expectation. (Polynomials, and more generally multinomials are dense in the space of continuous functions, and may be viewed as a special case of multilinear forms in n-dimensional space.)

9. Normative - Descriptive [7]

All science is descriptive not normative. It is based on the notion that knowledge is incomplete. It uses language and mathematics to understand, describe and predict events sometimes as a test of the accuracy of the theory. Events involve two things: 1) controllable and uncontrollable conditions (e.g. laws) and 2) people or objects characterized by matter, energy and motion influenced by and sometimes influencing these conditions. A missile's path is subject to uncontrollable forces like gravity and controllable forces like the initial aim of the missile, its weight, perhaps the wind, and others. The conditions are not determined by the objects involved. The idea is to get the missile from A to B by describing its path with precision.

Economics based on expected utility theory is predicated on the idea that the collective behavior of many individuals, each motivated by self interest, determines the market conditions which in turn influence or control each individual's behavior. In this case both the objects and the conditions are "up for grabs" because behavior is subject to rational influences that are thought to be understood. By optimizing individual behavior through rationality one can optimize the collective conditions and the resulting system, plus or minus some corrections in the conditions. But conditions are not all economic. Some are environmental, some social, some political and others cultural. We know little about their interactions. In attempting to include everything, normative theories treat intangible criteria as tangibles by postulating a convenient economic scale. It is hard to justify reducing all intangibles to economics in order to give the appearance of completeness. It is not clear that economic progress solves all problems. To the contrary, some believe that it can create problems in other areas of human concern. A normative theory requires criteria established by particular people external to the process of decision making. Experts often disagree on the criteria to judge the excellence of a normative theory and the decision resulting from it. For example, a basic criterion of Utility Theory is the principle of rationality which says that if a person is offered more of that which he values, he should opt to take more. It is precisely in response to this dictum that Herbert Simon [32] developed his idea of sufficiency (satisficing). Whenever we are saturated even with a highly valued commodity, there is a cutoff point where the marginal increase in total value is less than or equal to zero. A theory constructed to satisfy such a fundamental assumption will encounter difficulties in its applications. In such situations rank reversals would be appropriate in order to prevent the disadvantages of oversaturation.

The AHP is a descriptive theory in the sense of the physical sciences. It treats people separately from the conditions in which they find themselves, because so far we have no comprehensive and integrated theory of socio-economic-political-environmental-cultural factors that would enable us to deduce optimality principles for people's behavior. Completeness and optimality imply that there is an underlying order of which the solution of a problem simply elicits the relevant part of the order. There should be no surprises by changing rank due to some left out alternative particularly if it is "irrelevant".

The AHP does not insist that a decision is necessarily a wrong one unless it is done in some prescribed way and according to some rules. The purpose of the AHP is to assist people in organizing their thoughts and judgments to make more effective decisions. Its structures are based on observations of how influences are transmitted and its arithmetic derives from how psychologists have observed people to function in attempting to understand their behavior.

The AHP begins with the traditional concept of ordinal preference and advances further into numerical paired comparisons from which a ranking is derived. By imposing a multiplicative structure on the numbers ($a_{ij} \cdot a_{jk} = a_{ik}$), the reciprocal condition is obtained. Thus the AHP infers behavioral characteristics of judgments (inconsistency and intransitivity) from its basic framework of paired comparisons. It begins by taking situations with a known underlying ratio scale and hence known comparison ratios, and shows how its method of deriving a scale uniquely through the eigenvector gives back the original scale. Then through perturbation it shows that a derived scale should continue through the eigenvector to approximate the original scale providing that there is high consistency.

How then do we judge the soundness of a decision theory besides legislating normative standards? In the AHP the optimality of a decision depends on the value system and experience of the consistent decision maker and not on the rules and thoughts of experts creating scales. (S)He is assisted by mathematical procedures that produce the best rank order relative to the structure of his decision framework. In the AHP, as in any activity in life, the decision maker does not need to rely on an expert but rather becomes an expert through study and practice and the assistance of other decision makers.

10. Conclusions

J. Aczel [1] cites an anonymous quotation which says:

> "An economist is someone who cannot see something working in practice without asking whether it would work in theory."

As a descriptive rather than a prescriptive theory, the AHP will undergo adaptation by practitioners. Apart from the elicitation of judgment regarding dependence in the AHP, a uniform process is applied throughout to derive the priorities. The arithmetic operations in the AHP are based on the notion of dominance that is a prominent aspect of human thinking. These operations are also known in mathematics, the behavioral sciences, and generalizations in hierarchies and networks. In applications they give rise to what is known as an additive model in a hierarchy and a compound nonlinear model in a network. By increasing the number of levels and elements in each level, the former leads to a multilinear form, a tensor, which from its definition is nonlinear. With such forms one can approximate arbitrarily closely to any underlying measurements. Thus in a sufficiently elaborate hierarchy, and more generally throughout the AHP, an additive model is appropriate. As a descriptive theory, the AHP processes ranking through four general modes: 1) The absolute mode, to preserve rank or impose known standards on the alternatives, 2) The ideal mode, to preserve rank from irrelevant alternatives, 3) The distributive mode, to allow rank to change when the number and measurement of alternatives can affect preference among the alternatives by considering them as a set rather than one at a time, and 4) The supermatrix mode, to deal with dependence among the criteria or among the alternatives and between the criteria and the alternatives. The extension of the AHP to neural networks with Fredholm operators as generalizations of the eigenvalue formulation applied in the context of a hierarchy and a network appears in Chapter 13.

References

1.   Aczel, J., 1991, "Why, How and How Not to Apply Mathematics to Economics and to Other Social and Behavioral Sciences. An Example: Merging Relative Scores", Proceedings of the Seminar Debrecen-Graz, Grazer Math. Ber. 315.

2.   Bard, J. F., 1986, "A Multiobjective Methodology for Selecting Subsystem Automation Options", Management Science 32/12, pp. 1628-1641.

3.   Bauer, R.A., E. Collar and V. Tang, 1992, "Allocating Resources by Setting Priorities", Chapter 5 in: "The Silverlake Project - Transformation at IBM", Oxford University Press, New York.

4.   Blocksma, M., Reading the Numbers, A Survival Guide to the Measurements, Numbers, and Sizes Encountered in Everyday Life, New York: Viking-Penguin, Inc., 1989.

5.   ------------- and J.M. Alexander, Conflict Resolution: The Analytic Hierarchy Approach, New York, Praeger Publishers, 1989.

6.   Buede, D. M., 1992, "Software Review: Three Packages for AHP: Critcrium, Expert Choice and HIPRE 3+", J. of Multi-Criteria Decision Analysis 1, pp. 119-121.

7.   Cook, T., P. Falchi and R. Mariano, 1984, "An Urban Allocation Model Combining Time Series and Analytic Hierarchical Methods", Management Science 30/2, pp. 198-208.

8.   Coombs, C.H., 1964, A Theory of Data, John Wiley and Sons, New York.

9.   Communications of the Operations Research Society of Japan 31/8, 1986.

10. European Journal of Operational Research 48/1, Special Issue: Decision Making by the Analytic Hierarchy Process: Theory and Applications, 1990.

11. Forman, E.H., 1990, "Facts and Fictions about the Analytic Hierarchy Process", in: Multicriteria Decision Making by T.L. Saaty, RWS Publications.

12. Golden, B.L., E.A. Wasil and P.T. Harker (eds.), 1989, "The Analytic Hierarchy Process: Applications and Studies", Springer-Verlag, New York.

13. Hamalainen, R. P., 1988, "Computer Assisted Energy Policy Analysis in the Parliament of Finland", Interfaces 18/4, pp. 12-23.

14. Keeney, R.L. and H. Raiffa, 1976, Decisions with Multiple Objectives: Preference and Value Tradeoffs, Wiley, New York, NY.

15. Mathematical Modelling 9/3-5, 1987, R. Saaty and L. Vargas (eds.), Special Issue: The Analytic Hierarchy Process - Theoretical Developments and Some Applications.

16. Mathematical Modelling 17/4-5, 1993, L. Vargas and F. Zahedi (eds.), Special Issue: The Analytic Hierarchy Process.

17. "Proceedings of The 2nd International Symposium on The Analytic Hierarchy Process: Vol. 1 and 2", University of Pittsburgh, Pittsburgh, PA, 1991.

18. "Reprints of International Symposium on the analytic Hierarchy Process", Tianjin University, Tianjin, China, 1988.

19. Saaty, T. L., 1977, "Scenarios and Priorities in Transport Planning: Application to the Sudan", Transportation Research 11/5.

20. -------------, 1977, "The Sudan Transport Study", Interfaces 8/1, pp. 37-57.

21.   -------------, and L.G. Vargas, 1984, "Comparison of Eigenvalue, Logarithmic Least Squares and Least Squares Methods in Estimating Ratios", Mathematical Modelling 5/5, 309-324.

22.   -------------, 1987, "Risk: Its Priority and Probability, The Analytic Hierarchy Process," Risk Analysis 7/2.

23.   -------------, 1987, "Rank According to Perron: A New Insight," Mathematics Magazine 60/4, pp. 11-21.

24.   -------------, 1990, Multicriteria Decision Making: The Analytic Hierarchy Process, RWS Publications, 4922 Ellsworth Ave., Pittsburgh, PA.

25.   ------------- and K.P. Kearns, 1991, Analytical Planning, RWS Publications, Pittsburgh, PA.

26.   ------------- and L.G. Vargas, 1984, "Inconsistency and Rank Preservation", Journal of Mathematical Psychology 28/2, June.

27.   ------------- and L.G. Vargas, 1987, "Uncertainty and rank order in the analytic hierarchy process", European Journal of Operational Research 32, pp. 107-117.

28.   ------------- and L.G. Vargas, 1991, Prediction, Projection and Forecasting, Kluwer Academic, Boston.

29.   ------------- and L.G. Vargas, early 1993, "A Model of Neural Impulse Firing and Synthesis", forthcoming in Journal of Mathematical Psychology.

30.   Schoemaker, P.J.H. and C.C. Waid, 1982, "An experimental comparison of different approaches to determining weights in additive utility models", Management Science 28/2, pp. 182-196.

31. Shepard, R.N., 1972, "A Taxonomy of Some Principal Types of Data and of Multidimensional Methods for their Analysis", in Multidimensional Scaling, eds. R.N. Shepard, A.K, Romney and S.B. Nerlove, Seminar Press, New York.

32. Simon, Herbert A., 1955, "A Behavioral Model of Rational Choice", Quarterly Journal of Economics 69, pp. 99-118.

33. Simon, H.A., 1957, Models of Man, Wiley, New York.

34. -------------, 1977, The New Science of Management Decision. Englewood Cliffs, N.J.: Prentice Hall.

35. Socio-Economic Planning Sciences 20/6, Special Issue: The Analytic Hierarchy Process, 1986.

36. Socio-Economic Planning Sciences 25/2, Special Issue: Public-Sector Applications of the Analytic Hierarchy Process, 1991.

37. Vargas, L. G., 1990, "An Overview of the Analytic Hierarchy Process and its Applications", European J. of Operational Research 48/1, pp. 2-8.

38. Zahedi, F., 1986, "The Analytic Hierarchy Process--a Survey of the Method and its Applications", Interfaces 16/4, pp. 96-108.

CHAPTER TEN

FOUNDATIONS - AXIOMS AND CONSEQUENCES

1. Introduction

Three principles guide one in problem solving using the AHP: decomposition, comparative judgments, and synthesis of priorities.

The decomposition principle is applied by structuring a simple problem with elements in a level independent from those in succeeding levels. It works downward from the goal in the top level, to criteria bearing on the goal in the second level, followed by subcriteria in the third level, and so on. It starts at the more general (and sometimes uncertain) and moves toward the more particular and concrete. We make a distinction between two types of dependence which we call functional and structural. The former is the familiar contextual dependence of elements on other elements in performing their function whereas the latter is the dependence of the importance or priority of elements on the priority itself and number of other elements. Absolute measurement, sometimes called scoring, is used when it is desired to ignore structural dependence between elements while relative measurement is used in the alternative case.

The principle of comparative judgments is applied to construct pairwise comparisons of the relative importance of elements in some given level with respect to a shared criterion or property in the level above. This builds a reciprocal paired comparison matrix and its corresponding principal eigenvector.

The third principle is that of synthesizing the priorities. In the AHP priorities are synthesized from the second level down by multiplying local priorities by the priority of their corresponding criterion in the level above, and adding for each element in a level according to the criteria it affects. (The second level elements are multiplied by unity, the weight of the single top level goal). This calculation gives the composite or global priority of that element, which is then used to weight the local priorities of the elements in the level below when compared with respect to the element as a criterion or attribute, and so on to the bottom level. We will prove later that this method of composition is the optimal way to rank alternatives by capturing their separate ranks with respect to all the criteria.

2. The Axioms

Let $\mathfrak{A}$ be a finite set of n elements called alternatives. Let $\mathfrak{C}$ be a set of properties or attributes with respect to which elements in $\mathfrak{A}$ are compared. A property is a feature that an object or individual possesses even if we are ignorant of this fact, whereas an attribute is a feature we assign to some object: it is a concept. Here we assume that properties and attributes are interchangeable and generally refer to them as criteria. A *criterion* is a primitive.

When two objects or elements in $\mathfrak{A}$ are compared according to a criterion C in $\mathfrak{C}$, we say that we are performing binary comparisons. Let $>_C$ be a binary relation on $\mathfrak{A}$ representing "more preferred than" or "dominates" with respect to a criterion C in $\mathfrak{C}$. Let $\sim_C$ be the binary relation "indifferent to" with respect to a criterion C in $\mathfrak{C}$. Hence, given two elements, $A_i, A_j \in \mathfrak{A}$, either $A_i >_C A_j$ or $A_j >_C A_i$ or $A_i \sim_C A_j$ for all $C \in \mathfrak{C}$. We use $A_i \gtrsim_C A_j$ to indicate more preferred or indifferent. A given *family of binary relations* $>_C$ with respect to a criterion C in $\mathfrak{C}$ is a primitive. We shall use this primitive relation to derive the notion of priority or importance both with respect to one criterion and also with respect to several.

Let $\mathfrak{B}$ be the set of mappings from $\mathfrak{A} \times \mathfrak{A}$ to $\mathbb{R}^+$ (the set of positive reals). Let $f: \mathfrak{C} \rightarrow \mathfrak{B}$. Let $P_C \epsilon f(C)$ for $C \epsilon \mathfrak{C}$. P_C assigns a positive real number to every pair $(A_i, A_j) \epsilon \mathfrak{A} \times \mathfrak{A}$. Let $P_C(A_i, A_j) \equiv a_{ij} \epsilon \mathbb{R}^+$, $A_i, A_j \epsilon \mathfrak{A}$. For each $C \epsilon \mathfrak{C}$, the triple $(\mathfrak{A} \times \mathfrak{A}, \mathbb{R}^+, P_C)$ is a *fundamental* or *primitive scale*. A fundamental scale is a mapping of objects to a numerical system.

Definition - For all $A_i, A_j \epsilon \mathfrak{A}$ and $C \epsilon \mathfrak{C}$

$$A_i >_c A_j \qquad \text{if and only if } P_C(A_i, A_j) > 1,$$
$$A_i \sim_c A_j \qquad \text{if and only if } P_C(A_i, A_j) = 1.$$

If $A_i >_c A_j$ we say that A_i dominates A_j with respect to $C \epsilon \mathfrak{C}$. Thus P_C represents the intensity or strength of preference for one alternative over another.

Axiom 1 (Reciprocal). For all A_i, $A_j \epsilon \mathfrak{A}$ and $C \epsilon \mathfrak{C}$
$$P_C(A_i, A_j) = 1/P_C(A_j, A_i).$$

Whenever we make paired comparisons we need to consider both members of the pair to judge the relative value. The smaller or lesser one is first illustrated and used as the unit for the criterion in question. The other is then estimated as a not necessarily integer multiple of that unit. Thus for example, if one stone is judged to be five times heavier than another, then the other is automatically one fifth as heavy as the first because it participated in making the first judgment. The comparison matrices that we consider are formed by making paired reciprocal comparisons. It is this simple, yet powerful means of resolving multicriteria problems that is the basis of the AHP.

Let $A = (a_{ij}) \equiv (P_C(A_i, A_j))$ be the set of paired comparisons of the alternatives with respect to a criterion $C \epsilon \mathfrak{C}$. By Axiom 1, A is a positive reciprocal matrix. The object is to obtain a *scale of relative dominance* (or *rank order*) of the alternatives from the paired comparisons given in A.

There is a natural way to derive the relative dominance of a set of alternatives from a pairwise comparison matrix A.

Definition - Let $R_{M(n)}$ be the set of $(n \times n)$ positive reciprocal matrices $A = (a_{ij}) \equiv (P_C(A_i, A_j))$ for all $C \in \mathfrak{C}$. Let $[0,1]^n$ be the n-fold cartesian product of $[0,1]$ and let $\psi(A) : R_{M(n)} \rightarrow [0,1]^n$ for $A \in R_{M(n)}$, $\psi(A)$ is an n-dimensional vector whose components lie in the interval $[0,1]$. The triple $(R_{M(n)}, [0,1]^n, \psi)$ is a *derived scale*. A derived scale is a mapping between two numerical relational systems.

It is important to point out that the rank order implied by the derived scale ψ may not coincide with the order represented by the pairwise comparisons. Let $\psi_i(A)$ be the ith component of $\psi(A)$. It denotes the relative dominance of the ith alternative. By definition, for $A_i, A_j \in \mathfrak{A}$, $A_i >_C A_j$ implies $P_C(A_i, A_j) > 1$. However, if $P_C(A_i, A_j) > 1$, the derived scale could imply that $\psi_j(A) > \psi_i(A)$. This occurs if row dominance does not hold, i.e., for A_i, $A_j \in \mathfrak{A}$ and $C \in \mathfrak{C}$, $P_C(A_i, A_j) \geq P_C(A_j, A_k)$ does not hold for all $A_k \in \mathfrak{A}$. In other words, it may happen that $P_C(A_i, A_j) > 1$, and for some $A_k \in \mathfrak{A}$ we have

$$P_C(A_i, A_k) < P_C(A_j, A_k).$$

A more restrictive condition is the following:

Definition - The mapping P_C is said to be *consistent* if and only if $P_c(A_i, A_j)P_c(A_j, A_k) = P_c(A_i, A_k)$ for all i, j, and k. Similarly the matrix A is consistent if and only if $a_{ij}a_{jk} = a_{ik}$ for all i, j and k.

If P_C is consistent, then Axiom 1 automatically follows and the rank order induced by ψ coincides with pairwise comparisons.

Luis Vargas has proposed through personal communication with the author, that the following "behavioral" independence axiom could be used instead of the more mathematical reciprocal axiom that would then follow as a theorem. However, the reciprocal relation does not imply independence as defined by him, and unless one wishes to assume independence, one should retain the reciprocal axiom.

Two alternatives A_i and A_j are said to be mutually independent with respect to a criterion $C \epsilon \mathfrak{C}$, if and only if, for any A_k the paired comparison of the cluster $\{A_i, A_j\}$ with respect to A_k satisfies

and

$$P_C [\{A_i,A_j\},A_k] = P_C(A_i,A_k) \, P_C(A_j,A_k)$$

$$P_C [A_k,\{A_i,A_j\}] = P_C(A_k,A_i) \, P_C(A_k,A_j)$$

A set of alternatives is said to be independent if they are mutually independent.

Axiom 1´   All the alternatives in $\mathfrak{A}$ are independent.

Hierarchic Axioms

Definition - A *partially ordered set* is a set S with a binary relation $\leq$ which satisfies the following conditions:

(a) Reflexive: For all $x \epsilon S$, $x \leq x$,
(b) Transitive: For all $x,y,z \epsilon S$, if $x \leq y$ and $y \leq z$ then $x \leq z$,
(c) Antisymmetric: For all $x,y \epsilon S$, if $x \leq y$ and $y \leq x$ then $x = y$ (x and y coincide).

Definition - For any relation $x \leq y$ (read, y includes x) we define $x < y$ to mean that $x \leq y$ and $x \neq y$. y is said to *cover* (*dominate*) x if $x < y$ and if $x < t < y$ is possible for no t.

Partially ordered sets with a finite number of elements can be conveniently represented by a directed graph. Each element of the set is represented by a vertex so that an arc is directed from y to x if $x < y$.

Definition - A subset E of a partially ordered set S is said to be *bounded* from above (below) if there is an element $s \in S$ such that $x \leq s$ ($\geq s$) for every $x \in E$. The element s is called an upper (lower) bound of E. We say that E has a supremum (infimum) if it has upper (lower) bounds and if the set of upper (lower) bounds U (L) has an element $u_1(l_1)$ such that $u_1 \leq u$ for all $u \in U$ ($l_1 \geq l$ for all $l \in L$).

Definition - Let $\mathfrak{H}$ be a finite partially ordered set with largest element b. $\mathfrak{H}$ is a *hierarchy* if it satisfies the conditions:

(1) There is a partition of $\mathfrak{H}$ into sets called levels { L_k = 1,2,..., h }, where $L_1 = \{b\}$.
(2) $x \in L_k$ implies $x^- \subseteq L_{k+1}$, where $x^- = \{y \mid x$ covers $y \}$, $k = 1,2,..., h - 1$.
(3) $x \in L_k$ implies $x^+ \subseteq L_{k-1}$, where $x^+ = \{y \mid y$ covers $x \}$, $k = 2,3,..., h$.

Definition - Given a positive real number $\rho \geq 1$ a nonempty set $x^- \subseteq L_{k+1}$ is said to be ρ-homogeneous with respect to $x \in L_k$ if for every pair of elements $y_1, y_2 \in x^-$, $1/\rho \leq P_C(y_1, y_2) \leq \rho$. In particular the reciprocal axiom implies that $P_C(y_i, y_i) = 1$.

Axiom 2 Given a hierarchy $\mathfrak{H}$, $x \in \mathfrak{H}$ and $x \in L_k$, $x^- \subseteq L_{k+1}$ is ρ-homogeneous for $k = 1, ..., h$-1.

Homogeneity is essential for comparing similar things, as the mind tends to make large errors in comparing widely disparate elements. For example we cannot compare a grain of sand with an orange according to size. When the disparity is great, the elements are placed in separate clusters of comparable size giving rise to the idea of levels and their decomposition. This axiom is closely related to the well-known Archimedean property which says that forming two real numbers x and y with x < y, there is an integer n such that nx $\geq$ y, or n $\geq$ y/x.

The notions of fundamental and derived scales can be

extended to $x \epsilon L_k$, $x^- \subseteq L_{k+1}$ replacing $\mathfrak{C}$ and $\mathfrak{A}$ respectively. The derived scale resulting from comparing the elements in x^- with respect to x is called a *local derived scale* or *local priorities*. Here no irrelevant alternative is included in the comparisons and such alternatives are assumed to receive the value of zero in the derived scale.

Given L_k, $L_{k+1} \subseteq \mathfrak{H}$, let us denote the local derived scale for $y \epsilon x^-$ and $x \epsilon L_k$ by $\psi_{k+1}(y \mid x)$, $k = 2,3,\ldots, h$-1. Without loss of generality we may assume that $\Sigma_{y \in x^-} \psi_{k+1}(y \mid x) = 1$. Consider the matrix $\psi_k(L_k \mid L_{k-1})$ whose columns are local derived scales of elements in L_k with respect to elements in L_{k-1}.

Definition - A set $\mathfrak{A}$ is said to be *outer dependent* on a set $\mathfrak{C}$ if a fundamental scale can be defined on $\mathfrak{A}$ with respect to every $c \epsilon \mathfrak{C}$.

Decomposition implies containment of the small elements by the large clusters or levels. In turn, this means that the smaller elements depend on the outer parent elements to which they belong, which themselves fall in a large cluster of the hierarchy. The process of relating elements (e.g., alternatives) in one level of the hierarchy according to the elements of the next higher level (e.g., criteria) expresses the outer dependence of the lower elements on the higher elements. This way comparisons can be made between them. The steps are repeated upward in the hierarchy through each pair of adjacent levels to the top element, the focus or goal.

The elements in a level may depend on one another with respect to a property in another level. Input-output dependence of industries (e.g. manufacturing) demonstrates the idea of inner dependence. This may be formalized as follows:

Definition - Let $\mathfrak{A}$ be outer dependent on $\mathfrak{C}$. The elements in $\mathfrak{A}$ are said to be *inner dependent* with respect to $C \epsilon \mathfrak{C}$ if for some $A \epsilon \mathfrak{A}$, $\mathfrak{A}$ is outer dependent on A.

Axiom 3 Let $\mathfrak{H}$ be a hierarchy with levels $L_1, L_2, \ldots, L_h$. For each L_k, $k = 1, 2, \ldots, h\text{-}1$,

(1) L_{k+1} is outer dependent on L_k,

(2) L_k is not outer dependent on L_{k+1},

(3) L_{k+1} is not inner dependent with respect to any $x \in L_k$.

Principle of Hierarchic Composition. Later we show that if Axiom 3 holds, the global derived scale (rank order) of any element in $\mathfrak{H}$ is obtained from its component in the corresponding vector of the following:

$$\psi_1(b) = 1,$$
$$\psi_2(L_2) = \psi_2(b^- \mid b),$$
$$\vdots \qquad\qquad \vdots$$
$$\psi_k(L_k) = \psi_k(L_k \mid L_{k\text{-}1}), \psi_{k\text{-}1}(L_{k\text{-}1}), \qquad k = 3, \ldots, h.$$

Were one to omit Axiom 3, the Principle of Hierarchic Composition would no longer apply because of outer and inner dependence among levels or components which need not form a hierarchy. The appropriate composition principle is derived from the supermatrix approach of which the Principle of Hierarchic Composition is a special case [4].

A hierarchy is a special case of a system, the definition of which is given by:

Definition - Let $\mathfrak{S}$ be a family of nonempty sets $\mathfrak{C}_1, \mathfrak{C}_2, \ldots, \mathfrak{C}_n$, where $\mathfrak{C}_i$ consists of the elements $\{e_{ij}, j = 1, \ldots, m_i \}$, $i = 1, 2, \ldots, n$. $\mathfrak{S}$ is a system if it is a directed graph whose vertices are $\mathfrak{C}_i$ and whose arcs are defined through the concept of outer dependence; thus given two components $\mathfrak{C}_i$ and $\mathfrak{C}_j \in \mathfrak{S}$ there is an arc from $\mathfrak{C}_i$ to $\mathfrak{C}_j$ if $\mathfrak{C}_j$ is outer dependent on $\mathfrak{C}_i$.

Axiom 3´ Let $\mathfrak{S}$ be a system consisting of the subsets C_1, $C_2,...C_n$. For each C_i there is some C_j so that either C_i is outer dependent on C_j or C_j is outer dependent on C_i or both.

Note that C_i may be outer dependent on C_i which is equivalent to inner dependence in a hierarchy. Actually Axiom 3´ would by itself be adequate without Axiom 3. We have separated them because of the importance of hierarchic structures that are more widespread at the time of this writing than are systems with feedback.

Many of the concepts derived for hierarchies also relate to systems with feedback. Here one needs to characterize dependence among the elements. We now give a criterion for this purpose.

Let $D_A \subseteq \mathfrak{A}$ be the set of elements of $\mathfrak{A}$ outer dependent on $A \in \mathfrak{A}$. Let $\psi_{A_i,C}(A_j)$, $A_j \in \mathfrak{A}$ be the derived scale of the elements of $\mathfrak{A}$ with respect to $A_i \in \mathfrak{A}$, for a criterion $C \in \mathfrak{C}$. Let $\psi_C(A_j)$, $A_j \in \mathfrak{A}$ be the derived scale of the elements of $\mathfrak{A}$ with respect to a criterion $C \in \mathfrak{C}$. We define the dependence weight

$$\phi_C(A_j) = \sum_{A_i \in D_{A_j}} \psi_{A_i,C}(A_j)\, \psi_C(A_i) .$$

If the elements of $\mathfrak{A}$ are inner dependent with respect to $C \in \mathfrak{C}$, then $\psi_C(A_i) \neq \psi_C(A_j)$ for some $A_j \in \mathfrak{A}$.

Expectations are beliefs about the rank of alternatives derived from prior knowledge. Assume that a decision maker has a ranking, arrived at intuitively, of a finite set of alternatives $\mathfrak{A}$ with respect to prior knowledge of criteria $\mathfrak{C}$.

Axiom 4 (Expectations).

    (1)   Completeness : $\mathfrak{C} \subset \mathfrak{H} - L_h$, $\mathfrak{A} = L_h$.

    (2)   Rank : To preserve rank independently of what and how many other alternatives there may be. Alternatively, to allow

rank to be influenced by the number and the measurements of alternatives that are added to or deleted from the set.

This axiom simply says that those thoughtful individuals who have reasons for their beliefs should make sure that their ideas are adequately represented for the outcome to match these expectations; i.e., all criteria are represented in the hierarchy. It assumes neither rationality of the process nor that it can only accommodate a rational outlook. People could have expectations that are branded irrational in someone else's framework. It also says that the rank of alternatives depends on both the expectations of the decision maker and on the nature of a decision problem.

3. Results from the Axioms

Note that if P_C is consistent, then Axiom 1 follows, i.e., consistency implies the reciprocal property. The first few theorems below are based on this more restrictive property of consistency.

They show that paired comparisons and the principal eigenvector are useful in estimating ratios. We use perturbation arguments to demonstrate that the principal eigenvector solution is the appropriate way to derive rank order from inconsistent data. They also show that the eigenvector is stable to small perturbations in the data where the number of elements compared is small. These results are also obtained by means of graph theoretic arguments. Let $R_{C(n)} \subset R_{M(n)}$ be the set of all ($n \times n$) consistent matrices.

A few facts from matrix algebra will be useful.

If $|A|$ is the determinant of A, and if $\lambda_1, ..., \lambda_n$ are the eigenvalues of A, then $|A| = \lambda_1 \cdots \lambda_n$. This follows from the fact that the characteristic polynomial of A satisfies the relation, $|\lambda I - A| = (\lambda - \lambda_1) \cdots (\lambda - \lambda_n)$, and on putting $\lambda = 0$, we have $|A| = (-1)^n |A| = (-1)^n \lambda_1 \cdots \lambda_n$ and the result follows. It is now clear that a matrix is singular if and only if at least one of its eigenvalues is zero.

The trace of a matrix A denoted by Trace (A), is the sum of its diagonal coefficients. We want to show that Trace (A) is equal to the sum of the eigenvalues of A. We proceed by induction. When A is 2 by 2 we have $| \lambda I\text{-}A | = \lambda^2\text{-}(a_{11}+a_{22})\lambda\text{-}a_{21}a_{12}$. For a 3 by 3 matrix we extend the 2 by 2 case by a third row and third column and calculate the determinant by using either the third row or third column. Only the term $\lambda\text{-}a_{33}$ contributes to the terms λ^3 and λ^2. Multiplication by λ gives $\lambda^3\text{-}(a_{11}+a_{22})\lambda^2\text{-}a_{21}a_{12}\lambda$. Multiplication by $-a_{33}$ contributes $-a_{33}\lambda^2 + \cdots$. Hence, the coefficient of λ^2 would be $-(a_{11}+a_{22}+a_{33})$. It is clear that if this reasoning is true for $n=k$ it is also true for $n=k+1$ and hence it is true in general. Thus, $\lambda^{n-1}\sum_{i=1}^{n} a_{ii}$ equals the term $\lambda^{n-1}\sum_{i=1}^{n} \lambda_i$ in the expansion of

$$(\lambda\text{-}\lambda_1) \cdots (\lambda\text{-}\lambda_n), \text{ and Trace (A)} = \sum_{i=1}^{n} \lambda_i.$$

Theorem 10.1 (Consistency and Rank) *Let $A \in R_{M(n)}$. $A \in R_{C(n)}$ if and only if rank $(A) = 1$.*

Proof If $A \in R_{C(n)}$, then $a_{ij}a_{jk} = a_{ik}$ for all i, j and k. Hence, given a row of A, $a_{i1}, a_{i2}, \ldots, a_{in}$, all other rows can be obtained from it by means of the relation $a_{jk} = a_{ik} / a_{ij}$ and rank $(A) = 1$.

Let us now assume that rank $(A) = 1$. Given a row a_{jh} ($j \neq i$, $h = 1,2,\ldots,n$), $a_{jh} = Ma_{ih}$ ($h = 1,2,\ldots,n$) where M is a positive constant. Also, for any reciprocal matrix, $a_{ii} = 1$ ($i = 1,2,\ldots,n$). Thus, for $i=h$ we have $a_{ji} = Ma_{ii} = M$ and $a_{jh} = a_{ji}a_{ih}$ for all i, j and k, and A is consistent.

Theorem 10.2 (Consistency and the Principal Eigenvalue) *Let $A \in R_{M(n)}$. $A \in R_{C(n)}$ if and only if its principal eigenvalue λ_{max} is equal to n.*

Proof By Theorem 10.1 we have rank$(A) = 1$. Also, all

eigenvalues of A but one vanish. Since Trace $(A) = \sum_{i=1}^{n} a_{ii} = n$ and Trace $(A) = \sum_{k} \lambda_k = n$, then $\lambda_{max} \equiv \lambda_1 = n$.

If $\lambda_{max} = n$, then

$$n\lambda_{max} = \sum_{i,j=1}^{n} a_{ij} w_j w_i^{-1} = n + \sum_{1 \leq i < j \leq n} (a_{ij} w_j w_i^{-1} + a_{ji} w_i w_j^{-1})$$

$$\equiv n + \sum_{1 \leq i \leq j \leq n} (y_{ij} + 1/y_{ij}).$$

Since $y_{ij} + y_{ij}^{-1} \geq 2$, and $n\lambda_{max} = n^2$, equality is uniquely obtained on putting $y_{ij} = 1$, i.e. $a_{ij} = w_i/w_j$. The condition $a_{ij}a_{jk} = a_{ik}$ holds for all i, j and k, and the result follows.

Theorem 10.3 (Ratios and Consistency) *Let $A = (a_{ij}) \in R_{C(n)}$. There exists a function $\psi = (\psi_1, \psi_2, \ldots, \psi_n)$, $\psi : R_{C(n)} \rightarrow [0,1]^n$ such that*

    (i) $a_{ij} = \psi_i(A)/\psi_j(A)$,
    (ii) *The relative dominance of the ith alternative, $\psi_i(A)$, is the ith component of the principal right eigenvector of A,*
    (iii) *Given two alternatives A_i, $A_j \in \mathfrak{A}$, $A_j \gtrsim_c A_j$ if and only if $\psi_i(A) \geq \psi_j(A)$.*

Proof $A \in R_{C(n)}$ implies that $a_{ij} = a_{ik}a_{jk}^{-1}$ for all k, and each i and j. Also by Theorem 10.1, we have rank $(A) = 1$ and we can write $a_{ij} = x_i/x_j$, where $x_i, x_j > 0$ $(i,j = 1, 2, \ldots, n)$. Multiplying A by the vector $x^T = (x_1, x_2, \ldots, x_n)$, we have $Ax = nx$. Dividing both sides of this expression by $\sum_{i=1}^{n} x_i$ and writing $w = x/\sum_{i=1}^{n} x_i$, we have

$Aw = nw$ and $\sum_{i=1}^{n} w_i = 1$. By Theorem 10.2, n is the largest positive real eigenvalue of A and w is its corresponding right eigenvector. Since $a_{ij} = x_i/x_j = w_i/w_j$ for all i and j, we have $\psi_i(A) = w_i$, $i=1,2,...,n$ and (i) and (ii) follow.

By Axiom 1, for $A \epsilon R_{C(n)}$, $A_i \gtrsim_C A_j$, if and only if, $a_{ij} \geq 1$ for all i and j. Hence we have $\psi_i(A) \geq \psi_j(A)$ for all i and j.

It is unnecessary to invoke the Perron-Frobenius Theorem given at the end of this chapter, to ensure the existence and uniqueness of a largest positive real eigenvalue and its corresponding eigenvector. We have already proved the existence of an essentially unique solution in the consistent case. A similar result follows using the perturbation argument given below.

Theorem 10.4 *Let $A \epsilon R_{C(n)}$, and let $\lambda_1 = n$ and $\lambda_2 = 0$ be the eigenvalues of A with multiplicity 1 and $(n-1)$, respectively. Given $\epsilon > 0$, there is a $\delta = \delta(\epsilon) > 0$ such that if*

$$|a_{ij}+\tau_{ij}-a_{ij}| = |\tau_{ij}| \leq \delta \qquad for \ \ i,j = 1,2,...,n,$$

the matrix $B = (a_{ij} + \tau_{ij})$ has exactly $1 + (n-1)$ eigenvalues in the circles $|\mu - n| < \epsilon$ and $|\mu-0| < \epsilon$, respectively.

Proof Let $\epsilon_0 = n/2$, and let $\epsilon < n/2$. The circles C_1: $|\mu-n| = \epsilon$ and C_2: $|\mu-0| = \epsilon$ are disjoint. Let $f(\mu,A)$ be the characteristic polynomial of A. Let $r_j = \min |f(\mu,A)|$ for μ on C_j. Note that $\min |f(\mu,A)|$ is defined because f is a continuous function of μ, and $r_j > 0$ since the roots of $f(\mu,A) = 0$ are the centers of the circles.

$f(\mu,B)$ is a continuous function of the $1 + n^2$ variables μ and $a_{ij} + \tau_{ij}$, $i,j = 1, 2,..., n$, and for some $\delta > 0$, if $|\tau_{ij}| \leq \delta$, $i,j = 1,2,...,n$, then $f(\mu,B) \neq 0$ for μ on any C_j, $j = 1,2$.

From the theory of functions of a complex variable, the

number of roots μ of $f(\mu,B) = 0$ which lie inside C_j, $j = 1,2$, is given by $n_j(B) = \dfrac{1}{2\pi i}\displaystyle\int_{C_j}\dfrac{f'(\mu,B)}{f(\mu,B)}d\mu$, $j=1,2,$. This number is also a continuous function of the n^2 variables $a_{ij} + \tau_{ij}$ with $|\tau_{ij}| \le \delta$.

For $B = A$, we have $n_1(A) = 1$ and $n_2(A) = n\text{-}1$. Since $n_j(B)$, $j = 1,2$, is continuous, it cannot jump from $n_j(A)$ to $n_j(B)$ and the two must be equal and have the value $n_1(B) = 1$ and $n_2(B) = n\text{-}1$, for all B with $|a_{ij} + \tau_{ij} - a_{ij}| \le \delta$, $i,j = 1,2,...,n$.

Theorem 10.5 (The haunting theorem — Perturbation of the consistent case) *Let $A \in R_{C(n)}$ and let w be its principal right eigenvector. Let $\Delta A = (\delta_{ij})$ be a matrix of perturbations of the entries of A such that $A' + \Delta A \in R_{M(n)}$, and let w' be its principal right eigenvector. Given $\epsilon > 0$, there exists a $\delta > 0$ such that $|\delta_{ij}| \le \delta$ for all i and j, then $|w'_i - w_i| \le \epsilon$ for all $i = 1,2,...,n$.*

Proof By Theorem 10.4, given $\epsilon > 0$, there exists a $\delta > 0$ such that if $|\delta_{ij}| \le \delta$ for all i and j, the principal eigenvalue of A' satisfies $|\lambda_{max}\text{-}n| \le \epsilon$. Let $\Delta A = \tau B$. Wilkinson (1965) has shown that for a sufficiently small τ, λ_{max} can be given by a convergent power series $\lambda_{max} = n + k_1\tau + k_2\tau^2 + ...$. Now, $\lambda_{max} \to n$ as $\tau \to 0$, and $|\lambda_{max} - n| = o(\tau) \le \epsilon$.

Let w be the right eigenvector corresponding to the simple eigenvalue n of A. Since n is a simple eigenvalue, $(A - nI)$ has at least one nonvanishing minor of order $(n\text{-}1)$. Suppose, without loss of generality, that this minor lies in the first $(n\text{-}1)$ rows of $(A\text{-}nI)$. From the theory of linear equations, the components of w

may be taken to be $(A_{n1}, A_{n2}, ..., A_{nn})$ where A_{ni} denotes the cofactor of the (n,i) element of $(A - nI)$, and is a polynomial in n of degree not greater than $(n-1)$.

The components of w' are polynomials in λ_{max} and τ, and since the power series expansion of λ_{max} is convergent for all sufficiently small τ, each component of w' is represented by a convergent power series in τ. We have

$$w' = w + \tau z_1 + \tau^2 z_2 + ... \quad \text{and} \quad |w' - w| = o(\tau) \leq \epsilon.$$

By Theorems 10.4 and 10.5, it follows that a small perturbation A' of A transforms the eigenvalue problem $(A - nI)w = 0$ to the eigenvalue problem $(A' - \lambda_{max}I)w' = 0$.

Theorem 10.6 (Ratio Estimation). *Let $A \in R_{M(n)}$, and let w be its principal right eigenvector. Let $\epsilon_{ij} = a_{ij}w_iw_j^{-1}$, for all i and j, and let $1 - \tau < \epsilon_{ij} < 1 + \tau, \tau > 0$, for all i and j. Given $\epsilon > 0$ and $\tau < \epsilon$, there exists a $\delta > 0$ such that for all $(x_1,x_2,...,x_n)$, $x_i > 0, i = 1,2,...,n$, if*

$$1-\delta < \frac{a_{ij}}{x_i/x_j} < 1+\delta \qquad \text{for all } i \text{ and } j, \qquad (2)$$

then

$$1-\epsilon < \frac{w_i/w_j}{x_i/x_j} < 1+\epsilon \qquad \text{for all } i \text{ and } j, \qquad (3)$$

Proof Substituting $a_{ij}\epsilon_{ij}^{-1}$ for w_i/w_j in (3) we have

$$\left| \frac{w_i/w_j}{x_i/x_j}-1 \right| = \left| \frac{1}{\epsilon_{ij}}\frac{a_{ij}}{x_i/x_j}-1 \right| \leq \frac{1}{\epsilon_{ij}}\left| \frac{a_{ij}}{x_i/x_j}-1 \right| + \left| \frac{1}{\epsilon_{ij}}-1 \right|.$$

By definition $\epsilon_{ij} = 1/\epsilon_{ji}$ for all i and j, and we have

$$\left| \frac{w_i / w_j}{x_i / x_j} - 1 \right| = \epsilon_{ij} \left| \frac{a_{ij}}{x_i / x_j} - 1 \right| + \left| \epsilon_{ij} - 1 \right| < (1+\tau)\delta + \tau.$$

Given $\epsilon > 0$ and $0 < \tau < \epsilon$, there exists a $\delta = (\epsilon - \tau)/(1+\tau) > 0$ such that (2) implies (3).

This theorem says that if the paired comparison coefficient a_{ij} is close to an underlying ratio x_i/x_j then so is w_i/w_j and may be used as an approximation for it.

Theorem 10.7 *Let* $A = (a_{ij}) \in R_{M(n)}$. *Let* λ_{max} *be its principal eigenvalue and let w be its corresponding right eigenvector with* $\Sigma^n_{i=1} w_i = 1$, *then* $\lambda_{max} \geq n$.

Proof Let $a_{ij} = w_i w_j^{-1} \epsilon_{ij}$, $i, j = 1, 2, \ldots, n$. Since $Aw = \lambda_{max} w$, and $\Sigma^n_{i,j=1} a_{ij} w_j = \lambda_{max}$, we have

$$\lambda_{max} - n = \sum_{i,j=1}^{n} a_{ij} w_j - n = \sum_{i,j} \epsilon_{ij} - n.$$

by definition, the matrix $(\epsilon_{ij}) \in R_{M(n)}$. We have $\epsilon_{ii} = 1$ for all i, and $\epsilon_{ij} > 0$ for all i and j. Hence, we have $\Sigma^n_{i,j=1} \epsilon_{ij} - n = \Sigma_{i \neq j} \epsilon_{ij} > 0$ and the result follows.

Theorem 10.8 *Let* $A \in R_{M(n)}$. *Let* λ_{max} *be the principal eigenvector of A, and let w be its corresponding right eigenvector with* $\Sigma^n_{i=1} w_i = 1$. $\mu = (\lambda_{max} - n)/(n-1)$ *is a measure of the average departure from consistency.*

Proof For $A \in R_{C(n)} \subset R_{M(n)}$, by Theorem 10.2 we have $\lambda_{max} = n$, and hence, $\mu = 0$.

and hence, $\mu = 0$.

For $A \in R_{M(n)} - R_{C(n)}$, let $a_{ij} = w_i w_j^{-1} \epsilon_{ij}$ for all i and j. We have

$$\lambda_{max} = \sum_{j=1}^{n} a_{ij} \frac{w_j}{w_i} = \sum_{j=1}^{n} \epsilon_{ij},$$

$$n\lambda_{max} = \sum_{i,j=1}^{n} \epsilon_{ij} = n + \sum_{1 \le i < j \le n} \left[\epsilon_{ij} + \frac{1}{\epsilon_{ij}} \right],$$

$$\frac{\lambda_{max} - n}{n-1} = -1 + \frac{1}{n(n-1)} \sum_{1 \le i < j \le n} \left[\epsilon_{ij} + \frac{1}{\epsilon_{ij}} \right].$$

As $\epsilon_{ij} \to 1$, i.e., consistency is approached, $\mu \to 0$. Also, μ is convex in ϵ_{ij}, since $(\epsilon_{ij} + 1/\epsilon_{ij})$ is convex, and has its minimum at $\epsilon_{ij} = 1$, $i,j = 1,2,...,n$. Thus, μ is small or large depending on ϵ_{ij} being near to or far from unity, respectively, i.e. near to or far from consistency, and the result follows.

Note that $\sum_{i,j=1}^{n} a_{ij} w_j w_i^{-1} - n^2 = n(n-1)\mu$ is also a measure of the departure from consistency.

It is also possible to show that $(A-nI)w = 0$ is transformed into $(A' - \lambda_{max}I)w' = 0$ by means of graph theoretic concepts.

Definition - The intensity of judgments associated with a path from i to j called the *path intensity* is equal to the products of the intensities associated with the arcs of that path.

Definition - A *cycle* is a path of pairwise comparisons which terminates at its starting point.

Theorem 10.9 *If $A \in R_{C(n)}$, the intensities of all cycles are equal to a_{ii}, $i = 1,2,\ldots,n$.*

Proof $A \in R_{C(n)}$, implies $a_{ij}a_{jk} = a_{ik}$ for all i,j and k. Hence, we have $a_{ii} = a_{ij}a_{jk}a_{ki} = 1$ for all $i = 1,2,\ldots,n$. By induction, if $a_{ii_1}\ldots a_{i_{n-1}i} = 1$ for all $i_1\ldots i_{n-1}$, then $a_{ii_1}\ldots a_{i_{n-1}i_n}a_{i_ni} = a_{ii_n}a_{i_ni} = 1$ and the result follows.

Theorem 10.10 *If $A \in R_{C(n)}$, the intensities of all paths from i to j are equal to a_{ij}.*

Proof Follows from $a_{ij} = a_{ik}a_{kj}$ for all i,j and k.

Corollary 10.10.1 *If $A \in R_{C(n)}$, the entry in the (i,j) position can be represented as the intensity of paths of any length starting with i and terminating with j.*

Proof Follows from Theorem 10.10.

Corollary 10.10.2 *If $A \in R_{C(n)}$, the entry in the (i,j) position is the <u>average intensity</u> of paths of length k from i to j, and $A^k = n^{k-1}A$ $(k \geq 1)$.*

Proof According to Theorem 10.10, the intensity of a path of any length from i to j is equal to a_{ij}. An arbitrary entry of A^k is given by $a_{ij}^{(k)} = \sum_{i_1=1}^{n} \sum_{i_2=1}^{n} \cdots \sum_{i_{k-1}=1}^{n} a_{ii_1} a_{i_1 i_2} \cdots a_{i_{k-1} j}$.

Since $a_{ij} a_{jk} = a_{ik}$ for all i,j and k we have

$$a_{ij}^{(k)} = \sum_{i_1=1}^{n} \sum_{i_2=1}^{n} \cdots \sum_{i_{k-1}=1}^{n} a_{ij} = n^{k-1} a_{ij} .$$

By induction, if $a_{ij}^{(k)} = n^{k-1} a_{ij}$ for $k = 1,2,\ldots,m\text{-}1$, for $k = m$ we have

$$a_{ij}^{(m)} = \sum_{i_1=1}^{n} \cdots \sum_{i_{m-1}=1}^{n} a_{ii_1} \cdots a_{i_{m-1} j}$$

$$= n^{m-2} \sum_{i_{m-1}=1}^{n} a_{ii_{m-1}} a_{i_{m-1} j} = n^{m-1} a_{ij} .$$

Hence, we have

$$a_{ij} = \frac{1}{n^{m-1}} a_{ij}^{(m)} \qquad \textit{for all} \quad m \geq 1,$$

and the result follows.

A shorter proof would be to use Theorem 10.3 with $a_{ij} = w_i/w_j$ and induction.

Theorem 10.11 *If $A \in R_{C(n)}$ a_{ij} is given by the average of all path intensities starting with i and terminating with j.*

Proof By Corollary 10.10.2 of Theorem 10.10, we have

$$a_{ij} = \frac{1}{n^{m-1}} \sum_{i_1=1}^{n} \cdots \sum_{i_{m-1}=1}^{n} a_{ii_1} \cdots a_{i_{m-1}j} \; .$$

Hence, $a_{ij} = \lim\limits_{m \to \infty} \dfrac{1}{n^{m-1}} a_{ij}^{(m)}$,

and the result follows.

Theorem 10.12 *If $A \in R_{C(n)}$ the scale of relative dominance is given by any of its normalized columns, and coincides with the principal right eigenvector of A.*

Proof Let a^j be the jth column of A.

$$A \cdot a^j = \left[\sum_{k=1}^{n} a_{ik} a_{kj} \right] \quad (i,j=1,2,\dots,n),$$

and any column of A

$$= \left[\sum_{k=1}^{n} a_{ij} \right] = (n a_{ij}) \; (i,j=1,2,\dots,n),$$

(whether or not it is normalized to unity) is a solution of the eigenvalue problem $Ax = nx$. By Corollary 2 of Theorem 10.10 we have $A^k = n^{k-1}A$.

$$\psi(A) = \lim_{m \to \infty} \frac{1}{m} \sum_{k=1}^{n} \frac{A^k e}{e^T A^k e} = \lim_{m \to \infty} \frac{1}{m} \sum_{k=1}^{n} \frac{Ae}{e^T Ae} = \frac{Ae}{e^T Ae} \; .$$

Therefore,

$$\psi_i(A) = \sum_{j=1}^{n} a_{ij} / \sum_{i,j=1}^{n} a_{ij} = \frac{a_{ih}\left(\sum_{j=1}^{n} a_{hj}\right)}{\left(\sum_{i=1}^{n} a_{ih}\right)\left(\sum_{j=1}^{n} a_{hj}\right)} = \frac{a_{ih}}{\sum_{i=1}^{n} a_{ih}}$$

for all i and h, and the result follows.

Corollary 10.12.1 *The principal eigenvector is unique to within a multiplicative constant.*

Proof Follows from Theorem 10.12.

Theorem 10.13 *If $A \varepsilon R_{M(n)}$ the intensity of all paths of length k from i to j is given by*

$$\sum_{i_1=1}^{n} \sum_{i_2=1}^{n} \cdots \sum_{i_{k-1}=1}^{n} a_{ii_1} a_{i_1 i_2} \cdots a_{i_{k-1} j} \quad .$$

Proof It is known that the number of arc progressions of length k between any two vertices of a directed graph whose incidence matrix is V is given by V^k. If in addition each arc has associated a number ($\neq 1$) with it representing the intensity (or capacity) of the arc, then V^k represents the intensity of all arc progressions of length k between two vertices.

Let $V = A$. The entries of A^k give the intensity of all paths of length k between two vertices. Let $A^k = (a_{ij}^{(k)})$. By construction we have

$$a_{ij}^{(k)} = \sum_{i_1=1}^{n} \cdots \sum_{i_{k-1}=1}^{n} a_{ii_1} \cdots a_{i_{k-1}j}$$

and the result follows.

Corollary 10.13.1 Let $A \in R_{M(n)}$. If there is some k_o for which $a_{ih}^{(k)} \geq a_{jh}^{(k)}$ *for all h, then* $a_{ih}^{(k)} \geq a_{jh}^{(k)}$ *for all* $k \geq k_o$.

Proof If one row dominates another, multiplying both by a fixed set of priorities (columns of a matrix), yields a new matrix in which the same row dominance is preserved.

Note that this is a sufficient condition for convergence to the eigenvector, but not necessary. Here is a counterexample. Any reciprocal matrix whose principal eigenvector is the vector $(1,1,\ldots,1)$ converges to this vector without row dominance but oscillates from power to power as the following matrix does:

$$\begin{bmatrix} 1 & 2 & 1/2 \\ 1/2 & 1 & 2 \\ 2 & 1/2 & 1 \end{bmatrix}$$

It has no clear dominance nor do its powers.

Corollary 10.13.2 *Let* $A \in R_{M(n)}$. *If there is some k for which* $a_{ih}^{(k)} \geq a_{jh}^{(k)}$ *for all h, then* $a_{ih}^{(k)} \geq a_{jh}^{(k)}$ *for all* $k \geq K$. *The principal right eigenvector of A is given.*

Theorem 10.14 *Let* $\mathfrak{A}$ *be a finite set of n elements* $A_1, A_2, \ldots, A_n,$

and let C ∈ ℭ be a criterion which all the elements in 𝔄 have in common. Let A be the resulting matrix of pairwise comparisons. The ith component of the principal right eigenvector of the reciprocal pairwise comparison matrix A gives the relative dominance (rank order) of A_i, i = 1,2,...,n.

Proof The principal right eigenvector of A is given by

$$w_i = \lim_{m \to \infty} \frac{a_{ih}^{(m)}}{\sum_{j=1}^{n} a_{jh}^{(m)}}, \qquad i = 1,2,...,n,$$

for any h = 1,2,...,n. We also have

$$w_i = \lim_{m \to \infty} \frac{\sum_{j=1}^{n} a_{ij}^{(m)}}{\sum_{i,j=1}^{n} a_{ij}^{(m)}}, \qquad i = 1,2,...,n,$$

Thus, the relative dominance of an alternative along all paths of length $k \leq m$ is given by

$$\frac{1}{m} \sum_{k=1}^{m} \frac{a_{ih}^{(k)}}{\sum_{i=1}^{n} a_{ih}^{(k)}}.$$

Let

$$s_k = \frac{a_{ih}^{(k)}}{\sum\limits_{i=1}^{n} a_{ih}^{(k)}} \qquad and \qquad t_m = \frac{1}{m}\sum_{k=1}^{m} s_k \; .$$

It can be shown that if $\lim\limits_{k\to\infty} s_k$ exists then $\lim\limits_{m\to\infty} t_m$ also exists and the two limits coincide. By Theorem 10.14, we have $s_k \to w$ as $k \to \infty$, where w is the principal right eigenvector of A. Thus $t_m \to w$ as $m \to \infty$ and $\psi_i(A) = w_i$, $i = 1,2,\ldots,n$.

This theorem highlights the fact that the right eigenvector gives the relative dominance (rank order) of each alternative over the other alternatives along paths of arbitrary length. It holds for a reciprocal matrix A which need not be consistent.

In Chapter 2, we mentioned that deriving ratio scales in the AHP does not rely on the theorem of Perron because the AHP is based on ratio judgements and their perturbations. However, for completeness, we include the more general Perron-Frobenius Theorem and a short and elegant proof of that theorem due to J.P. Keener [1].

Theorem 10.15 *If the (nontrivial) matrix A has nonnegative entries, then there exists an eigenvector w with nonnegative entries, corresponding to a positive eigenvalue λ. Furthermore, if the matrix A is irreducible, the eigenvector w has strictly positive entries, is unique and simple, and the corresponding eigenvalue is the largest eigenvalue of A in absolute value.*

Proof Let Σ be the set of all nonnegative vectors with unit sum entries. for each vector s in the set Σ let σ^* be the positive number for which $As \leq \sigma s$ whenever $\sigma \geq \sigma^*$. If s has zero entries then σ^* may be infinite. Since Σ is a closed and bounded set, the smallest value of σ^* is attained for some vector s^* in Σ. To see that s^* is a positive eigenvector of A, suppose that $As^* \leq \sigma^* s^*$ but s^* is not an eigenvector of A. Then some, but not all, of the relations in the statement $As^* \leq \sigma^* s^*$ are equalities. (If there were no equalities, the number σ^* would be incorrectly chosen). After permutation, we can write the relations $As^* \leq \sigma^* s^*$ can be written as

$$A_{11}s_1 + A_{12}s_2 < \sigma^* s_1,$$
$$A_{21}s_1 + A_{22}s_2 = \sigma^* s_2$$

Since A is irreducible, (cannot be partitioned into the form $\begin{bmatrix} A_1 & 0 \\ A_2 & A_3 \end{bmatrix}$ where A_1 and A_3 are square matrices and 0 is the zero matrix) A_{21} is not identically zero, and one can reduce at least one component of the vector s_1, thereby changing at least one of the equalities to a strict inequality, without changing any of the original strict inequalities. After this change in s^* one rescales the vector to sum to one. Proceeding inductively, the vector s^* is repeatedly modified until all of the relations in $As^* \leq \sigma^* s^*$ are strict inequalities. But this contradicts the definition of σ^* and the first part is proven.

To prove uniqueness, one notes that a nonnegative eigenvector w must have all positive entries. Suppose there are two linearly independent eigenvectors of A, w_1 and w_2, satisfying $Aw_1 = \lambda_1 w_1$, and $Aw_2 = \lambda_2 w_2$, and suppose that w_1 has strictly positive entries. If the entries of w_2 are all of one sign, then without loss of generality they can be taken as positive. The vector $w(t) = w_1 - tw_2$ has nonnegative entries for all t in some range $0 \leq t \leq t_0$ with $t_0 > 0$, and $w(t_0)$ has some zero entries but is not identically zero, while for $t > t_0$, $w(t)$ has some negative entries. Then $Aw(t_0) = \lambda_1(w_1 - t_0\lambda_2/\lambda_1 w_2)$ has only positive entries. By the maximality of t_0, it must be that $|\lambda_2| < |\lambda_1|$. But if both w_1 and w_2 have only positive entries, we can interchange them in the above argument to conclude that $|\lambda_1| < |\lambda_2|$, a contradiction. Thus the positive eigenvector is unique and all other eigenvectors have eigenvalues that are smaller in absolute value. To see that the largest eigenvalue is simple, note that if w_2 is a generalized eigenvalue of A satisfying $A^k w_2 = \lambda_1^k r_2$ for some $k > 1$, then $A^k r(t_0) = \lambda_1^k w(t_0)$ is strictly positive, contradicting the definition of t_0.

References

1.   Keener, J.P., 1993, "The Perron-Frobenius Theorem and the Ranking of Football Teams", SIAM Review 35/1, pp. 80-93.

2.   Saaty, T.L., 1986, "Axiomatic Foundation of the Analytic Hierarchy Process", Management Science 32/7, pp. 841-855.

3.   -------------, 1987, "Rank According to Perron: a New Insight", Math. Magazine 60, pp. 211.

4.   -------------, 1990, "Multicriteria Decision Making", RWS Publications.

CHAPTER
ELEVEN

ADVANCED TOPICS

1. Introduction

In this chapter we study three advanced topics in the AHP:

• The Duality of Structure and Function

• Reciprocal Matrices with Random Coefficients

• Interval Judgments

2. The Duality of Structure and Function [15]

In what follows we need two abstract concepts from systems theory to deal with what Selznick [21] called structural-functional analysis. They are the dual concepts of form and activity or of structure and function, encountered frequently in the analysis of decisions when using AHP. Function generally is understood to be a criterion or property that can be used to describe behavior or change in a system. Piaget [12] defined structure as a set of parts or forms that relate together in a specific order to perform a function. Nagel [11] defined the functions of a system as those observed consequences, produced by a change in a state variable, that cause it to adapt or adjust. The variations must preserve the system in a particular state.

In the AHP, we often need to distinguish between the functions performed by the elements of a system and the structural aspects of that system. Structural aspects, such as the number of elements and their actual measurements under each criterion, are not reflected in information about the relative importance of the elements in performing various functions. This functional importance is often affected by structural information when relative measurement is used.

Here is an example of a structural criterion. Suppose an investment in stocks is made according to the priority of the sector of the economy to which each stock belongs. It is essential that the priorities of sectors be modified according to the relative number of stocks in each sector. Otherwise, an important sector with a large number of stocks would distribute a small priority to each stock, resulting in a higher priority of investment being assigned to stocks belonging to less important sectors. Here the number of elements in each sector must be considered as a structural criterion. With relative measurement, we can see that structural and functional information are inextricably linked.

The functional criteria depend on structural information. Such information cannot be included explicitly as a criterion but its influence is applied as a transformation on the weights of the functional criteria. To see this, let us denote our functional criteria by $C_1, ..., C_n$, and the set of alternatives of a decision by $A_1, ..., A_m$. Let A be an $n \times m$ matrix whose columns represent the unnormalized scales derived from paired comparisons of the alternatives with respect to each criterion given by,

$$A = \begin{array}{c} \\ A_1 \\ A_2 \\ \vdots \\ A_m \end{array} \begin{array}{c} C_1 \quad C_2 \quad \cdots \quad C_n \\ \begin{bmatrix} a_{11} & a_{12} & \cdots & a_{1n} \\ a_{21} & a_{22} & \cdots & a_{2n} \\ \vdots & \vdots & & \vdots \\ a_{m1} & a_{m2} & \cdots & a_{mn} \end{bmatrix} \end{array}$$

Normalization may be regarded as a structural criterion whose matrix is denoted by S_1 applied to adjust the vector of priorities of the criteria $x=(x_1, ..., x_n)$ derived from pairwise comparison of the importance of the functional criteria $C_1, ..., C_n$, with respect to higher goals. Normalization consists of multiplying each x_i by the reciprocal of the sum of the measurements in the column of A under criterion C_i. Instead of adjusting x_i and then using it to weight the corresponding columns of A, we simply multiply A on the right by the following diagonal matrix:

$$\text{Matrix } S_1$$

$$
\begin{array}{cccc}
 & C_1 & C_2 & \cdots & C_n
\end{array}
$$

$$
\begin{array}{c}
C_1 \\
C_2 \\
\vdots \\
C_m
\end{array}
\begin{bmatrix}
(\sum\limits_{i=1}^{m} a_{i1})^{-1} & 0 & \cdots & 0 \\
0 & (\sum\limits_{i=1}^{m} a_{i2})^{-1} & \cdots & 0 \\
\vdots & \vdots & \vdots & \vdots \\
0 & 0 & \cdots & (\sum\limits_{i=1}^{m} a_{in})^{-1}
\end{bmatrix}
$$

and then weight each column by its corresponding x_i.

Adjustment of criteria weights is also made when the number of alternatives under each functional criterion is not the same. Another structural criterion whose matrix is denoted by S_2, is applied to weight each criterion priority by the relative number of alternatives under that criterion. Let r_i be the number of alternatives under criterion C_i. Let N be the sum of the r_i. The priorities x_i must be multiplied by r_i/N. Again this operation is equivalent to multiplying by the diagonal matrix S_2.

$$
\begin{array}{cccc}
 & C_1 & C_2 & \cdots & C_n
\end{array}
$$

$$
S_2 =
\begin{array}{c}
C_1 \\
C_2 \\
\vdots \\
C_m
\end{array}
\begin{bmatrix}
r_1/N & 0 & \cdots & C_n \\
0 & r_2/N & \cdots & 0 \\
\vdots & \vdots & \vdots & \vdots \\
0 & 0 & \cdots & r_n/N
\end{bmatrix}
$$

In other problems the relevant number of alternatives may be regarded as opposing rather than favoring the importance of the criteria, and a different function r_i (such as N/r_i) may appropriately be used. Thus, before composing the weights of the alternatives with respect to $x_1, \ldots, x_n$, the adjustment may be carried out by multiplying A on the right by diagonal matrices representing the structural criteria and then multiplying that result on the right by the column vector x. We obtain the final weights of the alternatives from the matrix product: AS_1S_2x.

For our example of relative measurement with rank reversal, the calculations of the final weights have been arranged in two different ways - first by carrying out normalization of the alternatives directly and second by using the normalization weights to rescale the criteria weights. Thus, for example, following the theory above, if we write

$$\overset{A}{\begin{bmatrix} 3 & 1 \\ 1 & 2 \end{bmatrix}} \overset{S}{\begin{bmatrix} 1/4 & 0 \\ 0 & 1/3 \end{bmatrix}} \overset{x}{\begin{bmatrix} .5 \\ .5 \end{bmatrix}} = \begin{bmatrix} .54 \\ .46 \end{bmatrix}$$

we can either write $(AS)x$, which indicates normalization, or $A(Sx)$, which indicates rescaling of criteria weights.

Conditions For Rank Preservation in Relative Measurement

We now give conditions for preserving rank when an alternative is added or deleted. The first condition demonstrates that if the judgments are consistent and if one alternative dominates another in every matrix of comparisons with respect to the criteria, then it dominates the second overall. This rank remains unchanged if a new alternative is added or deleted. The second condition is more general than the first and leads to an inequality that must hold as a sufficient condition for rank preservation with consistent judgments. Here, unlike the first condition, an alternative need not dominate another everywhere. When the judgments are inconsistent there is no useful condition that continues to hold when the inconsistency is improved. Let us begin with the first condition.

Let the consistent pairwise comparison matrix of m

alternatives with respect to a given criterion be $A = (a_{ij})$, $i, j = 1$, ..., m. Now A is consistent, if and only if, $a_{ij} = w_i/w_j$ where w_i and w_j are the normalized priority weights of the ith and jth alternatives. Also, any two rows of A are constant multiples of one another and hence, if any alternative dominates another, its corresponding row dominates elementwise the row corresponding to the other alternative. Now assume that a new alternative is introduced and consistency is preserved. In that case the new matrix A', with $n+1$ alternatives, has the following form:

$$A' = \begin{bmatrix} w_1/w_1 & w_1/w_2 & \cdots & (w_1/w_n) & a_{1,n+1} \\ w_2/w_1 & w_2/w_2 & \cdots & (w_2/w_n) & a_{2,n+1} \\ \vdots & \vdots & & \vdots & \\ w_n/w_1 & w_n/w_2 & \cdots & (w_n/w_n) & a_{n,n+1} \\ 1/a_{1,n+1} & 1/a_{2,n+1} & \cdots & (1/a_{n,n+1}) & 1 \end{bmatrix}$$

The priorities of the $n+1$ alternatives are given by normalizing any column of A'. Let us first choose the first column. We have

$$w_i' = w_1 \sum_{i=1}^{n} \frac{w_i}{w_1} + \frac{1}{a_{1,n+1}} \qquad i = 1, \ldots, n$$

and

$$w_{n+1}' = \frac{1}{a_{1,n+1} \sum_{i=1}^{n} \frac{w_i}{w_1} + \frac{1}{a_{1,n+1}}}$$

Note that the denominator is the same constant for all w_i', $i = 1, \ldots, n$. If we use w_{hk} to denote the priority of the hth alternative with respect to the kth criterion, we have proved the following:

Lemma If for some pair of alternatives i and j, $w_{ik} \geq w_{jk}$, then also $w_{ik}' \geq w_{jk}'$.

Now we apply hierarchic composition with respect to the n criteria by multiplying by x_k (the weight of the kth criterion) and adding. We have for the composite weights

$$W_i \equiv \sum_{k=1}^{n} x_k w_{ik} \geq \sum_{k=1}^{n} x_k w_{jk} \equiv W_j.$$

Theorem 11.1 *If $w_{ik} \geq w_{jk}$ for $k = 1, \ldots, n$, then $w'_i \geq w'_j$.*

Proof Follows by using the lemma and applying hierarchic composition. Thus if an alternative dominates another under every criterion, introducing an additional alternative does not affect their rank order. A similar result can be proved if an alternative is deleted from the collection.

We now give a mathematical representation of rank reversal as a result of structural dependence of alternatives on criteria and derive a sufficient condition for rank preservation from this representation.

Let us take the simple case of normalized columns. Let $x = (x_1, \ldots, x_n)$ denote the vector of criteria weights and let $y = (y_1, \ldots, y_m)$, $y \in R$ be the vector of composite weights of the alternatives, ordered in such a way that $y_1 \geq y_2 \geq \ldots \geq y_m \geq 0$. Equivalently, we write $y_1 - y_2 \geq 0$, $y_2 - y_3 \geq 0$, $\ldots$, $y_{m-1} - y_m \geq 0$, $y_m \geq 0$, which is obtained by the transformation $Sy^T \geq 0$ where

$$S = \begin{bmatrix} 1 & -1 & 0 & \cdots & 0 & 0 \\ 0 & 1 & -1 & \cdots & 0 & 0 \\ \vdots & \vdots & \vdots & & \vdots & \vdots \\ 0 & 0 & 0 & \cdots & 1 & -1 \\ 0 & 0 & 0 & \cdots & 0 & 1 \end{bmatrix}$$

Let us call an alternative irrelevant only when its measurement under every criterion is zero. Assume this is the case for A. Now let us introduce a relevant alternative, A'_m, by changing these zeros to positive values. Let the columns of A be given vectors $a^1, \ldots, a^n \in R^m$ for which the last component is new. Thus, prior to introducing A'_m we have $(e^m)^T a^j = 0$,

$j=1, \ldots, n$ where $(e^m)^T = (0, 0, \ldots, 0, 1)$ is an m vector. Prior to A'_m we have

$$y^T = \sum_{j=1}^{n} x_j \frac{a^j}{e^T a^j}$$

with $e^T a^j$, $j=1, \ldots, n$ designating the column sums. By requiring that $Sy^T \geq 0$ we have

$$Sy^T = \sum_{j=1}^{n} x_j \frac{Sa^j}{e^T a^j} \geq 0.$$

Now if we change the last component of the vectors a^j from zero to $u_j \geq 0$, we replace a^j by $a^j + u_j e^m$, $j = 1, \ldots, n$. Thus we compute

$$\bar{y} = \sum_{j=1}^{n} x_j \frac{a^j + u_j e^m}{e^T (a^j + u_j e^m)}$$

Evidently $e^T(u_j e^m) = u_j$ and, hence, for rank preservation we need the first $(m\text{-}2)$ components on the right of the following expression to be nonnegative:

$$S\bar{y} = \sum_{j=1}^{n} x_j \frac{Sa^j + u_j Se^m}{e^T a^j (1 + \frac{u_j}{e^T a^j})} = \begin{bmatrix} \bar{y}_1 - \bar{y}_2 \\ \vdots \\ \bar{y}_{m-2} - \bar{y}_{m-1} \\ \bar{y}_{m-1} - \sum_j \frac{x_j}{e^T a^j + u_j} u_j \\ \sum_j \frac{x_j}{e^T a^j + u_j} u_j \end{bmatrix}$$

It is clear that $S\bar{y} \geq 0$ does not always hold and hence S is not isotone and therefore does not preserve rank. The following are sufficient conditions for rank preservations

Theorem 11.2 *Sufficient conditions that*
$\bar{y}_1 \geq \bar{y}_2 \geq \ldots \geq \bar{y}_{m-1}$ *holds are*

1. $a_k^j \geq a_{k+1}^j$ *for all j and for* $k = 1, \ldots, m-2$;
2. $u_i = u_j$ *for all i and j*;
3. $\bar{y}_k / \bar{y}_{k+1} \geq \dfrac{\max_j [e^T a^j + u_j]}{\min_j [e^T a^j + u_j]}$

More generally, with $\rho_j = \dfrac{\mu_j}{e^T a^j}$, $j = 1, \ldots, n$ we require that

$$\sum_{j=1}^{n} x_j \left(\frac{Sa^j}{e^T a^j} \frac{1}{1+\rho_j} + \frac{\rho_j}{1+\rho_j} Se^m \right) \geq 0, Se^m = \begin{bmatrix} 0 \\ \vdots \\ -1 \\ 1 \end{bmatrix}.$$

Let
$$b^j = \frac{Sa^j}{e^T a^j}$$

and recall that $\sum_{j=1}^{n} x_j = 1$, $x_j \geq 0$. The original condition $Sy^T \geq 0$

means that the point $\sum_{j=1}^{n} x_j b^j$ is in the simplex spanned by $b^1, \ldots, b^n$

in the positive orthant. The introduction of a new alternative changes the boundary edges of the cone, allowing for the possibility that the new cone contains points other than those in the positive orthant. These points correspond to rank reversals.

3. Reciprocal Matrices With Random Coefficients [24]

Our object here is to report on Vargas' work on reciprocal matrices whose entries are random variables. This would allow us to simulate the behavior of decision makers by establishing probability distributions of the resulting vector of priorities. These distributions would be useful in estimating the eigenvector in behavioral situations which involve a large number of decision makers with diverse opinions.

Distribution of the Principal Right Eigenvector: The Paradigm Case

We begin by analyzing the simplest case which is when the matrix of preferences X is consistent. In this case the entries of X satisfy

$$X_{ij}X_{jk} = X_{ik}, \quad i,j,k = 1,2,...,n.$$

The principal right (PR) eigenvector of this matrix is any one of its columns. Thus (n-1) judgments are sufficient to generate the entire matrix, since $X_{ji} = X_{ij}^{-1}$ implies $X_{ii} = 1$ for all i = 1, 2, ..., n. Also, the PR-eigenvector of a reciprocal matrix is unique up to a multiplicative constant. We have

$$w_k = \frac{X_{kj}}{\sum_{i=1}^{n} X_{ij}}, \quad for \ all \ j = 1,2,...,n; \quad k=1,2,...,n.$$

where

$$\sum_{k=1}^{n} w_k = 1,$$

and $0 < w_k \le 1, \ k = 1,2,...,n.$

Our object is to find the probability distribution of $(w_1, w_2...w_n)$ such that

$$\sum_{i=1}^{n} w_i = 1, \quad and \quad 0 < w_i \le 1, \ i = 1,2,...,n.$$

The first condition implies that (n-1) of the w_i's are independent. Thus, we are interested in the marginal probability distribution of

$(w_1, w_2...w_{n-1})$.

To solve this problem we must know the probability distribution of the coefficients of X, or in general the joint probability distribution of the matrix coefficients.

We may assume that the values of X_{ij} lie between 0 and infinity. However, in practice, it has been found useful and realistic to restrict the range of the scales. In the deterministic case, the X_{ij}'s take numerical values from $\frac{1}{9}, \frac{1}{8}, ..., \frac{1}{2}, 1, 2, ..., 8, 9$, the fundamental scale of the AHP. If two activities cannot be compared within the range of the scale, clustering is used. Clusters are sets of homogeneous objects or activities, which can be compared using this scale of absolute numbers. Naturally, if one were to use a different scale the cluster may differ in size and content. Let X be a consistent random reciprocal matrix, and let f(X) be its probability density function. Thus f(X) is the joint probability density function of the X_{ij}. Let $X_1, ..., X_n$ be independent and identically distributed random variables. The vector $(X_1, ..., X_n)$ could be any of the columns of X. We have

$$f(X) = f_1(X_1)...f_n(X_n).$$

Result: If X_i, i = 1, 2, ..., n, are gamma distributed random variables with parameters $\alpha_i > 0$, $\beta_i > 0$; the PR-eigenvector of X is a Dirichlet random variable with parameters $\alpha_1, ..., \alpha_n$. The proof can be found in [24]

Result: Let $(Y_1, ..., Y_{n-1})$ be an (n-1)-dimensional variable with a Dirichlet distribution of parameters $\alpha_1, ..., \alpha_n$. The variables Y_k, k = 1, 2, ..., n-1 are distributed according to a beta distribution,

$$B\left(\alpha_k, \sum_{\substack{i=1 \\ i \neq k}}^{n} \alpha_i\right).$$

The proof can be found in [24].

Generalization: The Inconsistent Case

Let us now consider an arbitrary random reciprocal matrix, X, i.e., there exist some i, j, and k for which $X_{ij}X_{jk} \neq X_{ik}$.

To obtain the distribution of the principal right eigenvector $\bar{w}$ of X, we must consider $n(n-1)/2$ independent random variables. In this case the PR-eigenvector must be obtained by solving the stochastic system of equations

$$\sum_{j=1}^{n} X_{ij}w_j = \Lambda_{max}w_i$$

i = 1, 2, ..., n, where Λ_{max} is the principal eigenvalue of X. Λ_{max} is also a random variable whose distribution depends on the distribution of the X_{ij}'s. There is no easy solution for this case. However, we can use an approximation of the PR-eigenvector to obtain an estimate of its distribution.

The average normalized columns of a reciprocal matrix provide a good estimate of the PR-eigenvector in the deterministic case, i.e.,

$$\hat{w}_i = \frac{1}{n}\sum_{j=1}^{n} \frac{X_{ij}}{\sum_{k=1}^{n} X_{kj}}, \quad i = 1, 2, ..., n.$$

If the X_{ij} are gamma random variables, then

$$X_{ij} \bigg/ \sum_{k=1}^{n} X_{kj}$$

follow a Dirichlet distribution. Thus, the distribution of $\hat{w}_i$ is the convolution of n Dirichlet random variables, which in general is not a Dirichlet distribution. A way of circumventing this problem is by examining the consistency of the matrix of expected values. We must decide when such a matrix is sufficiently consistent to justify the assumption that the PR-eigenvector would also be a Dirichlet random variable.

Thus, to construct a test of consistency, we must find the distribution of Λ_{max}. In the deterministic case, Λ_{max} represents the average of deviations from the consistent case. By the Central Limit Theorem, the distribution of the sample mean can be considered normal as long as the sample size is sufficiently large, and the population has a finite standard deviation. Since this is the case, Λ_{max} is defined according to a normal distribution. Consistency is defined as

$$X_\mu \equiv \frac{\Lambda_{max} - n}{n-1}.$$

Thus, X_μ is also normal as has been tested empirically in two different ways.

In the first experiment, for a given matrix size $(n = 3, 4, ..., 9)$, 500 matrices were generated from the scale $\frac{1}{9}, \frac{1}{8}, ..., \frac{1}{2}, 1, 2, ..., 8, 9$. All the values of the scale were considered equally probable. The Kolmogorov-Smirnov test was then applied at the 5% level of significance to the principal eigenvalue of the matrices to test for normality. For all the cases $(n = 3, 4, ..., 9)$, Λ_{max} followed a truncated $(\Lambda_{max} \geq n)$ normal distribution. The means and standard deviations for $n = 3, 4, ..., 9$, are given in Table 11.1.

Table 11.1

n	Interval of Variation		Λ_{max}	
			$\mu(n)$	$s(n)$
3	(3.0000,	9.7691)	4.0762	1.3695
4	(4.1013,	11.3006)	6.6496	1.8380
5	(5.3855,	15.3237)	9.4178	2.1032
6	(7.1376,	17.2361)	12.3129	2.1007
7	(10.6104,	20.3545)	15.0001	2.0305
8	(12.4807,	23.5383)	17.9518	1.9045
9	(14.9457,	25.3345)	20.5652	1.824

The second experiment used a specific (gamma) distribution to obtain the entries for the randomly generated matrices. The sample size in this case was $n = 100$. Once more Λ_{max} fit a truncated normal distribution at the 5% level of significance.

In general, let X_c denote a consistent reciprocal matrix whose entries are the expected values of gamma distributed variables. If we generate random matrices using X_c as the parameters of gamma distributions, then the average PR-eigenvector of the sample tends to the PR-eigenvector of X_c as inconsistency decreases.

If X_c is an arbitrary reciprocal matrix, then the distribution of its PR-eigenvector depends on its consistency; and the distribution of the average PR-eigenvector does not necessarily converge to that of X_c.

This analysis can be extended to a hierarchic structure to study its stability. The stability of a hierarchy can be analyzed from different points of view:

(a) Stability with respect to change in the composition of its levels (structural stability);

(b) Stability with respect to changes in judgment (sensitivity analysis); and

(c) Stability in time.

This analysis can be used to study the stability of a hierarchy from the second point of view. That is, if we assume that the priorities are fixed, what is the possible range of judgments that produces the same result; and given specific changes in the final composite vector, which judgments ought to be changed to attain the desired fluctuation maintaining consistency below a certain level.

In the school example of chapter 4, generating random reciprocal matrices based on those given earlier in this chapter, we obtain the average results shown in Table 11.2.

Table 11.2

Criteria	PR-E Upper Bound of Λ_{max}		Average PR-E Schools			Λ_{max}	Upper Bound of Λ_{max}
	∞	9	A	B	C		
L	0.24	0.32	0.20	0.53	0.27	3.04	3.1
CP	0.18	0.16	0.20	0.50	0.30	3.05	3.1
F	0.15	0.17	0.36	0.22	0.42	3.03	3.1
MC	0.16	0.15	0.69	0.11	0.20	3.02	3.1
VT	0.23	0.15	0.74	0.08	0.18	3.04	3.1
SL	0.03	0.05	0.46	0.08	0.46	3.03	3.1
Λ_{max}	10.016	8.939					

As the upper bound of Λ_{max} gets closer to n = 6, its consistent value, the PR-eigenvector, gets closer to the PR-eigenvector obtained in the deterministic case. The final priorities are obtained by multiplying the priorities of the schools with respect to the criteria by the weights of the criteria, and adding as in (Table 11.3).

Table 11.3

Schools	Priorities Upper Bound of Λ_{max}		Actual Priorities
	∞	9	
A	0.43	0.39	0.37
B	0.30	0.32	0.38
C	0.27	0.29	0.25

Despite the high inconsistency of the matrix of criteria, school A would have been selected even if all criteria were considered equally important. The stability of this example is good as implied by the proximity of the random priorities to the core value.

4. Interval Judgments [2,3,19]

When a decision maker is uncertain about his preferences,

what effect can this uncertainty have on the final decision? One would be inclined to think that there should be no concern if uncertainty leaves the rank of the alternative chosen unchanged. However that is not true. Even if the rank remains the same, the decision maker may have little confidence in his judgments. In such situations we need a measure of uncertainty to decide whether it is wise to proceed with the best choice or if more information is needed to remove some or all of the uncertainty.

There are two types of uncertainty: (a) uncertainty about the occurrence of events, and (b) uncertainty about the range of judgments used to express preferences. The first is beyond the control of the decision maker whereas the second is a consequence of the amount of information available to him and his understanding of the problem.

The concern here is with the second type of uncertainty. Ordinarily, it is possible to express a numerical judgment within a range or interval of values. Such judgments can give rise to several possible decisions creating uncertainty in the decision making process. This kind of uncertainty is commonly encountered in comparing projects with respect to criteria when we need to know how much resource to allocate to them according to priority.

To generate the paired comparisons one must answer the following kind of question: Given a criterion or property, which of two projects is more important according to this criterion, and how much more important is it? Cardinal judgments are numerical representations of the intensity of preference. After generating a matrix of paired comparisons for a criterion, we use it to derive a scale which represents the relative importance of the alternatives. When several criteria are involved, the final decision is based on a scale for comparing the criteria and on the several scales of the alternatives with respect to the criteria. The overall importance of the alternatives with respect to all criteria is obtained, if the criteria are independent from the alternatives [14], by multiplying the weights of the alternatives under each criterion by the relative importance of the criterion and adding over all the criteria. If there is uncertainty either in the judgments of the criteria, or in the judgments of the alternatives or both, the uncertainty is perpetrated to the derived scales and thus to the final outcome.

To capture the uncertainty experienced by the decision maker in making pairwise comparisons, an interval of numerical values is associated with each judgment and we refer to the pairwise comparison is known as an *interval pairwise comparison* or simply *interval judgment*.

The Arbel-Vargas approach leads to estimating the probability that an alternative or project exchanges rank with other projects. These probabilities are then used to calculate the probability that a project would change rank at all. Finally, they combine the priority of importance of each project with the probability that it does not change rank, to obtain the final ranking for resource allocation. It is this composite outcome that is of interest to both those who provide the judgments and those who allocate the resources. Statistical measures of dispersion can be used to refine the selection and break ties when necessary.

Interval judgments are not new in the literature. Earlier in the 1980's Saaty [13] proposed the use of a "bundle" of judgments; Vargas [23] assumed the judgments to be random variables; Laarhoven and Pedrycz [22] assumed the judgments to be fuzzy numbers with triangular membership functions; Buckley [6] extended fuzzy sets to hierarchical analysis; Saaty and Vargas [18] assumed interval judgments without any probabilistic or fuzzy properties; Boender, de Graan and Lootsma [5] extended Laarhoven and Pedrycz's approach; Arbel [1] introduced the concept of preference programming after formulating the prioritization process as a linear programming model; Salo and Hamalainen [19] extended Arbel's approach to hierarchic structures; Arbel and Vargas [2] formulated the hierarchic problem as a nonlinear model; and Moreno and Vargas [9] investigated how to find the most likely ranking of the alternatives from interval judgments.

Background

A typical matrix of interval pairwise comparisons is given

by

$$
\begin{bmatrix}
1 & [a_{12}^L, a_{12}^U] & [a_{13}^L, a_{13}^U] & \cdots & [a_{1n}^L, a_{1n}^U] \\
\vdots & 1 & [a_{23}^L, a_{23}^U] & \cdots & [a_{2n}^L, a_{2n}^U] \\
\cdots & \left[\dfrac{1}{a_{ij}^U}, \dfrac{1}{a_{ij}^L}\right] & \cdots & 1 & \vdots \\
\vdots & & & \ddots & \vdots \\
\vdots & & & & 1
\end{bmatrix}
$$

where $a_{ij}^L \le a_{ij}^U$ for all i, j = 1, 2, ..., n.

The problems which arise in working with interval judgments are of two types: (a) computational, and (b) theoretical.

Computationally, the problem is relatively intractable. It not only involves a method to determine the interval to which each judgment belongs and the distribution of the judgments in the interval, but also to derive the scales of relative values of which there can be a very large number due to the use of intervals. Consider five alternatives and the interval-judgments given in the following matrix:

$$
\begin{bmatrix}
1 & [2,5] & [1,4] & [2,6] & [3,5] \\
 & 1 & [2,6] & [\frac{1}{5},\frac{1}{3}] & [3,7] \\
 & & 1 & [5,7] & [4,4] \\
 & & & 1 & [\frac{1}{3},5] \\
 & & & & 1
\end{bmatrix}.
$$

Let us only consider the integers or reciprocals of the integers between the two bounds. For example, there are 4 integers in the interval [2,5]. The interval [⅓,5] has ⅓ and ½ as reciprocals of integers and 1, 2, 3, 4, and 5 as integers for a total of 7 judgments. Thus, the total number of possible combinations of judgments for this matrix is 378,000. Hence, 378,000 eigenvectors must be evaluated, if only integers or reciprocals of integers are considered and complete enumeration is used.

To cope with this difficulty there are two ways of processing interval judgments. One based on Simulation [16] and another based on Mathematical Programming [1]. The first approach assumes that the interval judgments are uniformly distributed and yields the priority vectors, and the underlying rank order, by randomly sampling from these distributions. This approach provides, in addition to the priority vectors, a probability distribution defined on the intervals of the components of the eigenvector. The second approach generates a region (if one exists) that encloses all priority vectors derived from inequalities representing the original interval judgments. This approach has already been generalized to the non-linear constraint case [2].

In sum, a reciprocal matrix with interval judgments is a matrix $A = (I_{ij})$ whose entries satisfy:

(i) $I_{ij} = \{x \mid l_{ij} \leq x \leq u_{ij}\}$, and
(ii) For all $x \in I_{ij}$ and $y \in I_{ji}$, $xy = 1$.

The problem is to find the range of values of each component of the principal right eigenvector. Let $I(w)$ the set of all principal right eigenvectors corresponding to the matrices constructed with values in the intervals I_{ij}, i.e.,

$$I(w) = \{w \mid Aw = \lambda_{max} w, \ A = (a_{ij}), \ a_{ij} \in I_{ij}\}.$$

In [17] this problem is studied using simulation. The problem is to determine the type of distribution to use for such simulation. From a theoretical point of view, the eigenvector is an n-dimensional variable, and statistical measures can be developed for each of its components, but not for the entire vector. For example, a vector, each of whose components is the sample average, can be formed and then used to construct confidence intervals for each component. The confidence intervals are then used to determine if two components can reverse rank and in turn if there is a chance that a rank reversal may occur in the entire vector.

It is clear that given i and j, if $I(w_i)$ and $I(w_j)$ do not have any elements in common, then whether $P[X_i > X_j] = 1$ or $P[X_i < X_j] = 1$ the two components will never reverse rank. This occurs if there are (n-1) independent components whose intervals $I(w_i)$ do not intersect. When the intervals intersect, there is not a unique ranking of the alternatives. If judgments were given at random from the intervals $[l_{ij}, u_{ij}]$, which ranking is more likely to be expressed by the decision maker?

Arbel [1] has solved this problem using linear programming but only in the case where the matrices are consistent. He considered a consistent matrix $A = (w_i/w_j)$, and formulated the following problem:

$$\textit{Minimize } w_0$$

$$\textit{subject to}$$

$$\Sigma w_i = 1$$

$$l_{ij} \le \frac{w_i}{w_j} \le u_{ij}, \; i,j = 1, 2, \ldots, n \tag{1}$$

$$w_i > 0, \textit{ for all } i$$

or

$$\textit{Minimize } w_0$$

$$\textit{subject to}$$

$$\Sigma w_i = 1$$

$$l_{ij}w_j - w_i \le 0, \; i,j = 1, 2, \ldots, n \tag{2}$$

$$-u_{ij}w_j + w_i \le 0, \; i,j = 1, 2, \ldots, n$$

$$w_i > 0, \textit{ for all } i.$$

The solutions of (2) are the eigenvectors of the consistent matrices in terms of which all other consistent matrices can be generated.

A problem that arises with this formulation is that the feasible region may be empty when the judgments are inconsistent. Hamalainen and Salo [19] extend Arbel's [1] approach to hierarchies. They introduce two dominance relations defined in terms of the weights of the alternatives. These weights are based on the decision maker's statements, and resemble those employed in multiattribute utility models (see e.g. Bana E. Costa [4], Hazen [7], Insua and French [8], Moskowitz et al. [10], Weber [25]). The dominance relations are revised after each new judgment providing the decision maker with an interactive decision support process that yields intermediate results even before most pairwise comparisons have been elicited.

Hamalainen and Salo give a computationally efficient solution to the problem of deriving dominance structures from interval judgments. They extend the results on the computation of weight intervals previously developed by them (Salo and Hamalainen [20]).

Let $V(x)$ be the weight interval of alternative x. An alternative x dominates another alternative y if any feasible combination of local priorities assigns to x a weight greater than that of y. They call this *absolute dominance*. Because the principle of hierarchical composition is based on the assumption that the weights of upper level criteria are independent of the judgments on the lower levels, finding the weight interval of an alternative can be decomposed into a series of linear programming problems.

Let the feasible region at criterion y be denoted by S_y. If $w^y \in S_y$ and $x \in y^-$, then w_x^y is the component of w^y corresponding to x. By definition the weight of the topmost element is one. For the other elements, the weights are recursively derived from the feasible local priorities $w^y \in S_y$, $y \in C$, the set of consistent matrices:

$$v(x) = \sum_{y \in x'} v(y) w_x^y.$$

For a given hierarchy **H** with levels L_1, L_2, ..., L_h, the maximum $\bar{v}_y(x)$ is called the *absolute upper bound*, and it is the

largest weight that x can have in the subhierarchy of **H** rooted at y. In the same way, the minimum for the weight of x can be found by computing the *absolute lower bounds* $\underline{v}_y(x)$ which are equal to the smallest weights that x can receive in the subhierarchies rooted at $y \in$ **C**. The following theorem summarizes the propagation of the weights in a hierarchy.

Theorem 11.3 *Let $x \in A$ be a decision alternative. For $y \in C$ such that $y \supset A$ define the absolute bounds*

$$\bar{v}_y(x) = \max_{w \in S_y} w_x$$

$$\underline{v}_y(x) = \min_{w \in S_y} w_x.$$

Proceed successively from level L_{h-2} upwards by recursively defining the absolute bounds

$$\bar{v}_y(x) = \max_{w \in S_y} \sum_{z \in y^-} \bar{v}_z(x) w_z$$

$$\underline{v}_y(x) = \min_{w \in S_y} \sum_{z \in y^-} \underline{v}_z(x) w_z$$

for the criteria $y \in L_i$, $1 \leq i < h-1$ ($y^- \not\subset A$). Then, $V(x) = [\underline{v}_b(x), \bar{v}_b(x)]$ is the set of weights assigned to x by feasible combinations of local priorities.

As before, when the weight intervals do not overlap, the dominance of the alternative is early distinguished.

To deal with the case when the weight intervals of two alternatives x and y overlap, they introduce the criterion of *pairwise dominance* ($\succ_p$):

$$x \succ_p y \Leftrightarrow min[v(x) - v(y)] > 0,$$

where the minimization is taken over all the feasible regions in the hierarchy.

Since absolute dominance implies pairwise dominance, the latter need not be checked for alternatives which have non-overlapping weight intervals. More specifically, the possible pairwise dominance of x over y must be checked only if the absolute bounds satisfy the inequalities

$$\bar{v}_b(x) > \bar{v}_b(y) >= \underline{v}_b(x) > \underline{v}_b(y),.$$

The transitivity of the relation $\succ_p$ can be exploited to further reduce the number of pairs for which pairwise dominance has to be determined. Pairwise dominance also can be computed from a series of linear programming problems. If $z \in L_{h-1}$, then an alternative x dominates another alternative y in the subhierarchy rooted at z only if $w_x - w_y > 0$ for all $w \in S_z$. The minimum for this difference,

$$\pi_z(x,y) = \min_{w \in S_z}(w_x - w_y),$$

is called the pairwise bound for the weight difference of x and y at z.

Theorem 11.4 *Fix* $x, y \in A$. *For* $z \in C$ *such that* $z^- \supset A$ *define the pairwise bounds*

$$\pi_z(x,y) = \min_{w \in S_z}(w_x - w_y).$$

Proceed successively from level L_{h-2} upwards by recursively defining the pairwise bounds

$$\pi_z(x,y) = \min_{w \in S_z} \sum_{t \in z^-} \pi_t(x,y)w_t$$

for the criteria $z \in L_i$, $1 \le i < h - 1$ ($z \not\subset A$). Then x dominates y, i.e. $x \succ_p y$, if and only if $\pi_b(x,y) > 0$.

To prevent the feasible regions from becoming empty, the decision maker needs guidance as he enters new comparisons and tightens earlier judgments. At criterion z the impact of the decision maker's earlier judgments can be characterized by the *consistency intervals* $\hat{I}_{xy} = [\hat{l}_{xy}, \hat{u}_{xy}]$. The bounds of these intervals are defined by

$$\hat{u}_{xy} = \max_{w \in S_z} \frac{w_x}{w_y}$$

$$\hat{l}_{xy} = \frac{1}{\hat{u}_{yx}},$$

where x and y are subelements of z, and the ratio in (3) is taken to be ∞ if $w_x > 0$, $w_y = 0$ and 0 if $w_x = w_y = 0$.

The decision maker can tighten the constraints on the feasible regions either through new comparisons or by narrowing the bounds of the earlier interval judgments. Both modifications can be modelled by assuming that the decision maker changes the interval I_{xy} to $I'_{xy} \subset I_{xy}$ (here $\supset$ denotes proper set inclusion) and that after this change the modified feasible region becomes $S'_z \subseteq S_z$. In such a situation, the modified feasible region inherits the property

$$x \in z^- \implies \exists w \in S_z \text{ such that } w_x > 0$$

(12) and becomes a proper subset of the earlier feasible region only if the intersection of the intervals I'_{xy} and $\hat{I}_{xy}$ is non-empty and a proper subset of $\hat{I}_{xy}$. In this way, the consistency intervals help the decision maker see the impact of the earlier judgments and allow him to effectively refine the preference description.

Hamalainen and Salo's approach is developed around the idea that to obtain a solution in the inconsistent case (i.e., the feasible region of (2) is empty) one needs to modify the interval judgments. Modification is done by extending the intervals until a consistent solution can be found. The simulation approach (Saaty and Vargas [18]) and the nonlinear approach (Arbel and Vargas [2]) do not modify the initial feasible region. The former is particularly attractive because in the process of estimating the priority intervals from interval reciprocal matrices one also estimates the probability of the different ranking (Moreno and Vargas [9]) that an interval reciprocal matrix can produce. Arbel and Vargas [3] show that when using a simulation, if one restricts sampling to the feasible region given by (2), the average converges to the average of the vertices of the feasible region.

Theorem 11.5 *Consider a solvable system of inequalities given by (2) having q vertices $\{w_1, w_2, ..., w_q\}$. If $\{\alpha_{1k}, \alpha_{2k}, ..., \alpha_{qk}\}$ is the kth random partition of the interval [0,1], then the point generated with these coefficients given by: $\alpha_{1k}w_1 + \alpha_{2k}w_2 + ... + \alpha_{qk}w_q$ converges to the arithmetic mean of the vertices as k tends to infinity.*

The priority intervals obtained from each interval reciprocal matrix can be easily used to compute the ranges of the priorities of the alternatives at the bottom of the hierarchy.

Finally, Arbel and Vargas [2] provide the solution for the inconsistent case. It is a nonconvex optimization problem. Its solution is not easy to obtain.

References

1. Arbel, A., 1989, "Approximate Articulation of Preference and Priority Derivation", European Journal of Operational Research 43, pp. 317-326.

2. ---------- and L.G. Vargas, 1990, "The Analytical Hierarchy Process with Interval Judgments", Proceedings of the IXth Int'l Symposium on Multicriteria Decision Making.

3. ---------- and L.G. Vargas, 1993, "Preference Simulation and Preference Programming: Robustness Issues in Priority Derivation", European Journal of Operational Research 69, 200-209.

4. Bana E. Costa, C.A., 1990, "An additive value function technique with a fuzzy outranking relation for dealing with poor intercriteria preference information", in: c.A. Bana E. cost (ed.), Readings in Multiple Criteria Decision Aid, Springer-Verlag, Berlin, pp. 351-382.

5. Boender, C.G.E., J.G. de Graan and F.A. Lootsma, 1989, "Multicriteria Decision Analysis with Fuzzy Pairwise Comparisons", Fuzzy Sets and Systems 17, pp. 233-247.

6. Buckley, J.J., 1985, "Fuzzy Hierarchical Analysis", Fuzzy Sets and Systems 17, pp. 233-247.

7. Hazen, G.B., 1986, "Partial information, dominance, and potential optimality in multiattribute utility theory", Operations Research 34, pp. 296-310.

8. Insua, D.R., and S. French, 1991, "A framework for sensitivity analysis in discrete multiobjective decision making", European Journal of Operational Research 54, pp. 176-190.

9. Moreno-Jimenez, J.M. and L.G. Vargas, 1983, "A Probabilistic Study of Preference structures in the Analytic Hierarchy Process", Mathematical and Computer Modelling 17/4-5, 73-81.

10. Moskowitz, H., P.V. Preckel and A. Yang, 1992, " Multiple-criteria robust interactive decision analysis (MCRID) for optimizing public policies", European Journal of Operational Research 56, pp. 219-236.

11. Nagel, E., 1956, "A Formalization of Functionalism", In: Logic Without Metaphysics. Free Press, New York.

12. Piaget, J., 1968, Structuralism, Harper & Row, New York.

13. Saaty, T.L., 1981, "Continuous, Recursive and Feedback Hierarchic Systems", Working Paper, KGSB, University of Pittsburgh.

14. -------------, 1986, "Axiomatic Foundation of the Analytical Hierarchy Process", Management Science 23/7, pp. 841-855.

15. -------------, 1987, "Rank Generation, Preservation, and Reversal in the Analytical Hierarchy Decision Process", Decision Sciences 18/2.

16. --------------, 1988, "Decision Making: The Analytic Hierarchy Process. Planning, Priority Setting, Resource Allocation."

17. ------------- and L.G. Vargas, 1984, "Comparison of eigenvalue, logarithmic least squares and least squares methods in estimating ratios", Mathematical Modelling 5, pp. 309-324.

18. ------------- and L.G. Vargas, 1987, "Uncertainty and Rank Order in the Analytical Hierarchy Process", European Journal of Operational Research 32, pp. 107-117.

19. Salo, A. and R.P. Hamalainen, 1990, "Processing Interval Judgments in the Analytic Hierarchy Process", Proceedings of the IXth Int'l Symposium on Multicriteria Decision Making.

20. -------- and --------------------, 1992, "Processing interval judgments in the analytic hierarchy process", Proceedings of the IX International Conference on Multiple Criteria Decision Making, Fairfax, Virginia, August 1990, Springer-Verlag.

21. Selznick, P., 1948, "Foundations of the Theory of Organizations", American Sociological Review 13, pp. 25-35.

22. van Laarhoven, P.J.M. and W. Pedrycz, 1983, "A Fuzzy Extension of Saaty's Priority Theory", Fuzzy Sets and Systems 11, pp. 229-241.

23. Vargas, L.G., 1982, "Prediction and The Analytic Hierarchy Process", Chapter. 10th IMACS World Congress on System Simulation and Scientific Computation, Montreal, Canada.

24. --------------, 1982, "Reciprocal Matrices with Random Coefficients", Mathematical Modelling 3, pp. 69-81.

25. Weber, M., 1987, "Decision making with incomplete information", European Journal of Operational Research 28, pp. 44-57.

CHAPTER TWELVE

DYNAMIC JUDGMENTS

1. Introduction

There are situations in which changes occur in the structure of a decision problem so that new criteria are added or old ones dropped. In others the judgments about the criteria change but the criteria remain the same. There are still others in which the judgments about the criteria remain the same but judgments about alternatives change. Finally, there are situations in which both the elements of the hierarchy and the judgments change. Here we give two examples to illustrate such ideas. Dynamic judgments were also studied briefly in my first book on the AHP.

There are at least two ways to introduce dynamics with respect to time in the AHP. The first is to provide numerical (static) judgments at various (perhaps regularly spaced) instances of time and generate trajectories from the hierarchy as functions of time. The first example below illustrates this idea in a pursuit problem. The other way is to generate time dependent judgment matrices. Each such judgment needs to be carefully analyzed according to its possible time trends and the results interpreted in some mathematically credible way. A technical problem that arises in relation to this approach is that because of the time dependence of the coefficients of the matrix, it is difficult to generate the eigenvector of priorities if the order of the matrix is more than four. The reason is that in these cases one must solve a polynomial equation to obtain the principal eigenvalue and derive the corresponding principal eigenvector. From Galois theory it is known that a quatric is the largest degree equation from which one can obtain the roots (eigenvalues in our problem) in closed form. This also means that for higher order matrices, the eigenvector must be derived numerically for each value of time. We have already derived expressions for the principal eigenvalue and eigenvector in the first book on the AHP. Still it is a relatively complicated process to weight and synthesize time dependent priorities for the alternatives. Each priority is a multilinear form as a function of time. Our second example uses this approach. Once we have the outcome, we can analyze its rate of change with respect to time by taking its derivative.

2. A Pursuit Problem

The following example was conceived by me and prepared by my former student Erik Wintner of Denmark. Consider a pursuit game in a plane where two players - the pursuer (P) and the evader (E) - are able to move according to some prespecified rules in the plane. The objective of the pursuer is to approach the evader within a specified distance in the shortest possible time. Consequently, the evader's objective is to maximize elapsed time before he is caught, and preferably to avoid capture at all. Elaborate models already exist for these games, so it is not the intention here to attempt something which will approach that level of sophistication. Rather, we will examine whether it is possible to model these games approximately in a simpler way by using prioritized hierarchies.

Let us assume that each player moves in the plane with constant speed - $|v_P|$ and $|v_E|$. We will consider the strategies available to the players at discrete time n to be $\{\Delta v_P\}$ and $\{\Delta v_E\}$. Thus each player can change his velocity by any one of the Δv's based on his own set of strategies. The simplest case is for each player to change his movement in an arbitrary direction as shown in Figure 12-1:

P   E

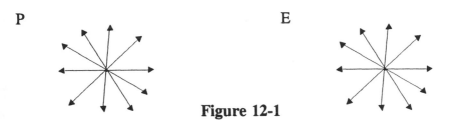

Figure 12-1

Here, the players' optimal strategies are obvious, both should move along the line PE, P towards E, and E away from P as in Figure 12-2:

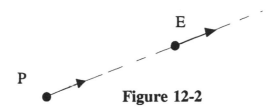

Figure 12-2

The optimal strategies are independent of the initial state of the system described by the players' positions and velocities. We will not get into a discussion of optimality here.

In the following we will assume that a player's strategies at an arbitrary time n, are as shown in Figure 3 and described in words below:

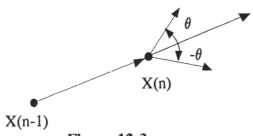

Figure 12-3

If the player was at point x(n-1) at time n-1, and he moves to x(n) at time n, then he has three possible strategies:

1)   to continue in the same direction with the previous velocity v,
2)   to change direction by an angle θ,
3)   to change direction by an angle $-\theta$,

where θ may be different for the two players.

The player's choice of strategy depends on

1) The information available about the opponent. For the game to be meaningful some information about the other player is needed. It may be that only the opponent's position at the time n is known; a player may know the opponent's position and velocity, or he may have information about the opponent's set of strategies as well.

2) A player's perception of how well each strategy will serve his ultimate objective (catch or evade). This may be done by instituting a set of lower level goals which are considered instrumental to the objective, and evaluate the strategies with respect to these operationally formulated goals.

At an arbitrary time n, each player can model his decision problem in the form of a hierarchy. Taking the evader as an example, it may look in Figure 12-4:

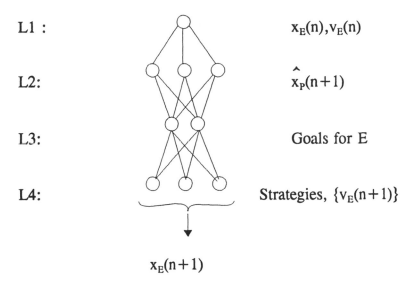

L1 : $x_E(n), v_E(n)$

L2: $\hat{x}_P(n+1)$

L3:   Goals for E

L4:   Strategies, $\{v_E(n+1)\}$

$$x_E(n+1)$$

Figure 12-4

The top level L1 signifies the present state of the evader: his position $x_E(n)$, and velocity $v_E(n)$. Level L2 is the set of potential positions at time $n+1$ of P, as perceived by E. Pairwise comparisons of the elements of L2, given L1, will yield E's probability distribution of P going to each of his potential positions. These comparisons should reflect the information E has about P. L3 contains the set of goals E believes to be instrumental for his objective. The relative contribution of these goals to the objective is estimated for each perceived potential position of P at time $n+1$. Examples of such goals could be: (1) to increase the distance between E and P, and (2) to make v_E perpendicular to v_P (this would be relevant if E could make "sharper turns" than could P). The lower level L4 is the set of available strategies. The relative contribution of these to each of the goals is estimated.

By multiplying the matrices of eigenvectors of each level with respect to the next higher level, the overall priority of the strategies is obtained. Picking the strategy with the highest priority, E goes to $x_E(n+1)$, and a new hierarchy is begun.

In a similar way a hierarchy is developed for P at each moment of time

EXAMPLES To illustrated the procedure, two numerical examples have been computed, using the following simplified hierarchies of Figure 12-5.

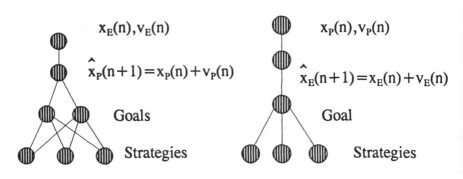

EVADER   PURSUER

$x_E(n), v_E(n)$ $x_P(n), v_P(n)$

$\hat{x}_P(n+1) = x_P(n) + v_P(n)$ $\hat{x}_E(n+1) = x_E(n) + v_E(n)$

Goals   Goal

Strategies   Strategies

Figure 12-5

EVADER   PURSUER

Goals: Goal:

Example 1: increase relative distance   - decrease (or get the
                                            smallest increase in)
Example 2: v_E perpendicular to v_P relative distance

Strategies: Strategies:

$\theta_E \in \{0°, 45°, -45°\}$ $\theta_P \in \{0°, 15°, -15°\}$

In the examples the goals of E were prioritized independently of the two players' states. At each moment of time E put the highest priority on goal (1). When it was impossible to get an increase in the relative distance, that strategy which gave the highest contribution to goal (2) was adopted.

The player's trajectories in the examples were computed by means of a computer program. The results are shown in Figures 6 and 7. It is seen that in example 1, E appears to be playing suboptimal. In example 2, P is playing less than optimal from the outset. He would probably have done better by using his first moves to get into a better position instead of chasing E right away. That he nevertheless captures E in the end is due to mistakes on the part of E.

In spite of the obvious shortcomings of these simple examples, refining the model by making the hierarchies time dependent, can yield significantly better results.

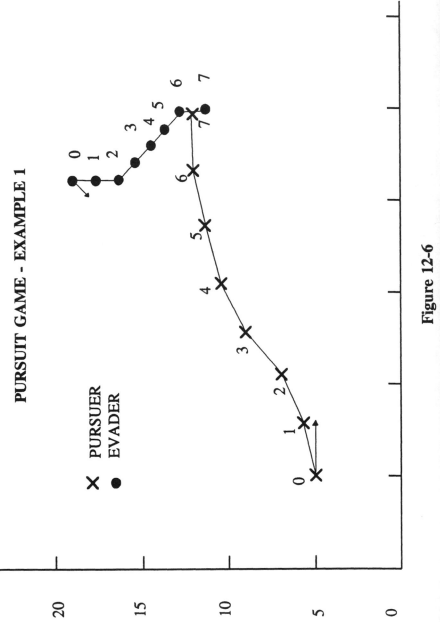

Figure 12-6

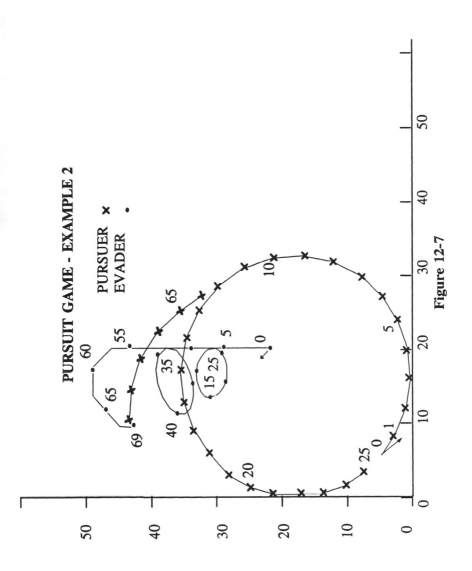

PURSUIT GAME - EXAMPLE 2

PURSUER ✕
EVADER •

Figure 12-7

THE EVADER

The hierarchy as used for the evader is shown in Figure 12-8:

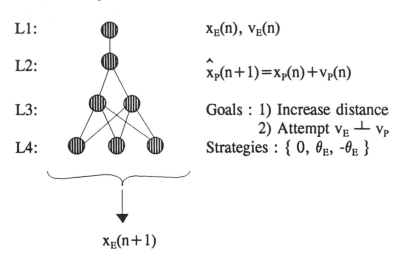

L1: $x_E(n)$, $v_E(n)$

L2: $\hat{x}_P(n+1) = x_P(n) + v_P(n)$

L3:   Goals : 1) Increase distance
                                               2) Attempt $v_E \perp v_P$

L4:   Strategies : $\{\ 0,\ \theta_E,\ -\theta_E\ \}$

$x_E(n+1)$

Figure 12-8

<u>L2, L1:</u> $A_{21} = \{\ 1\ \}$

<u>L3, L2:</u>   The relative importance of the goals G1 and G2,
                        given that the evader at time n judges the position of
                        the pursuer at time n+1 to be $\hat{x}_P(n+1)$ is given by
                        the following matrix :

$\hat{x}_P(n+1)$	G1	G2
G1	1	k
G2	1/k	1

$$\Rightarrow\quad A_{32} = \begin{pmatrix} \dfrac{k}{1+k} \\ \dfrac{1}{1+k} \end{pmatrix},$$

where k signifies a large positive number. It indicates that the evader judges that increase in distance, no matter how small, would have a far greater impact on his ultimate objective to delay capture for as long as possible - than has the second goal. In other words, the second goal is only effective if the first one cannot be achieved.

L4,L3:   To explain the computations, let us consider the following matrix of pairwise comparisons :

Goal 1	S_1	S_2	S_3
S_1	1		
S_2		1	
S_3			1

If a strategy S_i leads to a decrease in the expected distance, all off-diagonal elements of row i and column i are set to zero (element (i, i) is as usual = 1). It indicates that a comparison between S_i and the other strategies is meaningless, because S_i does not contribute to Goal 1. Correspondingly, in the eigenvector element i will be zero. In the case where all off-diagonal elements are zero, the eigenvector will be any $\{w_1, w_2, w_3\}$ which satisfies $w_1 + w_2 + w_3 = 1$. In other words, Goal 2 alone will determine which strategy to choose.

Using these judgments the computations become very simple

in practice. Let the state of the evader at time n be $x_E(n)$, $v_E(n)$. Having the set of available strategies $S_E = \{0, \theta_E, -\theta_E\}$, the set of potential positions for the evader at time $n+1$ becomes:

$$\{x_E(n)+v_{E,0}(n),x_E(n)+v_{E,\theta_E}(n),x_E(n)+v_{E,-\theta_E}(n)\}$$

where $v_{E,\theta_E}(n)$ is the velocity vector rotated through an angle θ_E. The estimated position of the pursuer at time $n+1$ is $x_P(n)+v_P(n)$.

We now compute

$$d_{\theta^*} = \max_{\theta \, \epsilon S_E}\{|x_E(n)+v_{E,\theta}(n)-\hat{x}_p(n+1)| - |x_E(n)-x_P(n)|\}.$$

If $d_{\theta^*} \geq 0$, then the strategy θ^* is taken. If $d_{\theta^*} < 0$, that is the distance to the pursuer cannot be increased, take that strategy θ^* for which $| v_P(n), v_{E,\theta}(n) |$ is minimum, that is the strategy which has the highest impact on Goal 2 (attempt $v_E \perp v_P$).

The Pursuer

The pursuer's hierarchy looks is shown in Figure 12-9:

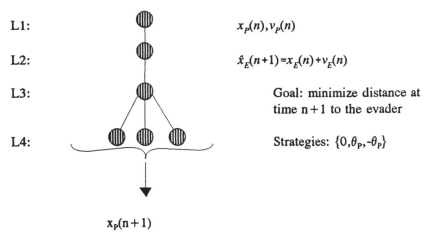

L1: $x_P(n),v_P(n)$

L2: $\hat{x}_E(n+1)=x_E(n)+v_E(n)$

L3:   Goal: minimize distance at time $n+1$ to the evader

L4:   Strategies: $\{0,\theta_P,-\theta_P\}$

$x_P(n+1)$

Figure 12-9

<u>L2, L1:</u> $A_{21} = \{1\}$

<u>L3, L2:</u> $A_{32} = \{1\}$

<u>L4, L3:</u>   There is only one goal, simply to choose that strategy
θ^* , $\theta^* \in S_P = \{ 0, \theta_P, -\theta_P\}$, which leads to the
pursuer being as close as possible to the evader at
time $n+1$. As the pursuer expects the evader to be
at $\hat{x}_E(n+1) = x_E(n) + v_E(n)$ at time $n+1$, the best
strategy at time n is found by using
$$d_{\theta^*} = \min_{\theta \in S_P}\{|\hat{x}_E(n+1)-(x_P(n)+v_{P,\theta}(n))|\}.$$

A Numerical Example

To illustrate the procedure in practice, let us consider
Example 3. In that example the initial conditions and the strategies
were as follows:

$x_P(0) = (5,5)$
$v_P(0) = (3,-3)$
$S_P \quad = \{ 0, 15°, -15° \}$

$x_E(0) = (20,20)$
$v_E(0) = (-1,1)$
$S_E \quad = \{ 0, 45°, -45° \}$

Using the previous described model, some of the computations are
given in Tables 1 and 2.

We have illustrated the process of paired comparisons in
dynamic problems, usually treated in continuous form.   This
approach could be useful in problems where a variety of factors and
judgments are involved. Some of the factors may be intangible and
relative values are derived for them and used in the model.

Table 12.1 EVADER

n	$x_E(n)$	$v_E(n)$	$\hat{x}_P(n+1)$	INCREASE DISTANCE			$\|v_{E,\theta}(n)\cdot v_P(n)\|$		
				0	θ_E	$-\theta_E$	0	θ_E	$-\theta_E$
0	20,20	-1,1	8,2	0.74	-0.33	1.61			
1	20,21.41	0,1.41	12.28,0.64	1.71	1.00	1.67			
2	20,22.83	0,1.41	16.76,0.34	1.65	1.22	1.34			
3	20,24.24	0,1.41	21.17,1.16	1.45	1.11	1.01			
...	...	...	...	...					
...	...	...	...	...					
6	20,28.49	0,1.41	31.50,9.36	0.24	0.39	-0.60			
7	19,29.48	-1,1	33.30,13.48	0.18	-0.26	-0.15			
8	18,30.49	-1,1	34.04,17.90	-0.11	-0.38	-0.61	2.27	2.31	5.53
9	17,31.49	-1,1	33.68,22.37	-0.47	-0.58	-1.12	3.55	0.90	5.93
10	15.59,31.49	-1.41,0	...	...					
...	...	...	...	...					

Table 12.2 PURSUER

n	$x_P(n)$	$v_P(n)$	$\hat{x}_E(n+1)$	EXPECTED DISTANCE		
				0	θ_P	$-\theta_P$
0	5,5	3,-3	19,20	21.95	20.93	22.92
1	8.64,2.82	3.64,-2.18	20,22.82	23.50	22.47	24.48
2	12.70,1.58	4.06,-1.24	20,24.24	24.12	23.08	25.11
3	16.93,1.37	4.24,-0.21	20,25.65	24.53	23.49	25.54
...	...	...	...		...	
...	...	...	...		...	
6	28.22,6.68	3.28,2.68	20,29.90	23.55	22.56	24.58
7	30.76,10.08	2.54,3.40	18,30.48	22.88	21.89	23.91
8	32.40,13.99	1.64,3.91	17,31.49	21.79	20.84	22.81
9	33.04,18.18	0.64,4.19	16,32.49	20.36	19.46	21.37
10	32.64,22.41	-0.39,4.22	...		...	
...	...	...	...		...	

3. Judgments as a Function of Time

How much of a woman's effort goes into satisfying herself and how much to her family? For the sake of a concrete example, let us take a married female whose primary concerns in life are her career, socializing and enjoying and taking care of a family. Let us further assume that the career duration of the woman is forty years, and that she gets married nearly around the same time when she begins hers service.

Concern for career means how much she cares for her career, her satisfaction with work and her efforts to improve her future prospects of promotion, salary raise, etc. Concern for socializing includes friends, group activities, political parties and the like. Concern for the family includes children, acquisition of assets, provision for the future after retirement, etc. It is assumed that these concerns will vary according to the stage of life one is at and the career one pursues. Thus they are time dependent. Further, how far she is able to satisfy her family depends upon the disposition of the family towards their concerns about life, i.e., how they look and derive satisfaction from these concerns. These too are time dependent. The hierarchy can be represented as in Figure 12-10. Individual matrices are developed at three points of time in order to express the pairwise comparisons in each matrix of the hierarchy in the form of functions of time. There is the time of start of a career, mid-career and end of career, which correspond to $t = 0$, 20 and 40 years respectively. It is assumed that the expressions would be continuous functions of time.

At the start of her career, the woman is young and right out of college, being more inclined to enjoy her newly earned independence in life. So her thoughts are mostly on career and on socializing. Her concern about the future of her career is not well crystallized, so it has a lower priority. Also, there may or may not be a family but its problems are not yet pressing for her to worry

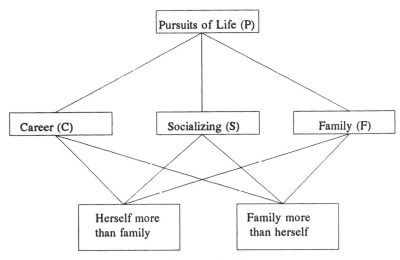

Figure 12-10

about. So the family has even less priority.

In her mid-career, when the career has taken a definite orientation, she has now specialized in a field and has expectations about higher achievements in the future. Also her family may have grown to include children with attendant concern for their education, health, etc. She tries to make savings and investments, own a house, etc. Hence, her family would occupy an equal share of her concern or attention. She would have less time and energy left for her other pursuits, and her pre-occupation with socializing would be less in comparison.

At the end of her career, she has less than previously to look forward to in her career, except maybe a good service record, retirement benefits and so on. She does not have much energy for friends and social life and may become a little isolated from old acquaintances. She devotes most of her time to her family as she has many worries about old age for herself, her husband, etc.

We assume that the three matrices at different points in her career are as in Table 12.3.

Table 12.3

P	C	S	F
C	1	0.5	2
S		1	3
F			1

P	C	S	F
C	1	3	1.5
S		1	0.5
F			1

P	C	S	F
C	1	1	0.2
S		1	0.2
F			1

Start Career
t = 0 years

Mid-Career
t = 20 years

End Career
t = 40 years

We also assume that the graphical representation of the changes in the ratios over time are as in Figure 12-11.

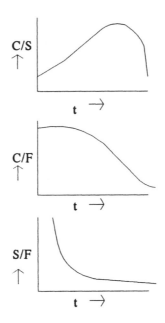

Figure 12-11

By a curve fitting method we can capture this time dependence in the following functions

$$a_{12}(t) = b_1 + b_2 t - b_3 t^2$$

$$a_{13}(t) = c_1 - c_2 e^{-c_3 t}$$

$$a_{23}(t) = d_1 - d_2 \ln d_3 t$$

Finally, by substituting the values of a_{12}, a_{13} and a_{23} for $t=0$, 20 and 40 in Table 12.3, respectively, in the above equations and solving for the coefficients we obtain the entries in the comparison matrix as functions of time.

$$a_{12}(t) = \frac{1}{2} + \frac{t}{4} - \frac{t^2}{160}$$

$$a_{13}(t) = \frac{37}{16} - \frac{5}{16} e^{-\frac{t}{20}}$$

$$a_{23}(t) = 3 - \frac{7}{16} \ln \frac{129}{8} t$$

This concludes the analysis of the second level in the hierarchy and we can now examine how far she is likely to satisfy herself at different times.

At the beginning of her career, her husband does not know much about her career, or how much she is going to stick to one. Hence her concern for her career is more likely to produce more satisfaction to her than to her family. In her mid-career, her husband and her family can identify themselves with her career obtaining greater satisfaction. Hence, although she will still be satisfying herself more, it would not be as great as in the earlier period where she was more needed to create and nurture a family. At the end of her career, the family would feel less enthused about her career exploits, so her satisfaction would be much higher than that of her family.

The three matrices for the pairwise comparisons of the alternatives if H=herself and FM=family are assumed to be as follows:

C	H	FM
H	1	2.33
FM		1

C	H	FM
H	1	1.5
FM		1

C	H	FM
H	1	4
FM		1

Start Career   Mid-Career   End Career
t = 0 years   t = 20 years   t = 40 years

We also assume that the time dependence of these ratios is as in Figure 12-12.

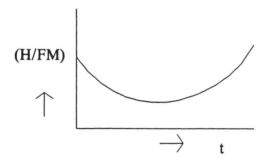

(H/FM)

Figure 12-12

Again by curve fitting we find that this graph is the representation of a function

$$a_{12} = b_1 + b_2 t + b_3 t^2$$

Substituting the values from the matrices above we obtain the time dependent entry

$$a_{12} = \frac{7}{3} - \frac{t}{8} + \frac{t^2}{240}$$

Socializing is usually shared by the spouse at least at the beginning and most of her friends are his friends also. Thus they both receive equal satisfaction from these activities. With the passing of time, however, he is probably more confined, and the woman's satisfaction from mixing with people is greater than the husband's. Her socializing becomes pronounced at the end of her career.

The matrices for pairwise comparisons would be as follows:

S	H	FM
H	1	1
FM		1

S	H	FM
H	1	2.5
FM		1

S	H	FM
H	1	4
FM		1

Start Career Mid-Career End Career
t = 0 years t = 20 years t = 40 years

The time dependence is assumed to be as in Figure 12-13 with the equation:

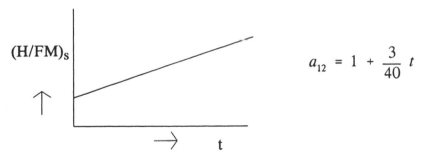

$(H/FM)_S$

$$a_{12} = 1 + \frac{3}{40} t$$

Figure 12-13

Finally, the woman's happiness in her family would be a source of great satisfaction to the family at all times. If this is uniformly over the years given by the matrix

F	H	FM
H	1	.25
FM		1

At all times for <u>all values of t</u>

then we have Figure 12-14 and its equation:

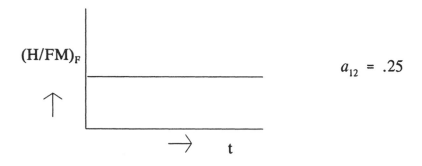

$$a_{12} = .25$$

Figure 12-14

Thus we can summarize all the time dependent matrices in the hierarchy as follows:

P	C	S	F
C	1	$\left(\dfrac{1}{2} + \dfrac{t}{4} - \dfrac{t^2}{160}\right)$	$\left(\dfrac{37}{16} - \dfrac{5}{16} e^{-\frac{t}{20}}\right)$
S		1	$\left(3 - \dfrac{7}{16} \ln \dfrac{129}{8} t\right)$
H			1

C	H	FM
H	1	$\left[\dfrac{7}{3} - \dfrac{t}{8} + \dfrac{t^2}{240}\right]$
FM		1

S	H	FM
H	1	$\left(1 + \dfrac{3}{40}t\right)$
FM		1

F	H	FM
H	1	.25
FM		1

Comparisons of H and FM indicate her expectations to satisfy herself more (or less) than her family.

We may utilize the above time-dependent pairwise comparison matrices to project the corresponding matrices at other time points in her career, say t = 10 and 30 years as follows:

At t = 10 years

P	C	S	F
H	1	2.375	2.123
S		1	0.776
F			1

C	H	FM
H	1	1.5
FM		1

S	H	FM
H	1	1.75
FM		1

At t = 30 years

P	C	S	F
H	1	2.375	2.242
S		1	0.296
F			1

C	H	FM
H	1	2.33
FM		1

S	H	FM
H	1	3.25
FM		1

By deriving the priorities in the hierarchy at different points in time using the matrices developed so far, we have the following values:

t	0	10	20	30	40
H	.51	.48	.49	.57	.37
FM	.49	.52	.51	.43	.63

t	0	10	20	30	40
C	.30	.48	.50	.56	.14
S	.54	.19	.17	.16	.14
F	.16	.33	.33	.28	.71

These numbers are revealing. They show that her concern for socializing has a fairly quick decline early in her career and this decline continues more slowly later on. Her concern for her career rises quickly and then rises steadily for quite some time, after which it falls quickly. Her concern for her family has a point of inflection beyond her mid-career, but rises very high at the end. Her "selfishness" and "neglect" of her family shows in the satisfaction levels where there is also a point of inflection. But in the end, she returns to her family.

The solution corresponding to the first level pairwise comparison matrices would be as follows:

$$\lambda_{max} = \left[\frac{\left[\frac{1}{2} + \frac{t}{4} - \frac{t^2}{160} \right] \left[3 - \frac{7}{16} \ln \frac{129}{8} t \right]}{\frac{37}{16} - \frac{5}{16} e^{-\frac{t}{20}}} \right]^{\frac{1}{3}}$$

$$+ \left[\frac{\frac{37}{16} - \frac{5}{16} e^{-\frac{t}{20}}}{\left[\frac{1}{2} + \frac{t}{4} - \frac{t^2}{160} \right] \left[3 - \frac{7}{16} \ln \frac{129}{8} t \right]} \right]^{\frac{1}{3}} + 1$$

$$\text{Let } A = \left[\frac{1}{2} + \frac{t}{4} - \frac{t^2}{160} \right] \left[3 - \frac{7}{16} \ln \frac{129}{8} t \right]$$

$$+ \left[\frac{37}{16} - \frac{5}{16} e^{-\frac{t}{20}} \right] (\lambda_{max} - 1)$$

$$B = \left[3 - \frac{7}{16} \ln \frac{129}{8} t \right] (\lambda_{max} - 1)$$

$$+ \frac{\left[\frac{37}{16} - \frac{5}{16} \cdot e^{-\frac{t}{20}} \right]}{\left[\frac{1}{2} + \frac{t}{4} - \frac{t^2}{160} \right]}$$

$$C = (\lambda_{max} - 1)^2 - 1$$

$$D = A + B + C$$

Hence the priorities w_C, w_S and w_H are $w_C = A/D$, $w_S = B/D$, $w_H = C/D$. The curves resulting from a plot of these expressions against the time t (in years) are shown in Figure 12-15.

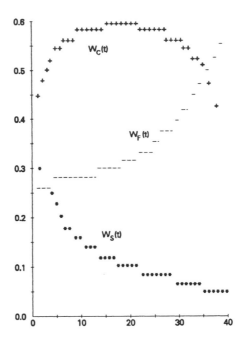

Figure 12-15

At the third level, there are three pairwise comparison matrices corresponding to the three factors at the second level.

The priorities for H in each of these matrices are given by:

$$w_H(C) = \frac{\dfrac{7}{3} - \dfrac{t}{8} + \dfrac{t^2}{240}}{\dfrac{10}{3} - \dfrac{t}{8} + \dfrac{t^2}{240}}$$

$$w_H(S) = \frac{1 + \dfrac{3}{40}t}{2 + \dfrac{3}{40}t}$$

$$w_H(F) = \frac{.25}{1.25} = .2$$

The composite third level priority of H with respect to the focus is given by:

$$w_H = w_C \cdot \frac{\dfrac{7}{3} - \dfrac{t}{8} + \dfrac{t^2}{240}}{\dfrac{10}{3} - \dfrac{t}{8} + \dfrac{t^2}{240}} + w_S \cdot \frac{1 + \dfrac{3}{40}t}{2 + \dfrac{3}{40}t} + w_F(.2)$$

$$w_{FM} = 1 - w_H$$

The curves resulting from a plot of these expressions against time t in years are shown in Figure 12-16. The intent of the example was simply to illustrate the kind of complexity that would be involved in the use of time dependent judgments.

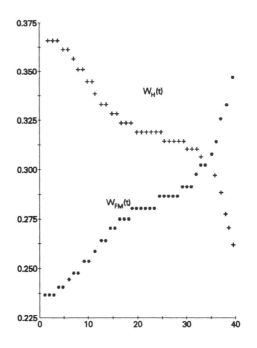

* The values of $W_{FM}(t)$ have been decreased by .4 to be able to plot them in the same figure as $W_H(t)$. Note that $W_{FM} = 1 - W_H$.

Figure 12-16

4. The Time Dependent Supermatrix

Now consider the case when the coefficients of the supermatrix and the weights of the components are time dependent. In that case it becomes difficult to derive the limiting priorities in closed form. Instead, one could fix small values for the time variable and solve the problem for each period by raising the supermatrix to powers and then approximate by curve fitting the several results of each element in the supermatrix. For some supermatrices that are sparse one may be able to derive the answer in analytical form. Many of the dynamic concepts from differential equations could be analyzed for the supermatrix and its limiting form, but one would be able to obtain meaningful interpretations only when the final results are known explicitly by curve fitting such as described above.

We have the following dynamic equations of a nonautonomous system in the supermatrix $A(t)$:

$$\frac{\partial X}{\partial t} = A(t)X \qquad\qquad with \quad X(0)=IC$$

Depending on what assumptions we make about the coefficients of A, we may look for periodic and almost periodic solutions of this system and for asymptotic stability of the linear part of the disturbed system

$$\frac{\partial X}{\partial t} = A(t)X + f(t,X)$$

In general we may be concerned with writing the above system as the sum of a linear part consisting of a spanning tree of the graph of a feedback network, plus a component that yields a disturbed system with feedback. Research in this area would be useful as an interface between physics models and using the AHP.

CHAPTER THIRTEEN

A MODEL OF NEURAL IMPULSE FIRING AND SYNTHESIS*

1. Introduction

Neurons are decision makers that decide from instant to instant whether to fire based on information received through neurotransmitter electric charge. In firing they accomplish two goals. First, they pass information to other neurons which in their turn make a decision to fire or not to fire. Second, their firing serves to express or posit electrically a part of the information received and highlighted - perhaps also modified by memory and other previously learned information based on what each neuron is best specialized to do. By receiving information from many neurons and firing, a neuron synthesizes this variety of signals to a new signal that is an amalgam of the old ones. How do these signals develop, how are they synthesized, and can they be used to create meaning from sense data is the concern of this work.

We develop an integral equation model to show that if a neuron follows basic assumptions used in making paired comparisons, it would be compelled to fire and its firings can be represented in terms of impulse functions or spikes rather in terms of oscillating continuous functions. We then use this impulsive behavior to investigate the response of many neurons whose collective firings could be interpreted as patterns of response by the different senses. We also propose that in order to evoke response output from a network of neurons, a stimulus must be represented as some kind of energy transform. We offer a speculative framework to relate the instant by instant signals generated by a cluster of neurons to a sensation defined by those signals. This work is concerned with how to construct a mathematical representation of action potentials rather than with the physiological phenomena underlying them.

Since Hodgkin and Huxley [20] gave a quantitative

expression for the biophysical mechanisms for the generation of action potentials, many workers have used differential equations to model the behavior of neurons and other cells which exhibit bursting activity in response to a stimulus, e.g., Both et al. [5]; Chay and Keizer [8]; Plant and Kim [31]; Plant [32]; and Rinzel [38].

Two other types of models, known as signal and systems models quantify passive electrical properties of neurons. The first deals with time-domain analysis of the neuronal voltage response. Here one of the most widely used signal models is due to Rall [36] in which the soma is approximated by a parallel combination of a resistor and a capacitor, and the dendrites are represented by a cable. Durand [13] modified Rall's model by suggesting that the somatic membrane resistivity could be lower than that in the dendrite. Other modifications and examples of signal models were studied by Carlen and Durand [7], Edwards and Mulloney [15], Perkel and Mulloney [29], Perkel et al. [30], Pottala et al. [35], Shelton [43], and others.

Systems models deal with the frequency-domain analysis of neuronal input impedance. Here the voltage response of a neuron stimulated by a relatively long current pulse is studied. For example, Durand et al. [14] and Bloomfield, et al. [2] represent the voltage response by the summation of exponential functions:

$$v(t) = I_{in} R_{in} + \sum_{i=1}^{N} C_{Li} e^{(-t/T_i)}$$

where I_{in} is the input current, R_{in} is the cell-input resistance, and N is the number of compartments used to represent the dendritic cable [9, 16, 17].

Another systems approach to the modelling of neural firings is to consider the inherent randomness of the inputs. Kohn [25] has developed a model in which the neuron consists of two compartments: the dendritic tree and the soma, and the trigger zone on the proximal region of the axon near the soma. The membrane potential due to a large number of randomly activated synapses is approximated by a a white Gaussian continuous time stochastic process. The dynamic description up to the time of a threshold crossing is given by the stochastic differential equation:

$$CdV(t) + R^{-1} V(t)dt = i(t)dt$$

$$V(t_o) = V_o, \quad V(t) < V_{th}$$

where $V(t)$ is the membrane potential, R^{-1} is the membrane conductance, C is the membrane capacitance, $i(t)$ is the output current from the dendritc/somatic model, V_o is the resetting or initial membrane potential, and V_{th} is the threshold potential.

When the multiple synaptic inputs happen on the soma, as a first approximation, $i(t)$ is modelled as a white Gaussian noise giving rise to what is known as the "leaky integrator" model used in many theoretical works in neurobiology, e.g., Holden [22] and Segundo et al. [41].

More recently there has been a surge of activity on artificial neural networks (ANN) initiated by the Parallel Distributed Processes (PDP) group [37] which resemble real neural networks but are investigated for their abstract engineering characteristics without regard to the physiological structure of neurons. ANN deal with the modeling of complex tasks by means of networks. The main idea underlying this approach is to find a way of coding information which can be replicated by the networks developed. The nodes of these networks are artificial neurons because they are given a threshold property, but they do not have physiological properties, and the networks constructed do not necessary reflect actual neural networks.

All these models with the exception of artificial neural networks study the production of action potentials and of trains of action potentials. They do not deal with the derived psychological properties of sensation and perception.

Our goal here is to mathematically show how the synthesis of impulses in neurons connected by chemical synapses can be interpreted as a meaningful representation of external stimuli. There are two basic assumptions in our model: (1) only those stimuli or inputs which maximize the overall response are selectively accumulated in the synthesis process, and (2) the response of networks of neurons have the property of being dense in the space of all responses. This implies that the output of a finite number of neurons is sufficient to approximate stimuli. This approximation would be our perception of the stimuli. We propose a method to synthesize signals, within and between neurons to put forth a mathematical theory of the synthesis of impulses in the brain.

Many authors have pointed to the difficulty of performing simultaneous measurements in different parts of the brain by means of electrodes and other devices to validate macro observations of neural activity. This chapter gives a global view of how neurons may work as a group to create images and impressions. We synthesize the solutions derived for the response of individual neurons, to obtain the general form of response of many neurons. To describe how a diversity of stimuli may be grouped abstractly into visual, auditory, sensual and other kinds of response, the outputs of such syntheses are interpreted as points of an inner direct sum of a space of functions of the form $\{t^{\alpha} e^{-\beta t}, \alpha, \beta \geq 0\}$ or more generally as distributions (generalized functions in the sense of Schwartz) that can be used to represent images, and perhaps other sensations.

2. Free and Forced Sequential Firings of a Neuron

In its simplest form measurement uses comparison by pairs of intensities of a stimulus. One element of the pair may be in memory, or as it is often the case, two stimuli share a property such as two apples with respect to redness. Grossberg [18, p.3] writes:

> "One illustrative type of psychological data that Helmholtz studied concerns color perception ... Helmholtz realized ... that the light we perceive to be white tends to be the average color of a whole scene ... Moreover, this averaging process must be nonlinear, since it is more concerned with relative than absolute light intensities ... we tend to see ... the relative amounts of light of each wavelength that they [objects] reflect, not the total amount of light reaching us from each point."

The problem before us is how to perform such measurement to enable us to take a certain stimulus and determine (or more accurately predict) the intensity of response to that stimulus. This means that to model neural activity one needs to carry out measurement on continua of both stimulus and response, because as Lerner [27, p.34] writes:

> "... the brain unlike today's digital computers, uses

continuous variables rather than discrete binary variables."

A number of researchers have studied the problem of measurement through ratio scales as a way of quantifying the relative response of an individual (or a neuron) to two levels of a stimulus. For a discrete number of responses to a stimulus, the problem has a matrix presentation. In that problem, a pair of objects (stimuli) i and j are compared according to a common attribute, the smaller or lesser one serving as the one possessing a unit amount of the attribute. The larger one is then compared with it as to how many times more it possesses that attribute and is given the value a_{ij}. Alternatively, one may seek the inverse comparison of the smaller object with respect to the larger one by writing down the reciprocal value $a_{ji} = 1/a_{ij}$. The matrix A is called consistent if the entire matrix can be constructed from the comparisons of a single row (or more generally a spanning tree). It satisfies the relation $a_{jk} = a_{ik}/a_{ij}$ or $a_{ij}a_{jk} = a_{ik}$. It is easy to see that a consistent matrix is reciprocal but not conversely. From the matrix A, a relative scale of ratio magnitudes is obtained by solving for the principal eigenvector $Aw = nw$ when A is consistent and hence has the form $A = (w_i/w_j)$ and $Aw = \lambda_{max}w$ when A is inconsistent (Saaty, 1988).

For application to neural firing in which it is assumed that a neuron compares neurotransmitter-generated charges in increments of time, we need to consider $K(s,t)$ the continuous counterpart of the matrix A. $K(s,t)$ is consistent or reciprocal if:
$K(s,t)K(t,u) = K(s,u)$ or $K(s,t) K(t,s) = 1$, for all s, t and u, respectively.

Thus, we select an interval of time [a,b] and our convention will be to choose a = 0. Let $0 = t_0 < t_1 < ... < t_{n-1} < t_n = b$ be a partition of the interval [0,b], $I_k \equiv t_k - t_{k-1}$, k=1,2,...,n. Let w(t), $t \in [0,b]$ be a single firing (voltage discharge) of a neuron in spontaneous activity. In simple terms, if G(t), $t \in [0,b]$ is the cumulative response of the neuron in spontaneous activity over time, given by $G(t) = \int_0^t w(u)du$, then $\dfrac{dG(t)}{dt} = w(t)$, where w(t)dt is the response during an infinitesimal period of time. Note that G(t) is monotone increasing

and hence $w(t)>0$ and
$w(0)= 0$. Let

$$K(I_i,I_j) \equiv \frac{G(t_i)-G(t_{i-1})}{G(t_j)-G(t_{j-1})}$$

be the relative comparison of the response of a neuron during a time interval of length Δt_i with another time interval of length Δt_j. Cross multiplication and summation over j yields:

$$\frac{1}{n} \sum_{j=1}^{n} K(I_i,I_j)[G(t_j)-G(t_{j-1})] = G(t_i)-G(t_{i-1}), \ i=1,2,...,n \qquad (1)$$

If $G(t)$ is of class $C^1[0,b]$, then as $\Delta t_k \to 0$ for all k, $K(I_i,I_j) \to$

$K(s,t)= \dfrac{w(s)}{w(t)}$, $s,t\in[0,b]$. Also because the left hand side of (1) is an

average, we obtain as $\Delta t_k \to 0$ for all k, and as $n \to \infty$:

$$\frac{1}{b} \int_0^b K(s,t)w(t)dt = w(s).$$

It is easy to show that b is the principal eigenvalue (i.e., the largest in absolute value) of the consistent kernel $K(s,t)$ [34] because all the other eigenvalues are zero, (the eigenfunctions being any function orthogonal to $w(t)$ on $[0,b]$.)   In general, if $K(I_i,I_j)$ is reciprocal but not consistent, the homogeneous equation takes the form given by:

$w(s) = \lambda_0 \int_0^b K(s,t)w(t)dt$ or in operator form $(I - \lambda_0 K)w = 0$, $w\in L_2[0,b]$

where I is the identity operator, and K is a compact integral operator defined on the space $L_2[0,b]$ of Lebesgue square integrable functions:

$$Kf(s) = \int_0^b K(s,t)f(t)dt, \ f\in L_2[0,b].$$

Because positive reciprocal kernels are non-factorable (the property that corresponds to irreducibility for non-negative matrices), there exists a unique positive simple eigenvalue λ_0^{-1} whose modulus dominates the moduli of all other eigenvalues.

As in the discrete case, there is an eigenfunction $w(s)$, that is unique to within a multiplicative constant, which corresponds to the simple maximum positive eigenvalue λ_0^{-1}.   w(s) is called the response function of the neuron in spontaneous activity.   From $K(s,t) > 0$, $K(0,t) = 0$ for all $t \neq 0$, it follows that $w(s) > 0$, for $s \neq 0$, and $w(0) = 0$ [42, p. 186].   If the reciprocal kernel $K(s,t) \geq 0$, on $0 \leq s, t \leq b$, is Lebesgue square integrable and continuously differentiable, and if $\lim_{\xi \to 0} K(\xi s, \xi t)$ exists, then:

$$w(t) = t^\alpha e^{g(t)} / \int_0^b t^\alpha e^{g(t)} dt \qquad (3)$$

satisfies (2) for some choice of g(t).   This solution of (2) assumes that the comparison process is continuous, but it is not meaningful to compare the response during an interval of length zero with the response during a non-zero interval no matter how small it is, for then the reciprocal comparison would be unbounded.   From a theoretical standpoint, one can study the problem using Lebesgue integration and allowing only one zero.

Because linear combinations of the functions $\{t^\alpha e^{-\beta t}, \alpha, \beta \geq 0\}$:

$$\sum_{i=1}^n \gamma_i t^{\alpha_i} e^{-\beta_i t} \qquad (4)$$

are dense in the space of bounded continuous functions C[0,b] we can approximate $t^\alpha e^{g(t)}$ by linear combinations of $t^\alpha e^{-\beta t}$ and hence we substitute $g(t) = -\beta t$, $\beta \geq 0$ in the eigenfunction w(t). Later we will see that such linear combinations are dense in even more general spaces worthy of consideration in representing neural responses to stimuli. The density of neural firing is not completely analogous to the density of the rational numbers in the real number system. The rationals are countable infinite, the number of neurons is finite but large.   In speaking of density here we may think of coming sufficiently close (within some prescribed bound rather than arbitrarily close).

The prediction provided by the classical Hodgkin and Huxley model can also be represented   by expressions as in (3).   In this model, the total current during a voltage clamp is given by linear combinations of exponentials.   When the voltage is allowed to vary, (4) is a more appropriate expression for representing the general solution of the two models given in their paper [20, 1952, pp. 519,

522).

Next we show that neuronal responses are impulsive and hence that the brain is a discrete firing system. It follows that the spontaneous activity of a neuron during a very short period of time in which the neuron fires is given by:

$$w(t) = \sum_{k=1}^{R} \gamma_k (t - \tau_k)^\alpha e^{-\beta(t - \tau_k)} \tag{5}$$

if the neuron fires at the random times τ_k, k=1,2, ..., R.

The empirical findings of Poggio and Mountcastle [33, p.288]:

> "The study of central neurons has confirmed ... that neural activity is a variable, a statistical affair that for quantitative evaluation must be treated from the probabilistic point of view."

support the assumption here that the variables R and τ_k are probabilistic. However, the parameters α and β vary from neuron to neuron, but are constant for each neuron as observed by F.J. Brinley [6, p.48]:

> "The expression "all or none" describes the ability of a nerve fiber, once a suprathreshold response has been applied to its surface, to initiate an action potential whose configuration is determined solely by the properties of the cell independently of the precise configuration of the exciting stimulus."

Non-spontaneous activity can be characterized as a perturbation of background activity taking place in the neural network. To derive the response function when neurons are stimulated from external sources, we consider an inhomogeneous equation to represent stimuli acting on the neuron in addition to existing spontaneous activity.

For that purpose, we solve the inhomogeneous Fredholm equation of the second kind given by:

$$(I - \lambda_0 K)W = f \tag{6}$$

where $f(t) \geq 0$, $f(t) \neq 0$ is a presynaptic action potential.

It is known that (6) has a solution if and only if the following orthogonality condition holds between f and v:

$$<f,v> \equiv \int_0^b f(t)v(t)dt = 0 \tag{7}$$

where $v(t)$ is the eigenfunction corresponding to the maximum positive eigenvalue λ_0^{-1} of the homogeneous equation associated with (2) given by:

$$(I - \lambda_0 K')v = 0 \tag{8}$$

where $K'v = \int_0^b K(t,s)v(t)dt$. Since f and v are required to be nonnegative, this condition cannot be satisfied unless v(t) or f(t) are zero almost everywhere. This is precisely the property of an impulse delivered through an action potential. A function f(t) is said to be impulsive if it is identically zero, except for a very short interval $t_1 \leq t \leq t_2$, its integral over this time interval is a given number $I_0 \neq 0$, not very small, and f(t) assumes large values in the interval $t_1 \leq t \leq t_2$ [4, p. 243]. Impulsive functions are studied mathematically as Schwartz's distributions.

The solution of (6) involves not simply distributions but also Lebesgue integrals of distributions. Stimuli or impulses are studied mathematically in more general spaces [28] than those of continuous functions. These are the spaces of Schwartz distributions $D'[0,b]$ defined on Sobolev spaces $W_p^k(\Omega)$, where Ω is an open subset of $\mathbf{R}^n$. $W_p^k(\Omega)$ is the space of distributions with derivatives of order k in $L_p(\Omega)$.

The Dirac distribution δ_θ is an example of how an impulsive function can be represented. It is defined by:

$$\int_{-\infty}^{+\infty} \delta_{t_\theta}(t)f(t)dt = f(t_\theta), \text{ for any } f \in W_2^1[0,b]$$

where t_θ is the time at which the potential in the neuron attains the threshold value and an action potential is produced. The orthogonality condition (7) is satisfied if $v(t_\theta)=0$. In other words, a forcing function of the inhomogeneous equation for which the orthogonality condition holds is the Dirac distribution and v(t) must vanish at the threshold point. Thus, to solve (6) we must first solve the associated homogeneous equation (8) to obtain v(t) and then show that $v(t_\theta)=0$ holds, from which we would conclude that w(t), the solution of (2), is impulsive because $w(t)v(t) = 1$ for consistent kernels.

Equation (2) in distributions is given by:

$$<w,\phi> = \lambda_0 <w,K'\phi>, \quad \phi \in W_2^1[0,b]$$

where

$$<w,\phi> = \int_0^b w(s)\phi(s)dt, \quad \phi \in W_2^1[0,b]$$

and

$$<w,K'\phi> = \int_0^b \left[\int_0^b K(s,t)w(t)dt \right]\phi(s)ds, \quad \phi \in W_2^1[0,b].$$

Its solution takes the form:

$$<w,\phi> = \sum_{i=1}^n \int_0^b \delta_{\tau_\theta}i(t)\phi(t)dt, \quad \phi \in W_2^1[0,b] \tag{9}$$

if the neuron fires n times during the interval [0,b]. All functions in $W_p^k(\Omega)$ can be approximated by linear combinations of smooth functions in $C^\infty(\Omega)$ [28, p.12]. Because $C^\infty(\Omega) \subset C(\Omega)$, and because the functions given in (4) are dense in $C(\Omega)$, it follows that the functions given in (4) are also dense in $W_p^k(\Omega)$ and their linear combinations can be used to approximate any function in these spaces. Since impulsive functions can be approximated by the linear combinations given in (4), (9) may be approximated by linear combinations as in (5). The density of the functions given in (4) implies that the output of a finite number of neurons is sufficient to approximate stimuli represented by distributions in Sobolev spaces.

The inhomogeneous equation (6) in distributions and its solution are, respectively:

$$<W,\phi> = <f,\phi> + \lambda_0 <W,K'\phi>, \quad \phi \in W_2^1[0,b] \tag{10}$$

and

$$W,\phi> = <f,\phi> + \lambda_0 <Hf,\phi> + <w,\phi>, \quad \phi \in W_2^1[0,b]$$

where $Hf = \int_0^b H(s,t)f(t)dt$ is the resolvent operator of (6) and $<w,\phi>$ is the solution of the homogeneous equation (2). The difference between the solutions of the homogeneous and the inhomogeneous equations are the instants of time at which an action potential takes place. They both have the same analytical form approximated as in (5).

3. Approximating an Impulse Function

For the purpose of intuitive understanding of how a function can be approximated by the linear combinations given in (4), we take a single term $\gamma \, t^{\alpha} e^{-\beta t}$ and estimate α and β to construct an approximation to the function

$$f_{\varepsilon}(t) = \varepsilon^{-1} \, e^{-t/\varepsilon} \tag{11}$$

which behaves like a Dirac distribution in the neighborhood of the origin for ε sufficiently small. Let τ_0 be the value at which $w(t) = \gamma \, t^{\alpha} e^{-\beta t}$ attains its maximum value M, and let $M \gg \tau_0$.

Let $V_{\theta}(t)$ be the voltage discharged by the neuron at the threshold θ, and let $\tau_1 > \tau_0$ be the time it takes for the voltage to go from its value at θ to the maximum value M and drop to the resting level. We have

$$V_{\theta}(\tau_1) = \gamma \int_0^{\tau_1} t^{\alpha} \, e^{-\beta t} dt + \gamma \int_{\tau_1}^{\infty} t^{\alpha} \, e^{-\beta t} dt$$

where the second term of $V_{\theta}(\tau_1)$ is sufficiently small. We assume, without loss of generality, that $V_{\theta}(\tau_1) = 1$. This yields $\gamma = \beta^{\alpha+1}/\Gamma(\alpha+1)$. Now, the maximum of the function $\gamma \, t^{\alpha} e^{-\beta t}$ is attained at $\tau_0 = \alpha/\beta$. If we substitute $t = \tau_0$ and $\Gamma(\alpha+1) \approx \alpha^{\alpha} e^{-\alpha}(2\pi\alpha)^{1/2}$ in $w(t) = \gamma \, t^{\alpha} e^{-\beta t}$ we obtain $\beta = 2\pi M^2 \tau_0$ and $\alpha = 2\pi M^2 \tau_0^2$. In addition, if we substitute $\varepsilon = M^{-1}$ and $t = \alpha/\beta$ in (11) we have:

$$|f_{\varepsilon}(\alpha/\beta) - w(\alpha/\beta)| = |Me^{-(\alpha/\beta)M} - M| < \varepsilon$$

because $M \gg \tau_0 = \alpha/\beta$ and hence $|e^{-(\alpha/\beta)M} - 1| < \varepsilon/M < \varepsilon$. Thus, $f_{\varepsilon}(t)$ can be approximated in $[0, \tau_1]$ by functions of the form $\gamma \, t^{\alpha} \, e^{-\beta t}$

or by linear combinations of them. The two figures given below show how, on appropriate choice of parameters, a single term and a linear combination behave.

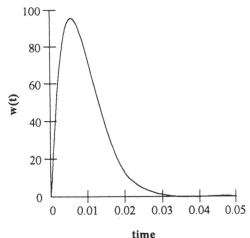

Figure 13-1: $w(t) = 197977.5 \, t^{1.5708} e^{-314.16t}$

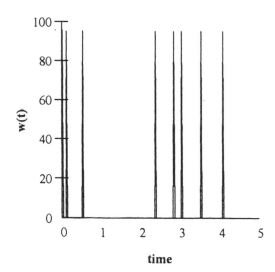

Figure 13-2: *An illustration of spikes generated by linear combinations with the same values for all α's and similarly for all β's.*

In Section 5 we show that the synthesis of both hierarchic and network arrangements gives rise to expressions as in (4) and hence again we have linear combinations that are dense. To illustrate how such dense functions can in fact give rise to all responses to ordered stimuli we must first consider the nature of the stimuli and the forms that the response takes.

4. Hierarchical and Network Synthesis of Sensation

There are three prevailing views about how to study neural activity classified according to the neural codes, the computing elements and the experimental tools [44]. The mass action theory in which neural activity is organized in definite cortical regions [23]; the cardinal cell hypothesis in which the activity is represented as trains of spikes [1]; and the cell assembly theory in which activity is the result of neurons arranged in patterns or assemblies [19]. In support of the last of the three theories, many researchers have observed that signal transmission in sensory neurons proceeds in a hierarchic fashion. Each set of neurons synapses into an adjacent set often funneling information through synthesis from detailed to composite.

To derive a general expression for the response of a group of neurons or cell assembly to a stimulus we use the method of steepest descent [10] to evaluate integrals of the form:

$$\int_{\Omega} g(z,t)dz$$

where $g(z,t)$ is a meromorphic function in z for $t \geq t_0$ and Ω is a contour in the complex z-plane. The method consists of finding the saddle points of $g(z,t)$. Such a point z_0 satisfies the first derivative condition $h'(z_0,t) = 0$, where $h(z,t) = \ln g(z,t)$. The above integral can be approximated at a given saddle point z_0 by

$$\int_{\Omega} g(z,t)dz \approx g(z_0,t) \int_{U(z_0)} e^{\frac{1}{2}h''(z_0,t)(z-z_0)^2} dz$$

where $U(z_0)$ is a neighborhood of z_0. The result for several saddle points is the sum of such expressions.

Thus we assume that the synthesis of response of several neurons is a consequence of the selection (filtering) of inputs that give rise to the maximum response from each neuron. This is in harmony with the concept that neurons will fire in response to suprathreshold stimuli.

Let $W_i(S,t)$ be the response function generated by the ith neuron in response to the stimulus S. Let $u_i(s) = d_i s^{p_i} e^{-q_i s}$, $\theta_1 \leq s \leq \theta_2$ be the relative strength of the response of the ith neuron to the stimulus $S \equiv [\theta_1, \theta_2]$. The overall synthesis of all signals from neuron i involved in the response to a range of S, and using the method of steepest descent with s_i denoting the saddle point, is given by:

$$w_i(S,t) = \int_S W_i(s,t) u_i(s) ds$$

$$= \int_{\theta_2}^{\theta_1} \sum_{k=1}^{R_i(s)} \gamma_{ik} (t-\tau_{ik})^{\alpha_i} e^{-\beta_i(t-\tau_{ik})} d_i s^{p_i} e^{-q_i s} ds$$

$$\approx \sum_{k=1}^{R_i(s_i)} \rho_{ik}(s_i)(t-\tau_{ik})^{\alpha_i} e^{-\beta_i(t-\tau_{ik})}.$$

The number of times, $R_i(s_i)$, a neuron fires is a representation of the intensity of the response to a stimulus.

Let N_S be the number of neurons activated by the stimulus S. The response of this set of neurons can be represented as a tuple of N_S dimensions:

$$\{w_1(S,t), ..., w_{N_S}(S,t)\}$$

which in turn can be written as:

$$W(S,t) = \sum_{i=1}^{N_S} w_i(S,t) = \sum_{i=1}^{N_S} \sum_{k=1}^{R_i(s_i)} \rho_{ik}(s_i)(t-\tau_{ik})^{\alpha_i} e^{-\beta_i(t-\tau_{ik})}. \qquad (12)$$

Here the frequency of firing of a neuron serves as the contribution of the neuron to the response of a group of neurons.

Due to the large number of neurons involved we represent (12) in continuous form. We assume that the neurons are packed so densely that the set of neurons $N(S)$ that responds to the stimulus S is compact. In this case, the response to the stimulus can be represented by:

$$W(S,t) =$$

$$\iint_{N(S)} \sum_{k=1}^{R(A(\omega),\Phi(\omega))} \rho_k[t-\tau_k]^{\alpha(A(\omega),\Phi(\omega))} e^{-\beta(A(\omega),\Phi(\omega))[t-\tau_k]} dAd\Phi.$$

where $R(A(\omega),\Phi(\omega))$ is the number of firings of the neuron in response to a stimulus with Fourier spectrum $A(\omega)$ and the phase angle $\Phi(\omega)$.

Synthesis of Signals in Feedback Networks

Let $W_{ij}(S,t)$ be the response of neuron i induced by neuron j due to a stimulus S, then:

$$W_{ij}(S,t) = \sum_{h=1}^{R_{ij}(S)} \gamma_i(t-T_{ijh})^{\alpha_i} e^{-\beta_i(t-T_{ijh})}.$$

where T_{ijh}, $h=1,2,...,R_{ij}(S)$ are the firing times. Let $U = (u_{ij} = W_{ij}(S,t))$ be the matrix of stimuli from neuron to neuron of a network. The entries of U^l represent the synthesis of stimuli from each neuron to all other neurons, where l is the length of the chains required to reach all neurons from a given one. An entry of U^2 is given by:

$$W_{ij}^{(2)}(S,t) =$$

$$\sum_{k=1}^{N_S} \left[\sum_{h=1}^{R_{ik}(S)} \gamma_i(t-\tau_{ikh})^{\alpha_i} e^{-\beta_i(t-\tau_{ikh})} \right] \left[\sum_{g=1}^{R_{kj}(S)} \gamma_i(t-\tau_{kjg})^{\alpha_i} e^{-\beta_i(t-\tau_{kjg})} \right]$$

Where N_S is the set of neurons that respond to the stimulus S.

For integer values α_i and α_k, $k=1,2,...,N_S$, we have:

$$W_{ij}^{(2)}(S,t) = \sum_{k=1}^{N_S} \sum_{m=1}^{\alpha_i} \binom{\alpha_i}{m} \sum_{h=1}^{R_{ik}(S)} (-\tau_{ikh})^{\alpha_i - m} e^{\tau_{ikh}\beta_i} t^m e^{-\beta_i t}$$

$$\bullet \sum_{n=1}^{\alpha_k} \binom{\alpha_k}{n} \sum_{g=1}^{R_{kj}(S)} (-\tau_{kjg})^{\alpha_k - n} \, e^{\tau_{kjg}\beta_k} \, t^n \, e^{-\beta_k t}$$

expanded in such a way as to show that it is again a linear combination of the functions $\{t^\alpha e^{-\beta t}, \alpha,\beta \geq 0\}$. The entries of U^3 are similarly obtained, and so on. In passing we note that hierarchic synthesis is a special case of the above result for networks [39].

5. Synthesis of Response to Several Stimuli

We have briefly examined the matter of several stimuli, like light and sound, experienced simultaneously, and how they may be perceived without being synthesized.

Let S be the space of stimuli, and let $S \subset S$ be a specific stimulus whose instances are impulses. Let $\{W_i(s,t), s \in S\}$ be the response function of the neuron N_i to the impulse s at time t. Let N(S) be the set of neurons that respond to S, and let W be the set of response functions of these neurons. The set of mappings from the space of stimuli S to the set of response functions W that assigns a response function to every neuron in N(S) for $S \subset S$ is a topological space which we denote by $L_N(S,W)$ with the norm:

$$\|W_i\|_s = \sup_t |W_i(s,t)|, \text{ for } s \in S.$$

We now define the norm in N(S):

$$\|N_i\| = \sup_{s \in S} \|W_i\|_s = \sup_{s \in S} \sup_t |W_i(s,t)|.$$

Let B be the set of all neurons in the cortex. To every subset $N(S) \subset B$, $S \subset S$, there corresponds a topological space $L_N(S,W)$. Let N and N´ be two subsets of B. Let $\| . \| : N \times N´ \rightarrow R$ (the set of real numbers) be the norm defined by:

$$(13) \quad \|(N,N')\| = \max \{\|N\|, \|N'\|\}$$

for $(N,N') \in N \times N´$. $N \times N´$ with the product topology induced by (13) is said to be the direct sum of N and N´ denoted by $N \oplus N´$. Every point of $N \oplus N´$ can be written as $N + N' \in N \oplus N´$. Thus to $N \oplus N´$ there corresponds a topological space $L_{N \oplus N´}(S,W)$.

A stimulus is a composite of more primitive types of stimuli.

Let S be a decomposable stimulus, $S = \bigcup_{i=1}^{m} S_i$, $S_i \cap S_j = \emptyset$, for all i and j, and let N_i, i=1,2,...,m be the set of neurons that respond to the stimulus S_i, i=1,2,...,m, respectively, and . Then the space of neural responses can be written as the direct sum of topological spaces:

$$L_{\oplus N_i}(S,W) = \bigoplus_{i=1}^{m} L_{N_i}(S,W)$$

where $L_{N_i}(S,W)$ is the space of neural responses to a stimulus associated with $N_i \subset B$, i=1,2,..., m.

We now study the form of the response function in these spaces. Let

$$w^{(i)}(S_i,t) = \iint_{N_i(S_i)} \sum_{k=1}^{R(s_i^0;x,y,z)} \rho_k(s_i^0;x,y,z)$$
$$\cdot [t-\tau_k(x,y,z)]^{\alpha(x,y,z)} e^{-\beta(x,y,z)[t-\tau_k(x,y,z)]} dxdydz$$

be the response function associated with the type of stimulus S_i, i=1,2,...,m. The total response to the stimulus $S = \bigcup_{i=1}^{m} S_i$, $S_i \cap S_j = \emptyset$, for all i and j, is given by:

$$w(S,t) = \sum_{i=1}^{m} w^{(i)}(S_i,t)$$

On n-dimensional Reciprocal Kernels

We assumed that stimuli can be separated from each other. The concept of reciprocal kernel can be generalized to synthesis accross several stimuli.   Let the response functions w(s) represent the response of the brain to a stimulus and let $w(s_1,s_2)$ represent its generalization to two stimuli s_1 and s_2.

2-Dimensional Kernels

Definition - A positive kernel $K(s_1,s_2;t_1,t_2)$ is said to be locally reciprocal if and only if it is reciprocal with respect to some of its variables, i.e.,

$$K(s_1,s_2;t_1,t_2)K(t_1,s_2;s_1,t_2) = 1$$

and/or

$$K(s_1,s_2;t_1,t_2)K(s_1,t_2;t_1,s_2) = 1$$

Definition - A positive kernel is said to be globally reciprocal if and only if

$$K(s_1,s_2;t_1,t_2)K(t_1,t_2;s_1,s_2) = 1$$

Definition - A reciprocal kernel $K(s_1,s_2;t_1,t_2)$ is said to be separable if and only if

$$K(s_1,s_2;t_1,t_2) = K_1(s_1,t_1)K_2(s_2,t_2).$$

Definition - A reciprocal kernel is said to be consistent if and only if $K(s_1,s_2;t_1,t_2) K(t_1,t_2;u_1,u_2) = K(s_1,s_2;u_1,u_2)$, for all s_i, t_i and u_i, i=1,2.

The 2-dimensional Fredholm equation of the second kind is given by:

$$(14) \quad w(s_1,s_2) = \lambda_0 \int_a^b \int_a^b K(s_1,s_2;t_1,t_2)w(t_1,t_2)dt_1 dt_2$$

Theorem 13.1 *If* $K(s_1,s_2;t_1,t_2)$ *is a separable kernel, the solution of* (14) *is given by:*

$$w(s_1,s_2) = w_1(s_1) w_2(s_2).$$

Proof Because the kernel is separable and reciprocal, it can be written as:

$$K(s_1,s_2;t_1,t_2) = K_1(s_1,t_1)K_2(s_2,t_2).$$

Let $w_i(s_i)$, i=1,2 be the principal eigenfunction of the equation given by:

$$w_i(s_i) = \lambda_i \int_a^b K(s_i,t_i)w_i(s_i)ds_i, \ i=1,2,$$

respectively. We have:

$$K(s_i,t_i) = [w_i(s_i)/w_i(t_i)]\varepsilon_i(s_i,t_i), \ i=1,2, \quad (15)$$

where

$$\lambda_i \int_a^b \varepsilon_i(s_i,t_i)dt_i = 1, \ i=1,2. \quad (16)$$

Substituting (15) and (16) into (14) we obtain $w(s_1,s_2)/\left[w_1(s_1)w_2(s_2)\right] = c$, where c is a constant. In addition, if $\int_a^b w_i(s)ds = 1$, i=1,2, then $\int_a^b \int_a^b w(s,\sigma)ds d\sigma = 1$ and the solution of the 2-dimensional equation for separable kernels is given by:

$$W(s_1, s_2) = W_1(s_1)\, W_2(s_2).$$

The definitions of locally and globally reciprocal, consistency and separability can be extended to n-dimensional kernels for considering n stimuli.

Let $K(s_1, s_2, ..., s_n; t_1, t_2, ..., t_n)$ be an n-dimensional reciprocal kernel. Let $w_i(s_i)$, i=1,2, ...,n, be the principal eigenfunction of the kernel $K_i(s_i, t_i)$, i=1,2, ..., n, respectively, corresponding to the principal eigenvalue λ_i, i=1,2, ..., n.

The corresponding n-dimensional Fredholm equation is given by:

$$W(s_1, s_2, ..., s_n) =$$

$$\lambda_0 \int_a^b ... \int_a^b K(s_1, s_2, ..., s_n; t_1, t_2, ..., t_n) W(t_1, t_2, ..., t_n) dt_1 dt_2 ... dt_n. \quad (17)$$

Theorem 13.2 *If the kernel of Equation (17) is separable, the solution corresponding to the principal eigenvalue is given by*

$$W(s_1, s_2, ..., s_n) = \prod_{1}^{n} w_i(s_i).$$

or

$$ln\{W(s_1, s_2, ..., s_n)\} = \sum_{k=1}^{n} ln\{w_k(s_k)\}.$$

Let us now consider a continuum number of stimuli X. Let $K(X,Y)$ be a compact reciprocal kernel, i.e., $K(x,y)K(y,x)=1$, for all $x \in X$ and $y \in Y$, where X and Y are compact subsets of the real numbers. Equation (2) is now written as:

$$w(X) = \lambda_0 \int_\Omega K(X;Y) w(Y)$$

Generalizing the solution of the n stimuli case to a continuum by introducing an integral instead of a sum, we have :

$$ln\{w(X)\} = \int_X ln\{w(s)\} ds$$

and

$$w(X) = \exp\{\int_X ln\{w(s)\} ds\}.$$

where $w(s)$ is given by:

$$W(s) = \sum_{i=1}^{n(s)} v_i \sum_{k=1}^{R_i(s)} \gamma_{ik} (t-\tau_{ik})^{\alpha_i} e^{-\beta_i (t-\tau_{ik})}$$

and $n(s)$ is the number of neurons that respond to the stimulus s, v_i is the relative contribution of the *i*th neuron in the response to that stimulus and $R_i(s)$ is the number of times the *i*th neuron fires.

6. Representation of Visual Response to Neural Firing

Factors that contribute to neural response to visual stimuli are: (a) the intensity of the background (Weber's law), (b) the target area (Ricco's law), (c) the target duration (Bunsen-Roscoe's law), (d) the wavelength, (e) the adaptation of the retina, and (f) the shape of the target. Hubel and Wiesel provide a suitable explanation to this questions for nature's way to make it possible for us to cope with the problem of portraying more than two dimensions on a two dimensional surface [22, p.96]:

"The cortex is dealing with at least four sets of values: two for the x and y position variables in the visual filed, one for orientation and one for the different degrees of eye preference. The two surface coordinates are used up in designating field position; the other two variables are accommodated by dicing up the cortex with subdivisions so fine that one can run through a complete set of orientations or eye preferences and meanwhile have a shift in visual field position that is small with respect to the resolution in that part of the visual world."

The parameters α and β, whose ranges are already fixed in a neuron's process of development, are related to particular ranges of the energy and frequency themselves as made explicit by the

Fourier transform. The values obtained here may be regarded as approximations to the actual values, the main point of this analysis being to illustrate that the synthesized response of many neurons has the density property, and hence to any impulsive stimulus there corresponds an organized response representing a particular sensation.

7. Energy Representation: The Fourier Transform

Neurons respond to several kinds of outside stimuli: (1) energy propagated as light and sound vibrations, heat and pressure, (2) energy in the form of electric charges, (3) fields such as gravity which generates the sensation of falling, (4) matter in the form of molecules creating actions and reactions according to the laws of Chemistry, (5) matter encountered physically in bulk, responding to it according to the laws Physics.

Both discrete and continuous stimuli can be represented as pulses which impact neural receptors which then fire in response. Stimuli are transformed into pulsations so that neurons can interpret them. One way to represent analytically the energy of stimuli is through their Fourier transform.

The Fourier transform of a function f(t) is given by:

$$F(f) \equiv F(t) = \int_{-\infty}^{+\infty} f(w)e^{-jtw}dw$$

which can also be written in the form:

$$F(f) = A(t)e^{j\phi(t)}$$

where $A(t)$ is the Fourier spectrum, $A^2(t)$ is the energy spectrum, and $\Phi(t)$ is the phase angle.

There is a useful link between forms which we perceive in nature and how these forms emanate energy as stimuli that enable us to sense them and respond to them through the firings of neurons. Because Fourier analysis gives periodic function approximation to functions with compact support, it is possible to use the Fourier transform to represent a periodic function as a sequence of pulsations which is what we want for representing stimuli as energy packets. That is, stimuli are periodic functions over short time intervals so that they can be quantized as forcing functions, the only condition under which there is a solution to the Fredholm equation (1).

In general we only recognize a stimulus by the impact of its intensity $x(t)$ and frequency ω on our senses. We denote by $f(x(t),\omega)$ the forcing function of (1) associated with that stimulus. To recognize a stimulus, its intensity must remain constant over a short duration t, and $x(t) = a$. According to (1) the response function during t is given by $W(x(t),\omega)$. It is a transformation of $f(x(t),\omega)$ given by:

$$W(x(t),\omega) = T[f(x(t),\omega)]$$

or $W(a,\omega) = T[f(a,\omega)]$. As an energy form, $f(a,\omega)$ may be written as a linear combination of pulsations (needed in this form for the solution of (1) as follows:

$$\overline{f}(a,\omega) = \tau \sum_{k=-\infty}^{\infty} f(a,k\omega_0)\delta(\omega-k\omega_0).$$

In fact, any function can be considered as an infinite aggregate of pulsations at each of its points of definition. But by using the Fourier transform of $\overline{f}$ we can determine the amplitude and frequency at each of these points, and by solving (1) we can relate the response parameters to the stimulus energy and wave parameters.

The Fourier transform of $\overline{f}(a,\omega)$ is given by:

$$F(\overline{f}) = \omega_0 \sum_{k=-\infty}^{\infty} f(a,k\omega_0)e^{-jk\omega_0 t}$$

which can also be written as:

$$F(\bar{f}) = \sum_{n=-\infty}^{\infty} F(a,t+\frac{2\pi k}{\omega_0})$$

where $F(f) = F(a,t)$ is the Fourier transform of $F(a,t)$. Conversely, if $f(a,\omega)$ is a periodic function with period ω_0, then it can be written as:

$$f(a,\omega) = \sum_{k=-\infty}^{\infty} \alpha_k e^{jk\tau\omega}, \tau = \frac{2\pi}{\omega_0}$$

where $\alpha_k = \omega_0^{-1} \int_{-\omega_0/2}^{\omega_0/2} f(a,\omega)e^{-jk\tau\omega}d\omega$, and its Fourier transform $F(f)$ is a sequence of equidistant pulses given by:

$$F(f) = 2\pi \sum_{k=-\infty}^{\infty} \alpha_k \delta(t-k\tau).$$

The right-hand side of equation (1) is the stimulus $f(a,\omega)$. We write (1) as:

$$W(a\omega) - \lambda_0 \int_{t_0}^{t_1} K(a,\omega,\xi)W(a,\xi)d\xi = f(a,\omega)$$

or as

$$W(\phi) = f(\phi) + \lambda_0 W(K'\phi), \phi \in W_2^1[t_0,t_1]$$

or as

$$W[(I-\lambda_0 K)\phi] = f(\phi), \phi \in W_2^1[t_0,t_1]$$

Its Fourier transform is given by:

$$F\{W[(I-\lambda_0 K)\phi]\} = F[f(\phi)], \phi \in W_2^1[t_0,t_1]$$

where $w_2^1[t_0,t_1]$ is the space of distributions with derivatives of order 1 in Lebesque space $L_2[t_0,t_1]$.

If $f(\phi) = f(a,\omega)$ is a periodic approximation to a given function in the interval $[t_0, t_1]$, then its Fourier transform $F[f(\phi)] = f(F\phi)$ is a sequence of equidistant pulses given by:

$$f(F\phi) = 2\pi \sum_{t_0 \leq k\tau \leq t_1} \alpha_k \delta_k(\phi)$$

where α_k is as given above which is our conjectured response of a neuron to a single stimulus. We represent this observation by writing:

$$W(\phi) = f(F\phi)$$

and

$$F\{W[(I - \lambda_0 K)\phi]\} = W\{F[(I - \lambda_0 K)\phi]\}$$

which yields $F[(I - \lambda_0 K)\phi] = \phi$, for all $\phi \in W_2^1[t_0, t_1]$ and neural response is an inverse Fourier transform.

8. Examples

We give three illustrations of how geometric figures can be represented using impulsive functions: (a) a sphere, (b) a flower, and (c) a bird.

We represent a perceived form by synthesizing the response of many neurons as a sum of functions given by:

$$\sum_{i=1}^{n} \gamma_i t^{\alpha_i} e^{-\beta_i t}$$

with the appropriate α's and β's which depend on the energy spectrum and the phase angle of the stimulus as variables. To do this for a sphere we take points (x, y, z) on the sphere. From $x^2 + y^2 + z^2 = r^2$ we can express z as a function of x and y. The Fourier transform $F(z)$ gives the desired energy form with the modulus of $F(z)$ and its argument as the energy spectrum and phase angle of the sphere, respectively.

We associate with each point (x,y,z) of the sphere an impulse whose maximum value z represents the intensity of the stimulus. The impulsive representation of z is obtained by taking the set of functions $\{ct^a e^{-bt}\}$ in two dimensions:

$$c(xy)^a e^{-b(x+y)}$$

The totality of such z is given by linear combinations of these functions where each term gives a spike at a given point while all other terms are negligible. To each point there corresponds a pair (a,b). The resulting three dimensional representation is given in Figure 13.3(a). The other two examples are two dimensional and shown in Figures 13.3(b) and 13.3(c).

9. Parameter Estimation

We now turn to the question of estimating α and β in the neural firing representation. If we think of the sphere as a cluster of n energy points we have for the Fourier transform of each point:

$$F(z_s) = \left[\frac{1}{n}\right]^{1/2} \sum_{r=1}^{n} z_r e^{2\pi j(r-1)(s-1)/n}, \quad s=1, 2, \ldots, n.$$

The correspondence between energy impulses from the sphere and neural firings need not be one-to-one. They could also be one-to-many. Many-to-one is simply a sequence of impulses from a stimulus received by a single neuron. Let us illustrate the calibration of α and β in the one-to-one case.

Each neuron fires several times in response to an energy impulse from a point on the sphere. The response function is given by:

$$w(S,t) \approx \sum_{k=1}^{R(s_0)} \rho_k(s_0)(t-\tau_k)^\alpha e^{-\beta(t-\tau_k)}.$$

(a) <u>A Sphere</u>

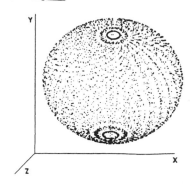

$$z = c_1 \, (xy)^{0.0062895} e^{-6.2895(x+y)}$$
$$+ c_2 \, (xy)^{0.00628935} e^{-6.28935(x+y)}$$
$$+ \ldots$$
$$+ c_{4869} \, (xy)^{0.00609354} e^{-6.09354(x+y)}$$

(b) <u>A Flower</u>

$$z = c_1 \, x^{0.00181} e^{-1.81x}$$
$$+ c_2 \, x^{0.00201} e^{-2.01x}$$
$$+ \ldots$$
$$+ c_{249} x^{0.00525} e^{-5.25x}$$

(c) <u>A Bird</u>

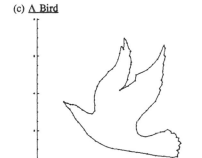

$$z = c_1 \, x^{0.00356} e^{-3.56x}$$
$$+ c_2 \, x^{0.00352} e^{-3.52x}$$
$$+ \ldots$$
$$+ c_{124} x^{0.00123} e^{-1.23x}$$

Figure 13.3

whose Fourier transform is given by:

$$F(w) = \sum_{k=1}^{R(s_0)} \rho_k(s_0) \int_{-\infty}^{+\infty} (t-\tau_k)^{\alpha} e^{-\beta(t-\tau_k)} e^{-j\omega_k t} dt$$

$$= \sum_{k=1}^{R(s_0)} \rho(s_0) e^{\beta \tau_k} \int_{-\infty}^{+\infty} (t-\tau_k)^{\alpha} e^{-(\beta+j\omega_k)t} dt$$

$$= \sum_{k=1}^{R(s_0)} \left[\left(\frac{\beta^2}{\beta^2+\omega_k^2} \right)^{\alpha+1} \right]^{1/2} e^{j[\varphi_k(\alpha+1)-\omega_k \tau_k]}$$

where $\varphi_k = \arctan\left[\dfrac{\omega_k}{\beta}\right]$.

By equating the spectra and phase angles of (2) and (3), we obtain two nonlinear equations in two unknowns α and β:

$$|F(z_s)| = |F(w)|$$

$$arg\{F(z_s)\} = arg\{F(w)\}.$$

Writing $A_k \equiv \left[\left(\dfrac{\beta^2}{\beta^2+\omega_k^2} \right)^{\alpha+1} \right]^{1/2}$ and $B_k \equiv [\varphi_k(\alpha+1)-\omega_k \tau_k]$, we have:

$$\left[\sum_{k=1}^{R(s_0)} A_k \cos B_k \right]^2 + \left[\sum_{k=1}^{R(s_0)} A_k \sin B_k \right]^2 = |F(z_s)|$$

$$\arctan\left\{ \left[\sum_{k=1}^{R(s_0)} A_k \cos B_k \right] \left[\sum_{k=1}^{R(s_0)} A_k \sin B_k \right]^{-1} \right\} = arg\{F(z_s)\}$$

When a single stimulus (e.g., a point on the sphere) causes the firing of several neurons, or when a stimulus from many points on the sphere causes many neurons to fire, each neuron fires with a pair of parameters (α, β). The problem is how to estimate these parameters.

In the classical approach [20] instead of considering density for the creation of sensation, continuity is used as a fundamental property underlying the emergence of large sensations from smaller ones gathered from separate neurons. In this approach the notion of infinitesimal generator is applied to the parameters α and β from which a Lie transformation group is derived to represent higher perceptions. Continuous variations in α and β give rise to the group of transformations. We believe that this is an elegant way to conceptualize (although not explicitly operationalize) the solution for α and β for all the neurons involved in the synthesis of a response. It is likely that for each neuron, α and β have a narrow range of statistical variation.

In closing, we make a useful observation about reciprocal kernels. The firings of a neuron in response to a stimulus are equally spaced in time, due to the refractory period. The Fourier transform of a stimulus as a generalization of a Fourier series has periodic properties. Because of these two facts neural response with a reciprocal kernel is an inverse transform and hence recovers the original form of the stimulus.

The density of neural firing is not completely analogous to the density of the rational numbers in the real number system. The rationals are countably infinite, the number of neurons is finite but large. In speaking of density here we must think of coming sufficiently close (within some prescribed bound) rather than arbitrarily close. The density of our linear combinations implies that the synthesis of the firings of groups of neurons can be used to approximate energy forms.

10. Summary and Conclusions

In this chapter we have examined the consequences of the assumption of reciprocal comparisons of neurotransmitter generated electric charges on the decision of a neuron to fire or not to fire. Our generalization on the discrete decision process leads us to consider positive reciprocal kernels of Fredholm integral operators [40] for the study of neural firings and their synthesis. We showed that neural response in both spontaneous and non-spontaneous firing give rise to generalized functions of the Dirac type. For spontaneous unstimulated firing we solved a homogeneous eigenvalue equation and obtained a family of gamma type functions. Finite linear combinations of these functions are dense in Sobolev spaces. The solution of the inhomogenous equation representing non-spontaneous firing belongs to these spaces. Next we observed that in harmony with known facts about neural networks, the forcing function of the inhomogeneous equation is a linear combination of such functions and can be used to represent the stimulus impacting a neuron causing it to fire. We also showed that the solution of the inhomogeneous equation representing neural response can be expressed as a linear combination of the basic functions. The need for a firing threshold, characteristic of the Dirac distribution, emerges as a necessary condition for the existence of a solution. We then studied the synthesis of the response of several neurons in both hierarchic and feedback network arrangements and again found that the same basic set of dense functions arises in the process. The analysis is then briefly generalized to examine response to several stimuli and represent it as a direct sum. We note that generalized functions are appropriate representations of neural firings and that understanding the structure of this representation is facilitated by the inevitable use of a fundamental set of dense functions to deal in mathematical terms with the operations of a very complex system. We are hopeful that the shortcomings of this work do not cause the reader to reject its basic findings, the natural way in which impulsive functions arise in conformity with the firing mode of neurons, and how their density may work in constructing sensation. We did not find it easy to model neural firings in a simpler way as the somewhat complex tools used here are a logical extension of their counterpart in discrete measurement processes.

REFERENCES

1. Barlow, H.B., 1972, "Single Units and Sensation: A Neuron Doctrine for Perceptual Psychology", Perception, 1, pp. 371-394.

2. Bloomfield, S.A., J.E. Hamos and S.M. Sherman, 1987, "Passive Cable Properties and Morphological Correlates of Neurons in the Lateral Geniculate Nucleous of the Cat", J. Physiology 383, pp. 653-692.

3. Blumenthal, A.L., 1977, The Process of Cognition, Prentice Hall, Englewood Cliffs.

4. Braun, M., 1983, Differential Equations and Their Applications, Springer-Verlag.

5. Both, R., W. Finger, and R.A. Chaplain, 1976, "Model Predictions of the Ionic Mechanisms Underlying the Beating and Bursting Pacemaker Characteristics of Mulloscan Neurons", Biol. Cybernetics 23, pp. 1-11.

6. Brinley, Jr., F.J., 1980, "Excitation and Conduction in Nerve Fibers", Chapter 2 in V.B. Mountcastle (Ed.), Medical Physiology. The C.V. Mosby Co.

7. Carlen, P.L. and D. Durand, 1981, "Modeling the Postsynaptic Location and Magnitude of Tonic Conductance Changes Resulting from Neurotransmitter of Drugs", Neuroscience 6, pp. 839-846.

8. Chay, T.R. and J. Keizer, 1983, "Minimal Model for Membrane Oscillations in the Pancreatic β-cell", Biophys. J'l. 42, pp. 181-190.

9. D'Aguanno, A., 1987, "The Passive Electrical Properties of Neuronal Membranes", M.A.Sc. Univ. of Toronto, Toronto, Ontario, Canada.

10. De Bruijn, N.G., 1958, "Asymptotic Methods in Analysis", North Holland.

11. Dollard, J.D. and C.N. Friedman, 1979, "Product Integration", Addison-Wesley.

12. Duffieux, P.M, 1983, "The Fourier Transform and Its Applications to Optics", New York: Wiley.

13. Durand, D., 1986, "The Somatic Shunt Cable Model for Neurons", Biophysics J. 46, pp. 645-653.

14. Durand, D., P.L. Carlen, N.Gurevich, A. Ho and H. Kunov, 1983, "Electrotonic Parameters of Rat Dendate Granule Cells Measured Using Short Current Pulses and HRP Staining", J. Neurophysiology 50, pp. 1080-1096.

15. Edwards, D.H. and B. Mulloney, 1984, "Compartmental Models of Electronic Structure and Synaptic Integration in an Identified Neuron", J. of Physiology 348, pp. 89-113.

16. Fu, P. and L. Bardakjian, 1988, "Cable Properties of Smooth Muscle: A System Model", Proceedings of IEEE EMBS 10th Annual Conf., New Orleans, LA.

17. Fu, P., L. Bardakjian, A. D'Aguanno and P. L. Carlen, 1989, "Computation of the Passive Electrical Parameters of Neurons Using a System Model", IEEE Trans. on Biomedical Engineering 36, pp. 55-63.

18. Grossberg, S., 1982, "Studies of Brain and Mind", BSPS 70. In R. Cohen and M.W. Wartofski (Eds.). D. Reidel Pub. Co.

19. Hebb, D.O., 1949, "The Organization of Behavior - A Neurophysiological Theory", New York: Wiley.

20. Hodgkin, A.L. and A.F. Huxley, 1952, "A Quantitative Description of Membrane Current and Its Applications to Conduction and Excitation in Nerve" J'l of Physiology 117, pp. 500-544.

21. Hoffman, W.C., 1970, "Higher Visual Perception as Prolongation of the Basic Lie Transformation Group", Mathematical Biosciences 6, pp. 437-471.

22. Holden, A.V., 1976, "Model of the Stochastic Activity of Neurons, Springer Verlag.

23. John, E.R., 1972, "Switchboard Versus Statistical Theories of Learning and Memory", Science 177, pp. 850-864.

24. Kandel, E.R. and J.H. Schwartz, 1985, "Principles of Neural Science", Elsevier/North-Holland.

25. Kohn, A.F., 1989, "Dendritic Transformations on Random Synaptic Input as Measured from a Neuron's Spike Train–Modeling and Simulation", IEEE Trans. on Biomedical Engineering, 36, pp. 44-53.

26. Lentz, T.L., 1983, Encyclopedia Britannica: Macropedia, 12, pp. 991.

27. Lerner, E.J., 1984, "Why Can't a Computer Be More Like a Brain?", High Technology 4, pp. 34-41.

28. Maz'ja, V.G., 1985, Sobelev Spaces, Springer Verlag.

29. Perkel, D.H. and B. Mulloney, 1978, "Calibrating Compartmental Model of Neurons", American Journal of Physiology 235, pp. 93-98.

30. Perkel, D.H., B. Mulloney and R.W. Budelli, 1981, "Quatitative Method for Predicting Neuronal Behavior", Neuroscience 6, pp. 823-827.

31. Plant, R.E. and M. Kim, 1976, "Mathematical Description of a Bursting Pacemaker Neuron by a Modification of the Hodgkin-Huxley Equations", Biophysics J. 16, pp. 227-244.

32. Plant, R.E., 1981, "Bifurcation and Resonance in a Model for Bursting Nerve Cells", J. of Math. Biology 11, pp. 15-32.

33. Poggio, G.F. and V.B. Mountcastle, 1980, "Functional Organization of Thalamus and Cortex", Chapter 9 in V.B. Mountcastle (Ed.), Medical Physiology, The C.V. Mosby Co.

34. Pogorzelski, W., 1966, "Integral Equations and Their Applications", Pergamon Press.

35. Pottala, E.W., T.R. Colburn and D.R. Humphrey, 1973, "A Dendritic Compartmental Model of Neuron", IEEE Trans. Biomed. Eng., BME-20, pp. 132-139.

36. Rall, W., 1977, "Core Conductor Theory and Cable Properties of Neurons", Chapter 3 in Handbood of Physiology – The Nervous System, Bethesda, MD:Amer. Physiol. Soc.

37. Rumelhart, D.E., J.L. McClelland and the PDP Research Group, 1989, "Parallel Distributed Processing. Cambridge: The MIT Press.

38. Rinzel, J., 1984, "Bursting Oscillations in an Excitable Membrane Model", In B.D. Sleeman, R.J. Jarvis and D.S. Jones (Eds.), Proceedings of the 8th Dundee Conference on the Theory of Ordinary and partial Differential Equations. Springer-Verlag.

39. Saaty, T.L., 1988, "The Analytic Hierarchy Process", Pittsburgh: RWS Publications.

40. Saaty, T.L. and L.G. Vargas, 1987, "Stimulus Response with Reciprocal Kernels: The Rise and Fall of Response", J'l of Math. Psychology 31, pp. 83-92.

41. Segundo, J.P., D.H. Perkel, H. Wyman, H. Hegstad and G.P. Moore, 1962, "Input-Output Relations in Computer-Simulated Nerve Cells", Kybernetik 4, pp. 157-171.

42. Shaposhnikova, T.O., R.S. Andersen and S.G. Mikhlin (Eds.), 1975, "Intergral Equations", Leyden Noordhoff.

43. Shelton, D.P., 1985, "Membrane Resistivity Estimates for the Purkinje Neuron by Means of a Passive Computer Model", Neuroscience 14, 111-131.

44. Vaadia, E., H. Bergman and M. Abeles, 1989, "Neuronal Activities Related to Higher Brain Functions – Theoretical and Empirical Implications", IEEE Trans. on Biomedical Eng. 36, pp. 25-43.

APPENDIX

This appendix deals with five topics: 1) the motivation for the AHP; 2) the stability of the eigenvector and how it requires that the number of elements compared be small and homogeneous; 3) how to combine readings from the same scale of measurement under different criteria; 4) the consistency index of a feedback system and 5) how to do structural adjustment for both criteria and alternatives.

For a comprehensive bibliography and list of PH.D. dissertations on the Analytic Hierarchy Process see the Expert Choice, Inc., home page on the internet: www.expertchoice.com and click on Support and on References.

1. The Motivation for the AHP

Most of the time people would have decided on what is important to them in the abstract and look for alternatives to satisfy their criteria, in which case the criteria do not depend on the alternatives as in a hierarchic structure. At other times the criteria derive some of their importance from the alternatives and depend on them and on other factors as in a network structure.

This section is concerned with the measurement of what has so far been known as intangibles to make possible the allocation of resources to them side-by-side with tangibles.

There are essentially two ways to create measurement. The first is the widely familiar one universally used today; it is to use a scale of measurement with an arbitrary unit performing the measurement in a uniform fashion by obtaining multiples and fractions of that unit. The other is to derive measurement in the form of priorities by performing relative comparisons. Derived measurement can be shown mathematically to give rise to ratio scales which when appropriately normalized become pure numbers that belong to an absolute scale, invariant under the identity transformation.

In order to get to the point quickly and not tax the reader's patience we need to make an important observation regarding the relation between adding absolute numbers obtained as measurements of activities under more than one criterion. To obtain the correct correspondence between absolute numbers and their conversion to relative numbers under different criteria, one cannot normalize and add. Consider two criteria, investment in stocks and investment in bonds by individuals, as advised by a broker who then tallies the relative values of these investments. First assume that there is one person A for whom the money is divided as follows:

	Stocks	Bonds	Total
Dollars	10,000	5,000	15,000
Relative values	$\dfrac{10,000}{15,000}$	$\dfrac{5,000}{15,000}$	$\dfrac{15,000}{15,000}$
or	$\dfrac{2}{3}$	$\dfrac{1}{3}$	1

Two thirds of the total investment for A is placed in stocks and one third in bonds. Now let us add a second person B so that we can look at what one would do in the case of the total for two people. We have:

	Stocks	Bonds	Total	Relative Total
Dollars: A	10,000	5,000	15,000	3/10
B	20,000	15,000	35,000	7/10
Total	30,000	20,000	50,000	1

Relative Values:				Relative Total
A	$\dfrac{10,000}{30,000}$	$\dfrac{5,000}{20,000}$		7/12
B	$\dfrac{20,000}{30,000}$	$\dfrac{15,000}{20,000}$		19/15

and the two Relative Total columns are different. For them to be the same, we must multiply the numbers in the first column of the Relative Value numbers by 30,000/50,000 and the numbers in the second column by 20,000/50,000. These two numbers correspond to the relative share or importance of investment in stocks and in bonds respectively. These values are lost to us if we were dealing with relative numbers only in each column without knowledge of the actual quantities. The question then is: "Can we determine these ratios without knowing the original dollar values and how reliable would the outcome be if we were to estimate them?"

Let us now make a second observation. Assume that we increase the number of investors and note the average total investment of all of them successively as we go along. How do these relative values of investment in stocks and in bonds change and do they stabilize so that one number can be used for each as a reliable working average?

We note that when we only had one investor A the relative investments were 2/3 and 1/3 whereas when we had both A and B these values were 3/5 and 2/5 respectively. There is a tendency for people, guided by the broker, to invest slightly more in stocks than in bonds. The question is whether there is a definite trend that affirms this bias and converges to a reliable average as we increase the sample of investors? Now let us try three investors:

		Absolute
	Stocks	Bonds
A	10,000	5,000
B	20,000	15,000
C	50,000	40,000
Total	80,000	60,000

Total		
(Rel.)	$\dfrac{80,000}{140,000}$	$\dfrac{60,000}{140,000}$
	or	
	$\dfrac{4}{7}$	$\dfrac{3}{7}$

The set of average relative numbers as importance indicators for stocks and bonds as the number of investors is increased to three is as follows:

Investor	Stocks	Bonds
A	2/3 = .67	1/3 = .33
A & B	3/5 = .60	2/5 = .40
A & B & C	4/7 = .57	3/7 = .43

The series under each criterion converges if the coefficients are uniformly bounded and if each of the individual series (with positive entries) satisfies

$$\sum_{i=1}^{n+1} x_i / \sum_{i=1}^{n} x_i \rightarrow 1 \text{ as } n \rightarrow \infty.$$

Even when the criteria depend on the alternatives, what we deem to be important always derives from our own system of values and how they affect how we regard the alternatives and thus these criteria also derive importance from our higher system of values.

That is why the network approach with the supermatrix is essential for this kind of decision making.

For better insight how people derive importance for the criteria independently from the alternatives driven by their intuition we need ideas from measure theory as it is applied to uncountable sets. It appears that people's experience provides them with a dense set of alternatives in terms of which all alternatives and in particular extreme or limiting ones are representable. They are led to derive the weights of the criteria as measures that do not depend on the alternatives (because the contribution of each alternative has measure zero). Thus, the criteria weights are determined independently in terms of the entire set rather than in terms of each of the alternatives. The reader may wish to consult the literature on measure theory to understand how important a part of our make up this kind of abstraction is. We know in fact that people can and do determine weights for the criteria independently of any particular set of alternatives. In fact people walk the world projecting the idea that they know what is important and what is not without ever looking at things. They are more accurate when they structure their decisions with an understanding of the details of their criteria and alternatives, but accuracy again depends on someone else's system of values.

2. How to Combine Readings from the Same Scale of Measurement under Different Criteria

In the AHP one needs to be careful with criteria measured on the same absolute scale. Criteria measured in dollars are a common example of this. The priority of each criterion must be equal to the sum of the measurements of its alternatives divided by the sum of the measurements of the alternatives with respect to all such criteria. Only then can one normalize the measurements of the alternatives, weight them by these priorities and add to obtain the relative weights of the alternatives with respect to all these criteria. This group of criteria with the alternatives having a single composite weight under them collectively are now identified as a single criterion such as "economic" that is then pairwise compared with the other criteria that

Note that we would not obtain these weights if we normalize the alternatives' weights under each criterion first and then perform the weighting and adding composition. That would give us 0.44 and 0.56 for the respective weights of the alternatives, a reversal of the real ranks obtained above. This shows what we said above that when the alternatives are measured on the same scale of numbers under different criteria, they must be combined in the way we described. Incidentally, the supermatrix approach would yield the correct outcome. We have for the supermatrix:

	C_1	C_2	A_1	A_2
C_1	0	0	0.89	0.5
C_2	0	0	0.11	0.5
A_1	0.67	0.2	0	0
A_2.	0.33	0.8	0	0

The numbers 0.89 and 0.11 are obtained by normalizing the weighted first row in the first matrix above. Thus we have under A_1 $0.5 \times 8 / (0.5 \times 8 + 0.5 \times 1) = 0.89$ and $0.5 \times 1/ (0.5 \times 8 + 0.5 \times 1)$ $=0.11$. Similarly to obtain 0.5 and 0.5 under A_2 we have $0.5 \times 4/ (0.5 \times 4 + 0.5 \times 4) = 0.5$ and $0.5 \times 4/ (0.5 \times 4 + 0.5 \times 4) = 0.5$.

The limiting supermatrix obtained by raising the above supermatrix to large odd powers (in order to have the non-zero blocks fall in the same positions as in the original matrix) is given by:

	C_1	C_2	A_1	A_2
C_1	0	0	0.71	0.71
C_2	0	0	0.29	0.29
A_1	0.53	0.53	0	0
A_2	0.47	0.47	0	0

We note that the final priorities of A_1 and A_2 are again 0.53 and 0.47 respectively as we obtained originally by using the correct procedure to go from absolute to relative numbers. The new values for the weights of the criteria (0.71 and 0.29) can also be justified by examining the ratio of the total value of the alternatives with respect to criterion C_1 (8 + 4=12) and to that of C_2 (1+4=5) to rescale the original weights to the new weights $0.5 \times 12/(12 + 5)$ and $0.5 \times 5/(12 + 5)$ that are then normalized.

3. Stability of the Eigenvector Requires a Small Number of Homogeneous Elements

The question often arises as to how sensitive are the priorities given by the eigenvector components to slight changes in the judgment values. Clearly, it is desirable that the priorities do not fluctuate widely with small changes in judgment. There are essentially three ways to test this sensitivity: (1) by finding a mathematical estimate of the fluctuation; (2) by deriving answers based on a large number of computer runs appropriately designed to test the sensitivity; (3) by a combination of the two, particularly when it is not possible to carry out the full demonstration analytically.

We have already pointed out, in the case of consistency, that λ_{max} is equal to the trace of the matrix which consists of unit entries. In this case one would expect the eigenvector corresponding to the perturbed matrix to undergo an overall change by an amount inversely proportional to the size of the matrix.

In general, the eigenvalues of a matrix lie between its largest and smallest row sums. Changing the value of an entry in the matrix changes the correspondence row sum and has a tendency to change λ_{max} by an equal amount. However, since a change in the eigenvector should also be influenced by the size of the matrix, we expect that the larger the matrix, the smaller the change in each component.

We begin the analytical treatment of the question by considering a matrix A with the characteristic equation

$$\det(A - \lambda I) = \lambda^n + a_1 \lambda^{n-1} + \cdots + a_n = 0$$

Following standard procedures, let $A+\varepsilon B$ be the matrix obtained by introducing a small perturbation in A. The corresponding characteristic equation is

$$\det(A+\varepsilon B-\lambda I) = \lambda^n+a_1(\varepsilon)\lambda^{n-1}+\cdots+a_n(\varepsilon) = 0$$

where $a_k(\varepsilon)$ is a polynomial in ε of degree $(n-k)$, such that $a_k(\varepsilon) \rightarrow a_k$ as $\varepsilon \rightarrow 0$.

Let λ_1 be the maximum simple eigenvalue corresponding to the characteristic equation of A. It is known in matrix theory that for small ε, there exists an eigenvalue of $A+\varepsilon B$ which can be expressed as the sum of a convergent power series, i.e.,

$$\lambda_1(\varepsilon) = \lambda_1+k_1\varepsilon+k_2\varepsilon^2+\cdots$$

Let w_l denote the eigenvector of A corresponding to λ_1 and let $w_1(\varepsilon)$ be the eigenvector of $A+\varepsilon B$ corresponding to $\lambda_1(\varepsilon)$. The elements of $w_1(\varepsilon)$ are polynomials in $\lambda(\varepsilon)$ and ε, and, since the power series for $\lambda_1(\varepsilon)$ is convergent for small ε, each element of $w_1(\varepsilon)$ can be represented as a convergent power series in ε. We may write

$$w_1(\varepsilon) = w_1+\varepsilon z_1+\varepsilon^2 z_2+\cdots$$

If the matrix A has linear elementary divisors, then there exist complete sets of right and left eigenvectors $w_1, w_2, .., w_n$ and $v_1, v_2, ..., v_n$, respectively, such that

$$v_i^T w_j = 0 \qquad i \neq j$$

Note that w_j and v_j are the jth eigenvectors (right and left), and not the jth components of the vectors.

The vectors z_i can be expressed in terms of the w_j as

$$z_i = \sum_{j=1}^{n} s_{ij} w_j$$

which, when substituted in the formula for $w_i(\varepsilon)$, gives

$$w_1(\varepsilon) = w_1+\sum_{i=2}^{n} \sum_{j=1}^{n} t_{ij} \varepsilon^j w_i$$

where the t_{ij} are obtained by dividing the s_{ij} by the coefficient of w_l.

The first order perturbations of the eigenvalues are given by the coefficient k_1 of $\lambda_1(\varepsilon)$.

We now derive the expression for the first order perturbations of the corresponding eigenvectors.

Normalizing the vectors w_j and v_j by using the euclidean metric we have

$$|v_j^T| \, |w_j| = 1$$

We know that

$$(A+\varepsilon B)w_1(\varepsilon) = \lambda_1(\varepsilon)w_1(\varepsilon)$$

If we substitute the expressions for $\lambda_1(\varepsilon)$ and $w_1(\varepsilon)$ obtained above and use $Aw_1 = \lambda_1 w_1$, we have

$$\sum_{j=2}^{n} (\lambda_j - \lambda_1)t_{j1}w_j + Bw_1 = k_1 w_1$$

Multiplying across by V_j^T and simplifying, we obtain

$$k_1 = v_1^T Bw_1 / v_1^T w_1 \quad \textit{for } j=1$$

and

$$t_{j1} = (v_j^T Bw_1 / (\lambda_1 - \lambda_j)v_j^T w_1) \quad \textit{for } j \neq 1$$

where, as noted above, k sub 1 is the first order perturbation of λ_1 and

$$|k_1| = (v_1^T Bw_1 / v_1^T w_1) \leq [B] / v_1^T w_1$$

where [B] is the sum of the elements of B.

Thus for sufficiently small ε the sensitivity of λ_1 depends primarily on $v_1^T w_1$. $v_1^T w_1$ might be arbitrarily small.

The first order perturbation of w_1 is given by

$$\Delta w_1 = \varepsilon \sum_{j=2}^{n} t_{j1}w_j$$

$$= \varepsilon \sum_{j=2}^{n} (v_j^T Bw_1 / (\lambda_1 - \lambda_j)v_j^T w_j)w_j$$

$$= \sum_{j=2}^{n} (v_j^T(\Delta A)w_1 / (\lambda_1 - \lambda_j)v_j^T w_j)w_j \quad \textit{where } \Delta A \equiv \varepsilon B$$

The eigenvector w_l will be very sensitive to perturbations in A if λ_l is close to any of the other eigenvalues. When λ_l is well separated from the other eigenvalues and none of the $v_i^T w_i$ is small, the eigenvector w_i corresponding to the eigenvalue λ_l will be comparatively insensitive to perturbations in A. This is the case, for example, with skew-symmetric matrices ($a_{ji} = -a_{ij}$).

The $v_i^T w_i$ are interdependent in a way which precludes the possibility that just one $1/v_i^T w_i, i=1,2,...,n$ is large. Thus if one of them is arbitrarily large, they are all arbitrarily large.

However, we want them to be small, i.e., near unity. To see this let

$$w_i = \sum_j c_{ij} v_j \quad and \quad v_j = \sum_j d_{ij} w_j$$

where $|w_i| = |b_i| = 1, i = 1,2,...,n$. It is easy to verify by substitution that

$$c_{ij} = w_j^T w_i / v_j^T w_j$$

and

$$d_{ij} = v_j^T v_i / v_j^T w_j$$

Then

$$v_i^T w_i = \sum_j d_{ij} w_j^T \sum_j c_{ij} v_j$$

$$= \sum_j (w_j^T w_i)(v_j^T v_i)/v_j^T w_j.$$

for $i = j$

$$w_i^T = v_i^T v_i = 1$$

and

$$v_i^T w_i = (v_i^T w_i)^{-1} + \sum_{j \neq i} (w_j^T w_i)(v_j^T v_i)(v_j^T w_j)^{-1}$$

Since

$$w_j^T w_i = \cos \theta_{ij} \quad and \quad v_j^T v_i = \cos \varphi_{ij}$$

we have

$$|(v_i^T w_i)^{-1}| \le |v_i^T w_i)| + \sum_{j \ne i} |(v_j^T w_j)^{-1}|$$

$$\le 1 + \sum_{j \ne 1} |(v_j v^T w_j)^{-1}|$$

which must be true for all $i = 1, 2, .., n$. This proves that all the $v_i^T w_i$ must be of the same order.

We now show that for consistent matrices $(v_1^T w_1)^{-1}$ cannot be arbitrarily large. We have in the case of consistency

$$v_1^T = (1/w_{11},...,1/w_{1n})/\sum_{i=1}^{n} 1/w_{1i}$$

$$w_1^T = (w_{11},...,w_{1n})$$

Therefore

$$(v_1^T w_1)^{-1} = [(1/w_{11},...,1/w_{1n})(w_{11},...,1_{1n})^T/\sum_{i=1}^{n} 1/w_{1i}]^{-1}$$

$$= [n/\sum_{i=1}^{n} 1/w_{1i}]^{-1} > n$$

since $n/\sum_{i=1}^{n} 1/w_{1i} < \sum_{i=1}^{n} w_{1i}/n$.

Now $(v_1^T w_1)^{-1}$ is minimized when all w_{1i} are equal since

$$\sum_{i=1}^{n} w_{1i} = 1.$$

In practice, to keep $(v_1^T w_1)^{-1}$ near its minimum we must deal with relatively comparable activities so that no single w_{1i} is too small.

To improve consistency the number n must not be too large. On the other hand, if we are to make full use of the available information and produce results which are valid in practice, n should also not be too small. If, for example, we reject the values $v_1^T w_1 \le 0.1$, then we must have $n \le 9$.

Under the assumption that the number of elements being compared is small and that they are relatively comparable, i.e., their weights differ by a multiple of their number, we can show that none of the components of w_I is arbitrarily small and none of those of v_I is arbitrarily small, and hence the scalar product of the two normalized vectors cannot be arbitrarily small.

With large inconsistency one cannot guarantee that none of the w_{Ii} is arbitrarily small. Thus, near-consistency is a sufficient condition for stability. Note also that we need to keep the number of elements relatively small, so that the values of all the w_{Ii} are of the same order.

4. The Consistency Index of a System

This section relates to supermatrix models with feedback and dependence. In such models we want to represent both the inconsistency in chains beginning with a goal and the inconsistency in cycles. For chains we want the initial not the limiting priorities of the elements. For cycles we want the limiting priorities of the elements. We need to weight inconsistency by the weight of the corresponding elements. Also we need the impact priority of a component containing an element used to compare elements in another component, on that component. We also need to weight by the priority of the supercriterion in the control hierarchy.

$$C_S = \sum_{\substack{control \\ criteria}} K_C \sum_{\substack{all \\ chains}} \sum_{j=1}^{h} \sum_{i=1}^{n_{ij+1}} w_{ij}\mu_{ij+1}$$

$$+ \sum_{\substack{control \\ criteria}} K_C \sum_{k=1}^{S} \sum_{j=1}^{n_k} w_{jk} \sum_{h=1}^{|C_h|} w_{(k)(h)}\mu_k(j,h)$$

where $n_j = j = 1, 2, ..., h$ is the number of elements in the jth level and $\mu_{i,j+1}$ is the consistency index of all elements in the $(j+1)^{st}$ level with respect to the ith criterion of the jth level. In the second term, $w_{(k)(h)}$ is the priority of the impact of the hth component on the kth component. w_{jk} is the limiting priority of the jth element in the kth component. In case of a hierarchy there are no cycles and the second term is equal to zero. As in the measurement of consistency of a hierarchy, this index must be divided by the corresponding index with random inconsistencies.

5. Structural Adjustment for Both Criteria and Alternatives

There has been no definitive theory about structural adjustment and the situations that lead to it. Perhaps the best thinking on the subject has been done by Diederik J.D. Wijnmalen of the TNO Physics and Electronics Lab., Div. for Operational Research & Business Management, PO Box 96864, 2509 JG The Hague, The Netherlands. The following is the material he has written. His five figures at the end of the discussion are more or less self-explanatory and support it nicely.

In incomplete hierarchies there exists at least one level whose nodes are not connected to all the nodes on its adjacent higher or lower level. In such hierarchies a structural imbalance occurs if this incompleteness results in node clusters of unequal sizes on the same level, or if there are paths of unequal length from the goal to the bottom level. We distinguish between incompletely connected levels of criteria nodes and missing connections between the alternatives and their covering criteria. In both cases the structural imbalance can be resolved by adjusting weights. Since alternatives and criteria are different in nature (synthesis reduces to taking the sum of globally weighted local alternative priorities), the cases must be treated somewhat differently.

Let us first focus on incompletely connected criteria levels. Pairwise comparison of the importance results in weights that sum to unity. The weight of a criterion itself, in turn, represents the relative importance of its subcriteria with respect to their grand-parent. This relative importance should also be reflected in the average weight of that parent's children. However, the average weight $1/n$ of the children depends on the family size n, given the fixed unit sum, and so does each individual child's weight. As a consequence, the global weights of the lowest-level criteria depend on the sizes of their (ancestor-) families and as a result so do the priorities of the alternatives. Conceptually, equivalent hierarchies, having different family structures (i.e. different clusterings of nodes) can result in non-equivalent final priorities of the alternatives. This phenomenon of "structural bias" is most obvious when one assumes, for example, equally important criteria clustered together in equally important families but of unequal sizes and incompletely connected. The global weights of the bottom level of criteria will not be equal after clustering. The core of the problem is the node-wise unit sum-to-one normalization in a hierarchy. While holding onto normalization, a solution can be based on weight adjustment taking family sizes into account. The adjustment could be done locally by focusing on two adjacent levels at a time. Since the aim is to obtain the correct priorities for the alternatives, the adjustment needs to be global so as not to let the family averages of bottom-level global weights be distorted by the hierarchy's structural imbalance.

The normalized local weight of each node above the lowest level of criteria nodes of the hierarchy is adjusted as follows. Count the number of lowest-level criteria within the descending sub-hierarchy of the given node and count the total number of the hierarchy's lowest-level criteria. Divide the first by the second and multiply the given node's original local weight by this ratio. When the weights of all nodes of a family have thus been adjusted, re-normalize them to sum to unity. This procedure leads to giving greater weight to larger families, and less weight to smaller ones; thus avoiding weight dilution by large families.

The foregoing adjustment procedure will not always restore distorted *individual* weights. If one knows that a criterion X is, say, twice as important as another criterion Y, but as a result of a clustering process both find themselves in different families with structurally biased global weights, the adjustment would not necessarily restore their original weight ratio of 2:1 (assuming perfect consistency). In order to achieve this balance, a full adjustment based on the real "weighting mass" of each family would be needed. First re-normalize by dividing the original local weights of the subcriteria of a given criterion by their maximum in order to make them independent of family size. Then, for each node above the lowest level of criteria nodes compute an adjustment factor by multiplying the re-normalized local weights along each path from that node to the lowest-level criteria of its descending sub-hierarchy and add those products; adjust the re-normalized local weight of the node by multiplying it with the adjustment factor. After normalization of the adjusted weights, carry out the synthesis.

Adjustment of the structural bias may perhaps not be necessary when a hierarchy is constructed from the top downwards, with sub-nodes strictly defining their parent nodes no matter how many are needed. The assumed fairness of a situation where families with more children would have less to spend on each child than smaller families with equal income, would be another example.

The second problem of missing connections between the alternatives and the covering criteria is that the global weights of the covering criteria of an alternative with missing connections do not sum to unity. That alternative will therefore not assemble the full weighting sum of its local priorities and thus is penalized for receiving a zero priority value for a missing connection. If this is considered to be unfair, the solution is as follows. On each lowest-level criterion, divide the priorities of the alternatives by their local maximum in order to make them independent of family size. Carry out the synthesis for each alternative in turn, after temporarily assigning a zero weight to the criterion-node to which the given alternative is not connected and re-normalizing the weights of its remaining covering criteria to sum to unity. If desired, this would be followed by the other structural adjustment described above. When syntheses are completed, the final priorities of the alternatives are in turn re-normalized.

Author's note: With regard to incomplete hierarchies I believe that one needs to consider the alternatives first to determine the number of nodes to which each is connected and assign it the reciprocal of that value to get for it the fractional allocation through each of the nodes to which it is connected. This avoids multiple counting. One then moves up to the covering criteria and assigns them the sum of the numbers attached to their alternatives. Again one divides this number by the number of criteria to which that subcriterion is attached and so on upwards in the same way.

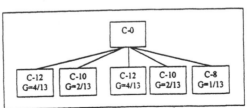

Figure 1: A model for sharing pocket money based on age among
5 children of 2 families (C-x denotes a child of age x, x=8,10,12; G
denotes the share)

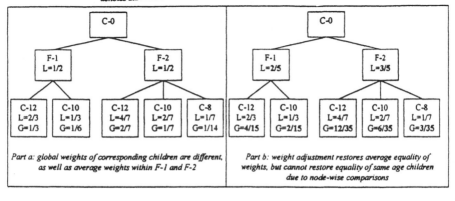

Part a: global weights of corresponding children are different,
as well as average weights within F-1 and F-2

Part b: weight adjustment restores average equality of
weights, but cannot restore equality of same age children
due to node-wise comparisons

Figure 2: Figure 1 continued, but families and their children modeled explicitly; part a shows the
structural weighting bias; part b shows structural weight adjustment in bold (L denotes the
local share within a family)

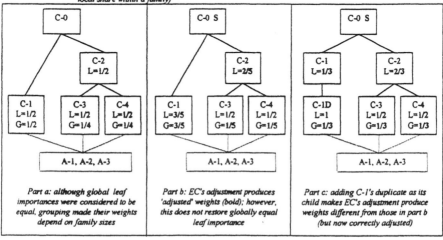

Part a: although global leaf
importances were considered to be
equal, grouping made their weights
depend on family sizes

Part b: EC's adjustment produces
'adjusted' weights (bold); however,
this does not restore globally equal
leaf importance

Part c: adding C-1's duplicate as its
child makes EC's adjustment produce
weights different from those in part b
(but now correctly adjusted)

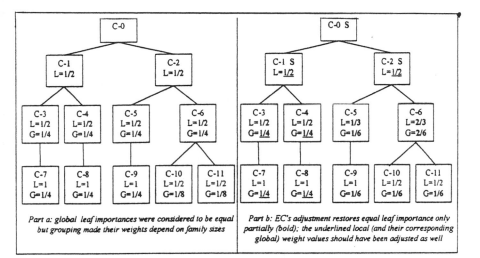

Figure 4: The "Structural Adjust" of AHP's Expert Choice is a local (i.e. 2-level) mechanism (S denotes that the structural adjustment has been turned on for that element; L=local weight; G=global weight)

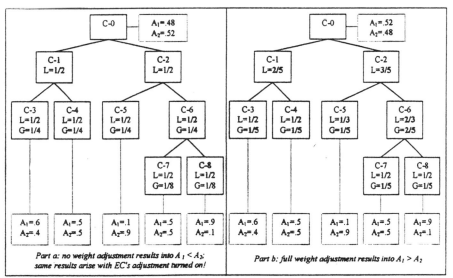

Figure 5: Weight adjustment can reverse the final order of the alternatives; EC's adjustment produces equal results compared with the situation of no adjustment

Books on the Analytic Hierarchy Process (AHP)

Dyer, R.F. and E.H. Forman, 1991, *An Analytic Approach to Marketing Decisions*, Prentice-Hall, Englewood Cliffs, NJ. 368 pp.

Golden, B.L., E.A. Wasil and P.T. Harker (eds), 1989, *The Analytic Hierarchy Process*, Springer-Verlag, New York. 265 pp.

Rabbani, S.J. R., and S. R. Rabbani, 1996, *Decisions in Transportation with the Analytical Hierarchy Process*, Center of Science and Technology, Federal University of Paraiba, Brazil, 100 pp.

Saaty, T.L., 2000, *The Brain, Unraveling the Mystery of How It Works, The Neural Network Process*, RWS Publications, 4922 Ellsworth Ave., Pittsburgh, PA 15213. 481 pp.

------------, 1996, *The Analytic Network Process, Decision Making with Dependence and Feedback*, RWS Publications, 4922 Ellsworth Ave., Pittsburgh, PA 15213. 370 pp.

------------, 1995 (revised 2000), *Decision Making for Leaders*, (also available in Spanish from RWS Pub.) RWS Publications, 4922 Ellsworth Ave., Pittsburgh, PA 15213. 315 pp.

------------ and L.G. Vargas, 1994, *Decision Making in Economic, Political, Social and Technological Environments*, RWS Publications, 4922 Ellsworth Ave., Pittsburgh, PA 15213. 330 pp.

------------, 1993(revised 2000), *Fundamentals of Decision Making and Priority Theory with the Analytic Hierarchy Process*, RWS Publications, 4922 Ellsworth Ave., Pittsburgh, PA 15213. 527 pp.

------------ and E. Forman, 1993, *The Hierarchon*, RWS Publications, 4922 Ellsworth Ave., Pittsburgh, PA, 15213. 510 pp.

------------, 1992, *Multicriteria Decision Making - The Analytic*

Hierarchy Process, RWS Publications, 4922 Ellsworth Ave., Pittsburgh, PA 15213. 479 pp.

------------- and K. Kearns, 1991, *Analytical Planning*, RWS Publications, 4922 Ellsworth Ave., Pittsburgh, PA 15213. 208 pp.

------------- and L.G. Vargas, 1991, *The Logic of Priorities*, RWS Publications, 4922 Ellsworth Ave., Pittsburgh, PA 15213. 299 pp.

------------- and L.G. Vargas, 1991, *Prediction, Projection and Forecasting*, Kluwer Academic Publishers, Boston, Mass. 251 pp.

------------- and J.M. Alexander, 1989, *Conflict Resolution - The Analytic Hierarchy Process*, Praeger, NY. 252 pp.

Books on the Analytic Hierarchy Process in other languages:

ARABIC:
Saaty, T.L., 2000, *Decision Making for Leaders*, translated by Asma Bahurmoz, Professor, King Abdulaziz University, Jeddah, Saudi Arabia.

CHINESE:
Saaty, T.L., 1989, *Analytic Hierarchy Process - Applications to Resource Allocation, Management and Conflict Resolution*, Thomas L. Saaty, translated by Shubo Xu, Press of Coal Industry, China. 334 pp.

Xu, Shubo, 1988, *Applied Decision Making Methods - Analytic Hierarchy Process*, Press of Tianjin University, Tianjin, China. 230 pp.

Zhao, Huan Chen, Shubo Xu and Jinsheng He, 1986, *The Analytic Hierarchy Process - A New Method for Decision Making*. Science Publishers, Beijing. 116 pp.

Wang, Lianfen and Shubo Xu, 1989, *The Analytic Hierarchy Process*, People's University Publishers, Beijing, China. 389 pp.

FARSI:

Saaty, T.L., 2000, *Decision Making for Leaders*, translated by Ali Asghar Tofigh, Chancellor, University of Applied Science, Tehran, Iran.

FRENCH:

Merunka, D., 1987, *La prise de decision en management*, Vuibert Gestion, 63 Bd. St. Germain, Paris. 264 pp.

Saaty, T.L., 1984, *Decider Face a la Complexite*, Enterprise moderne d'edition, 17 Rue Viete, 75017 Paris. 231 pp.

GERMAN:

Richter, K. and G. Reinhardt, 1990, *Haben Sie heute richtig entscheiden?*, Verlag Die Wirtschaft Berlin. 109 pp.

Weber, K., 1993, *Mehrkriterielle Entscheidungen*, R. Oldenbourg Verlag GmbH, Munchen. 218 pp.

INDONESIAN:

Saaty, T.L., 1991, *Pengambilan Keputusan Bagi-Para Pemimpin*, PT Pustaka Binaman Pressindo, Jakarta, Indonesia. 270 pp.

JAPANESE:

Tone, K., 1986, *The Analytic Hierarchy Process - Decision Making*, Japanese Scientific and Technical Press, Tokyo. 218 pp.

Tone, K. and R. Manabe, 1990, *AHP Applications*, Japanese Science and Technology Press, Tokyo. 248 pp.

Kinoshita, E., 1991, *Science for the Imagination: Fuzzy and Intangible*, Denki Shoin Publishing Co., Tokyo, Japan. 173 pp.

Kinoshita, E., 1991, *Like or Dislike Mathematics: Decision Making with Mathematics*, Denkishoin, Tokyo. 171 pp.

Kinoshita, E., 1992, *Decision Making Theory*, Keigaku Publications Company, Tokyo.

Kinoshita, E., 1993, *AHP Method and Applications*, Sumisho Publishing Co., Tokyo. 233 pp.

KOREAN:
Saaty, T.L., 2000, *Decision Making for Leaders*, translated by Keun Tae Cho, PH.D., Seoul, Korea.

PORTUGUESE:
Saaty, T.L., 1991, *Metodo de Analise Hierarquica*, translated by Wainer Da Silveira E. Silva, Ph.D., McGraw-Hill, Ltda. e Makron Books, Brasil. 367 pp.

RUSSIAN:
Saaty, T.L. and K. Kearns, 1991, *Analytical Planning: The Organization of Systems*, translated by Revaz Vachnadze, Radio Moscow, Moscow. 224 pp.

Saaty, T.L., 1993, *The Analytic Hierarchy Process*, translated by Revaz Vachnadze, Radio Moscow, Moscow. 314 pp.

THAI:
Saaty, T.L., 2000, *Decision Making for Leaders*, translated by Viton Tansirikongkol, Merit Capital Management Ltd., Liberty Square Building, 287 Silom Road, Bangrak, Bangkok, Thailand.

Special Journal Issues Dedicated to the AHP:

Wasil, E.A. and B.L. Golden (eds.), 1991, Public-Sector Applications of the Analytic Hierarchy Process, *Socio-Economic Planning Sciences* 25/2. 8 articles.

Harker, P.T. (ed.), 1986, The Analytic Hierarchy Process, *Socio-Economic Planning Sciences* 20/6. 13 articles.

Vargas, L.G. and R.W. Whitaker (eds.), 1990, Decision Making by the Analytic Hierarchy Process: Theory and Applications, *European Journal of Operational Research* 48/1. 18 articles.

Vargas, L.G. and R.W. Saaty (eds.), 1987, The Analytic Hierarchy Process - Theoretical Developments and Some Applications, *Mathematical Modelling* 9/3-5. 25 articles.

Vargas, L.G. and F. Zahedi (eds.), 1993, Analytic Hierarchy Process, *Mathematical and Computer Modelling* 17/4-5. 19 articles.

Manabe, R. (ed.), 1986, Analytic Hierarchy Process (in Japanese), *Communications of the Operations Research Society of Japan* 31/8. 12 articles.

Decision Making and the Analytic Hierarchy Process, Chinese Systems Engineering Association, Beijing, China. (Biannual Publication started in 1989).

SUBJECT INDEX